THE PRAXIS OF MY SYSTEM

Illustrated by 109 games from my contests
with many illustrative articles and introductory talks
and 132 diagrams

A Text-Book on Practical Chess

BY

A. NIMZOVICH

Translation by
J. DU MONT

Introduction by W. H. WATTS

DOVER PUBLICATIONS, INC.
NEW YORK

This Dover edition, first published in 1962, is an unabridged and unaltered republication of the work originally published in 1936 by Printing Craft, Ltd. This edition is published by special arrangement with Printing Craft, Ltd.

Standard Book Number: 486-20296-8

Manufactured in the United States of America
Dover Publications, Inc.
180 Varick Street
New York, N. Y. 10014

AUTHOR'S PREFACE.

The Modern Chess Master is not secretive. Positional play has its own technique, as has every branch of the art, and this technique can be acquired. This is the object and the justification of my book.

It is to teach positional play; the stratagems already indicated in my first book are treated here with studious care (by interspersed articles) and illustrated by games from master-play. Yet the book is entirely independent of " My System," and at no time is any sort of knowledge of the principles of " My System " presupposed. Where deemed necessary this has been expounded very shortly. It is not at all difficult to employ " prophylaxis," " over-protection," etc., but one must get to know about them.

The book has also its value as a collection of games, for, apart from those already published in "My System " and in the "Blockade," which are not repeated, there are here 109 of my best games.

A few words concerning the lay-out of the book. We have refrained from self-praise, for we have arrived at the conclusion that this foible, which comes down to us from the so-called classic period, is as much out of place as, for instance, the 3 ......, P–QB4; variation and others which were praised at the time to the skies. Self-praise is allowable only when deserved recognition is unjustly withheld. In all other cases it is both in bad taste and demoralising.

This time there is no lack of Indexes. Besides a detailed table of contents there is an index to games and one to the openings. Furthermore, as we divide the matter only under the more important stratagems, such as Centralisation, Blockade, etc., and not the minor stratagems, such as Open Lines, 7th Rank, etc., we thought it wise to introduce a register of guerilla tactics. That this could not be exhaustive is obvious, but the opportunity is given for the chess amateur to study the tactical elements which are of special interest to him (lines, passed pawn, etc.).

Finally. I would have liked to see each game provided with 4 or 5 diagrams to facilitate the study of the variations which often are particularly intricate, but obese volumes are not in favour now-a-days (slimming is the watchword). However, there is a simple as well as effective means, which we warmly recommend to the student; let him, when playing over a game, use two chess boards (say one ordinary set and a pocket board) and play the games on one board and the variations on the other. It is much easier than one might imagine, and valuable variations are not overlooked.

I think that is all there is to be said, and we must let the book speak for itself.

A. NIEMZOWITSCH.

INTRODUCTION.

After the lamented death of the Master, Aaron Niemzowitsch, I was almost persuaded to drop the idea of publishing an English translation of his Praxis, but a well-known player of the highest rank assured me that a very great advance in the strength of English players would follow its publication here. This remark made such a great impression on my mind that eventually I resolved to make some investigation for myself. My knowledge of German was limited to a few words and phrases and just a smattering of chess terms, so that nothing short of a translation would be of much use. When this became available I examined the work carefully and was immediately convinced of the correctness of the prophecy : there is nothing like it in the whole of chess literature. No other author or player has so scientifically reduced chess playing to the application of a number of clearly defined principles and rules. Compared with this, chess playing has heretofore been without system —just a haphazard exhibition of natural aptitude or skill or the want of it. Chess players were born, not made, but now that era has finished; Niemzowitsch has systematised chess play. It is now possible to make good, strong players out of the most unpromising material and players of master strength out of those who possess a natural aptitude for the game. Niemzowitsch's System comes as near as can be to making Chess an exact science.

Future generations, doubtless, will develop and improve his system. They will divide and sub-divide his classifications, they may improve on his technique, but the fact remains that he was the great pioneer, for what was unwritten law for the master players of his time is now set forth in his Praxis for the benefit of any and every aspirant to chess prowess. All the known methods of treatment, whether attack or defence, of the various types of positions are named, tabulated and described. There is a snag, of course; the player has to decide for himself as to the precise category in which to place the position with which he is dealing; but even so the system takes him at least one step nearer to complete mastery and a thorough grasp of the principles so carefully outlined by the author should reduce any error in this direction to a minimum.

The Translation is the work of Mr. J. Du Mont and amongst those who have assisted in the proof correcting special thanks are due to Messrs. V. L. Wahltuch and V. O. Knowles.   W. H. WATTS.

November, 1936.

CONTENTS.

(TABLE OF CONTENTS.)

Page

PART I.   Centralisation (Games 1-23 inclusive)   1
  1. Neglect of the central squares complex (games 1-3)   2
  2. Sins of omission in central territory (games 4-6)   10
  3. The vitality of centrally placed forces (games 7-8)   17
  4. A few complicated forms of centralisation (games 9-15) ...   24
  5. A mobile body of pawns in the centre (games 16-17)   46
  6. Giving up the pawn-centre (games 18-20)   52
  7. Centralisation as " deus ex machina " (games 21-23)   61

PART II. Restriction and Blockade (Games 24-52)   71
  1. Restriction of liberating pawn advances (games 24-25)   73
  2. Restricting a body of pawns in the centre (games 26-28) ...   79
  3. Restriction of a qualitative majority (games 29-30)   91
  4. Restriction in the case of the doubled-pawn complex (games 31-36)   99
  5. From the workshop of the Blockade   123
      a. Spreading the Blockade Net.
      b. The formation of gaps is prevented by prophylactic
         means (games 37-48.)
      c. The Blockade Net in action
      d. Blockade by Sacrifice.
  6. My new treatment of the problem of the pawn-chain. The
     Dresden Variation (games 49-52)   158

PART III. Over-protection and other forms of prophylaxis (games
     53-60)   173

PART IV. The isolated QP, the two hanging pawns, the two Bishops
     (games 61-70)   199

PART V.   Alternating manœuvres against enemy weaknesses when
     possessing advantages in space (games 71-77)   229

PART VI. Excursions through old and new territory of hyper-modern
     Chess (games 78-109)   255
  1. Concerning the thesis of the comparative inefficiency of the
     massed pawns advance (games 78-79)...   256
  2. The elastic treatment of the opening (games 80-83)   261
  3. Wing play and the centre (games 84-88)   272
  4. The small but secure centre (games 89-91)   288
  5. Asymmetric treatment of symmetrical variations (games (92-94)   298
  6. The Bishop with and without outpost (games 95-97)   309
  7. The weak square-complex of a specified colour (games 98-99)   321
  8. The triumph of the " bizarre " and " ugly " move (games
     100-101)   328
  9. The defence on heroic lines (games 102-106)   336
  10. Combinations which " slumber beneath a thin coverlet "
     (games 107-109)   354

      Index to Games...   365
      Register of Stratagems   367
      Index to Openings   369

CHESS   PRAXIS

PART I.

CENTRALISATION.

Excellent results can be achieved in tournament play by " centralisation." The fact that proper control of the central squares, in all circumstances of paramount necessity, is up to the present not widely known, and so it happens frequently that even experienced players show the centre " a clean pair of heels."

We, however, have seen to it that any and every omission in central territory on the part of the opponent should also carry its punishment.

The sins of omission in the centre spring either from habitual neglect of strategical necessities (in other words— *sit venia verbo*—strategic carelessness) or from a passionate fondness of the idea of an attack on the wings! In the first case the opponent allows the mastery in the centre to be wrested from him, in the second he gives it up of his own free will, in order to try his luck in a bold raid on the flank.

But a flank attack only affords a real chance when the centre is closed or else if it can be held against diversions by a minimum of forces. In the contrary case the attack is bound to die of inanition, for it is unthinkable that it should be possible to link up a difficult attacking formation with an exceedingly difficult defensive formation !

Game No. 3 provides a clear illustration of this point. There a central break-through leads to a complete paralysis— I could almost say demoralistion—of the attacking troops on the flank.

The technique of centralisation works (after the necessary preventive precautions in the case of a mobile enemy pawn centre), with a view to surround more and more closely the central square-complex. In this sense we rejoice in the capture of any line or diagonal, be it never so modest, as long as it leads over the centre of the board.

But when we succeed in turning to account these slightly theoretical potentialities, in that we establish some of our pieces in the centre, then we can be well satisfied with the results of our policy of centralisation.

A concentration of forces achieved in the centre in the course of the middle-game (as sketched above) can be exploited strongly by flank attacks, for, after all is said and done, centralisation is not an end in itself; it is for us the most rational way of accumulating forces available for action on the wings. (See Game No. 8). At any rate it can be stated definitely that a reasonably centralised position can in any circumstances be taken as secure.

But, in spite of all, even a centralised position is not altogether proof against all dangers.   For instance, the opponent could evolve the idea of suppressing the centralised pieces by means of exchanges. In this case the problem is to preserve a sufficient balance of centralisation into the end-game (Game 7). Another danger would accrue, should the opponent sacrifice one of his blockading units in order suddenly to extend the central territory. The danger alluded to should be averted by an immediate adaptation to the new circumstances; frequently a counter-sacrifice, with the object of an energetic exploitation of a central diagonal, is particularly effective (see Game No. 8).

We shall confine ourselves to the foregoing short remarks for the time being; all else will be made clear by the games themselves and their introductory notes.

I.—NEGLECT OF THE CENTRAL SQUARES COMPLEX AS A TYPICAL AND OFT-RECURRING FAILING.

The Idea of the Central Forces.

Games I—3.

In Nos. 1 and 2, the central territory is neglected for no apparent reason, in No. 3, for the sake of a flank attack; such strategy can only succeed against faulty counter-play. Compare our remarks on pages 1 and 9.

Our focussing lens is perhaps an imaginary, but certainly a very effective instrument, which reveals in every case whether or not the intended move will add to the cumulative effect of all our forces.

Had Brinckmann made use of this central focussing lens in our tournament game, Berlin, 1928, he would hardly have chosen 5 ...., Q–Kt3; as his move. 1 P–Q4, P–Q4; 2 Kt–KB3, P–K3; 3 B–B4, Kt–KB3; 4 P–K3, P–B4; 5 P–B3, and after 5 ...., Q–Kt3; 6 Q–Kt3, Kt–B3; 7 QKt–Q2, the centralising ...., B–Q3; proved

impossible. Now he should at least have played ....,
B–K2; but he chose the decentralising ...., Kt–KR4.
There followed a short but effective punitive expedition.
8 Q × Q, P × Q; 9 B–B7, P–B5; 10 B × KtP, and Black was
compelled to recall his Kt with loss of time, therefore
10 ...., Kt–B3; (this also parries the threat P–K4). There
followed 11 B–B7, with advantage.

Without Black's 7 ...., Kt–KR4; White would have
no sort of justification for his marauding raid, e.g., 7 ....,
B–K2; (instead of ...., Kt–KR4.) 8 Q × Q, P × Q;
9 B–B7, P–B5; 10 B × KtP, Kt–Q2; and Black has the
attack. We shall find further opportunities of testing the
usefulness of our lens.

Game No. I.—Berlin, 1928.

Black: K. Ahues.

1	P–QB4	Kt–KB3
2	Kt–QB3	P–B3
3	P–K4	P–Q4
4	P–K5	P–Q5
5	P × Kt	P × Kt
6	KtP × P	....

6 ....   KtP × P

KP × P; was clearer. And why? Because the development B–Q3; Castles; and R–K1; could no longer be
prevented. This disposition would mean centralisation and
therefore the greatest possible safeguard against all surprise.
Matters are very different after the move in the text (........,
KtP × P;). No doubt Black soon obtains a "proud" pawn
centre, but it is doubtful whether this pawn centre gives a
good reason for being proud of anything. Let us examine:

the mobility of the pawn centre is small, e.g., 6 ...., KtP×P; 7 Kt–B3, P–K4; 8 P–Q4, P–K5?; 9 Kt–R4!, P–KB4; 10 P–Kt3, together with Kt–Kt2, and B–B4, with blockade effect. But withholding the centre here also proves weak as shown in the note to move 9. Therefore, 6 ...., KP×P; was the proper procedure.

$$\text{7 Kt–B3} \qquad \text{P–QB4}$$

Positionally, P–K3 with a defensive position in the centre looks better.

$$\text{8 P–Q4} \qquad \text{Kt–B3}$$
$$\text{9 B–K2} \qquad \text{P–B4}$$

To be considered was 9 ...., P–K4; with the intention of staying there (=a waiting policy). The sequel would be 10 B–K3, Q–R4; (or 10 ...., P–Kt3; 11 Castles, with Q–Q2, QR–Q1; and White exerts pressure on the Q file) 11 Castles, Q×BP; 12 P×KP, (far better than 12 R–B1, which only drives the Q back for the defence via R4 to B2) 12 ...., P×P; (if 12 ...., Kt×P; 13 Q–Q5!) 13 Kt–Kt5, B–B4; 14 B–R5, B–Kt3; 15 B×B, RP×B; 16 Q–Q5, and wins. The move in the text (P–B4;) is a grave mistake which abandons the whole of the centre. Relatively best was 9 ...., R–KKt1; though even then White retains an advantage, e.g., 9 ...., R–KKt1; 10 P–Kt3, B–R6; 11 R–QKt1, Q–B2; 12 Q–R4, B–Q2; 13 Q–B2, etc.

$$\text{10 P–Q5} \qquad \text{Kt–R4}$$
$$\text{11 Kt–K5} \qquad ....$$

This decides the game.

$$\text{11 ....} \qquad \text{B–Q2}$$

Or 11 ...., B–Kt2; 12 Q–R4ch., K–B1; (12 ...., B–Q2?; 13 Kt×B, B×Pch.; 14 B–Q2, B×R; 15 Kt–B6 db. ch., K–B1; 16 B–K6, mate). 13 P–B4, P–B3; 14 Kt–B3, with complete positional mastery.

$$\text{12 B–R5} \qquad \text{B–Kt2}$$
$$\text{13 Kt×P} \qquad \text{Q–Kt3}$$
$$\text{14 Kt×Rch.} \qquad \text{K–B1}$$
$$\text{15 Kt–B7} \qquad ....$$

White unhesitatingly gives back the whole of his material gain but obtains a giant Knight on K6. That is how it should be done. Do not always wish to hold on blindly to your gains. To play with freedom (turn one advantage into another), that is the watchword.

15	B–K1
16 Kt–Kt5	B × Pch.
17 K–B1 !	....

Not 17 B–Q2, because of B × B; 18 Q × B, B × Bch.;
19 K × B, Q–Kt7ch.

17	B × R
18 Kt–K6ch.	K–Kt1
19 B × B	R × B
20 Q–R5	R–R1
21 Q × P	Q–Kt5
22 P–Kt3	Q × Pch.
23 K–Kt2	Q–K7
24 B–Q2	....

More exact would be 24 R–K1 ! Q × R; 25 Kt–Kt5,
B–Kt2; 26 Q–B7ch., K–R1; 27 B–Kt2 ! and wins.

| 24 .... | Kt–B5 |

Or 24 ...., Q × B; 25 Kt–Kt5, B–Kt2; 26 Q–K6ch.,
with a smothered mate.

| 25 R–K1 | Q × B |
| 26 Kt–Kt5 | Kt–Q3 |

The remainder of the game is sheer murder, which we
give reluctantly, as we are not of a bloodthirsty nature.

27 Q × Pch.	K–B1
28 Q × Pch.	K–Kt1
29 Q–R7ch.	K–B1
30 Q–R6ch.	K–Kt1
31 Q–Kt6ch.	B–Kt2

Poor Bishop, your hour has come. But there is one
consolation, you die at home !

32 Q–R7ch.	K–B1
33 Kt–K6ch.	K–K1
34 Kt × B db. ch.	K–Q1
35 Kt–K6ch.	K–K1
36 R–K5	Resigns.

Game No. 2.—London, 1927.

White: Bogoljubow.

1 P–QB4	P–K3
2 Kt–QB3	Kt–KB3
3 P–K4	P–B4
4 P–KKt3	....

The following continuation, suggested by Bogoljubow,
is worthy of consideration : 4 Kt–B3, Kt–B3; 5 P–Q4,
P × P; 6 Kt × P, B–Kt5; 7 Q–Q3.

4	P–Q4
5 P–K5	P–Q5
6 P × Kt	P × Kt
7 QP × P	....

There was no fault to find with 7 KtP × P, e.g. 7 KtP × P,
Q × P; 8 P–Q4, (8 ...., P × P; 9 P × P, B–Kt5ch.;
10 B–Q2, Q × P; 11 B × B, Q–K5ch.; 12 B–K2, Q × R;
13 Q–Q6, Kt–B3; 14 B–KB3, and wins). However, the move
in the text is also playable as Black's pawn majority will
hardly be able to assert itself.

| 7 .... | Q × P ! |
| 8 Kt–B3 | .... |

Here B–Kt2, had to be taken into serious consideration,
e.g.: 8 B–Kt2, Kt–B3; 9 Kt–K2, P–K4; 10 Castles, with
P–B4.   After the text-move the Bishops will have much
more difficulty in making the most of the centralising effect
of their diagonals.

8	P–KR3
9 B–Kt2	B–Q2 !
10 Kt–Q2	....

Herewith the mistake on move 8 is remedied to a certain
extent.

10	B–B3
11 Kt–K4	Q–Kt3
12 Q–K2	B–K2

Not ...., P–B4; because of the reply: B–B3, with
Kt–Q2, and Black's K4 remains permanently weak.

We see that the problem which White has to solve here
is a complex one: 1—The Black pawn majority must be
blockaded; 2—The supremacy in the centre is to be established.   This compound problem can in fact be solved, but
only through the most accurate use of all available means.

| 13 Castles | Castles |

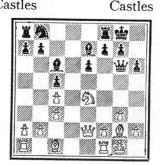

14 P–KR4

He neglects the centre! Why not: 14 P–B4! If then
........., Kt–Q2; 15 B–Q2, K–R1; 16 QR–K1, Kt–B3;
17 B–B1, (intending Kt–Q2–B3–K5,). After the wholesale
exchanges on K4, after move 17, we still cannot perceive any
chance for Black to assert his pawn-majority.

14	P–B4
15 Kt–Q2	B × B

He avoids the trap: 15 ...., B × P; 16 Kt–B3.

16 K × B	Kt–B3
17 Kt–B3	....

Intending B–B4.

17 ....   P–B5

Barring the gate. There follows a last attempt at
consolidation and the White position collapses.

18 R–K1	R–B3
19 Q–K4	P × P
20 P × P	B–Q3

The weakness of White's KKtP, his insufficient
development and exposed King, are more than even a
centralised position could stand. It is seen clearly what
damage 14 P–KR4, has caused.

21 P–KKt4	Q × Q
22 R × Q	QR–KB1
23 R–K3	R–B5

The less experienced reader should observe the " work "
in the open file.

24 P–Kt5   ....

24 R × P, R × Pch.; 25 K–B2, Kt–K4; leads to disaster
for White.

24	R–Kt5ch.
25 K–R1	....

Or 25 K–B2, Kt–K4; 26 K–K2, R–Kt7ch.; 27 K–B1,
R–Kt6; winning a piece.

25	P × P
26 P × P	K–B2
27 Kt–Kt1	....

After 27 P–Kt6ch., the best continuation would be
K–B3; (not K–K2; because of Kt–R2, R–KR1; R–K2,
R(Kt5)–R5?; B–Kt5ch.)

27	R–R1ch.
28 Kt–R3	K–K2
29 P–Kt3	B–B5

With the Black King at B2, a pin by R–B3; would now be on, hence Black's 28th move.

                30 R–B3   Kt–K4
Resigns.

Game No. 3.—Ostend, 1907.

Black: von Scheve.

    1 Kt–KB3   P–Q4
    2 P–Q3   Kt–QB3
    3 P–Q4!   ....

For now the Black QBP is blocked by a Kt.

    3 ....   P–K3
    4 P–K3   Kt–B3
    5 P–B4   B–K2
    6 Kt–B3   Castles
    7 B–Q2   Kt–K5

Correct play; observe that 7 B–Q3, (instead of 7 B–Q2,) would scarcely have prevented this penetration, e.g.: 7 B–Q3, Kt–QKt5; 8 B–K2, P–QB4; etc.

    8 B–Q3   P–B4

Not very good. A stonewall is not playable with a Knight at QB3. Black should have been content with: 8 ...., Kt×B; 9 Q×Kt, Kt–Kt5; 10 B–K2, P×P; 11 B×P, P–QB4.

    9 P–QR3   B–B3
    10 Q–B2   K–R1
    11 Castles KR   P–QR3

Probably in order to prevent Kt–QKt5, at some future time. It was called for, however, to give up all thought of stonewall attacks (as by P–KKt4;). With the simple 11 ...., Kt×B; 12 Q×Kt, P×P; 13 B×P, P–K4; 14 QR–Q1! P–K5!; Black could still have nearly equalised (15 Kt–K1, R–K1; 16 P–B3, P–B5!), and why not? With moves such as White's P–Q3, then P–Q4, P–QR3, a position exerting pressure cannot be built up as a matter of course; then too, Black has achieved something; the diversion by the Kt has secured him the two Bishops. Therefore it is not surprising that there should still have been a possibility of balancing the position.

12 QR–B1   P–R3
13 KR–Q1   P–KKt4

This would be playable only if White were not in a position to open up the central lines. With an open centre, however, an attack on the wing would appear hopeless.

14 B–K1   P–Kt5
15 Kt–K5   ………

The Q file now becomes active.   See next note.

15 ………   B × Kt
16 P × B   Kt–Kt4

If 16 ………, Kt × KP; 17 P × P, P × P; 18 B × Kt, BP × B; 19 R × P, etc.

17 Kt–K2   Q–K1
18 B–B3   P × P
19 B × QBP   ………

The Q file becomes powerful. Black cannot obtain an attacking position.

19 ………   B–Q2
20 Kt–B4   R–Q1
21 P–Kt4   P–Kt4
22 B–Kt3   Kt–K2
23 B–Q4   P–B3
24 Q–R2   Kt–Kt3

If 24 ………, Kt–Q4; 28 B × Kt, BP × B; 29 R–B7, etc.

25 Kt–R5   Kt–R5
26 Kt–B6   ………

Compare the two positions : White has two centre files, two central Bishops, a strongly posted Knight, with the Black pawns on the sixth rank all hanging. Black has two raiding Knights . . . and nothing else. No wonder that the impending attack by Black will be beaten off with frightful losses.

26	Q–Kt3
27 B–Kt6	Kt(R5)–B6ch.
28 P×Kt	R×Kt
29 B×R	Kt×Pch.
30 K–B1	R–B2
31 B–B6ch.	R×B
32 P×R	Kt×Pch.
33 K–K1	Kt–B6ch.
34 K–K2	P–B5
35 R×B	Resigns.

2.—SINS OF OMMISSION IN CENTRAL TERRITORY.

In Game No. 4, Black had broken through, but, with correct play, White could have re-established his position— from the centre (Move 21). He neglected this to his cost.

In Game No. 5, White was threatened with a K side attack, but he had the opportunity of launching a counter-attack in the centre. He neglected this attack, as it did not appear to him to promise an immediate success, and rightly succumbed to the hostile K side attack.

In Game No. 6, Black was on the point of occupying several centre-squares. White should have opposed this, for central points should never be conceded without a fight. But he underestimated the peril, so that his opponent was enabled to build up a powerful position in the centre.

The faults described above, must be attributed not only to insufficient knowledge, but also to a panicky temperament. And the moral? Well, even in a critical position, salvation can often enough be evolved from the centre, therefore : "Centralise and don't lose heart."

Game No. 4.—Ostend, 1907.

White: Erich Cohn.

1 P–Q4	Kt–KB3
2 Kt–KB3	P–Q3
3 B–B4	Kt–R4

Already in 1907 I went my own way.

4 B–Q2	Kt–KB3
5 P–B4	QKt–Q2
6 B–B3	....

Or 6 Kt–B3, P–K4; 7 P–K4, B–K2; and the lost tempo is shown to be a "quantité négligeable."

6	P—K3
7 P–K3	P–Q4

Better would be P–QKt3; with B–Kt2.

| 8 P–B5 | .... |

This is playable.

8	Kt–K5
9 B–Q3	P–B4
10 P–QKt4	P–KKt3
11 B–Kt2	B–Kt2
12 Kt–B3	....

The positional requirements would be met by 12 Castles, with Kt–K5, and P–B3.

12	Castles
13 Q–B2	P–B3
14 Kt–K2	Q–K2
15 Castles KR	....

Kt–K5, would please us better.

15	P–K4
16 P × P	Kt × KP
17 Kt × Kt	B × Kt
18 Kt–Q4	B–Q2
19 P–B3 !	Kt–B3
20 QR–K1	QR–K1
21 P–K4	....

The decisive mistake; correct was: 21 P–B4, B–B2; (B × Kt; B × B,) 22 Kt–B3, with B–Q4, and the White position is consolidated; the move in the text leads to ruin at express speed.

21	BP × P
22 P × P	Q–Kt2 !
23 P × P	Kt–Kt5
24 Q–B4	B × Pch.
25 K–R1	R × R
26 P × P dis. ch.	....

If 26 R × R, Kt–B7ch.; and mate in 4.

26	B–K3
27 Q × Bch.	R × Q
28 R × Rch.	Q × R
29 Kt × R	Q–B7

Resigns.

Game No. 5.—Carlsbad, 1923.

White: R. Spielmann.

1 P–K4	P–QB3
2 P–Q4	P–Q4
3 P × P	P × P
4 P–QB3	Kt–QB3
5 B–KB4	B–B4

An innovation.

6 Kt–B3	P–K3
7 Q–Kt3	Q–Q2
8 QKt–Q2	P–B3

Secures his K4 and prepares for a general advance on the K wing. A strategic diversion here is justified, as his own centre appears reasonably secure, for his K3 is well covered and the diagonal from his KB4 to QKt8 makes a pretty picture. That a flank attack, when your own centre is insecure, is inadmissible, we have emphasised already more than once.

9 B–K2	....

Here 9 P–B4, was indicated, e.g.: 9 P–B4, B–QKt5; 10 P × P, P × P; 11 B–QKt5, with an even game; or 9 ...., Kt–Kt5; 10 R–QB1, and White has nothing to fear.

9	P–KKt4
10 B–Kt3	P–KR4
11 P–KR3	KKt–K2
12 Castles KR	....

P–B4, would no longer improve matters; e.g.: 12 P–B4, P × P; 13 B × P, Kt–Q4; with a strong Knight in centre; nevertheless this line was preferable to the text.

12	B–R3
13 Kt–K1	P–Kt5
14 Q–Q1	B × Kt

This wins a pawn.

15 Q × B	P × P
16 Kt–Q3	P–Kt3
17 KR–K1	P–R5
18 B–R2	K–B2

Not Castles QR ; because of Kt–K5 !

19 P–KKt4	....

Other moves also lose.

19	P × P e.p.
20 B × P	P–R7ch.
21 K–Kt2	B–K5ch.

The win was more clearly demonstrated as follows :—
21 ...., P–K4; 22 P × P, B–K5ch.; 23 P–B3, QR–KKt1 ;
24 P–K6ch., Q × P; 25 Kt–B4, Q–Kt5 !; or 24 (instead of
P–K6ch,) Q–B4, Kt–B4; 25 P × B, Kt × B; 26 Q × Pch.,
K–K1; 27 P–K6, P–R8(Q)ch.; 28 R × Q, Kt × R dis. ch.;
and wins.

22 B–B3	....

With P–B3, White would have held out a little longer.

22	Kt–B4 !
23 B × B	P × B
24 Kt–B4	....

If R × P, Q–Q4 ; etc.

24	P–K4
25 Kt–K2	Kt–R5ch.
26 B × Kt	Q–Kt5ch.

and mates in a few moves.

Game No. 6.—London, 1927.

White: F. D. Yates.

1 P–K4	P–QB4
2 Kt–KB3	Kt–KB3
3 P–K5	Kt–Q4
4 B–B4	Kt–Kt3
5 B–K2	Kt–B3

White has lost time with the B ; on the other hand,
Black's Kt is not too well placed at QKt3, so the manœuvre
with the B is not to be condemned.

6 P–B3	P–Q4
7 P–Q4	....

We would have given P × P e.p., the preference.

7 ………	P × P
8 P × P	B–B4
9 Castles	P–K3
10 Kt–B3	B–K2
11 Kt–K1	………

If the attack intended with this move, P–B4, with P–KKt4, and P–B5, were really feasible, it would prove Black's 8 ………, B–B4; to be wrong and that surely cannot be.

The fact is that Kt–K1, does not achieve much and that this diversion should have been abandoned in favour of a properly thought-out plan on the QB file; e.g., 11 B–K3, Castles; 12 R–B1, followed by P–QR3, P–QKt4, and Kt–Q2–Kt3–B5, and the outpost advocated in " My System " is established.

11 ………	Kt–Q2
12 B–Kt4 !	………

Ingenious play: After 12 P–B4?, there would follow Kt × QP; 13 Q × Kt?, B–B4. Also unfavourable would be : 12 B–K3, because of Kt(Q2) × P; 13 P × Kt, P–Q5; 14 B–Q2, P × Kt; 15 B × P, Q–B2; with some advantage in position for Black.

By means of the move in the text (12 B–Kt4,) Yates is able to play the desired P–B4, in an astounding manner !

12 ………	B–Kt3
13 P–B4	Kt × QP
14 Kt × P !	Kt–QB3 !

If 14 ………, B–QB4; 15 P–Kt4, would be strong. 14 ………, P × Kt; would be altogether bad, because of B × Ktch., followed by Q × Kt.

15 Kt × B	Q–Kt3ch.
16 K–R1	Kt × Kt

17 Q–R4	………

Here we have the typical mistake of which we spoke in our preliminary note. Black clearly intends to occupy the central points and, as a matter of course, White should fight for them instead of running away from the centre with Q–R4. Therefore: 17 Q–K2, (intending B–K3,) Kt–Q4; 18 B–B3, Q–B4; 19 B–Q2, Kt(Q2)–Kt3; 20 R–B1, Q–K2; and now perhaps 21 B–K3, and White controls more of the centre than Black. But even if this " more " had been unattainable, what matter? Even then White should have put up a fight! Now a just punishment overtakes him.

    17 ....   P–KR4
    18 B–R3   ....

Compulsory, for after 18 B–B3, there follows Kt–KB4; with further gain in territory. Moreover a threat of mate would arise via P–R5; and Kt–Kt6ch.

    18 ....   B–B4
    19 Q–R3   Q–Kt4

Making room for the Kt, which aims at Q4 via QKt3.

    20 K–Kt1   Kt–QKt3
    21 Q–KB3   Kt(Kt3)–Q4
    22 P–QKt3   Q–Kt3ch.

    23 R–B2   R–QB1

This move, in connection with the next, causes one of the Rooks to be decentralised, and creates a flaw in a position so harmoniously built up in other respects.

    23 ...., Castles QR ! on the other hand, held out the promise of perfect balance. After 24 ...., K–Kt1; and 25 ...., P–Kt3; nothing stood in the way of deploying the Rooks centrally; therefore: 26 ...., R–Q2; and 27 ...., R–QB1.

    Even better seems: 23 ...., B–Kt5; e.g.: 24 B × B, P × B; 25 Q × P, R × P; 26 Q × KtP, Castles QR; 27 K × R, Q × R; 28 Kt–Q3, Q–K7; and Black must win.

Finally, a combination of both lines of play is possible:
23 ...., Castles QR; 24 B–R3, and now B–Kt5; if then
25 R–B1ch., K–Kt1; 26 B–B5, Q×B; 27 R×Q, B×Q;
28 R×B, R–QB1; capturing the QB file with a winning
advantage.

	24 B–Q2	R–R3

Interesting and, after all, a centralised position can afford
an adventurous expedition. But 24 ...., Castles; with
P–KKt3; and KR–Q1; was more correct.

25	R–Q1	B×B
26	Q×B	Kt–B4
27	Q–Q3	R–Kt3
28	Kt–B3	R–Kt5
29	P–KR3	R–Kt6
30	P–QR4	Kt–R5

Black, in view of his disposition of forces is torn between
two opposite aims; the fact that the two Rooks are separated
makes a mating attack appear desirable, but the rest of the
army is better placed for the end-game. The Kt at Q4 is
formidable for that purpose and Black would be in
undisputed possession of the White squares.

31	K–B1	R–B3

In order to make the threat Q–R7, and Q–Kt8ch.
nugatory: the Rook vacates the first rank in good time.
Black must in any event watch both wings carefully.

32	P–R5	Q–Q1
33	K–Kt1	Kt–B4
34	K–R2	P–R3
35	Q–Kt1	....

Threatening Kt–Q4.

35	....	Q–K2

He submits to the threat with an eye on QB4 (Q–B4;).

36	Kt–Q4	....

This loses. R–QB1, was better.

37	....	Q–R5

As the separated units could not rejoin the main body,
the main body rejoins them.

37	B–K1	....

If Kt×R, R×RPch.; and mate in two.

37	....	Kt×P

Again a mating threat, this time through R×KtPch.;
etc.

| 38 R × Kt | R × RPch. |

The simplest way.

| 39 P × R | Q × Rch. |
| 40 K–Kt2 | Kt–K6ch. |

and Mate in two.

For this game Black was awarded a prize, " for the best played game."

3.—THE VITALITY OF CENTRALLY PLACED FORCES.
Games 7—8.

The notes to Game No. 7 give us an opportunity of observing how centralisation, which threatens to obtain results in the middle-game, can be turned into centralisation advantageous in the end game. This stratagem is not only of importance as a defensive measure (we have the case in mind in which the defender attempts to get rid of the adverse forces established in the centre by means of exchanges), but also when it becomes necessary to progress slowly but surely.

In Game No. 8, Black has succeeded, by a pretty Pawn sacrifice, in circumventing his opponent's attempt at blockading the centre, and many nice open lines are beckoning him. Here too, he has reckoned without his host (vulgo the vitality of forces in the centre), the seemingly dead blockade returns to life and renewed strength, and throttles him.

Games No. 7.—Played in Oslo, 1921.
White: 3 Norwegian Amateurs.

1 P–K4	P–K3
2 P–Q4	P–Q4
3 Kt–QB3	B–Kt5
4 P × P	P × P
5 Kt–B3	B–Kt5
6 B–K2	Kt–K2
7 Castles	QKt–B3
8 B–KB4	B–Q3
9 Kt–K5	....

Here Q–Q2, looks more natural.

9	B × B
10 Kt × B	B × Kt
11 B × B	Kt × B
12 P × Kt	....

Now both sides have a pawn majority on a flank, but White's majority impresses one as less mobile.

12	Q–Q2
13 P–KB4	Castles QR
14 P–B3	K–Kt1
15 Q–Kt3	P–QB4
16 QR–K1	....

Here QR–Q1, was preferable.

16	P–KR4 !
17 K–R1	Kt–B4

And now the mobility of White's pawn majority has
shrunk almost to nothing. But there is a long way to go yet
before it can be rolled up.

18 Kt–Kt1	P–R5
19 Kt–R3	P–Q5
20 P × P	P × P
21 Q–Q3	Kt–K6
22 R–B2	Q–Q4

Black, at all events, has achieved something, a well-
centralised position, a valuable passed pawn, even though it
is blockaded, and the possibility of P–B3.

23 P–R3	P–B3

Black might have played KR–K1; first, and possibly
P–R3; in order to lift the blockade by Q–Kt4; but the move
in the text is thoroughly sound and clearly demonstrates
Black's superiority.

24 P × P	P × P
25 P–B5 !	....

25	KR–Kt1

The problem was to prevent White's obviously intended
Kt–B4, or to make it harmless. The preventive measure
25 ...., KR–K1; was to be recommended. If then 26
Kt–B4, there follows Q × P; (even stronger and immediately
decisive would be the combinative refutation of 26 Kt–B4,

by Kt–Kt5!); 27 Q×Q, Kt×Q; 28 R×R, R×R; 29 Kt–Q3, Kt–Q3!; 30 R×P, K–B2; and all the Black forces are in readiness to support the QP.

The strategical basis of the foregoing variation could be characterised as follows : Black's centralisation has been passed on from the Middle-Game to the End-Game, a stratagem to be warmly recommended in all suitable cases.

It must be added, in truth, that the move in the text, 25 ...., KR–Kt1; conforms to the requirements of the stratagem described and is therefore thoroughly sound.

If 25 ...., KR–K1; (instead of Kt1;) 26 KR–K2, Kt×KtP; 27 R×R, Kt–B5 dis. ch.; 28 Q–K4, R×R; and wins.

26 Kt–B4   Q–B3

Here the manœuvre mentioned several times could have been carried out by the simple continuation : 26 ...., Q×P; e.g., 27 Q×Q, Kt×Q; 28 Kt–R5, KR–K1; 29 R–QB1, Kt–K6; 30 Kt×P, R–K3. If we now compare this position with that shown in Diagram 7, it must be conceded that raising the blockade of the QP represents for Black a clear gain. It will be noted that the centralisation has taken on an End-Game character, but without losing in intensity.

There could follow : 31 Kt–Q7ch., K–R1; 32 Kt–B5, R–QB3; 33 Kt–Q3, R×Rch.; 34 Kt×R, P–Q6!; 35 Kt–Kt3, (if R–Q2, R–KB1; or if Kt×P, P–R3; 36 R–Q2, Kt–Kt5; and wins) Kt–B5; 36 Kt–Q2, Kt×KtP; 35 R–B4, P–Kt4; followed by Kt–B5; and wins. Therefore 26 ...., Q×P; was the correct move affording an easy transition into the End-Game with a legacy of contralisation. With the move in the text a clarification of the position is not attained without trouble.

27 Kt–Kt6   ....

The correct move was K–Kt1, for, after the text move, Black had a clear win by means of an elegant combination : 27 Kt–Kt6, P–R6; 28 Kt–K7, Q–B2; 29 Kt×R, Kt–Kt5; 30 Q–KKt3, Q×Q: 31 P×Q, Kt×Rch.; 32 K–Kt1, Kt–Q6; 33 R–Q1, P–R7ch.; 34 K×P, Kt–B7; 35 R–KB1, Kt–Kt5ch.; with R×Kt; to follow. After 27 K–Kt1, it would not have been so easy to demonstrate an advantage, e.g. : 27 K–Kt1, R–Kt4; 28 Q–K2, (if instead R×Kt?, Q–B8ch.;) 28 ...., QR–Kt1; 29 Kt–Kt6, R×Kt; 30 P×R, R×P; 31 Q–Q2, Q–K5; and Black has an

imposing position, with, however, Middle-Game responsi-
bilities not altogether desirable.

27	········	QR–K1

A mistake due to time difficulties. Black was playing
three games simultaneously and had to make three times 20
moves in the hour. As demonstrated, P–R6; won easily.

28	Kt × P	R–Kt5
29	Kt–B3	Q–Q4
30	KR–Q2	KR–Kt5
31	Kt × P	Kt × KtP

This ought not to have succeeded. After Black's
mistake on the 27th move, he had a lost game. But the gods
are kind.

32	R × R	R × R
33	Kt–B6ch.	········

This is clearer than 33 Kt–B3, Q × Q; 34 R × Q,
Kt–K6; 35 R–Q4, R–K1; 36 K–Kt1, followed by K–B2.

33	········	P × Kt
34	Q × Q	P × Q
35	K × Kt	R–K4
36	R–KB2	·········

Through this one weak move, the smouldering glow of
Black's centralisation is enabled to blaze up anew. The
correct continuation was: 36 P–KR4, and if R × P; then:
37 R–KB2, R–R4; 38 K–R3, P–B4; 39 R–Q2, or 36 P–KR4,
K–B2; 37 K–Kt3, K–Q3; 38 P–R5, R × P; 39 R–R2,
R–Kt4ch.; 40 K–B4, K–K3; 41 P–R6, R–Kt1; 42 P–R7,
R–KR1; 43 P–Kt4, and White wins.

36	········	K–B2
37	K–Kt3	K–Q3
38	K–Kt4	R–K5ch.
39	K–R5	········

If 39 R–B4, K–K4; 40 R × Rch. ; K × R ; and wins.

39	P–Q5
40 K–Kt6	K–K4
41 P–Kt4	R–Kt5ch.
42 K–B7	**R–B5**
43 R × R	....

A bad mistake, of course, but White was lost in any case.

43	K × R
44 K × P	P–Q6
45 K–Kt6	P–Q7
46 P–B6	P–Q8(Q)

and wins.

Game No. 8.—Carlsbad, 1911.

Black: Löwenfisch.

1 P K4	P–K3
2 P–Q4	P–Q4
3 P–K5	P–QB4
4 P–QB3	Kt–QB3
5 Kt–B3	P–B3

Strategically unsound; a pawn-chain should only be attacked at its base, here at White's Q4. Correct is accordingly : 5 ...., Q–Kt3; 6 B–K2, P × P; 7 P × P, B–Q2; with pressure on the QP.

| 6 B–QKt5 | B Q2 |
| 7 Castles | Q–Kt3 |

Not 7 ...., Kt × KP; because of 8 Kt × Kt, B × B ; 9 Q–R5ch., K–K2 ; 10 Q–B7ch., K–Q3 ; 11 P × Pch., K × Kt; 12 R–K1ch., K–B4 ; 13 Q–R5ch., P–Kt4 ; 14 P–Kt4, mate.

| 8 B × Kt | P × B |
| 9 P × KBP | Kt × P |

Here I should have given P × BP ; the preference.

10 Kt–K5	B–Q3
11 P × P	B × P
12 B–Kt5	....

This move, which leads to a complete blockade of the Black Pawn position, is the point of White's tactics from move 8 onwards.

12	Q–Q1
13 B × Kt	Q × B
14 Q–R5ch.	P–Kt3
15 Q–K2	R–Q1
16 Kt–Q2	Castles

17	QR–K1	KR–K1
18	K–R1	B–Q3
19	P–KB4	P–B4
20	P–B4	B–KB1

It is always difficult to bridge the gap between subtle blockade play and the open attacking game for which the opponent strives. This was perhaps best accomplished by 20 Q–R6, e.g.: 20 Q–R6, B–Kt1; 21 Kt–Kt3, Q–K2; 22 Kt–R5, or 20 Q–R6, Q–K2; 21 QKt–B3, and White threatens to play Q × P, or Kt–Kt5, according to circumstances.

The continuation in the text costs Black a pawn but this is not a serious loss, for now the Bishops become effective. White will not find it easy to re-adjust his game, which is laid out for blockade.

21	P × P	B–B1
22	Kt–K4	Q–Kt2
23	P × P	....

With P–Q6, the character of the game would be maintained, but White wished to try out the pawn sacrifice. 23 P–Q6, gave an easy win.

23	....	B × P

24	Q–R6	K–R1
25	R–Q1	B–Kt1
26	P–QKt3	R–Q5
27	R × R	P × R
28	Q–R5	....

White takes good care not to provoke the mighty Bishops by a possible excursion by the Knights (Kt–Kt5,). The move in the text prevents R–Q1; but allows the occupation of the QB file. The contest now becomes quite dramatic.

28	R–B1
29 R–Q1	R–B7
30 P–KR3	Q–Kt2
31 R × P	B–B4

The attack by Black appears to become overpowering.

| 32 Q–Q8 !! | .... |

With the surprising point : 32 ...., B × R ; 33 Q × B, Q–Kt2 (other replies would be worse); 34 Kt–Q6 ! and 35 Kt–K8, with an immediate win.

The question may be suggested : must this saving clause be attributed purely to chance ? The answer is, No, the whole procedure is typical. If the opponent has succeeded in thwarting the central blockade by the sacrifice of a pawn, you must maintain yourself in the centre nevertheless, and wait for the opportunity of making a central diagonal the object of a counter sacrifice. This sacrifice will then be decisive.

32	B–K2
33 Q–Q7	Q–R3
34 R–Q3	....

Intending Q–Q4, again the blockade diagonal.

| 34 .... | B–B1 |
| 35 Kt–B7ch. | B × Kt |

If 35 ...., K–Kt2; 36 Q–Q4ch., and mate in two.

| 36 Q × B | R–B1 |

A complete débâcle.

| 37 R–Q7 | Resigns. |

This game comprises two parts : I. A central blockade, surprisingly carried out. II. An interesting repulse of an attempt to shatter this blockade by violent means.

The first part, at the time the game was played, was unexplored territory, the second part still is.

4.—WE LEARN TO KNOW THE CENTRAL TERRITORY MORE THOROUGHLY. A FEW COMPLICATED FORMS OF CENTRALISATION.

Games 9—15.

In Game No. 9 we observe a form of centralisation already seen in No. 7; but in this case the blockader is brought to the ground by direct assault.

In No. 10 the centre is built up on original lines, whilst in No. 11 the most striking feature is the building up of the centre-kernel in depth.

That a centralised position can control very definitely points far away on the wings (No. 7) is a fact based on the nature of centralisation.

But at times this more or less automatic radiation of power is not sufficient in itself, and it becomes desirable to build up an attack on the wing concurrently with the attack in the centre. Such a procedure is illustrated in game No. 12. That it is not absolutely necessary to give this diversion the character of an attack can be seen in Game No. 13; there the play on the wing pursued only defensive aims.

It is of importance to state that this combined play (in the centre and on the flank at the same time) requires the greatest possible firmness in the general lay-out of your own position; viewed in that light the collapse of this combined action in game No. 14 can easily be understood; the attacker's Queen's wing was weak.

We submit the extremely critical No. 15, seeking by it to define the maximum advantage obtainable, from a centralised position.

Game No. 9.—Semmering, 1926.

White: Yates.

1 P–K4	P–K3
2 P–Q4	P–Q4
3 Kt–QB3	B–Kt5
4 P×P	P×P
5 B–Q3	Kt–K2
6 Kt–K2	Castles
7 Castles	B–Kt5
8 P–B3	B–KR4

Now a small weakness has developed at White's K3, which, however, can only be demonstrated by P–QB4; a risky-looking move.

9	Kt–B4	B–Kt3
10	QKt–K2	B–Q3
11	Q–K1	....

This move can be classified under the heading: " Neglect of the central complex." Our " central focus " clearly points to B × B, after which the central squares QB5 and K5 appear to be fixed.

11	....	P–QB4
12	P × P	B × Pch.
13	K–R1	QKt–B3
14	B–Q2	R–K1
15	Kt × B	RP × Kt
16	P–KB4	....

A flank attack with an inferior central position. Relatively the best was: 16 Q–R4, Kt–B4; 17 Q × Q, QR × Q; with only a small end-game advantage for Black.

16	....	Kt–B4
17	P–B3	P–Q5
18	P–B4	Q–Kt3

Black's position is clearly superior.

19	R–B3	B–Kt5

Conquest of Black's K6 for his own pieces.

20	P–QR3	B × B
21	Q × B	P–R4
22	Kt–Kt1	R–K6
23	R–Q1	QR–K1
24	Q–KB2	....

The central territory in this position reminds us of game No. 7. There, as here, the Black pawn at his Q5 forms the kernel of the centralised action; in logical connection are the

point K6 and the K file. In both games the Black pressure
in the centre leads or should lead to the elimination of the
White blockader at Q3.

24	Q–Kt6
25 R–Q2	Kt–Q3
26 P–QB5	Kt–B5
27 B × Kt	Q × B

Black has succeeded; the blockader has fallen. The
student should now proceed as follows : let him first set up,
on a second board, the position in Diag. 7 from Game No. 7
with the added moves : 25 ...., KR–Kt1 ; 26 Kt–B4. He
should then study the note to the last move. This done, let
him compare the procedure which we shall be able to observe
in the present game, moves 24–27. Finally he should try to
establish in his own mind the difference in the strategical
method employed in each case. Our conclusions will be set
out at the end of the present game.

| 28 R–B2 | Q–Q4 |
| 29 R–B1 | Q–K5 |

Now the following continuation is in the air : R × R ;
Q × R, Q × Q ; Kt × Q, R–K7 ; and the seizure of the seventh
rank should be decisive.

| 30 P–B5 | .... |

An ingenious attempt to save the situation.

30	R × R
31 Kt × R	Q × P
32 P–QKt4	P × P
33 P × P	Kt × P

Not bad would be the continuation 33 ...., Kt–K4 ;
34 R–K1, R–K3.

| 34 Q × P | Kt–Q6 |
| 35 R–B2 | .... |

Not R–B3, because of R–K8ch. ; followed by Q–B8ch. ;
and Kt–B7 ; mate.

| 35 .... | R–QB1 |

Tempting, but unsound, would be : 35 ...., Kt–K8 ;
because of 36 R–K2, R × R ; 37 Q–Q8ch, K–R2 ; 38
Kt–Kt5ch., K–R3 ; 39 Kt × Pch., K–R4 ; 40 Q–R8ch., with
Q–R3ch., Q–Kt3ch., Kt–Q6ch., winning the Queen.

| 36 R–B3 | Kt × P |

It should be clear that the sequence of moves 34–37 is
to be taken as a centralising manœuvre, the basis of which
is the central diagonal from Black's KB4–QKt8.

The rest is a matter of technique (the technique of the strategic retreat especially).

37	P–R4	P–Kt3
38	Kt–Kt5	R–B1

No false shame. The retreat is only of short duration.

39	R–B3	Q–Q2
40	Q–QB4	Kt–K3
41	R–Q3	Q–B1
42	Q–Kt5	....

The Rook End-Game after 42 Q × Q, R × Q; 43 Kt × Kt, P × Kt; 44 R–Q6, R–Kt1; 45 R × KP, K–B2; is hopeless for White.

42	....	Q–B8ch.
43	K–R2	Q–B5ch.
44	P–Kt3	Q–B7ch.
45	K–R1	Q–B8ch.
46	K–R2	Kt–B4

Resigns.

Answer to the query set out in the note to move 27 : In game No. 9 the blockader falls in the course of defensive manœuvres, in game No. 7 in the course of an attack which his side was compelled to undertake. White's attack in game No. 7 can be termed involuntary, because without it he would have been crushed as by a tank by Black's central attack and its consequent effect on White's KKt2.

The power to compel the decentralised opponent to undertake a premature flank-attack is typical of a position highly centralised.

Game No. 10.—Marienbad, 1925.
White: Réti.

The opening moves lead through hyper-modern looking byways to a pawn-formation well-known in the exchange variation of the French.

1	P–QB4	P–K4
2	Kt–KB3	P–K5
3	Kt–Q4	Kt–QB3
4	Kt–B2	B–B4
5	Kt–B3	Kt–B3
6	P–Q4	P × P e.p.
7	P × P	P–Q4
8	P–Q4	B–K2
9	P–B5	

Played in enterprising blockade style.

9 ....   B–B4

Breaking-up attempts beginning with ...., P–QKt3; would have been premature; e.g., 9 ...., P–QKt3; 10 P–QKt4, P–QR4; 11 P–Kt5, and P–B6.

10 B–Q3   ....

Here the natural combination would have . been 10 B–QKt5, followed by B × Ktch.

10 ....   B × B
11 Q × B   P–QKt3

Here this move is in order.

12 Castles

Now 12 P–QKt4, P–QR4; 13 P–Kt5, fails on account of 13 ...., Kt–QKt5; with the gain of a tempo.

12 ....   Castles
13 B–Kt5   P–KR3
14 B–R4   P × P
15 P × P   Kt–K4
16 Q–Q4   Kt–Kt3
17 B–Kt3   P–B3

Black has a good QP (poorly blockaded) and the possibility of attacking the White QBP. Against this White's control of the Diagonal from KKt3 to QKt8 does not seem to afford an equivalent. White should clearly have played 10 B–QKt5.

18 Kt–Kt4   R–B1
19 P–KR3   R–K1

Making room for the Knight and at the same time preparing for the occupation of the central file, which White cannot dispute because of his difficulties at QB5.

20 QR–Q1   Kt–B1
21 Kt–Q3

21 ....   Q–R4

White saw that 22 Q–QR4, is now forced, and had prepared a highly original centralisation manœuvre in reply.

22 Q–QR4

Bad would be : 22 P–Kt4, Q–R6; 23 R–Kt1, Kt–K3; 24 Q–K5, Kt–Q2; 25 Q–K1, KKt×P; 26 P×Kt, B–B3.

| 22 .... | Q×Q |
| 22 Kt×Q | Kt–K5 |

Now the Kt occupies the centre, which has become free after the deflection of the defending forces.

| 24 B–R2 | Kt–K3 |

What can the Kt want?   The QBP is easy to defend.

| 25 P–QKt4 | Kt–Q5 |

A quite extraordinary co-operation ! Two Knights, of which one can easily be driven away (P–B3), and the other is undefended, and yet they control the board.

| 26 KR–K1 | .... |

If 26 P–B3, Kt–K7ch. ¡ followed by Kt–Kt6ch.

| 26 .... | B–R5 |

The third ally.

| 27 B–K5 | .... |

White was in difficulties. This move loses a pawn.

27	R×B
28 Kt×R	B×Pch
29 K–B1	B×R
30 R×Kt	B–Kt6
31 Kt–KB3	R–K1
32 R–Q1	R–K3
33 R–B1	K–B1

The King goes to the threatened wing.

34 Kt–B3	Kt×Kt
35 R×Kt	R–K5
36 P–R3	K–K1
37 R–Q3	....

A fine move. If now K–Q2; P–Kt5.

37	P–R3
38 R–Q4	P–B4
39 P–QR4	K–Q2
40 P–Kt5	....

This fails now on account of a finesse worthy of an End-Game study.

40	....	RP × P
41	P × P	P × P
42	R × Pch	K–B3

As in game No. 1 the extra material is returned with thanks.

43	R–Q4	....

If 43 R × P, P–Kt5; etc.

43	....	K × P

and Black won.

Game No. II.—Wilna, 1912.

White: Löwenfisch.

1	P–K4	P–QB3
2	P–QB4	P–K3
3	Kt–KB3	P–Q4
4	KP × P	KP × P
5	P × P	P × P
6	B–Kt5ch	Kt–B3
7	Castles	B–Q3

This allows the undisturbed development of all the forces.

8	P–Q4	Kt–K2
9	B–Kt5	P–B3
10	B–KR4	Castles
11	QKt–Q2	B–KKt5
12	B × Kt	Kt × B
13	Q–Kt3	B–Kt5

Refutes White's attempt to demonstrate instability in the Black position.

14	Kt–K5	....

Directed against Black's Q–Kt3; with attendant threats.

14	....	Kt × Kt

The continuation: 14 ...., B × Kt; 15 Kt × B, P–KKt4; 16 B–Kt3, P–B4; 17 Q × P, Q–B1; would fail because of the piquant answer 18 B–K5. 18 ...., Kt × B; 19 Q × Q, with Kt × Kt, to follow and White has an extra pawn.

15	Q × B	Kt–Q6
16	Q × P	B–K7

| 17 KR–Kt1 | R–B1 |

The centralisation effected in the heart of the hostile position strikes one as humorous.

18 Kt–B1	P–KKt4
19 B–Kt3	P–B4
20 B–K5	R–KB2
21 Q–R6	P–B5
22 R–K1	....

He rebels against fate, for 22 P–B3, R–B7; appeared unbearable : 22 R–Q1, would be just as hopeless.

22	Kt × R
23 Q × B	Kt × P
24 Kt–Q2	Kt–R5
25 Kt–B3	Kt–Kt3

Consolidation by concentrating the retreating troops after a successful raid is particularly called for. Frequently such raids bring about a measure of disorganisation (the units losing touch with one another).

26 K–R1	P–Kt5
27 Kt–Q2	Q–Q2
28 R–KKt1	R–B7

The last straw !

| 29 P–KR3 | P–Kt6 |
| Resigns. | |

A jolly little game.

Game No. 12.—London, 1927.

White: Dr. Tartakower.

1	P–Q4	P–K3
2	Kt–KB3	Kt–KB3
3	P–K3	P–QKt3
4	B–Q3	B–Kt2
5	QKt–Q2	P–B4
6	Castles	Kt–B3
7	P–B3	R–B1
8	Q–K2	B–K2 !
9	P×P	P×P
10	P–K4	P–Q4
11	P×P	P×P

Black has laid out his game on original lines (moves 8 and 11). The positions are approximately even; yet, already at this stage, Black possesses a few preferential shares in the central territory, though they are as yet hardly negotiable.

12	B–R6	B×B
13	Q×B	Castles
14	R–Q1	Q–B2
15	Kt–B1	R–Kt1
16	Q–K2	KR–Q1

As consolidating the position is now of paramount importance KR–K1; is discarded. The valuable QP is worthy of an escort in keeping with its standing!

17	B–K3	P–KR3

Centralisation tactics; Black endeavours to take nearly all the central squares from his opponent. White's only centre square, KB5, is now so to speak depreciated (for on Kt–Kt3–B5, there would follow simply B–B1; and White has no useful attacking continuation, for B–Kt5, is no longer available).

18	Kt–Kt3	B–B1
19	Q–B2	Kt–KKt5

Black is out for central points (K4).

20	Kt–B1	QKt–K4
21	Kt×Kt	Kt×Kt
22	P–QKt3	....

22 ....   P–QR4

The flank attack built up on centralisation.

23 R–Q2   P–B5

Another and possibly sounder continuation would have been : R–Q2; with QR–Q1; and P–R5; if then P×P, Kt–B5; with an irruption by the Rooks via the QKt file.

24 P×P   ....

A better defence would have been : 24 QR–Q1, and if Kt–Q6; the sacrifice of the exchange on Q3.

24 ....   Kt×P

25 R–Q3   P–R5 !

With P–R6; an important point of entry is to be created at White's QKt2.

26 Kt–Q2   Kt×B !

27 P×Kt   ....

If 27 R×Kt, P–Q5; 28 R–Q3, B–Kt5; and White is in a worse plight.

27 ....   Q–R2

28 R–Kt1   R×Rch

29 Q×R   B–B4

30 K–B2   R–Kt1

31 Q–B2   Q–Q2

The weaknesses in the White camp, PK3, square QKt2 and the vulnerable position of the King are now dealt with according to the rules of the art.

(See technique of alternation in preceding chapter).

32 Kt–B3   ....

If instead : 32 P–B4, P–Q5 !

32 ....   Q–K3

33 Q–K2   ....

If here : 33 Q×P, B×Pch. !

| | 33 .... | P–R6 |

At last !

34 R–Q2	R–Kt8
35 Kt–Q4	Q–B3ch
36 Q–B3	Q–K4

With this move Black has attained the peak of power on the straight as well as diagonally. For what could be more central than K5, and what could compare in outflanking power with a Rook on the eighth, which moreover has potential control of the seventh?

| 37 P–Kt3 | .... |

A mistake which should have been immediately fatal. The only possibility was : 37 Q–Kt3, whereupon the sequel would have been : B × Kt; 38 BP × B, Q–K3; and White could still have made some show of resistance. A plausible variation would have been : 39 Q–B7, (in order to prevent Q–B3;) Q–R3; 40 Q–Q8ch., K–R2; 41 Q × P, Q–B8ch.; 42 K–Kt3, R–Kt7; and wins.

Noteworthy is the decisive co-operation of the QRP.

| 37 .... | B × Kt ? |

Here 37 ...., R–B8; won immediately. If then 38 Kt–K2, B × Pch.; and if 38 Kt–B6, Q × P; and wins.

| 38 BP × B | Q–K3 |
| 39 K–Kt2 | .... |

Affords some counterplay on the KB file after R–KB2; but White's game cannot be held nevertheless.

| 39 .... | R–Kt7 |

Black's main trump.

| 40 R–KB2 | P–B4 |
| 41 K–Kt1 | R–Kt8ch |

Time difficulties! The correct play was: 41 ...., K–R2; 42 K–Kt2, (the BP could not be captured, e.g.: 42 Q × BPch., Q × Q; 43 R × Q, R × QRP; 44 R × P, R–Kt7; and forces the QRP through) K–Kt3; 45 K–Kt1, Q–K5; and wins more or less as in the actual game.

| 42 K–Kt2 | P–Kt3 |

This is by far less enduring than the indirect protection of the KBP (see previous note).

43 Q–B4	Q–K5ch
44 Q × Q	QP × Q
45 R–K2	....

Now Black's clock again runs smoothly. After P–Kt4, it would have stopped altogether, e.g.: 45 P–Kt4, P × P; 46 R–B6, R–Kt7ch.; 47 K–Kt3, (whatever he does, not the first rank!) and White need not lose. It is easy to see now that this heaven-sent saving clause never really was " on," for, after ...., K–R2; and 42 ...., K–Kt3; Black could have exchanged Queens and White would have no chance whatsoever of breaking through.

45 ....   K–B2

There now follows an ending, attractive in its simplicity, a parallel case to that treated in " My System," that of the " absolute seventh "; the " absolute " seventh rank plus passed pawn nearly always wins. (" Absolute " applied to the seventh rank implies that the Rook on the seventh also helps to confine the opposing K to the eighth).

46	K B2	K–K3
47	R–Q2	K–Q4
48	K–K2	R–Kt7

The sealed move. Black foresaw the whole of the ensuing break-through.

49 K–Q1   ....

Threatens to annihilate the troublesome gate crasher at QKt2.

49 ....   P–Kt4

The supporting manœuvre on the other wing (if R × R, P × R; K–B2, P–B5; White is lost).

50	R–QB2	P–B5
51	KtP × P	P × P
52	R–B5ch	K–Q3
53	P × P	R × QRP

Now we have the " absolute seventh " plus passed pawn.

54	R–QR5	P–K6
55	K–K1	R–R8ch
56	K–K2	P–R7
57	P–B5	R–R8

And Black won in a few moves. In spite of the omission on Move 41, the main idea stands out clearly, namely : the combination of pressure in the centre and an out-flanking manœuvre—a very instructive example.

Game No. 13.—Berlin, 1928.

White: Sämisch.

1	P–K4	P–K3
2	P–Q4	P–Q4
3	Kt–QB3	Kt–KB3
4	B–Kt5	B–K2
5	P–K5	Kt–Kt1

With this move, which has a bad name, Black introduces a new and noteworthy plan of campaign.

6	B–K3	P–QKt3

This is the point: it is intended to exchange the White Bishops after B–QR3.

7	Q–Kt4	P–Kt3
8	P–KR4	P–KR4
9	Q–Kt3	B–R3
10	Kt–B3	B × B
11	K × B	Q–Q2

There now threatens, *inter alia*, the diversion Q–B3; followed by ...., P–QKt4–Kt5. One notices that White's QB2, QB4 and QKt5, all White squares labour under a certain weakness. This was the reason for the exchange of the White Bishops.

12	P–QR3	Kt–QB3

Black can be content with the success of his Queen's diversion (to Q2): White's P–QR3, after all creates a weakness.

13	QR–Q1	....

He defends his game prophylactically: this adds to the interest. Sämisch, incidentally, is one of the few players who fight for central points. He is indeed, strategically speaking, endowed with brilliant talent.

13	....	Kt–R4
14	Kt–KKt5	Kt–R3
15	B–B1	Castles QR
16	Q–Q3	K–Kt1
17	R–R3	....

The White position appears now to be well consolidated; the danger of Black's Kt–B5, is purely local, and on P–QB4; P × P, there would always be a sufficient defence, based on the Q file; the most important point is that the Kt at KKt5 exerts pressure on the whole K side, nor can it be exchanged without affording the White QB the run of a splendid diagonal.

　　　17 ………　　　　　　QR–KB1
As will be seen shortly, this move is not without sting.
　　　18 K–Kt1　　　　　………
He underrates the danger; the R had to play to B3 at once, for now its retreat is cut off. Even on 18 R–B3, there would follow Kt–B4; 19 P–KKt3, P–KB3; 20 P × P, B × P; (threatening Kt–B3; and P–K4;) 21 R–K1, R–K1; 22 R–B4, B × Kt; (not P–K4; because of the sacrifice of the exchange by : P × P, B × P; Kt × P, B × R; B × B,) 23 P × B, Kt–B3; and Black would still have slightly the best of it because of a possible break-through by P–K4. The opening, was, after all, in favour of Black.

　　　18 ………　　　　　　Kt–B4
　　　19 Kt–K2　　　　　　Q–Q1
Now 19 ………, P–KB3; would have been less strong because of 20 Kt–B3.
　　　20 P–KKt3　　　　　………
The threat was Kt × RP; (see the first part of Note 18).
　　　20 ………　　　　　　P–B4
　　　21 P × P　　　　　　　P × P
　　　22 K–Kt2　　　　　　Q–Kt3
The idea is to attack the KP intensively until White plays P–KB4, after which B × Kt; is to follow at last. Then the QB can no longer recapture, and the problem of the Kt at White's KKt5 is solved.

23 P–KB4 ....

He need not have made this move yet; but Sämisch, to whom consolidation has become a psychological necessity, cannot bear to see a pawn unprotected.

23 ....   B × Kt
24 RP × B   R–B1
25 R–R2   KR–Q1

The Rooks, now available, are positively hungry for work.

26 K–R3   P–Q5

A gradual advance of the central mass, accompanied, step by step, by the centralisation of the supporting pieces.

27 Q–KB3   R–Q4
28 P–Kt3   P–B5 !
29 P–QKt4   Kt–B3
30 P–B3   P–Q6

With this move, a beautiful and apparently sound combination is initiated, and yet, from a practical point of view, it would have been advisable to give preference to a strategy of simplification as illustrated by us at various times : without particular effort Black would have been able to retain some of the advantages of centralisation into the End-Game, as follows : 30 ...., QR–Q1; (instead of ...., P–Q6;) 31 P × P, QKt × P ; 32 Kt × Kt, Kt × Kt ; Now 33 Q–K4, (counter centralisation) would fail because of 33 ...., Kt–B4; and on 33 Q–B2 ; 33 ...., Kt–Kt6; would follow with : 34 B–K3, Q–Kt2; and an overwhelming advantage in position.

31 Kt–Kt1   P–Q7
32 KR × P   R × R
33 B × R   R–Q1
34 Q–K2   ....

If 34 B–B1, R × R; 35 Q × R, Q–B7; 36 Kt–K2, K–B1;
37 Q–R4, Q–B6; and wins; or 37 P–R4, QKt–K2–Q4–K6;
winning at once.

34	R–Q6
35 Kt–B3	Q–Q1
36 R–KB1	Q–Q4
37 R–B2	P–R5

Triumph of the centralising idea, carried out here in
Middle-Game style; White now loses the Queen.

38 P × P	QKt–Q5
39 P × Kt	Kt × QP
40 Q × R	....

He has nothing better. Black should win the ending
with ease, but weariness (which would hardly have set in had
he played 30 ...., QR–Q1; instead of sacrificing the
pawn) caused him to make a bad blunder which nearly
robbed him of the good results of his play.

40	P × Q
41 Kt × Kt	Q × Kt
42 K–Kt3	Q–K5 ?

Here Q–R8; K–B3, Q × P; K–K3, K–B2; would have
won easily.

43 R–R2	K–Kt2
44 P–R4	K–B3
45 P–QR5	K–Q4
46 P–R5	P × P
47 R × P	....

Now there begins, so to speak, a new game. Black
succeeds in winning after Sämisch missed a chance to draw.

47	Q–K7
48 R–R2	Q–Q8
49 R–B2	K–K5
50 K–R2	K–B4
51 R–Kt2	Q–KB8
52 K–Kt3	K–K5
53 R–B2	Q–KR8
54 R–Kt2	K–Q5
55 R–R2	Q–Q8
56 R–Kt2	K–B5
57 R–B2	Q–KR8

58	R–R2	Q–K5
59	R–B2	K–Kt6
60	R–R2	K–B7
61	R–B2	K–Q8
62	R–R2	Q–B3
63	K–Kt4	Q–B7
64	K–Kt3	Q × B

The only chance.

65	R × Qch.	K × R
66	P–B5 !	K–K6
67	P–Kt6	BP × P
68	P–B6	....

Frightened of ghosts. P × KP, would have made it a draw, e.g.: 68 P × KP, P–Q7; 69 P–K7, P–Q8 (Q); 70 P–K8 (Q), Q–B3ch.; 71 K–R2, K–B7?; 72 Q × P.

68	....	P–Q7
69	P–B7	P–Q8(Q)
70	P–B8(Q)	Q–Kt8ch.
71	K–R3	K–K5
72	P–Kt5 ?	Q–R8ch.
73	K–Kt3	Q–K8ch.
74	K–Kt4	Q × P
75	Q–Q6	Q–Kt3
76	K–Kt5	Q × P
77	K–B6	Q–B8ch.
78	K–Kt7	Q–B4
79	Q–B6ch.	K × P
80	Q–B5ch.	K–K5
81	Q × P	P–K4
82	Q–Kt1	K–Q4
83	Q–Q1ch.	K–B4
84	Q–QB1ch.	K–Kt4 !
85	Q–Kt2ch.	K–B3
86	Q–B3ch.	K–Q2
87	Q–Q2ch.	K–K1
88	Q–Q5	....

With Q–R5, White could have held out longer.

| 88 | .... | Q–Q2ch. |

Resigns.

An interesting Q End-Game.

Game (Ending) No. 14.—St. Petersburg, 1913.

White: Alekhin.

   1 R–B4 ....

Compare this position with Game No. 12, after Black's
33rd move; the difference lies in the type of wing attack; in
Game 12 the advanced P was supported on a file and here on
a diagonal; the diagonal is less forcible.

   1 .... R–B5

The combinative play intended by White in the centre
and on the K wing fails on account of the weakness of his
own Q side (See preliminary note). Instead of the text-
move, it was also possible to oppose the Queens by:
1 ...., Q–R1; 2 Q–Kt7, Q×Q; 3 P×Q, P–KR4;
4 P–KKt4, R–KKt1; 5 P×P, P×P; 6 R×RP, R×Pch.;
7 K–B3, and now perhaps 7 ...., P–R4; with P–Kt4;
eventually. Black could probably hold this ending, but the
move actually made is far stronger.

   2 R–R1 ....

One makes such a move with reluctance, but 2 Q–Kt7,
is parried by P–B4; e.g.: 3 Q–K5, R×RP; 4 Q×KP,
R–K2; 5 Q–B6, Q–Q2; and Black has the better position.

   2 .... R–B3
   3 R–B6 ....

Here 3 Q–Kt7, would not be without danger because of
3 ...., P–B4; 4 Q–K5, Q–Kt4; 5 R–R1, R–K2; with
R–B5; to follow.

3	....	Q–QKt1
4	Q–K3	R–K2
5	Q–B3	Q–K1 !
6	P–KKt4	Q–Q2
7	R–K1	R–B2

Black has made headway; his KBP is well covered, White can hardly get to KKt7 and his QRP is under fire.

	8 P–Kt3	....

This weakens his Q side still further.

8	....	K–R2
9	P–Kt5	Q–Q3
10	Q–Q3	Q–R6

With this move Black takes up the attack.

11	Q–B2	Q–Kt5
12	R–QB1	Q–R6
13	R–K1	Q–Kt5
14	R–QB1	Q–R6
15	R–K1	Q–Kt5
16	R–QB1	Q–Q3
17	Q–Q3	Q–R6
18	R–QKt1	....

If again Q–B2, Black plays R–B3; followed by KR–B2.

18	....	Q–R7
19	R–B3	P–K4

After the break-through, the White position, weakened on all sides, can no longer be held.

20	R–K3	P–K5
21	Q–Q1	P–B4 !
22	P×P e.p.	R–B2
23	R–R1	Q–Kt7
24	R–Kt1	Q–R6
25	P–QB4	R×KBP
26	P×P	QR—B2
27	R–K2	Q–Q3
28	Q–B2	Q×P

Black has now obtained a mighty K side attack.

29	K–B1	P–K6
30	R×P	Q–R8ch.

Better than R×Pch.

31	K–K2	R×Pch.
32	K–Q3	Q–Q4
33	Q–B8	R–Q2

White resigns.

For after 34 R–K4, Black's reply R–B6ch.; 35 K–Q2, Q–Kt4ch.; leads to Mate.

Game No. 15.—Semmering, 1926.

Black: Dr. Alekhin.

1 P–K4	Kt–KB3
2 Kt–QB3	P–Q4
3 P–K5	KKt–Q2
4 P–B4	P–K3
5 Kt–B3	P–QB4
6 P–KKt3	Kt–QB3
7 B–Kt2	....

Black's K side appears to be somewhat hemmed in, but his centre is all the more mobile.

7	B–K2
8 Castles	Castles
9 P–Q3	Kt–Kt3

Bad would be 9 ...., P–Q5; because of 10 Kt–K4, with centralisation; but 9 ...., P–B3; was strongly to be considered: e.g., 9 ...., P–B3; 10 P × P, B × P; and Black has full control of the centre.

10 Kt–K2	P–Q5 !?

Black wants to stigmatise White's last move as a mistake for the Kt can no longer reach his K4. This is an error of judgment, and 10 ...., P–B3; would have replaced the text-move advantageously, e.g., 10 ...., P–B3; 11 P × P, B × P; 12 P–B3, P–K4; 13 P × P, Kt × P; and Black has quite a good game.

11 P–KKt4	P–B3

This move, twice passed over by Black, now leads to undesirable results because of the weakness at his K4. Defence by preventive tactics was preferable, e.g., 11 ...., R–K1; 12 Kt–Kt3, B–B1; 13 Kt–K4, Kt–Q4; (preventing P–B5,).

12 P × P	P × P

With 12 ...., B × P; 13 Kt–Kt3, P–K4; 14 P–B5, Black would also not have been particularly happy.

13 Kt–Kt3	Kt–Q4

Black seeks to safeguard the threatened wing from the centre; he should not have succeeded.

14 Q–K2	B–Q3
15 Kt–R4	....

Threatening B × Kt, and Kt–B5.

15	QKt–K2
16 B–Q2	....

Here Kt–R5, would have been more energetic; e.g.:
16 Kt–R5, Kt–KKt3; 17 B × Kt, P × B; 18 Kt–B5, with a
winning attack.

    16 ....   Q–B2
    17 Q–B2   ....
Kt–R5, was still preferable.

    17 ....   P–B5
    18 P × P   Kt–K6

With this ingenious diversion, Dr. Alekhin succeeds
in bringing his opponent's attack to a standstill for the time
being.

    19 B × Kt   P × Kt
    20 Q–B3   Q × P

The position has become clearer : Black has a passed
pawn, not in the best of health, but highly insured against
death; we mean by that the diagonals from Black's QB3–
KR8 (after B–Q2–B3;) and QB4–KKt8 would afford compensation for the loss of the passed pawn. It would therefore
be of greater moment for White to pursue his K side attack
(P–Kt5,) rather than to hunt for the doubtful advantage of
winning this pawn. Through this omission White gets the
inferior game.

    21 Kt–K4   B–B2
    22 P–Kt3   Q–Q5
    23 P–B3   Q–Kt3
    24 K–R1   ....

White has localised the enemy break-through.

    24 ....   Kt–Q4

No doubt B–Q2; was better.

    25 P–B5   ....

He neglects the opportunity of advancing P–Kt5, which
would have won, e.g.: 25 P–Kt5, P × P; 26 Kt × P, R × P;
27 Q–R5, or 25 P–Kt5, P–B4; 26 Q–R5, P × Kt; 27 B × P,
etc.

    25 ....   Kt–B5
    26 KR–Q1   K–R1

According to H. Wolf, the better continuation was:
26 ...., P–K7; 27 R–Q2, Q–Kt4; with eventually Q–K4.

    27 B–B1   P × P
    28 P × P   B–K4
    29 R–K1   B–Q2

Now matters develop exactly as described in the Note to move 20 : White captures the pawn, but Black exerts pressure on the two diagonals.

  30 R × P   B–B3
  31 QR–K1   Kt–Q4

With 31 ...., R–KKt1 ; Black could have intensified the pressure.

  32 R–Q3   ....

....   Kt × P

Pretty but not sufficient. It is true, accepting the sacrifice would spell disaster, but White has a counter-combination which can be truly termed amazing.

  33 Kt–Kt6ch.   P × Kt
  34 Q–Kt4 ! !   ....

The point. Hitting out at once would be bad ; e.g. : 34 P × P, K–Kt2 ; 35 Q–R3, R–R1 ; 36 R–Q7ch., B × R ; 37 Q × Bch., K × P ; and White is threatened with mate on KR2.

  34 ....   R–B2

Here R–KKt1 ; was called for. The continuation would be : 35 P × P, K–Kt2 ; 36 R–Q7ch., B × R ; 37 Q × Bch., K × P ; 38 B–Q3 ! K–R3 ; 39 Q–R3ch., K–Kt2 ; 40 R–Kt1ch., Q × Rch. ; and the win for White would still be far away.

  35 R–R3ch.   K–Kt2
  36 B–B4 !   B–Q4
  37 P × P   Kt × Kt
  38 P × R dis.ch. K–B1
  39 R × Kt   ....

A simpler way to win is : 39 Q–Kt8ch., K–K2 ; 40 P–B8(Q)ch., R × Q ; 41 R–R7ch., K–K1 ; 42 Q × B.

39	B × Rch.
40 Q × B	K–K2
41 P–B8(Q)ch.	....

The passed pawn's urge to expand.

| 41 .... | R × Q |
| 42 Q–Q5 | Q–Q3 |

The alternative 42 ...., Q–B3; would not exchange but would lose the Q; e.g.: 43 R–R7ch., K–K1; 44 B–Kt5.

43 Q × Pch.	K–Q1
44 R–Q3	B–Q5
45 Q–K4	R–K1
46 R × B	Resigns.

5.—A MOBILE BODY OF PAWNS IN THE CENTRE. HOW THE CONTACT IS MAINTAINED BETWEEN ADVANCED CENTRE PAWNS AND THEIR SUPPORTING PIECES.

Games 16—17.

We have already seen the procedure in Game No. 13 (see moves 26 and 27 as well as the variation given in the note to Move 30, namely: 30 ...., QR–Q1; 31 P × P, etc.): in that position, it may be said that the pawn advance was no isolated, self-contained process. On the contrary, it derived its strength from the readiness of the pieces behind them to occupy central squares; it was a case, therefore, of centralising action prepared behind the scenes.

In Games 16 and 17, the procedure is similar. In Game 16, the characteristics are the subtle central moves Q–K4–Q4–Q5, together with the powerful deployment on the flanks (QKt6 and KKt7); only centralisation made the advance P–Q6, possible.

Also in Game 17, the effective work of the centrally placed pieces is noteworthy.

Besides the voluntary giving up of the QB file, the positional try: 32 ...., P–KR4; is worthy of note. This latter manœuvre is particularly typical; in positional games by efficient masters, a strong central lay-out frequently manifests itself in this manner.

Game No. 16.—London, 1927.

Black: Romih.

1	P–Q4	P–Q4
2	P–QB4	P–K3
3	Kt–QB3	Kt–KB3
4	B–Kt5	QKt–Q2
5	P–K3	P–B3
6	P × P	KP × P
7	B–Q3	B–Q3

Better would be B–K2.

8	Q–B2	P–KR3
9	B–R4	....

Black now suffers from Castling troubles. By this we mean that Castles KR would be hazardous, and Castles QR would be very difficult to carry out. In these circumstances the waiting strategy chosen by Romih, in that he retains the option of Castling on either wing, must be held to be entirely appropriate.

9	....	Q–R4
10	Castles	B–Kt5
11	KKt–K2	B–K2

The art of marking time at its best! Black desires to divert the White Knight from the route KKt1–B3–K5. Certainly a fine manœuvre, betraying more Chess instinct than many a brilliant assault, be is never so cleverly carried out.

12	K–Kt1	Kt–B1
13	P–KR3	....

In order, eventually, to retire the B to Kt3 without having to fear Kt–R4.

13	....	B–K3
14	P–B3	P–R3
15	P–R3	....

The initiation of an enduring attack here is not easy; e.g.: 15 P–K4?, Kt × P; 16 B × B, Kt × Ktch.; followed by K × B.

15	....	B–Q2

Preparing for the excursion Kt–K3, B2, Kt4.

16	B × Kt!	B × B
17	P–K4	Kt–K3
18	P–K5	B–K2
19	P–B4	....

The mobile pawn centre.

19	....	Kt–B2
20	P–B5	Kt–Kt4

21	KR–B1	....

Contact is being established (compare preliminary note).

21	....	Q–Kt3

If 21 ...., B × RP; it was White's intention to reply
22 B × Kt, RP × B; 23 P × B, Q × P; 24 Q–R2, which would
fail because of B × Pch.; had White not played 21 KR–B1.
The contact is already noticeable.

A better continuation than the move in the text would
have been the exchange on QB6 and Castles QR; e.g., 21
........., Kt × Ktch.; 22 Kt × Kt, Castles QR; 23 Kt–R4,
K–Kt1; 24 P–QKt4, Q–B2; 25 K–R2, and White's attack
would not be easy to conduct.

22	B × Kt	RP × B
23	Kt–B4	P–Kt5
24	QKt × P	....

The point.

24	....	P × Kt

Or if 24 ...., P–Kt6; 25 Q–K4, with a strong attack.

25	Kt × P	Q–R4
26	Kt–B7ch.	K--Q1
27	Kt × R	Q × Kt

Compulsory, for on 27 ...., P × P; liquidation would
follow by 28 P–Q5, P × P; 29 Q–B7ch.; Q × Q; 30 Kt × Q,
K × Kt; 31 P–Q6ch., and wins.

28	P–Q5	Q–B1
29	Q–K4	....

Placing the Q centrally considerably enhances the
dynamic value of the advanced pawns.

29	R–K1
30 R–B1	Q–Kt1
31 P–K6!	....

There appears to be now at Q6 a dead square over which the pawns cannot pass. It would be so were it not for the Q in the centre! As it is, the obstacle is surmounted with the greatest ease.

| 31 .... | B–QKt4 |
| 32 Q–Q4 | .... |

Threatens Q–Kt6ch.

| 32 .... | P–QKt3 |
| 33 P–Q6! | .... |

If now 33 ...., Q × P; then 34 KR–Q1. If, however : 33 ...., B × P; 34 KR–Q1, K–K2; 35 Q × KKtP, R–KB1; 36 Q × P, with an early decision. Note that the Q from Q4 acted equally towards KKt7 and QKt6, the usual corollary of centralisation.

33	B–KB3
34 P–K7ch.	K–Q2
35 Q–Q5	B × R
36 Q–B6 mate.	

Game No. 17.—Kecskemet, 1927.

White: Grünfeld.

1 P–Q4	Kt–KB3
2 P–QB4	P–K3
3 Kt–QB3	B–Kt5
4 Q–B2	P–Q3

A playable move in this position is : 4 ...., P–QKt3; e.g. : 5 P–K4, B × Ktch.; 6 P × Kt, P–Q3; 7 P–KB4, and now KKt–Q2; subsequently Black will develop his forces with QKt–B3 (later perhaps to R4), B–Kt2; P–KB4; (never P–K4.) Q–B2; and Castles QR; Black has a defendable game.

| 5 B–Kt5 | QKt–Q2 |
| 6 P–QR3 | .... |

Loss of a tempo. The best continuation appears to be : 6 P–K3, e.g., ..., P–QKt3; 7 B–Q3, B–Kt2; 8 P–B3.

6	B × Ktch.
7 Q × B	P–KR3
8 B–R4	P–QKt3

Very good too would be : 8 ...., Castles; for, if then :
9 P–B3, (as in the actual game) simply 9 ...., P–Q4; etc.

>9 P–B3   B–Kt2
10 P–K4   ....

The disposition of the White forces has, at most, only
defensive value, for if e.g.: 10 ...., P–K4; 11 B–B2,
P–B4; 12 P–Q5, (or 12 P×BP, QP×P; with Q–K2; QKt–
Kt1–B3; and P–Q5;) 12 ...., P–KKt4; and White's two
Bishops are quite inoffensive; at the same time Black's attack
will hardly carry through.

10 ....   Kt × P

High spirits !

11 B × Q   Kt × Q
12 B–R4 !   ....

Less good would be : 12 B × P, K–K2; 13 P × Kt,
KR–QB1; 14 B × Pch., K × B; because White's QBP cannot
be held against R–B2; QR–QB1; Kt–Kt1; and B–R3; but
now, after 12 B–R4 ! Black has to give up a piece.

12 ....   Kt–R5

At this stage, Black bethought himself of the American
motto : "Make the best of it !" Not to despair, to find the
relatively best chance in the worst circumstances ! To make
the win as difficult as possible. So thinks the American, and
this way of thinking has its points ! This can be seen in the
present game.

13 P–QKt3   P–QB4 !
14 P × Kt   ....

Weak. 14 P–Q5, was called for, although in that case
also Black would have assumed a defensive position difficult
to disturb, e.g.: 14 P–Q5, P × P; 15 P × Kt, P × P; 16 B × P,
P–Q4; 17 B–QKt5 !, P–Kt4; 18 B–Kt3, Castles QR ; after
the move in the text White actually drifts into an inferior
position.

14 ....   P × P
15 Kt–K2   P–K4
16 Kt–B1   Kt–B4

Black has now two extra pawns with a strong position;
he moreover has definite prospects of winning two more
Pawns; he has therefore already secured the advantage.

17 P–R5   P × P

This Pawn helps to cover important squares and its
value is by no means to be despised.

18 Kt–Q3   Kt–Q2

The correct retreat whereby his K4 is kept under observation, e.g., 19 P–B5, P × P; and the KP is protected. Accordingly 18 ...., Kt–K3; would be bad for the reply 19 P–B5, would have had disagreeable consequences for Black, as follows: 18 ...., Kt–K3; 19 P–B5, Kt × P; 20 Kt × Kt, P × Kt; 21 B–Kt5ch., and White has an open game.

19	B–K2	B–R3
20	Castles KR	B × P
21	B–K1	P–R5
22	B–Kt4	P–Q4
23	KR–K1	P–B3

No chances must be given of a sacrifice on White's K5,

24	Kt–Kt2	B × B
25	R × B	K–B2

The alternative 25 ...., QR–B1; 26 Kt × P, K–B2; was also playable, but Black voluntarily abandons the QB file in order to advance his centre the more quickly. The further course of the game proves him to be right.

26	R–QB1	Kt–Kt3
27	R–B7ch.	K–Kt3
28	KR–QB2	P–K5

See previous note.

29	R(B2)–B6	P–Q6
30	R–K6	KR–K1
31	R × R	R × R
32	K–B1	......

If 32 R × P, the reply is ...., R–QB1 !

32	......	P–KR4

Feeling for an opening. New weaknesses are to be created.

33	P–R3	......

Black was probably in a position to force this move sooner or later (attacking threats of P–R5–R6) but White should not have given in without a fight, for now there is a dreadful hole at KKt3.

33	......	P–R5
34	K–Kt1	K–B4
35	K–B2	P–K6ch.
36	K–B1	P–Q7
37	K–K2	P–Q5

$$\text{38 Kt–Q3} \qquad \ldots\ldots\ldots$$

The state of blockade is illusory as is shown by the following Kt manœuvre.

38	Kt–Q4
39 R–B5	....

If 39 R–B4, Kt × B ; is decisive. 40 Kt × Kt, (if R × Kt, R–QB1 ;) R–Q1 ; 41 Kt–Q3, R–QKt1 ; 42 R–Kt4, R × R ; 43 Kt × R, K–B5 ; and K–Kt6.

39	R–Q1
40 B–R5	R–Q2
41 R–B4	Kt–B5ch.
42 Kt × Kt	K × Kt
43 B–B3	....

Or B–B7ch., K–B4, etc.

43	K–Kt6
44 R × QP	R × R
45 B × R	K × P
46 B × KP	K × RP
47 B × QP	K–Kt7

Resigns.

6.—GIVING UP THE PAWN-CENTRE.
Games 18—20.

This need not be a catastrophe; as we have seen in the examples given up to date, there is only one question that matters : are the central squares under adequate control? Under strong control by the opposing forces, the mobility of the free pawn-centre is reduced to an alarming degree, and the pawn-centre itself might in the end become the object of an attack.

In Game 18, Steiner neglects the opportunity of establishing pressure against his opponent's free pawn-centre. In

Game 19, we have an attempt, based on insufficient grounds, to paralyse a strong and elastic centre, which attempt is, in a manner of speaking, blown to atoms; at least the chief actors, first the P at QB4, and soon after the P at K4.

In Game No. 20, we have, in quick succession— 1 : Abandonment of the centre; 2 : Reconquest of the centre, though with a loss in pawns; 3, The deficiency in material is balanced by centralisation on the White squares; and 4 : Black should have obtained the advantage, only his 33rd move takes the game out of its logical course, whereby it loses some of its didactic value.

Game No. 18.—Niendorf, 1927.

Black: L. Steiner.

1	P–K4	P–K4
2	Kt KB3	Kt–QB3
3	Kt–B3	Kt–B3
4	B–Kt5	P–Q3
5	P–Q4	B–Q2
6	B × Kt	B × B
7	Q–Q3	Kt–Q2
8	B K3	P × P
9	B × P	....

Black's difficulty is not so much the problem of the Pawn-centre as the fact that White's centralised Bishop keeps the KtP under fire.

    9 ....   P–B3 ?

The move appears to us to be the decisive mistake. The correct continuation was : 9 ...., Kt–B4; at once, e.g., 10 Q–K2, Kt–K3; 11 Castles QR, B–K2; 12 Kt–Q5, Castles; 13 B–B3, R–K1; followed by B–B1; with entirely sufficient central effect. Or else : 12 ...., B × Kt; (instead of Castles); 13 P × B, Kt × B; 14 Kt × Kt, Castles; with B–B3; and Black has a good game.

    10 Kt–KR4   ....

A diversion in no way premature.

10	....	Kt–B4
11	Q–K2	Kt–K3
12	Kt–B5	....

Now Black can no longer obtain a satisfactory development; e.g. : 12 ...., B–K2 ?; 13 Kt–Q5, B × Kt; 14 P × B, Kt × B; 15 Kt × Kt, with decisive control of K6.

| 12 .... | Q–Q2 |

Futile would be 12 ...., P–KKt3; because of : 13 Castles QR, K–B2; 14 Q–B4.

| 13 Castles KR | .... |

Not merely a developing but also a waiting move.

For Black is in all circumstances compelled to create a new weakness if he wishes to arrive at a reasonable development, and White can afford to wait until Black decides to play either P–QR3; or P–QKt3.

Therefore, 13 Castles KR, which looks like a developing move, was in reality a tentative waiting move similar to 32 ...., P–KR4; in Game 17.

| 13 .... | P–QKt3 |

The alternative, 13 ......, P–QR3; also had its drawbacks. Entirely bad, however, would be : 13 ...., Castles QR ; e.g. : 14 B × RP, P–QKt3; 15 P–QR4, K–Kt2; 16 P–R5, K × B ; 17 P × P db. ch., K–Kt1 ; 18 R–R7, B–Kt2 (the only move); 19 R × Bch., K × R ; 20 R–R1, P × P; 21 Q–R6ch., K–B3; 22 Q–Kt5ch., K–Kt2; 23 Q–Q5ch., Q–B3; 24 R–R7ch., and wins. Instead of creating a weakness by P–QR3; or P–QKt3; a Steinitz would no doubt have tried 13 ...., B–K2; e.g. : 14 Kt–Q5, B–Q1; 15 P–QB4, Castles KR; 16 B–B3, R–K1; and the Black position is terribly constricted, yet not easy to undermine.

| 14 P–QR4 | .... |

Now everything is set.

| 14 .... | P–QR4 |
| 15 Kt–Q5 | Kt × B |

If 15 ...., Castles ; 16 B × KtP.

16 Kt × Kt	B–Kt2
17 Kt–K6	R–B1
18 Q–R5ch.	P–Kt3
19 Kt × KBPch.	K–B2
20 Kt × Q	P × Q
21 Kt(Q7) × B	Resigns.

It is clear that Black's game could have been held, as shown, by 9 ...., Kt–B4; and perhaps later even with 13 ...., B–K2; and 14 ...., B–Q1; (though this required the defensive powers of a Steinitz). Also 10 ...., Kt–K4; possessed strength. Giving up the centre is not necessarily a catastrophe.

Game No. 19.—Carlsbad, 1911.

White: Alapin.

1	P–K4	P–QB3
2	P–QB4	P–Q3
3	P–Q4	Kt–B3
4	Kt–QB3	QKt–Q2
5	P–B4	P–K4
6	Kt–B3	P × QP
7	Q × P	Kt–B4

In order to tame the tiger; *vulgo* the centre, ready to spring. If 8 P–K5, P × P; and White has nothing.

8	B–Q3	Q–Kt3

Here Kt × B; came into consideration (the " Two Bishops.")

9	B–B2	B–K2
10	Castles	Castles
11	K R1	R Q1

The taming continues.

12	QR–Kt1	B–K3

This is the counter-chance; a rolling up process sets in against QB5; the reason why this must be so lies deep : why should the White QBP imagine that it could paralyse the elastic and strong Black centre (PQ3) ! For this presumption it will be severely punished.

13	P–B5	....

A heavy surrender, for now the White centre loses considerably in mobility. Against other moves the rolling-up process mentioned above would set in, e.g. : 13 B–K3, Q–R3; 14 P–QKt3, P–QKt4; (or ...., P–Q4; 15 BP × P, BP × P; 16 P–K5, KKt–K5;) or else 13 P–QKt4, Kt–R3; 14 Q–Q3, Kt × KtP; 15 Q–K2, Q–B4.

13	....	QB–B1
14	B–Kt5	QKt–Q2
15	Q–Q2	P–QR3
16	P–QKt3	Q–B2
17	QR–Q1	P–Kt4

The storm breaks.

18	KR–K1	Kt–K4
19	P × P	RP × P

That pompous White QBP, has passed away, unwept, unhonoured and unsung.

        20 B–Kt1   B–Kt2
        21 Q–B1   Q–Kt3
        22 P–KR3   ....
Sounder would be B–K3, Q–R4; B–Kt1.

        22 ....   Kt × Kt
The beginning of a deep-laid combination.
        23 P × Kt   Q–B7
        24 Q–K3   Q–Kt6
        25 P–B4   Q × Q
        26 R × Q   P–R3
        27 B–R4   P–Kt5
    The last two pawn moves are the key to the combination.
The White centre will now be conquered in a surprising
manner.
        28 Kt–R4   Kt × P !
        29 R × Kt   B × B
        30 R × KtP   R–R2
and, with his two Bishops—the White pawn position being
torn up—Black has a won game.
        31 B–K4   B–K2
        32 B–B3   P–Q4
        33 KR–Q4   R–Q3
        34 K–R2   R–B3
        35 B–Kt4   B–Q3
        36 R–QB1   P–R4
        37 K–Kt3   ....
    If 37 B × P, Black wins a piece by : R × P; 38 B–Kt4,
R × P.

37	....	P × B
38	P × P	P–Kt4
39	P × P e.p.	P × P
40	P–Kt5	R–B4
41	K–B3	R–R1
42	Kt–B5	B × Kt
43	R × B	R × RP

Resigns.

Game No. 20.—Kecskemet, 1927.

White: Alekhin.

1	P–K4	P–K3
2	P–Q4	P–Q4
3	Kt–QB3	Kt–KB3
4	P × P	Kt × P
5	Kt–K4	....

Thus early Black finds himself in the not necessarily unpleasant position of having to fend without a pawn-centre. For the next seven moves he solves this problem quite satisfactorily.

5	....	Kt–Q2
6	Kt–KB3	B–K2
7	B–Q3	P–QKt3
8	Castles	Kt–Kt5
9	B–QB4	B–Kt2
10	Q–K2	Castles
11	P–QR3	Kt–Q4
12	R–Q1	....

A preventive measure against Black's P–QB4.

| 12 | .... | P–QB4 |

Nevertheless Black lets himself be tempted to open up the game prematurely. It would have been wiser to open it up slowly by 12 ...., P–QB3; followed by Q–B2; KR–Q1; and only then P–QB4; a restricted position should not be liberated too suddenly. In Chess too, liberty, absorbed in deep, quick draughts, is intoxicating. With 12 ...., P–QB3; Black's game could have become strong and full of life. (After 12 ...., P–QB3; 13 ...., Q–B2; even Kt–B5; might have become possible after B–Q3, at some future time).

13 B–QKt5	Kt–B2
14 B × Kt	....

Clearly Alekhin would not have allowed: 14 P × P, Kt × B; 15 Q × Kt, B × Kt; 16 R × Kt, Q–K1; 17 P–B6, R–B1.

14	Q × B
15 P × P	Q–B3
16 Kt–Q6 !	....

He scorns the gain of a pawn by: 16 P × P, P × P; 17 R–K1, because of 17 ...., Kt–Q4; (18 P–B4, Kt–B3; 19 Kt × Ktch., B × Kt; with two splendid diagonals for the Bishops) and Black would obtain a powerfully centralised game; e.g.: 17 ...., Kt–Q4; 18 Kt–K5, Q–B2; 19 Kt–Q3, QR–B1; 20 P–QB3, KR–Q1; and, if anything, Black is better.

16	B × Kt

There is nothing better. If 16 ...., B–R3; 17 P–B4, P × P; 18 Kt–K5, Q–R5; there follows: 19 B–R6, B × Kt; 20 R × B, P × B; 21 Q–Kt4ch., K–R1; 22 R–Q7, with a winning position.

17 P × B	Kt–K1
18 B–Kt5	....

Again, a move of the utmost cunning.

18	Kt–B3
19 R–Q4	Kt–Q2
20 B–K7	KR–B1
21 P–B3	P–K4

And now it is shown that in spite of all subtleties, Black's centralisation has stood firm. In addition the White B at K7 is a little shaky, whereas Black's B at Kt2 shows a lively disposition. The games are equal and White's Pawn plus is of no great importance.

22 R–KKt4	....

The object of this move is to give the Bishop a possible field of action. Incidentally it frees the Kt as the KKtP is now covered.

22	Q–Q4
23 R–Kt3	R–B5

24 R–Q1 ....

Here White believes that he could have taken the position by storm as follows : 24 Kt–Kt5, P–KR3 ?; 25 R–Q1, Q–B3; 26 Kt × P, K × Kt; 27 Q–R5ch., K Kt1; 28 Q–Kt6. There is, however, the resource : 24 ......, P–Kt3; 25 R–Q1, Q–B3; 26 R–B3, P–B4; and the decisive move 27 R × P, has become impossible because of the threatened mate at KKt2. After the move in the text Black has an unusual manœuvre by which he forces a welcome exchange of Rooks.

24	Q–K5
25 Q–B1	Q–B7
26 R–Q2	Q–R5
27 R–K2	....

After 27 P–R3, which Alekhin subsequently recommended as the better move, Black had considered, *inter alia*, a change of front by B–K5–Kt3; etc. It is noteworthy that Black's manœuvres in the centre all use the point K5.

27	R–K5
28 R × R	Q × R
29 Q–B1	P–KR3
30 P–R3	K–R2
31 Q–Q1	P–Kt3

Not to be thought of was : 31 ...., P–B4; because of the sacrifice Kt–Kt5ch., with Q–R5ch., and Q × P.

32 R–Kt4	Q–Q4
33 Q–B2	....

An excursion by the R : R–QB1–B5; appeared to Black to be both tempting and risky. Risky because of the threat by White of Kt–R4×P, and tempting on a question of " System." For Black's K5 is here the most valuable point strategically and should attract the forces as a magnet. (See Over-Protection). After 33 ...., R–QB1; there could follow: 34 Kt–R4, P–K5; 35 P–B3, Q–B4ch.; and now either 36 K–R1 or K–R2. On 36 K–R1, Q–K6; 37 P×P, P–KR4; 38 R–Kt5, Q–K8ch.; with the gain of a piece.

On 36 K–R2, Black has the choice between 36 ...., Q–K6; (37 P×P, R–B5;) or 36 ...., Kt–K4; e.g.: 36 ...., Kt–K4; 37 R–B4, Q–K6; 38 P–KKt3, P×P; 39 R×Pch., K–Kt1; and White has no defence against the threat Q–K7ch. As this short analysis shows, 33 ...., R–QB1; was a suitable move to show conclusively that White's advantage was illusory.

33	R–KKt1
34 R–KR4	....

Threatening B–Kt5.

34	P–B3
35 P–B4	Q–K3
36 Kt–Q2	Q–B4
37 Q–Q1	P–KKt4

As Alekhin rightly says: 37 ...., P–KR4; was preferable, as the Rook now gains the open. Both players were short of time.

38 R–Kt4	Q–Kt3
39 R–Kt3	P–B4
40 R–QB3	P–K5

Here a draw was agreed to, specially on account of time difficulties. After 41 Kt–Kt3, followed by P–B5, White appears again to have the advantage. From a thorough study of this game, the learner will be able to develop the feeling for "weak squares of a stated colour," (here the White squares at White's KKt2, K4, QB4, Q7).

7.—CENTRALISATION AS "DEUS EX MACHINA." (THE SUDDEN CONCLUSION).

Games 21—23.

We would beg the reader, who is objectively interested, not to treat this subject lightly. It may be that the centralisation, when arising suddenly, so to speak as a last minute saviour, is not as typical as the centralisation arrived at slowly, methodically. Against that the first-named is psychologically and pedagogically all the more important. What is impossible to the gradually developed centralisation, the sudden centralisation will achieve. And that is : to instil an unbounded faith in the value of centralisation. And nothing matters more ; it is not enough to have acquired the technical details, it is essential to believe in the power of centralisation to work wonders. The faith is essential, only he who has faith will succeed !

Game 21.—New York, 1927.

Black: Marshall.

1 Kt–KB3	Kt–KB3
2 P–K3	P–Q4
3 P–QKt3	B–Kt5
4 B–Kt2	QKt–Q2
5 P–KR3	....

This Pawn move makes Castling on the K side at a later state none too desirable, and therefore reduces White's resources. 5 B–K2, and Castles, was good enough.

5	B–R4
6 P–Q3	P–KR3
7 QKt–Q2	P–K3
8 Q–K2	....

If 8 B–K2, and 9 Castles, White had to anticipate an assault by Pawns : e.g., 8 B–K2, B–Q3 ; 9 Castles, Q–K2 ; 11 R–B1, P–KKt4 ; (White lost in a similar manner against Vidmar in the same tournament).

8	....	B–QKt5
9	P–KKt4	B–Kt3
10	Kt–K5	Kt × Kt
11	B × Kt	B–Q3
12	Kt–B3	Q–K2
13	B–KKt2	Castles QR
14	Castles QR	B × B
15	Kt × B	B–R2
16	P–QB4	....

This move loosens the White position, but a line of communications had to be established in the second rank.

16	....	Kt–Q2
17	Kt × Kt	R × Kt
18	P × P	P × P
19	Q–Kt2	P–KB4

White has succeeded in securing his K position by preventive measures such as 16 P–QB4, and 19 Q–Kt2, but at the cost of weaknesses on the other wing; it simply was impossible to " prevent " on both wings at the same time, and he had unfortunately to submit to ...., P–KB4.

20	R–Q2	R–B1
21	P × P	B × P
22	KR–Q1	Q–Kt4
23	P–B4	Q–Kt6

24 Q–K5   ....

This unexpected centralisation saves the game!   The honour is shared by centralisation and the " prophylactic " (=preventive) method, as Q–K5, can be said to be a corollary to 19 Q–Kt2.

24	B × RP

The alternative: 24 ...., P-B3; 25 R-QB2, is no better.

25 B × P	Q-Kt3
26 B-K4	Q-KB3
27 Q × Q	R × Q
28 R-Kt1	B-B4
29 R(Q2)-KKt2	....

Matters appear to develop according to programme—first centralisation and now a positionally well justified flanking movement to the right wing.

29	B × B
30 P × B	R-Q6
31 R × P	R × KP
32 R-Kt8ch.	....

The flank attack has developed into a break-through.

32	K-Q2
33 R(Kt1)-Kt7ch	K-B3
34 R(Kt7)-Kt6	R-Q3

This attempt, imaginative in itself, of forcing the White King into a cul-de-sac, is hardly sufficient.

35 P-K5	R-K8ch.
36 K-Kt2	R-K7ch.
37 K-R3	R × R
38 R × Rch.	K-Q4
39 R × P	P-R4
40 R-R7	R-QB7

If instead: 40 ...., K-B3; there follows: 41 R-K7, P-Kt4; 42 P-Kt4, R-K6ch.; 43 K-Kt2, P × P; 44 P-B5, and the White King has escaped at the cost of a pawn, which, in view of his united passed pawns is quite a negligible loss.

41 R-K7	P-Kt4
42 P-Kt4	....

Not 42 P-B5, because of 42 ...., P-B3; 43 P-Kt4, K-B5; and Mate to follow.

42	P-R5?

There was a slight chance of a draw by: 42 ...., P × Pch.; 43 K × P, R-B5ch.; 44 K × P, P-B3ch.; with R × P; to follow. After the move in the text, Black is utterly lost.

43 P-B5	P-B4

44 P–B6   ....

A heavy blunder; 44 P–K6, won easily, e.g., 44 P–K6, R–B6ch.; (44 ...., K–B5?; R–QB7,) 45 K–Kt2, P × P; 46 R–Q7ch., K–B3; 47 R–Q8, R–K6; 48 P–B6, and wins.

44 ....   R–B6ch.
45 K–Kt2   P × P
Drawn.

For if 46 P–B7, the draw is forced after P–R6ch.; 47 K–Kt1, R–B6; 48 P–K6, R–B8ch.; 49 K–B2, R–B7ch.; 50 K–Q3, P–Kt6; 51 P × P, P–R7; 52 R–R7, K × P; etc.

The White centralisation would have won easily but for the blunder on Move 44.

Game (Ending) No. 22.—Kecskemet, 1928.

Black: Vukovic.

The Black position, with the K exposed, and the pawns isolated, would appear decidedly unsound, were it not for the centralised Queen. As it is all is well, and Black even plans an advance, P–B5; and P–K5; or P–B5; and if Q–QB2, R–Kt1; but White succeeded, to begin with, in decentralising his opponent.

37 Q–R5 ....
Threatens R × P.

37 .... R–K2
Or if 37 ...., K–Kt2; 38 R–B3.

38 R–Q1 Q–KKt3

He has nothing better and White now occupies the central diagonal which he has filched from his opponent.

39 Q–B3 ....
Winning a tempo as well; mate is threatened.

39 .... K–Kt2
40 Q–Q5 ....
And, at a stroke, the situation has altered entirely.

40 .... Q–R4
41 R–Q3 Q–B2
42 R–Kt3ch. K–R1
43 Q × P Q–B8ch.
44 Q–Kt1 R–KB2

White has now gained a pawn though he had to give up his central position in exchange for it. However the pawn is sound; the retreat was voluntary and the Rook End-Game is won without much trouble.

45 P–R3 P–K5
46 K–R2 R–B7
47 Q × Q R × Q
48 R–K3 R–R8
49 P–Kt4 K–Kt2
50 K–Kt3 K–Kt3
51 K–B4 P–R4
52 P × Pch. K × P
53 K × P

and White won.

Game No. 23.—San Sebastian, 1912.

Black: Duras.

1 P–K4 P–K3
2 P–Q4 P–Q4
3 P–K5 P–QB4
4 Kt–KB3 ....

At the present time we think that Q–Kt4, is better.

4 .... Q–Kt3
5 P–B3 Kt–QB3
6 B–Q3 ....

Here B–K2, is preferable.

6	P × P
7 P × P	B–Q2
8 B–K2	KKt–K2

A better choice is, we think, Kt–R3.

9 Kt–R3	Kt–Kt3

This move is against tradition—the usual move is Kt–B4; with pressure on White's QP—and thus sets up an interesting and novel problem, which could be formulated as follows: " Can the move 9 ...., Kt–Kt3; be termed decentralising?" A pawn-chain (here the White pawns at Q4 and K5 against the pawns at Black's K3 and Q4), can normally only be attacked at the base (White's Q4); less advisable would be to attack its spear-head (White's K5). So much about pawn-chains in general. In this specific case, however, we see matters in a different light; we notice White's Kt at QR3 and shudder to think how utterly useless it is once Black has played P–B3. Therefore the move Kt–Kt3; seems intended to initiate an action in the centre which, in a sense, appears justified. Should it accordingly be classed as decentralising? The judgment on this question must be reserved.

10 Castles	....

To be considered was: 10 P–R4, B–Kt5ch.; 11 K–B1, P–B3; 12 P–R5, but this raid, evolved as a punitive expedition, would be of doubtful value, because Black has two replies: 12 ...., KKt–K2; 13 P–R6, P × KP; 14 P × KtP, KR–Kt1; 15 P × P, R × P; or, in combinative style: 12 ...., KKt × KP; 13 P × Kt, P × P; 14 Q–B2, (best) B–B4; (not 14 ...., Castles KR; because of 15 B–K3, followed by Kt–KKt5,) and White has a poor game.

10	B–K2

Here P–B3; at once was playable, but Duras likes to disguise his plans as much as possible.

11 Kt–B2	....

If instead 11 R–K1, B–Kt5; and the R would have to wander back to B1 (12 B–Q2, Kt × QP;).

11	P–B3
12 B–Q3	Castles QR

Now the question must be decided whether Black's action against White's K5 is effective or not.

13 P–QKt4	....

With the object of relieving White's position by P–Kt5. Consolidation by means of R–K1, was also good. If any event, both moves will have to be made, and it matters little in which order.

13 .... P × P

Thereby White obtains the square Q4 for his QKt and the premise for the soundness of the whole of the P–B3; attack collapses (see note to 9 ...., Kt–Kt3;). More correct would be 13 ...., K–Kt1; with 14 ...., R–QB1. A plausible variation after 13 P–QKt4, would be K–Kt1; 14 R–K1, R–QB1; 15 R–Kt1, (not 15 P–Kt5, because of Kt–R4; and Kt–QB5; eventually) but White would then have the advantage because he has a strong initiative (B–Q2, and P–QR4–QR5,) and Black is hemmed in. This main line of play confirms the impression that, after all, the manœuvre 9 ...., Kt–Kt3; was hardly justified. If, in addition, one weighs up the fact there was the manœuvre 9 ...., Kt–B4; available, which, from the centralising point of view, can be given full marks, one has to admit that the term " decentralising " must be applied to 9 ...., Kt–Kt3.

14 B × Kt P × B
15 Kt × P ? ....

With this move White loses the whole of his advantage; the correct continuation was : 15 P × P, e.g., 15 ...., Kt × KtP; 16 B–K3, (not 16 R–Kt1, because of B–R5;) with 17 QKt–Q4, though White would lose a pawn, but the truly imposing central island, together with the chances of attack on the open lines, would soon have yielded a strong advantage. The text-move 15 Kt × P, is faulty, for on the one hand the Black Rook obtains the square at his KR5 with effect on the centre, on the other the B at Q2 becomes active. If that were not enough, 15 Kt × P, ran contrary to the principle which says : " For the blockaded player, any exchange of pieces spells relief." White has now, at the most, drawing chances.

15 .... Kt × Kt
16 P × Kt B–R5
17 Q–Q2 ....

The only chance; on 17 ...., P–Q5; the intention is to continue with 18 B–Kt2, P–Q6; 19 Kt–Q4, and if 19 ...., R × Kt; 20 Q–B3ch.

17 ....   K–Kt1 ?

This makes up for White's blunder on the 15th move.
With 17 ...., R–R5; 18 B–Kt2, B × P; 19 Kt × B, Q × Kt;
20 QR–B1ch., K–Q2; he could have won a pawn and also
kept his Q5 under permanent control.

18 Kt–Q4   ....

Intending to centralise even at the expense of a pawn,
and this sudden and daring insistence on the central idea
saves the White game, which was on the point of collapse.
Had White thought earlier of the possibility of this pawn
sacrifice, he would not have failed to play 15 P × P, but at
that stage he may not have been in a state of mind for heroic
measures.

18 ....   R–R4

If 18 ...., B × P; White would have played 19 Q–Q3,
followed by B–K3, and R–Kt1, obtaining a position harmoniously blended with both attack and blockade, not unlike the
line of play shown in the note to move 15.

19 Q–Q3   QR–R1
20 P–KR3   P–Kt4
21 B–K3   P–Kt5

On one side thorough-paced centralising moves (Kt–
Q4, Q–Q3, B–K3.) on the other, rather futile blows on the
wing; in these circumstances it is not difficult to forecast the
winner.

22 Kt–B5   B–QKt4

Or 22 ...., Q–Q1; 23 Kt × B, Q × Kt; 24 Q–Q4, with
Q × KtP.

23	Q–R3	Q–R3
24	Q × Q	B × Q
25	Kt × B	B × R
26	R × B	P–KKt4

Black now puts up a stubborn if hopeless defence.

27	P–B3	P × RP
28	P–Kt4	KR–R2
29	B × P	R–K1
30	K–R2	K–B2

A Rook ending after exchanges on his K2 would be hopeless for Black.

31 R–B1ch.
and White won on the 46th move.

An important game from the point of view of centralisation and we warmly recommend its careful study.

PART II.

RESTRICTION AND BLOCKADE.

With the tactics of Restriction and Blockade, as with those of Centralisation, excellent results can be achieved and I warmly recommend their study to all players, irrespective of class! It is a surprising fact that, frequently, a player of an inferior class handles the blockade with greater freedom and gusto than those in the first class. This applies particularly to my own speciality the "Blockade-sacrifice." Here the first-class amateur, grown grey in the worship of pawn-material, fails more easily than many a second-class player. Consider the play in the following game, played by two amateurs.

1	P–Q4	P–Q4
2	P–QB4	P–K4
3	P×KP	P–Q5
4	P–QR3	B–KB4
5	P–K3	P–B4
6	P×P	Kt–QB3

A most surprising sacrifice, intended to effect a Blockade.

7	P–Q5	Kt×P
8	Kt–KB3	B–Q3
9	B–K2	Kt–K2
10	Castles	Q–B2

White's extra pawn is, for the time being, inactive; the centralisation of the Black forces, however, provides an excellent basis for the process of tying up the opponent slowly but surely.

11	Kt×Kt	B×Kt
12	P–B4	....

Thus Black's pressure on his diagonal Q3–KR7 has led to a loosening of the White position.

12	....	B–Q5ch.
13	K–R1	Castles QR
14	Kt–B3	P–QR3

Still better would have been B×Kt; with R–Q3; any attack on the open Kt file would have been warded off easily after P–QR4, by P–QKt3; and P–QR4; etc.

15 P–KKt4 ....

A better line is : B–Q2, and P–QKt4.

15	B × Kt
16 P × KB	B–K5ch.
17 B–B3	B × Bch.
18 Q × B	P–B4 !
19 P–R3	P–KKt3

Loss of time ! P × P, was not to be feared and K–Kt1 ; at once should have been considered.

20 B–K3	K–Kt1

Room for the blockader ! The Knight is making for Q3.

21 QR–Kt1	....

Better was Q–B2.

21	Kt–B1
22 R–Kt3	Kt–Q3

White's position looks helpless. QB4 and K4 are weak, the P at Q5 is blockaded, and with it the long White diagonal.

23 KR–QKt1	K–R1
24 R–Kt6	KR–K1
25 Q–B2	R × B !
26 R × Kt	QR–K1
27 R(Q6)–Kt6	R–K7
28 Q–B1	Q–K2
29 R(Kt6)–Kt2	Q–K5ch.
30 K–Kt1	Q–Q6

Resigns.

Herr Karl Jacobsen, of Copenhagen, who was Black in this game, had been learning for three months, and had just been promoted into the second class.

With the stratagem shown in this game, the subject of restrictive strategy is by no means exhausted. Restriction covers a great deal of ground, and, for that reason, is not easy to assimilate.

It is of paramount importance to grasp its inner meaning.

If a hostile pawn phalanx wishes to march forward, we try to thwart this tendency by working against the threatened advance. Does the process, as described here, sufficiently explain the nature of restriction ? No.   In reality restriction is only a part of an attack in steady course of preparation. Restriction is only effective in the long run, when a decided attacking idea is linked up with it : if the restrictive action is based on a diagonal, then the wing, under fire by the restricting Bishop, will ultimately be attacked.

The understanding of the latent, inner value of restriction from an attacking point of view (No. 26—28) will do much to widen the horizon of the Chess student.

Our next task will be gradually to sharpen the learner's eye for the varying degrees of dynamic weakness of a pawn or a constellation of pawns. To this end we shall show how, in a number of games, various doubled pawns, in spite of a measure of freedom at first, end up in a state of complete immobility. We think this a good subject for practice. Dynamic weakness cannot be better illustrated than by such a complex of doubled pawns.

After these preliminary exercises, we can at last cope with the problem of the blockade, to which restriction is the first step.

And so we shall learn to spin a blockading web, and also to avoid the dangers to which any defect in that web might expose us. In this respect prophylactic, or preventive measures are particularly to be recommended.

Finally we bring forward two recent and very original variations (my own Dresdener triangle variation, and the French defence with an audaciously obstructed QB pawn) and we seek to bridge the gap between these variations and the line of thought underlying the Blockade.

We wish to reiterate our advice to the student to devote thought to the whole of this second part; there is much to be learned there.

I.—RESTRICTION OF LIBERATING PAWN ADVANCES.

The strategy of restriction gives here the first demonstration of its power, so to speak, a first appearance : as yet we do not expect any extensive plans of blockade, but are satisfied with the minimum requirement—" Liberating pawn advances must be undermined." We will now see whether " restriction " will stand the first test.

Game No. 24.—Gothenburg, 1920.

Black: Breyer.

1	P–K4	P–K4
2	Kt–KB3	Kt–QB3
3	Kt–B3	Kt–B3
4	B–Kt5	P–Q3
5	P–Q4	B–Q2
6	B × Kt	B × B
7	Q–Q3	Kt–Q2
8	P–Q5	....

In Game No. 18, White played 8 B–K3, at this stage. Here White succeeds in exerting pressure on the extreme Q wing by exploiting the weakness of Black's QRP.

8	....	Kt–B4
9	Q–B4	B–Q2
10	P–QKt4	Kt–R3
11	B–K3	B–K2
12	Castles KR	Castles
13	P–QR4	K–R1
14	Kt–QKt5	Q–Kt1

An alternative which afforded some counter-play on the K wing was the pawn-sacrifice by: 14 ...., P–KKt3; and 15 Kt × RP, P–KB4; 16 Kt–QKt5, P–B5.

15	P–B3	....

Prevents the liberating move P–QB3; e.g.: 15 ...., P–QB3; 16 P × P, P × P; 17 Kt × QP, B × Kt; 18 Q × Kt, and the QKtP is covered.

15	....	P–R3

On P–KB4; at once, White replies comfortably with B–Kt5.

16	Kt–Q2	....

In order to reply to 16 ...., P–KB4; with 17 P–B4, and White is better. (Black has only one R in play).

16 ....   P–Kt4

Now the problem is how to prevent P–KB4; or, alternatively, how to make it ineffective.

17 KR–K1   P–KB4
18 P × P   B × P
19 Kt–B1   ....

Still simpler would be: 19 P–B3, and 20 Kt–K4, and White is strong on the White squares and, last but not least, on the K file. White's slightly puzzling 17th move is particularly characteristic.

19 ....   R–Kt3
20 Kt–Kt3   B–B3
21 P–B3   B–Kt2

It looks now as if White could start a rolling-up process with P–R4. This attack would fail because Black's attempt, already given up for dead, to free himself by P–B3; would suddenly blossom forth into life, e.g.: 22 P–R4, P–B3; 23 QP × P, P × BP; 24 Q × P, P × P; and the situation is not clear. Note the vitality of possible (or impossible) attempts at liberation; it only seldom happens that such attempts are permanently eliminated; it happens far more frequently that they persist under the surface as possible future threats.

The correct restrictive strategy, directed against P–B3; in the present case, consisted in the sequence: 22 R–K2, and 23 R–Q1, (not 22 QR–Q1, at once, because of the awkward reply B–B7;). Then P–R4, could no longer be held up. Even so matters were still not quite straightforward, as Black could still undertake counter-measures. An instructive instance would be: 22 R–K2, K–R2; (in order to follow up with B–B2; which move, without K–R2; first, would fail on account of 23 Q–K4, with enduring centralisation. But now, after 23 QR–Q1, the diversion by B–B2; would be quite effective, for 24 Q–K4ch., would be useless because of 24 ...., B–Kt3; 23 P–R4, (this move is possible with the Black King at his R2) 23 ...., P–B3; 24 QP×P, P×P; 25 P–KR5, threatening P×B, with check: White wins. From the foregoing it follows convincingly that 22 R–K2, was sound.

| | 22 R–R2 | .... |

This move provides Black with the opportunity of freeing his game, without, however—so bad was his position —giving any real hope of salvation.

| | 22 .... | B–B2 |
| | 23 Kt–K4 | .... |

Making a virtue of necessity. This sacrifice of the exchange should win for White.

	23	P–B3
	24 QKt×QP	B×P
	25 Q–K2	B×R
	26 Q×B	Q–B2
	27 P–Kt5	P×P
	28 P×P	Kt–Kt1
	29 Q–K6	....

With his powerful centralisation, excellent development, and the chance of a direct attack with P–R4, White has enough to win.

	29	P–QR3
	30 P–R4	RP×P
	31 P×P	R—R3
	32 R–Q1	....

If 32 P×P, B–B3.

| | 32 .... | Q–B5 |

Black puts up an ingenious defence and actually succeeds in surviving the middle-game, though only to obtain a lost end-game position.

| | 33 Q×Q | P×Q |
| | 34 P×P | B–B3 |

Hereabouts White appears to lose his hold on the game and to drift into a drawn position.

	35 R–Kt1	P–Kt3
	36 B×P	Kt–Q2
	37 B–K3	B–R5
	38 Kt×P	....

There was an easy win by: 38 R–Kt7, Kt–B3; 39 Kt–B7ch., R×Kt; (best) 40 R×R, Kt×Kt; 41 P×Kt, R–R6; 42 B–Q2, R–R7; 43 R–Q7.

38	Kt–B3
39 Kt×Kt	B×Kt
40 Kt–Q2	....

Here again the direct attack with 40 R–Kt7, would have won. 40 ...., R–B3; 41 Kt–Kt6, R×P; 42 Kt–Q7, R–KB2; 43 R–Kt8ch., K–R2; 44 Kt–B8ch., K–R1; 45 B–Kt5, R–Kt6; 46 R–K8, and wins. Or, 40 R–Kt7, P–K5; 41 P×P, B×P; 42 P K5, R–QB3; 43 Kt–Q6, and White must win. White neglects the direct attack—a sign of depression.

40	R–KKt1
41 Kt–K4	B–R5
42 K–R2	R R7
43 B–Q2	B–Kt6ch.

Now White can no longer win.

44 K–R3	B–B5
45 Kt–B6	R–KB1
46 B×B	P×B
47 R–Kt6	R–R8
48 K–Kt4	R–KKt8
49 K×P	R×P
50 K–B5	R–KR7
51 K–Kt6	R–Kt7ch.
52 Kt–Kt4	R–Kt6
53 R–Kt7	....

The seventh rank should have been exploited earlier; now it is too late.

| 53 .... | R(Kt6)×P |

Drawn.

Game No. 25.—Gotenburg, 1920.

Black: Dr. Tartakower.

1 P–Q4	P–KB4
2 P–K3	Kt–KB3
3 Kt–KB3	P–K3
4 B–K2	P–KKt3
5 P–B4	B–Kt2
6 Castles	Castles
7 P–QKt4	....

In order to transfer the main field of battle to the Q side.

7	....	P–Q3
8	QKt–Q2	QKt–Q2
9	B–Kt2	Q–K2
10	P–B5	....

White has a clear advantage in position for now 10 ...., P–K4; would fail on account of the sequence of moves: 11 BP × P, BP × P; 12 P × P, P × P; 13 Kt–B4, with Q–Kt3, QR–B1, and KR–Q1.

10	....	P–QR4
11	P × QP	P × QP
12	P–Kt5	Kt–Kt3
13	Kt–B4	Kt × Kt
14	B × Kt	P–Q4
15	B–Q3	B–Q2
16	P–QR4	KR–B1
17	Kt–K5	B–K1
18	Q–Q2	....

This leads to Bishops of opposite colours.

18	....	Kt–K5
19	B × Kt	B × Kt
20	P × B	QP × B
21	QR–B1	R–Q1

Black must avoid further exchanges because of his Q side pawns, which otherwise could not be held.

22	B–Q4	P–Kt4

How can the liberating advance P–B5; be prevented?

23	R–B4	....

Quite simply, because now the answer would be P × P, and Q × BP.

23	....	Q–KB2
24	Q–K2	....

Here P–B5 should still have been prevented; a suitable move would be 24 Q–B2, for after 25 R–B1, White could exploit the open QB file. After the text-move, the nimble-witted Tartakower escapes his fate.

24	P–B5
25 P × P	Q × P
26 Q–K3	QR–B1

White labours under a temporary weakness in his first rank and on this seemingly unimportant circumstance Tartakower builds up a plan which saves the situation.

27 KR–B1	R × R
28 R × R	Q × P !
29 P–R4	Q–B5
30 P × P	P–K4

Now the game must end in a draw.

31 Q × Q	P × Q
32 B–Kt6	R–Q8ch.
33 K–R2	R–Kt3
34 B × P	P–K6
35 R–B8ch.	K–B2
36 R–B7ch.	K–K3
37 P × P	P × P
38 B–Kt4	R–Q5
39 B–B5	R × P
40 R–K7ch.	K–Q4
41 B × P	R–K5

Drawn.

2.—RESTRICTING A BODY OF PAWNS IN THE CENTRE.

Games 26—28.

As we have found that "restriction" is well able to prevent a threatened advance by hostile pawns, we shall now put its efficiency to a harder test. The problem will be to hold up a mobile body of central pawns. How difficult this is has been shown in the games versus Grünfeld and Romih. This laborious process can be made less onerous if some sort of attack, be it never so modest, be co-ordinated with the more or less passive method of restrictive strategy. The idea is illustrated in the games versus Alapin and Steiner (No. 18 and No. 19). A typical case is found in the Steinitz Defence of the Ruy Lopez, where the White pawns at K4 and KB2 are opposed to the Black pawns at Q3 and KB2 : Black, on the K file, works against White's threatened P–K5, and at the same time threatens the White KP at his K4.

In modern practice it is frequently found that the restrictive manœuvres and the co-ordinated attack occur in different territory. In Game 27, for instance, Black restricts in the centre, but attacks on the Q side. A similar case is found in Game No. 28. In Game 26, the " brilliancy " against Marshall, this segregation is entirely absent, (restrictive and attacking operations both take place exclusively in central territory,) but only because White abandons the centre entirely as he wished to concentrate his attack on the Q side.

To sum up : if restrictive operations are based on an open file, they should be confined to the centre; if a diagonal is our only restrictive instrument, then it behoves us to look beyond the centre for further fields of activity. How this is done can be seen in the following three games.

Game No. 26.—New York, 1927.

Black: Marshall.

1	P–QB4	Kt–KB3
2	P–Q4	P–K3
3	Kt–KB3	P–B4

This results in a cramped position.

4	P–Q5	P–Q3
5	Kt–B3	P × P
6	P × P	P–KKt3 !

The KB assumes the control of the central point at Black's K4, and with it the duty to prevent the advance of a central body of pawns (perhaps two pawns at White's K4 and KB4).

7 Kt–Q2   ....

Many readers will think it regrettable that White, in a manner of speaking, avoids the problem of central restriction which Black has set, instead of trying to solve it as follows : 7 P–K4, B–Kt2; 8 B–Q3, Castles; 9 Castles, P–QR3; 10 P–QR4, R–K1; 11 P–R3. But White estimated that this position, speaking generally, is more or less balanced,

and in particular, that the possibility 11 ...., P–Kt3;
with R–R2–K2; had to be considered. Besides Black could
also have played B–Kt5; on the 10th move with B × Kt; to
follow; in that case what could be done against the restrictive
development by Q–B2; and the doubling of Rooks on the K
file? The friendly reader will understand after this why
White preferred to play for complications with the move in
the text, rather than to play 7 P–K4, with the probable outcome that, after completing their development, both players
would have reached a deadlock.

7	....	QKt–Q2
8	Kt–B4	Kt–Kt3
9	P–K4	B–Kt2

Here 9 ...., Kt × Kt; 10 B × Kt, B–Kt2; could have
been played, e.g.: 11 Castles, Castles; 12 P–KR3, R–K1;
13 Q–Q3, P–QR3; 14 P–QR4, B–Q2; and now Black would
have been in a position to complete his development with
Q–B2; and the doubling of Rooks on the K file.

10	Kt–K3	....

Black had not reckoned with this move : White intends
to advance P–QR4–R5, and to post his Kt anew on QB4.
From this point White appears to have the advantage.

10	....	Castles
11	B–Q3	Kt–R4
12	Castles	B–K4
13	P–QR4	Kt–KB5
14	P–R5	Kt–Q2
15	Kt–B4	Kt × B
16	Q × Kt	P–B4
17	P × P	R × P
18	P–B4	....

As White allowed his opponent a free hand, Black was
able to roll up the White pawn centre. But White remains
strongly centralised (the Kt at QB4) and also has chances
on the Q side. Instead of the combinative move in the text,
18 Kt–K4, was also very good.

18	....	B–Q5ch.
19	B–K3	B × Kt
20	Q × B	Kt–B3
21	Q–Kt3	....

White obtains compensation for the lost QP.   Note, *inter alia*, that Black's Q side is difficult to develop.

| 21 .... | R × QP |

The answer to 21 ...., Kt × P; would be 22 QR–K1, which prevents B–K3; because of B × P. Black would then be helpless and White would win with B–Q2, and the doubling of the Rooks on the K file.

| 22 P–B5 | P × P |
| 23 B–Kt5 | .... |

This move contains an unusual point. For if 23 ...., B–K3; (and White had to reckon with this parry above all), there follows 24 Q × P (threatening to win a piece by B × Kt,) R–B1; 25 QR–K1, and the B can no longer protect both Rooks against the threat B × Kt.

23	R–Q5
24 Kt–Kt6dis.ch	P–B5
25 Q–QB3	P × Kt
26 Q × R	K–Kt2
27 QR–K1	P × P
28 R–K8	....

The shortest way.

28	Q × R
29 Q × Ktch.	K–Kt1
30 B–R6	Resigns.

Game No. 27.—Carlsbad, 1923.

White: Sämisch.

1 P–Q4	Kt–KB3
2 P–QB4	P–QKt3
3 Kt–QB3	B–Kt2
4 Q–B2	Kt–B3
5 P–Q5	....

Or : 5 Kt–B3, P–Q3 ; 6, P–Q5, Kt–QKt1 ; more or less
as in the game, except that now, after the further moves :
P–KKt3, and B–Kt2, and possibly Kt–Q4, White would
have a better game than he actually obtained.

5	………	Kt–QKt5
6	Q–Q1	P–QR4

In order to keep open a carefree retreat via QR3 and
QB4 if White play P–QR3.

7	P–K4	………

Here and subsequently Sämisch shows his will power
backed up by scientific earnestness : how many players, in
his place, would have succumbed to the temptation to drive
away the offending Kt, even at the expense of weakening
their own position ?

7	………	P–K4
8	P–KKt3	P–Kt3
9	B–Kt2	B–Kt2
10	KKt–K2	Castles
11	Castles	P–Q3
12	P–B4	P × P
13	P × P	………

13	………	R–K1
14	Kt–Kt3	Kt–Q2

The White centre is now hemmed in. To this slightly
passive restrictive procedure White now seeks to add an
attack on the extreme Q flank (see preliminary discussion).

We owe the careful reader an explanation : we have up
to now deliberately ignored the existence of the Black K file
and considered the restrictive action as based only on the
long Black diagonal.   Is this the proper way of looking at
it ? Answer : From a broader point of view, undoubtedly Yes ;
for the K file is of no importance at all as an instrument of

attack, as White's K4 is thoroughly over-protected; the real factors are, on the one side, the White centre, filled with the urge to expand, and, on the other side, the black diagonal, highly effective for the purpose of restriction, and as will be seen shortly, of attack as well.

15 Q–B3   ....

That Sämisch has left the Black Kt unmolested at Kt5 is to be commended; that he allows him free access to his B7 seems, however, unnecessary. Play in the centre by B–K3, was called for: e.g., 15 B–K3, P–KB4?; 16 P–QR3, Kt–R3; 17 B–Q4, or 15 B–K3, Q–B3; (to prevent B–Q4); 16 P–K5, P×P; 17 QKt–K4, Q–Q1; 18 P–KB5, with a strong attack.

15 ....   P–R5

The diagonal begins to make itself felt (threat P–R6)

16	B–Q2	B–QR3
17	Kt–Q1	Kt–B7
18	R–B1	Kt–Q5
19	Q–R3	....

There is no good square for the Q.

19 ....   Kt–QB4

The break-through P–QKt4; was sufficiently prepared and could have taken place at once.

20 Kt–B2   P–B4

The wrong objective; the Q side, as before was the right one, e.g.: 20 ...., P–QKt4; 21 B–Kt4, P×P; 22 B×Kt, P×B; 23 Q×BP, Q–Q3; 24 Q×Q, P×Q; and White's QKtP is tottering.

21	P×P	P×P
22	Kt–R5	....

If now 22 ...., Kt–K7ch.; followed by Kt×R; White would, at the proper time, obtain the advantage by the attacking move Q–KKt3.

22 ....   Q–K2

The defence by B–R1; and K–B2; was also playable.

23 Kt×B   ....

After this move, White should again get the worst of it. He would have preserved equality by 23 K–R1, B–R1; 24 Q–R3.

23	....	Q×Kt
24	K–R1	R–K7
25	B–QB3	B×P

Now Black threatens a Q sacrifice at KKt7. 26 ....,
Q × Bch.; 27 K × Q, B × Pch.; 28 K–R3, R–K6ch.;
29 K–R4, Kt–B6ch.; 30 K–R5, B–B2ch.; etc.

On 26 R–KKt1, there would follow K–B2; 27 B–B3,
Q × Rch.; and Kt × B; with advantage to Black. The most
striking feature, however, is the fact that this Q sacrifice, in
a more refined form, was "on" again later, as shown in the
note to move 26.

26 B–B3   ....

26 ....   K–B1

An oversight due to pressure of time. The Q sacrifice
was still very strong, e.g.: 26 ...., Kt × B; 27 B × Q,
B × QP; and White is practically helpless, for instance:
28 B–R6, K–B2; 29 QR–Q1, R–Q7; 30 R × R,
Kt × R dis.ch.; 31 K–Kt1, R–Kt1ch.; 32 B–Kt5, Kt–B6ch.;
33 K–Kt2, Kt × B dis. ch.; 34 K–Kt3, Kt–B6 dis. ch.;
35 K–R3, Kt–Q7; 36 R–Q1, B–Kt7ch.; 37 K–R4,
Kt–B6ch.; 38 K–R5, Kt–K3; 39 Q–K3, R–Kt3; or
39 Kt–R3, R–Kt5; and wins.

If 28 K–Kt2, (instead of B–R6,) K × B; 29 K–R3, R–K3;
(30 R–Kt1ch., K–B2;) Black, with a very small disadvantage in material, would have maintained a very strong
attack which would probably have proved decisive. Consequently Black could have forced a decision on the 26th move
in very elegant fashion.

27 B × Kt   ....

White quickly returns the compliment by also making
a mistake, of course under time pressure. 27 QR–Q1,
Kt–Q6; 28 B × Kt, Q × B; 29 B × R, Kt × Ktch.; 30 R × Kt,
Q × R; 31 B × B, would have decided the game in White's
favour.

27	Q × B
28 B × R	B × B
29 Q–R3	....

There is hardly anything better.

29	Q × Pch.
30 K–Kt1	B × R
31 Q–R6ch.	K–K1
32 K × B	K–Q2
33 Q × RPch.	K–B3

Black should now win without difficulty.

34 Q–R3	R–KKt1
35 P–Kt4	P × P e.p.
36 P × P	K–Kt2
37 R–B3	R–QR1
38 Q–B3	R–R8ch.

This makes the win considerably more difficult; the R should have stayed at R1 for the time being. Kt–K5; at once would have won easily.

39 K–Kt2	Kt–K5
40 Kt × Kt	P × Kt
41 R × Pch.	....

The resource made possible by 38 ...., R–R8ch.

41	K × R
42 Q–B3ch.	K–Kt2
43 Q–Kt7ch.	K–B3
44 Q × R	P–K6 dis. ch.

Now follows a most instructive Q ending in which Black has a slight advantage.

45 K–Kt3	Q–Q7
46 Q–R8ch.	K–B4
47 Q–R3ch.	K–Q4
48 Q–R4	Q–K8ch.
49 K–Kt4	Q–K7ch.
50 K–Kt3	P–Kt4
51 Q–Kt4	Q–B8
52 P–R4	....

52 P–B5, afforded drawing chances, e.g. : 52 P–B5, K–K4 ; 53 Q–B3ch., K–K5 ; 54 Q–B6ch, with a drawn result.

52	Q–B7ch.
53 K–Kt4	Q–Kt7ch.
54 K–B5	Q–B7ch.
55 K–Kt4	K–K3

White had overlooked this move; if now 56 Q × P, Q–Kt7ch.; 57 K–R5, Q–Q4ch.; and wins.

56 P–B5ch.	Q × Pch.
57 K–Kt3	P–K7
58 Q–B3	Q–B8
59 Q–K3ch.	K–B2
60 Q–R7ch.	K–Kt3
61 P–R5ch.	K × P
62 Q–R7ch.	K–Kt4

Now the King escapes to his QKt7; but he will need the cover of his QP which has to go to Q4 to shield the K from the rear.

63 Q–Kt7ch.	K–B4
64 Q–B7ch.	K–K4
65 Q–K7ch.	K–Q4
66 Q–Kt7ch.	K–Q5
67 Q–Kt6ch.	K–K5

The flight to QB7 would be useless as yet.

68 Q–B6ch.	P–Q4

The shield!

69 Q–K6ch.	K–Q5
70 Q–Kt6ch.	K–Q6
71 Q × Pch.	K–B7

Resigns.

If Black's P stood at Q3 instead of Q4, Q–B4ch., would draw.

To sum up: After 23 K–R1, instead of Kt × B, Black could hardly have exploited the K file. But against this, the correct advance of ...., P–QKt4; on the 19th or 20th move as indicated in the preliminary note would have won fairly easily for Black.

Game No. 28.—London, 1927.

White: V. Buerger.

1 P–QB4	Kt–KB3
2 Kt–QB3	P–B4
3 P–KKt3	P–KKt3
4 B–Kt2	B–Kt2
5 P–Q3	Castles
6 B–Q2	P–K3

Black does not fear the threat of Q–B1, and B–R6, and therefore scorns the unimaginative P–KR3; and K–R2.

7 Q–B1	P–Q4
8 Kt–R3	....

There is a sound idea behind this move! Kt–B4; is to force a decision in the centre. White rightly does not commit himself to 8 B–R6, P–Q5; 9 Kt–Q1, Q–R4ch.

8	P–Q5
9 Kt–R4	Kt–R3
10 P–R3	Q–K1
11 P–Kt3	P–K4
12 Kt–Kt2	B–Kt5

In order to prevent White's Castling on the Q side. But, as I think to-day, ..., B–B4; is better. This was, however, difficult to discern over the board.

13 Kt–Kt5	....

Very adroit. The Knight hovers round K4 at the same time evading the attack by the Bishop and so White is ready to continue the sustained forward thrust on the extreme Q wing. In other words: in the centre White passively opposes Black's threatened advance of the KP, but to this procedure there is to be added a sharp Q side attack.

13	R–Kt1
14 P–Kt4	P–Kt3
15 P–Kt5	Kt–B2
16 P–QR4	B–B1

In order to exchange Bishops.

17 P–R5	B–Kt2
18 P–B3	....

Simpler would have been: B × B, R × B; P × P, P × P; Castles. The QR file may not be of immediate moment, but it would have required constant watching by the opponent and so have helped to divert forces from the K wing.

18	Kt–K3
19 P–R6	....

Up to a short time ago, I thought this playable. To-day, however, I think that White's defence, now exclusively passive, must collapse sooner or later. 19 P × P, was imperative.

19	B–R1

Here the B is dead; but Black is counting on the breakthrough by P–K4; after due preparation.

20 P–R4	....

Weakening the position still further; comparatively better was Kt–Q1–B2, directed against Black's P–K5; a preventive measure which, however, would also have proved insufficient. White's whole defence is too passive.

20	Kt–R4
21 Kt × Kt	Q × Kt
22 P–Kt4	Kt–B3

To be considered was the P sacrifice by : 22 ...., Kt–B5; 23 B × Kt, P × B; 24 Q × P, B–K4; 25 Q–Q2, Q–Q3; followed by B–B5; etc.

23 B–R3	Q–Q3
24 Kt–Q1	P–R4
25 P–Kt5	Kt–R2
26 Kt–B2	P–B3
27 P × P	....

A little better is 27 R–KKt1, and after P × P; P × P, and White could have maintained his QB to cover KB4 where the enemy will break through, which is not the case in the actual game. At the same time, if 27 R–KKt1, Black replies with P–B4; which connects up all his pieces with his K5, the Kt via B1, K3, B2, K1, to Q3; the Q would be best placed at QB2, the Rooks on the K file. Finally the break-through by P–K5; would be carried out with decisive effect.

27	KB × P
28 B–Kt5	B × B
29 P × B	R–B5

See the first part of the previous note.

| 30 R–KKt1 | QR–KB1 |

Poverty-stricken would be the gain of a pawn by 30 ...., Q–K2; 31 Q–Q2, Kt × P; 32 Castles.

| 31 B–B1 | R–R5 |

Preventing 32 Kt–R3, because of the possibility
32 ...., P–K5; 33 QP × P, Q–R7; winning a piece.

32 Q–Q2	R–R7
33 R–Kt2	....

Compulsory. The R on the seventh exerts too severe a
pressure.

33	R × R
34 B × R	P–K5

The point of the exchange of Rooks.

35 QP × P	Q–Kt6

Not only breaking through, but breaking in.

36 K–B1	....

If 36 B–B1, then B × P; etc.

36	Kt × P
37 K–Kt1	....

If 37 Kt–R1, then Kt × KP; 38 Kt × Q, Kt × Qch.;
followed by Kt × QBP, and the cloistered B has Q4 at his
disposal.

37	R × P

Here Black considered for twenty minutes whether
P–R5; would win more speedily. But the sequel would have
been : 37 ...., P–R5; 38 Kt–R1, Kt–R6ch.; 39 K–B1,
Q–R7; 40 B × Kt, Q × Ktch.; 41 K–B2, Q × R; and now
there would be awkward complications for Black if White
attacks with Q–R6. But 41 ...., Q × B; 42 R–KKt1,
Q–R7ch.; 43 R–Kt2, Q–B5; and here too Black has an easy
win.

38 Q × Kt	Q × Q
39 P × R	Q–K6
40 R–Q1	Q–Kt6
41 R–QB1	P–Kt4
42 K–R2	Q–K6
43 R–B1	Q–K7
44 Kt–R3	P–Q6
45 Kt–B2	P–Q7
46 K–Kt1	Q × QBP
47 R–Q1	Q–B8
48 B–R3	P–Kt5
49 P × P	B × P

At last the B emerges from retirement.

50 P × P	B–B6

Resigns.

3.—RESTRICTION OF A QUALITATIVE MAJORITY (ESPECIALLY A CHAIN MAJORITY).

We shall begin with an explanation which should elucidate the meaning of " qualitative majority." As I wrote in my treatise, " The Blockade," a majority, say three pawns against two, has of course to be restricted; in this sense, a majority must also be allowed to such positions in which the pawn predominance on a wing is not one of numbers.

In the writer's game v. Bernstein (White : Niemzowitsch), Carlsbad, 1923, after the moves 1 Kt–KB3, Kt–KB3; 2 P–Q4, P–Q4; 3 P–B4, P–K3; 4 Kt–B3, B–K2; 5 P–K3, Castles; 6 P–QR3, P–QR3; 7 P–B5, P–B3; 8 P–QKt4, QKt–Q2; 9 B–Kt2, Q–B2; 10 Q–B2, P–K4; 11 Castles, P–K5; a position has arisen in which White, on the Q side and Black on the K side, possess a qualitative majority. Why? Because Black's P at his K5 is of greater value than White's at his K3. Conversely White's P at QB5 is superior to Black at his QB3. If Black was left unhindered, he would eventually obtain an attack with P–KB4; P–KKt4; and P–KB5; which would, in intensity, equal a storm by an actual pawn majority. Here too, the wedge formation is threatened (P–B6); as well as the opening of lines (P × KP); together with the ultimate capture of White's KP, which will be laid bare diagonally (not frontally).

Now, to recognise a majority, as such, implies undertaking something against it. Accordingly there followed : 12 Kt–KR4, Kt–QKt1; (to prevent Kt–B5,) 13 P–Kt3, Kt–K1; 14 Kt–Kt2, P–B4; 15 P–KR4, and the King's wing, which seemed ready to advance, is now paralysed. After a few further moves restriction developed into a blockade (by Kt–B4,).

So far the disquisition in my treatise " The Blockade." We should like to add the following remark : the superiority of Black's pawn at his K5 over White's pawn at K3 has its reason in the fact that White's KP was blockaded on the way to the centre (a painful matter for a centre pawn) whilst Black's KP has at least gone beyond the centre line.

The restrictive methods to adopt against qualitative majorities were shown so clearly in Games 13 and 27 that we think it sufficient to refer to them.

But our conscience as a teacher requires that we should

expound carefully a stratagem which we have not yet discussed: " The King's flight as a palliative."

The following scene of action can be called typical : a qualitative majority, which rolls on gradually, threatens to smash up the opposing pawn-chain. This break-through would, at the same time, expose the King and be, therefore, doubly unpleasant.

The palliative measure would be to seek to hold up the advancing qualitative majority until the King has escaped; the attack is therefore not prevented but reduced in effect. Games 29 and 30 show this procedure clearly.

Game No. 29.—Ostend, 1907.

White: Van Vliet.

1	P–Q4	P–Q4
2	Kt–KB3	P–QB4
3	P–K3	P–K3
4	P–QKt3	Kt–KB3
5	B–Q3	Kt–B3
6	P–QR3	B–Q3
7	B–Kt2	Castles
8	Castles	P–QKt3
9	Kt–K5	B–Kt2
10	Kt–Q2	P–QR3
11	P–KB4	………

In the opening stage White shows a desire to exert pressure at K5. Now Black thinks the time has come to start counter-measures.

11	………	P–QKt4
12	P × P	B × P
13	Q–B3	………

Anyone with a knowledge of centralisation strategy will interpret White's last two moves as an attempt to control the central squares, which have now become free, by means of pieces and also to occupy them in the further course of play. It is clear that Black is not going to look on passively, but will himself contend for mastery in the centre.

13	………	Kt–Q2

This move, attacking the Kt which, thanks to 12 P × P, seems uprooted, has the appearance of being strictly logical. And yet the move is not the best. A central Knight (and a Kt at KB3 can be called that in the fullest sense of the word, as it controls his K5 and secures the Castled King's Field) a central Knight, we say, must not be disturbed except in case of the direst necessity, which does not apply here. Instead, a sound central action was available by 13 ...., R–B1; in a game Dus-Chotimirski-Niemzowitsch, Carlsbad, there followed: after 13 ...., R–B1; 14 Q–Kt3, Kt×Kt; 15 B×Kt, B–Q3; 16 B–Q4, Q–K2; 17 P–Kt4, P–Kt3; 18 Q–Kt5, and Black could have equalised easily by 18 ...., Kt–Q2; 19 Q×Q, B×Q; 20 P–K4, Kt–B3; it is interesting to note that instead of 13 ...., Kt–Q2; the immediate advance ...., P–Q5; might be thought playable. This attempt fails on account of : 13 ...., P–Q5; 14 Kt×Kt, P×P; 15 Kt–K4, Kt×Kt; 16 Kt×Q, P–K7 dis. ch.; 17 K–R1, P×R(Q)ch.; 18 R×Q, Kt–B7ch.; 19 Q×Kt, B×Q; 20 Kt×B. In spite of its unsoundness, this variation is highly instructive; the advance 13 ...., P–Q5; must be prepared for, so this abortive attempt tells us. Therefore : 13 ...., R–B1; and if then 14 Q–Kt3, either 14 ...., Kt×Kt; as against Dus, or else 14 ...., P–Q5; 15 P–K4, Kt×Kt; 16 P×Kt, Kt–Q2; 17 Kt–B3, with chances for either side. After the move in the text, Black has a most difficult game.

| 14 Kt×QKt | B×Kt |
| 15 Q–Kt3 | Kt–B3 |

If 15 ...... P–B3; White occupies the central squares by : 16 Q–R3, P–B4; 17 P–QKt4, B–K2; 18 Kt–Kt3, B–B3; 19 Kt–Q4, but then Black can put up a stout defence with Q–B1; P–Kt3; and Kt–Kt3. Accordingly 15 ...., P–B3; seems to be the right move after all. After the move in the text Black's position is such, that with any sequence of moves—it need not be the strategic plan which was foreshadowed—White would retain the initiative.

| 16 QR–Q1 | .... |

An obviously colourless move. Surely the central strategy with 16 P–Kt4, followed by Kt–Kt3, was fairly obvious?

| 16 .... | P–QR4 |

Black exerts himself to the utmost : now P–Kt4, is no longer possible, and the RP also looks weak. Notwithstanding it is difficult to make an impression on White because he has a powerfully centralised position.

| 17 Q–R3 | .... |

Played in humdrum style. A " system " player would

rather have considered the "pawn sacrifice for blockade," namely: 17 Kt–B3, B×Pch; 18 K–R1, and White will occupy the squares Q4 and K5. The black pawn plus, not being mobile, would be of no positive value, and would only act in a negative sense, that is, blocking its own pieces. But, as we said before, Q–R3, is also very strong.

17 ....   P–R3

Intending to provoke P–KKt4, and thus to intensify the struggle. Another possibility was: 17 ...., P–Q5; 18 P–K4, P–K4; 19, P×P, B–Q2; (not Kt–Q2; because of P–K6), 20 Q–Kt3, Kt–Kt5; 21 QR–K1, but in this position White's game is no doubt preferable.

18 P–KKt4   P–Q5

In order to force the interlocking of the pawns, a stratagem which we shall learn to know later on under the heading "from the workshop of the Blockade."

19 P–K4   Q–Q2

Meaning to answer P–Kt5, with P–K4. It is a moot question whether 19 ...., P–K4; was better, e.g.: 19 ...., P–K4; 20 P×P, Kt–Q2; 21 Kt–B3, Q–K2; 22 Q–Kt3, QR–K1; 23 P–Kt5, P–KR4; and Black's game hardly inspires confidence.

20 QR–K1   P–K4
21 P–B5   ....

21 ....   Kt–R2

Black exerts himself to the utmost against the threat of P–Kt5, (after a Q move and P–KR4,) but plans already the King's subsequent flight. Now the following question is strategically of the greatest interest: Would it not have been simpler to prepare for this flight by Q–K2; Kt–Q2; and P–B3; would this arrangement, compared with the manœuvre in the text, have saved two Tempi? (For in the text the Kt makes the round trip Kt–R2–B1–Q2. Answer: White replies, after 21 ...., Q–K2; with 22 Kt–B3, Kt–Q2; 23 Kt–R4, and P–B3; and the King's flight would have been prevented. Moreover, the threat 24 P–B6, with Kt–B5, would have been awkward to meet.

In the manœuvre, so warmly recommended by us in the preliminary notes: " Keep up restrictive measures until the King has retreated," speed is less essential than enticing the opponent to advance his pawns, and it lies in the nature of an advance by pawns that, for a time at least, pieces are out of the picture, and that squares are made inaccessible to them. This circumstance will be highly welcome to the player who wishes to move his King away into safety. Compare note to move 24.

22	Kt–B3	Q–K2
23	Q–Kt3	KR–K1
24	P–KR4	P–B3

The storming by the White pawns has cost the pieces an important square. Kt–R4, is no longer available.

25	R–R1	Q–Kt2
26	KR–K1	K–B2
27	R–K2	R–R1
28	K–Kt2	Kt–B1
29	P–Kt5	RP×P
30	P×P	Kt–Q2

Black's position is now fairly solid: a nice resting place awaits the K at his Q3 (alternatively at QB1), and he has control of the KR file: for the end-game the White QRP is an easy mark. Nevertheless, it is still very difficult to make headway.

31	P×P	....

In order to occupy KKt6 with the Kt. The book of the Tournament queries this move. We think the plan quite playable, and see no reason to find fault with the move. It may be that 31 R–KKt1, looks better, but what remains for White to do after 31 ...., K–K2; with QR K1; and K–Q1–B1;? and White's QRP is helpless. No, 31 P×P, deserves no adverse criticism; the White position still looks very good, but dry-rot has set in, and neither 31 P×P, nor 31 R–KKt1, can alter this to any great extent.

31 ………	P × P
32 Kt–R4	QR–KKt1
33 Kt–Kt6	R–R4
34 K–B2	Kt–B1
35 R–KKt1	R–Kt4

All this is correctly played by Black, and White can
hardly maintain himself at KKt6. Possible was also
35 ………, Kt × Kt; 36 P × Ktch, K–Kt2; followed by
R–KR1.

| 36 Q–R4 | ……… |

Q–R2, appears necessary here.

| 36 ……… | R × R |

He disdains the chance solution 36 ………, Kt × Kt;
which would not have been playable had the White Q retired
to R2, and goes in for the main line of play.

37 K × R	Kt × Kt
38 Q–R5	K–B1
39 P × Kt	Q–Kt2
40 R–Kt2	R–R1
41 Q–K2	………

| 41 ……… | R–R5 |

He is on the wrong tack (which he would have thought
right up to 1925, see " Blockade ").   Black imagined
erroneously that White's KP could not be held because of
a discovered check by the Black KB being in the air. On
the contrary, the game could be won simply enough by an
attack directed against Kt3. Namely: 41 ………, R–R3;
42 Q–Kt4, B–Q2; 43 Q–Kt3, B–K1; and wins.

| 42 B–B1 ! | R × P !? |
| 43 Q–Q2 ? | ……… |

He sees not that Dame Fortune smiles at him ! But then
Teichmann, myself and everyone else failed to see the saving

clause. White would most likely secure the draw by the Q
sacrifice: 43 Q × R, B × Q; 44 B × B, with the threat
R–R2–R7, as the disc. ch. by P–Q6; leads to nothing after
K–B1. After the text-move all is over for White.

43	R–R5
44 Q × P	Q–Q2
45 P–Kt7ch.	K–Kt1
46 B–B4ch.	P × B
47 Q × B	R–R8ch.
Resigns.	

A task for the reader: let him take the black pieces in
the position after Black's 30 ...., Kt–Q2. Let an opponent
—of equal playing strength—play 31 R–KKt1. Now try to
hold the black position together. Begin, as shown, with
K–K2; followed by QR–K1; and K–Q1–B1; the crux of the
problem, however, is: with what speed and under what
compulsion will the exchanges, which are in favour of Black,
take place? Can White push on to Kt7 without permitting
exchanges in the end? Or will the game drift slowly but
surely into an ending in which Black would have the
advantage? This exercise is interesting as well as instructive.

Game No. 30.—London, 1927 (Imperial Chess Club).

Black: Buerger.

1 P–QKt3	Kt–KB3
2 B–Kt2	P–K3
3 P–KB4	P–Q4
4 Kt–KB3	B–K2
5 P–K3	QKt–Q2
6 B–Q3	....

In order to reply to Kt–B4; with Castles; after Kt × B;
there would follow P × B, with P–Q4, P–Q3, Kt–K5, and
play on the QB file.

6	Kt–K5
7 Kt–K5	Castles
8 Castles	Kt × Kt
9 KB × Kt	Kt–Q2
10 KB–B3	B–B3

The game looks drawish.

11 Kt–B3	P–B4
12 Q–K1	....

If 12 Q–K2, P–Q5; 13 Kt–K4?, P–Q6! 14 Kt × Bch, Q × Kt; 15 B × Q, P × Q; and wins.

12	P–QKt3
13 P–KKt4	B–R3
14 P–Q3	P–Q5

This only results in a stiffening of the pawn-skeleton, whereas Black should work towards opening up the game. Correct was: 14 ...., R–B1; with, eventually P–B5; to follow.

15 Kt–K4	R–B1
16 Kt × Bch.	Kt × Kt
17 P–K4	P–K4
18 P–B5	P–R3
19 Q–Kt3	R–K1

The position now has some similarity with that in Diag. 33. Here as there the King's flight is indicated, and in both cases White's advance by P–Kt5, after P–KR4, can in no way be prevented. In the case of Diag. 33 (Game No. 29), Black, by slow methods, had practically to provoke the storming by hostile pawns, for this led to the blocking up of squares for the White pieces (square KR4 for the White Knight) and thus allowed the King's flight to be carried out unhindered. In the present case there was no danger of the Black King's flight being prevented by the White pieces, so the deliberate process of slowing-up, as far as it was deliberate, only spelt unnecessary loss of time. Correct was: 19 ...., Kt–Q2; at once with P–B3; and K–B2; e.g.: 20 P–KR4, P–B3; 21 B–B1, K–B2; 22 P–Kt5, RP × P; 33 P × P, R–KR1; and Black will bring his K without trouble to QKt1 via Q3. Later on he would be able to consider an attack by P–QKt4; and P–B5; which is " on " in this position. To sum up Black has the opportunity completely to consolidate his position. After the faulty move in the text the Black King no longer succeeds in escaping from the burning castle, and dies a pitiful death in the flames. (Who says that death by burning is beautiful?!)

20	P–KR4	Kt–R2
21	B–B1	P–B3
22	R–B2	R–B2
23	R–Kt2	Q–K2
24	Q–R3	R–B3
25	B–Q2	R–Q1
26	K–R1	R(Q1)–Q3
27	P–R4	....

Black's P–QKt4; up to now would always have been refuted by P–QR4, but as White, at this stage, requires the QR on the K side, he first uses this preventive measure on the Q side.

27	....	B–B1
28	QR–KKt1	P–R3
29	R–R2	....

Now P–Kt5, can no longer be prevented.

29	....	K–R1
30	P–Kt5	BP × P
31	P × P	P–Kt4
32	P × KtP	P × KtP
33	Q–R4	P–B5

There is no defence.

34	P × RP	Q × Q
35	P × Pch.	Resigns.

There could follow: 35 ...., K–Kt1; 36 R × Q, R–Q1; 37 B–QR5, R–K1; 38 B–R5, R–K2; 39 B–B7ch, R × B; 40 R × Kt, K × R; 41 P–Kt8 (Q) ch, etc. Moral: do not provoke an assault by pawns unless the hostile pieces, in consequence of the advance of the pawns, lose mobility and so help the flight of the King. If that is not the case, take to your heels at once, for a deliberate slowing-down as in game 29 would be quite useless.

4.—RESTRICTION IN THE CASE OF THE DOUBLED-PAWN-COMPLEX (FOR SHORT DOUBLE-COMPLEX).

a. Position: White: Pawns at QR2, QB3, QB4, Q3 and K4. Black: Pawns at K4, Q3, QB2, QKt2, QR2. (Games 31-34).

b.   The fixed doubled pawn at QB2, QB3 (for White or
     Black).   White: pawns at QB2, QB3, Q4, KP
     at K3 or K5.   Black: pawns at QB5, Q4, K3
     (Game 35).
c.   The doubled P at QB2 and QB3 blockaded by a Kt
     on the same file.   (Game 36).

Concerning a):
Unless White be willing, Black will hardly succeed in
urging the pawn-complex, rolled up like a hedgehog, to
unroll by P–Q4,—it will rather remain rolled up, "staying
put." At the same time, such a practice of abstention will
not contribute to the potentialities of the White position;
quite the contrary. (Game 31)—Once the complex has come
out of its shell, there will nearly always be further develop-
ments; on P–Q4, there will ultimately follow P–Q5, and the
complex is permanently compromised.   This continued
advance can be attributed to nerves (due to the disagreeable
pressure specially on the K file), whilst obejctive reasons can
hardly be adduced.
     Compare the opening of the following game between
Tartakower (White) and the author, Berlin, 1928: 1 P–Q4,
Kt–KB3; 2 P–QB4, P–K3; 3 Kt–QB3, B–Kt5; 4 B–Kt5,
B × Ktch.; 5 P × B, Q–K2; 6 Q–B2, P–Q3; 7 P–K4, P–K4;
8 B–Q3, P–KR3; 9 B–K3, Castles; 10 Kt–K2 (or Kt–B3, as
in No. 33), 10 ...., Kt–B3; 11 P–Q5. There is no
objective reason for this move; the unimportant threat P × P;
P × P, Kt–QKt5; could have been parried equally well by
R–QKt1.
     We shall also see, in connection with No. 33 (see Note
to Black's 13th move), what powers of resistance the double-
complex has when extended by P–Q4. Against that, the
complex weakness stands out clearly after P–Q5, and that
without Black having taken extreme measures by P–QB4;
(see Game 32, note to 39th move). The possibilities arising
out of P–QB4; P–Q5, are elucidated in Games 33 and 34.

Concerning b):
The double weakness, namely, the isolated QRP and
the doubled QBP, taken together, provides a not too happy
picture; for the existence of this blockaded doubled pawn
makes the isolated pawn appear more isolated than ever
and cut off from the main body (No. 35). Where the White

chain of pawns extends to K5, White has of course counter-chances, and in such cases a prophylactic defence of the complex has to be considered, as shown later in the Games v. Kmoch (Niendorf, 1927) and Vajda (Kecskemet, 1927) Nos. 50 and 49.

Concerning c):
Compare the following two openings: White: Morrison, 1927: 1 P-K4, P-K3; 2 P-KKt3, P-Q4; 3 Kt-QB3, Kt-QB3; 4 P×P, P×P; 5 P-Q4, B-KB4; 6 P-QR3, Q-Q2; 7 B-Kt2, Castles; 8 KKt-K2, QKt-K2; 9 Kt-B4, Kt-KB3; 10 P-R3, P-KR4; 11 Kt-Q3, Kt-K5; 12 B-K3, Kt×Kt; 13 P×Kt, Kt-B3; 14 Kt-Kt4, B-K3; 15 Q-K2, Kt-R4; and: White: Leonhardt, Berlin, 1928: 1 P-K4, P-K3; 2 P-Q4, P-Q4; 3 Kt-QB3, B-Kt5; 4 P×P, P×P; 5 B-Q3, Kt-QB3; 6 Kt-K2, KKt-K2; 7 Castles, Castles; 8 B-KB4, B-Kt5; 9 P-KR3, B-R4; 10 Q-B1, B-R4. If now 11 P-R3, (to prevent K-Kt5;) then 11 ...., B×Kt; 12 P×B, Kt-R4; and Black's double manœuvre with the Bishop has brought the White QRP forward whereas, at QR2, it would have been less vulnerable.

Game No. 31.—Dresden, 1926.

Black: Sämisch.

In this game Black does not succeed in getting the adverse double complex to advance (White stays "put") and therefore the symptoms of the malady are not clearly distinguishable. There is compensation however, in the observation of a typical secondary symptom, the helplessness of the White pieces.

These pieces would, in the ordinary way, be quite ready to attack, but the enthusiasm for an attack is damped by the consciousness that the co-operation of the "pawn-party" cannot altogether be depended upon. As the incriminated body of pawns is unreliable also in a defensive sense, (for there always is a danger of its being rolled up by P-QB3; and P-Q4;), the undecided attitude of the pieces (10 Q-B2, 11 Q-Q2,) is sufficiently explained. And so the hidden weakness of the pawns is projected to a plane where it is clearly noticeable by the learner, and the study of the game is made highly valuable.

1 P–QB4	P–K4
2 Kt–QB3	Kt–KB3
3 Kt–B3	Kt–B3
4 P–K4	B–Kt5
5 P–Q3	P–Q3
6 P–KKt3	B–Kt5
7 B–K2	....

This is not as inconsistent as it may appear, for P–KKt3, was primarily intended to cover a Kt move to KR4, and, on the other hand, B–Kt2, would permit ...., Kt–Q5.

7	P–KR3
8 B–K3	B × Ktch.
9 P × B	Q–Q2
10 Q–B2	....

White realises that the mobility of his centre pawns is small, as P–Q4, and still more so P–Q5, would paralyse him on account of the weakness at QB5. Therefore he seeks to adapt the movements of his pieces to his modest circumstances in space. In this sense he could also have played 10 Kt–Q2 (to effect a strategic retreat with P–B3,) e.g., 10 Kt–Q2, B × B; 11 Q × B, Kt–KKt5; 12 P–B3, Kt × B; 13 Q × B, Castles KR; 14 Castles KR, with an approximately even position. But 10 Q–Q2, must be looked upon as a misuse of the modest space available, for that square should remain open and the Q, in any event, would be better placed at QB2 with an eye on QR4, and the eventual threat of P–Q4, in view. After 10 Q–Q2, we recommend: 10 ...., Kt–QR4; 11 Q–B2, Castles KR; followed by KR–K1; P–B3; and P–Q4; and Black has the better position.

| 10 .... | Castles KR |

Here too we should prefer Kt–QR4; (P–Q4?, Kt × BP).

| 11 Q–Q2 | .... |

Now in order as Black's Castled position is in jeopardy.

| 11 .... | Kt–R2 |

In order to play P–B4; but this proves impracticable, and the only result is a decentralised KKt on R2.

| 12 P–KR3 | .... |

Kt–R4, would also have been sufficient.

| 12 .... | B × P |

This loses a piece. Black had only reckoned with 13 B×KRP, which, by the way, would also have been strong, e.g., 13 B×KRP, B–Kt7; 14 R–R2, B×Kt; 15 B×B, P×B; 16 Q×P, P–B3; 17 B–Kt4, etc.

13	Kt–Kt1	B–Kt5
14	P–B3	B–K3
15	P–Q4	....

Black cannot save the piece.

15	....	P×P
16	P×P	P–Q4
17	BP×P	B×P
18	P×B	Q×P
19	R–Q1	KR–K1
20	K–B2	Kt–B3

The decentralised Kt returns in sackcloth and ashes.

21	R–R4	Kt–K2
22	B–Q3	Kt–B4
23	B×Kt	Q×B
24	K–Kt2	R–K2
25	B–B2	QR–K1
26	R–B4	Q–Kt3
27	P–Q5	R–K4

If 27 ...., R–Q2; 28 Q–R5, etc.

28	R–Q4	R–Q1
29	Q–R5	Kt–R4
30	Q×BP	QR–K1
31	P–Q6	Resigns.

Game No. 32.—London, 1927.

Black: Colle.

The double complex of the previous game, extended through P–Q4,—and weakened thereby—provides the theme of the present struggle. Taking it all in all, the White advance, P–Q4, may have had a stimulating effect on White's game, but as far as the complex itself is concerned, it was the first step downhill. And P–Q5, was the second and last. Let us be quite clear about this point: the fortunes of the complex need not necessarily merge into those of the game as a whole, though they usually do. It is noteworthy how, willy nilly, White had to play P–Q5, in the end.

1	P–Q4	Kt–KB3
2	Kt–KB3	P–K3
3	P–B4	P–QKt3
4	P–KKt3	B–Kt2
5	B–Kt2	B–Kt5ch.
6	Kt–B3	....

Deliberately setting the problem of the double-complex.

6	....	Castles
7	Castles	B × Kt
8	P × B	P–Q3
9	P–QR4	....

The intention is to induce P–QR4; and so to prevent the possible manœuvre: Kt–QB3–R4.

9	....	P–QR4

Or 9 ...., Kt–B3; 10 Kt–Q2, Kt–QR4; 11 B × B, Kt × B; 12 Kt–Kt3, and the complex is of good cheer.

10	B–QR3	QKt–Q2
11	Kt–Q2	B × B
12	K × B	P–K4
13	P–K4	....

Now we can see, in life-size, the complex of Game No. 31, but in extended form.

13	....	R–K1

Threatens P × P; and Kt × P. Usually this threat is sufficient to force P–Q5, but here it is easy for White to cover the KP.

14	P–B3	Kt–B1

The Black KR now has a preventive function: it hinders P–B4.

15	R–B2	Q–Q2
16	Kt–B1	Kt–Kt3
17	B–B1	K–R1
18	Kt–K3	Kt–Kt1
19	P–R4	Q–B3
20	P–R5	Kt(Kt3)–K2
21	Q–Q3	R–KB1
22	P–Kt4	P—Kt3!

| 23 B–Q2! | P × RP |
| 24 Kt–B5 | .... |

The idea of preventing P–B4; even at the cost of a pawn is sound but the question is whether this could not have been achieved more incisively by 24 R–R1, e.g.: 24 R–R1, Q × RP; 25 R × P, P–KB3; 26 K–Kt3, with trebling on the KR file. However, White, heading for the first prize, preferred to tread warily.

24	Kt × Kt
25 KtP × Kt	Kt–B3
26 P–Q5	....

He does it after all; at all events the complex has rendered sterling service by marking time.

26	Q–Q2
27 Q–K3	R–Kt1ch.
28 K–R1	Q–K2
29 R KR2	R–Kt2
30 B–K1	Kt–Q2

Because of the threatened B–R4.

| 31 R × P | .... |

Simpler would be: 31 B–R4, P–B3; 32 Q–R6, Q–B2; followed by recurring moves by the R (R–Q1, R–R1, R–Q1).

31	QR–KKt1
32 B–B2	P–KB3
33 R–KR2	....

By which move White consolidates his position.

33	R–Kt4
34 B–R4	R–R4
35 R–KKt1	Q–B1
36 R–Kt4	Q–R3
37 Q × Q	R × Q
38 B–B2	....

38 R × Rch., with B–B2, clearly brought about the draw.

| 38 .... | R × Rch. |
| 39 K × R | .... |

| 39 .... | R–Kt1 |

It is typical of the great weakness of a confirmed double-complex, that the opponent can afford to play for a win in spite of the fact that his own pawns are none too secure (his pawns here are on squares of the same colour as the opposing Bishop). And not only with the move in the text but also with : 39 ...., R–QB1 ; 40 R–Kt1, P–B3 ;—this challenge of the advanced complex is particularly expedient when it is hemmed in :   first   the   advance   will   be   provoked, P–Q3–Q4–Q5, and then comes the reckoning by means of ...., P–QB3 ; it is true that in the present case this method of procedure is not carried out undisturbed, because White's direct K side attack has created weaknesses in the enemy camp—41 R–Kt1, P × P ; 42 BP × P, R × P ; 43 B × P, R × P ; 44 B × P, Kt–B4 ; now the position is exceedingly open, with the odds a shade in favour of Black.

40 R–Kt1	Kt–B4
41 R–QR1	K–Kt2
42 B–K3	K–B2
43 R–R2	Kt–Q6

White's last two preventive moves were directed against this; Black should be content with a draw.

44 R–Q2	Kt–K8
45 K–Kt3	R–Kt1ch.
46 K–B2	Kt–Kt7
47 B–R6 !	....

The parry which in certain circumstances culminates in the capture of the Kt, namely : 47 ...., Kt–R5 ; 48 K–K3,

R–Kt6; 49 R–KR2; Kt×P; 50 K–B2, Kt×R; 51 K×R, Kt–B8ch.; 52 K–Kt2, and the Kt has no escape.

47 .... Kt–B5

This costs a pawn and, after a tenacious ending, the game as well; with Kt–R5; K–K3, Kt–Kt7ch.; Black could easily have drawn the game which he had played so well. The end-game is a most instructive example of "7th rank absolute."

48	B×Kt	P×B
49	R–Q1	K–K2
50	R–KR1	R–Kt2
51	R–R4	P–B3

A belated challenge, but the reply is not easy to find.

52	R×BP	P–R4
53	R–R4	R–R2
54	R–R1!	K–Q2
55	R–KKt1	P×P
56	BP×P	P–R5
57	R–Kt8	P–R6
58	R–QR8	R–R3
59	R–R7ch.	K–B1

It is done; the R holds the "7th rank absolute," whilst the K will do the blockading.

60	K–Kt1	P–R7ch.
61	K–R1	R–R6

Now it all depends on who gets there first.

62	R–KB7	R×P
63	R×P	K–Q2
64	R–B7ch.	K–K1
65	R–QKt7	R×QBP
66	R×P	K–K2
67	R–Kt7ch.	....

Always the same "Leit-Motif" the 7th rank.

67	....	K–B1
68	R–QR7	R–B5
69	R×P	R×KP
70	R–R7	R–KB5
71	P–R5	R×P
72	P–R6	....

Triumph of the "7th rank absolute."

72 .... R–B8ch.

If 72 ...., R×P; White wins by 73 R–QKt7, R–QR4; 74 P–R7, with R–Kt8ch.

73	K × P	R–R8
74	R–R8ch.	K–Kt2
75	K–Kt3	R–R5
76	K–B3	K–B3
77	P–R7	K–Kt2
78	K–K3	Resigns.

Game No. 33.—St. Petersburg, 1914.

White: Janowski.

1	P–Q4	Kt–KB3
2	P–QB4	P–K3
3	Kt–QB3	B–Kt5
4	P–K3	P–QKt3
5	B–Q3	B–Kt2
6	Kt–B3	B × Ktch.
7	P × B	P–Q3

A playable alternative is 7 ...., P–B4; with Kt–B3.

8	Q–B2	QKt–Q2
9	P–K4	P–K4

Black appears to have a solid position. But the B at QKt2 plays a doubtful rôle; on the one side his power is not sufficient to enforce White's P–Q5, and on the other its absence from the original long diagonal will soon have a disagreeable effect. The transition to an open game has been too sudden.

10	Castles	Castles
11	B–Kt5	P–KR3
12	B–Q2	R–K1
13	QR–K1	....

| 13 | .... | Kt–R2 |

With 13 ...., R–K3; which looks a little strange, followed by Q–K1 ; Black could have attempted to counteract White's "marking time," and so to enforce P–Q5. The continuation could be : 13 ...., R–K3; 14 Kt–R4 (to exploit the weakness of White's KB4), P–Kt3; 15 P–B4 (if B × P, Kt–Kt5), P × BP; 16 B × P, and now Black has the choice between : 16 ...., P–KKt4; 16 ...., Kt–R4; and 16 ...., Q–K1. Black's strategic object is most clearly shown by 16 ...., Q–K1 ; e.g. : 17 P–Q5, R–K2; 18 B × RP, Kt–Kt5; 19 B–Kt5, P–KB3; 20 B–B1, KKt–K4; and White though a pawn up, does not lie on a bed of roses; his double complex is paralysed and Black controls central points. Even more illuminating is the variation : 16 ...., Kt–R4; 17 Q–B2 ?, R–B3; 18 P–Kt3, P–KKt4; 19 P–K5, Kt × B; 20 P × Kt, R × P; and wins, or 16 ...., Kt–R4; 17 B–Kt3, Kt × B; 18 P × Kt, Q–Kt4; followed by QR–K1; and Black has nothing to fear. But the answer to 13 ...., R–K3; would probably have been : 14 R–K2, and after 14 ...., Q–K1; 15 KR–K1, and White, with the utmost perseverance, continues the policy of marking time. However, Black has also a score to register; the chance for White to play P–B4, has receded into the dim future.

Besides 13 ...., R–K3; ...., Kt–B1; also deserved consideration, e.g., 13 ...., Kt–B1; 14 P–KR3, Kt–Kt3; 15 Kt–R2, R–K2; 16 P–B4?, P × BP; 17 B × P, Q–K1; and P–Q5 is compulsory at last. Finally 13 ...., P–QB4; was playable, but then 14 P–Q5, would cause a general block.

| 14 P–KR3 | .... |

After 14 K–R1 (recommended in the book of the tournament) the reply, *inter alia*, could be QKt–B3; e.g., 15 Kt–Kt1, Kt–Kt4; and the advance P–KB4, is no longer feasible.

| 14 .... | KKt–B1 |

Here too 14 ...., QKt–B3; etc., could have been played.

15 Kt–R2	Kt–K3
16 B–K3	P–QB4
17 P–Q5	Kt–B5

Instead of the chances on the Q side, lost through P–QB4; Black now has opportunities on the K side.

| 18 B–K2 | Kt–B1 |
| 19 B–Kt4 | B–B1 |

At last the B lands on the right diagonal.

| 20 Q–Q2 | B–R3 |

Kt–Kt3; would have been simpler but Black has no confidence in his own K side attack; that he could not enforce P–Q5, without making concessions to the enemy—and P–QB4; was conceding something—has had a depressing effect. So he is content to effect a strategic retreat and by doing so nearly wins the game.

21 P–Kt3	Kt(B5)–Kt3
22 B–K2	Kt–R2
23 P–KR4	Kt–B3
24 B–Q3	R–Kt1

As a preventive measure the R is played to K2.

25 Q–K2	R–Kt2
26 B–B1	QR–K2
27 K–R1	B–B1
28 R–Kt1	K–B1
29 P–R5	Kt–R1
30 P–Kt4	Kt–R2
31 B–B2	R–Kt2
32 P–B4	P–B3

At last White has succeeded in carrying out the intended advance; but, in so doing, he had to give up several important points, for instance, KKt5; this will react against him later on.

| 33 P × P | QP × P |

33 P–Kt5, leads nowhere, e.g.: 33 P–Kt5, BP × P; 34 P × KtP, P × P; 35 R–Kt3, Kt–B2; 36 Kt–B3, P–Kt5.

34 Kt–B3	Kt–B2
35 QR–B1	K–Kt1
36 Kt–R4	Kt–Q3
37 Kt–B5	B × Kt
38 KtP × B	Kt–KKt4

Compare note to move 32.

| 39 B × Kt | RP × B |
| 40 B–R4 | .... |

He troubles not about his own exposed KRP but attempts to roll up the hostile Q wing (B–B6, P–QR4–R5,). In connection with other games, we shall see that this manœuvre is in the nature of a punitive expedition, (retribution for the questionable 16 ...., P–QB4) that Janowski, in spite of weak points in his own position, boldly attempts to show up the flaws in the opponent's camp deserves praise.

He had a wonderfully keen chess-sense. The tournament
book blames him for it and holds the resultant loss of a pawn
to be decisive. But even should it be so, which we doubt,
the merit of the variation, in one sense, remains to be dis-
proved. For Janowski's manœuvre, correct or otherwise,
unveils the mystery of the position !

40	R–B1
41 B–B6	R–Kt1
42 P–R4	K–B2
43 K–Kt2	R–R1
44 R–KR1	R–R3
45 R–R1	Q–B2
46 K–B2	QR–KR1
47 K–K3	K–Kt1
48 K–Q3	Q–B2
49 P–R5	R × P
50 R × R	R × R
51 P × P	R–R6ch.
52 K–B2	P × P
53 R–R8ch.	K–R2
54 R–Q8	Q–R2
55 R QR8	Q–KB2

56 K–Kt3   ....

Here White trips up. For how could Black win after
56 R–Q8? Examine: 56 R–Q8, Q–R2; 57 R–QR8,
Q–QB2; 58 K–Kt3, R–R5; 59 Q–QR2, R × P; 60 R–KB8,
Kt × KBP; 61 Q–R8, Kt–Q3; 62 R–Q8, etc. or 60 ....,
P–Kt3; (instead of Kt × KBP;) 61 Q–R8, P × P;
62 R–R8ch., K–Kt3; 63 B–K8ch., K–Kt2; 64 B–R5, and
mate in a few moves. It appears therefore that the rolling-up
develops into a turning movement, and that the book of
the Tournament errs in pronouncing the loss of the pawn as

decisive. It is true that after the faulty move in the text
Black should have won easily.

56	Q–R4
57 Q × Qch.	R × Q
58 B–K8	Kt × B ?

Black misses an immediate win which was assured by
58 ...., R–R3; if then 59 R–Q8, P–Kt5; etc., but if
59 B–Kt6ch., Black wins with 59 ...., R × B ; 60 P × Rch.,
K × P ; 61 K–B2, Kt × KP ; 62 K–Q3, K–B4 ; (overlooked by
Black in his calculations). After the text move it is probably
impossible to prove a win for Black.

59 R × Kt	R–R7
60 R–R8	P–Kt5
61 R–R1	K–R3
62 K–R4	K–Kt4
63 K–Kt5	K–B5
64 R–KKt1	....

The best reply, as K × P ; allowed ...., K–B6, and a
rapid advance of the passed pawns.

64	K × P
65 R × Pch.	K × P
66 R × P	R–Kt7ch.
67 K–B6	P–K5
68 P–Q6	R–Q7
69 P–Q7	P–K6
70 K × P	....

White would lose by K–B7.

70	P–K7
71 R–K7	R × P
72 R × P	R–Q6
73 R–QB2	R–Q8

and the game was drawn after a further twelve moves. A
difficult struggle.

Game No. 34.—Dresden, 1926.

White: Johner.

This game has already appeared in " My System," but
with different notes, and we repeat it here because its relation
to No. 33 makes it essential for us to do so.

1 P–Q4	Kt–KB3
2 P–QB4	P–K3
3 Kt–QB3	B–Kt5
4 P–K3	Castles

In the previous game P–QKt3; was played here.

5 B–Q3	P–B4
6 Kt–B3	Kt–B3
7 Castles	B × Kt
8 P × B	P–Q3
9 Kt–Q2	....

A fine move. If now 9 ...., P–K4; there follows 10 P–Q5, Kt–K2; (not ...., Kt–QR4; because of 11 Kt–Kt3,) 11 P–K4, with the pawn formation we have seen in the previous game (move 22); the only appreciable difference lies in the fact that here Black's QKtP is still at home and the rolling up by P–QR4–R5, therefore is not threatened. On the other hand will this pawn be able to remain at QKt2 in view of the open file?

9	P–QKt3

To make QKt2 available for the Kt; Black intends to play ...., P–K4; P–Q5, Kt–QR4; and if Kt–Kt3, Kt–Kt2.

10 Kt–Kt3	....

Here 10 P–B4, was indicated. If then 10 ...., P–K4; 11 BP × P, QP × P; 12 P–Q5, Kt–QR4; 13 Kt–Kt3, Kt–Kt2; 14 P–K4, Kt–K1; followed by KKt–Q3; the pawn formation of Game No. 33 (after move 36) is attained, which formation, generally speaking, has a deadening effect on the game.

10	P–K4
11 P–B4	P–K5

This move would also have been the reply to 11 P–Q5, e.g., 11 P–Q5, P–K5; 12 B–K2, Kt–K4; with centralisation. Alternatively: 11 P–Q5, P–K5; 12 P × Kt, P × B; with advantage to Black. The interesting point about this seemingly uneventful battle (moves 9—11) is that it was in fact, most intensely fought; White played P–KB4, one move too late and the Black KP only just escaped retribution. Had Black played 11 ...., Q–K2; instead of P–K5; and retired, after 12 BP × P, QP × P; 13 P–Q5, the Kt to Q1; (13 ...., P–K5; is better), the sequel would again be 14 P–K4, Kt–K1; with general mummification. After the move in the text, 13 ...., P–K5; Black has to solve a new and very difficult problem: restriction of White's K side (BP, KtP, and RP).

12 B–K2   ....

12 ....   Q–Q2

A most difficult and complicated restrictive manœuvre
is initiated with this move. Another restrictive possibility
was: 12 ...., Kt–K1; but after: 13 P–Kt4, P–B4;
14 P–Q5, Kt–K2; 15 P–Kt5, this would again lead to a
deadlock; we miss the squares at Black's QB4 and KB4 for
the Knight's. To conduct restrictive operations, whilst
avoiding the deadlock, makes the problem exceedingly
difficult to solve.

13 P–KR3   Kt–K2
14 Q–K1   ....

One is tempted to ask whether White's attack will be
sufficient even to ensure a deadlock. Let us examine:
14 B–Q2, Kt–B4; (this square is a strong one from which to
start new operations, for instance, there now threatens
Kt–Kt6; with the exchange of the White KB which covers
the QBP); 15 Q–K1, P–Kt3; 16 P–Kt4, Kt–Kt2; 17 Q–R4,
Kt(B3)–K1; 18 P–QR4 (*inter alia*, to prevent Q–R5;) P–B4;
19 P–Kt5, with P–Q5, and the position arrived at is difficult
to assess, e.g., 19 P–Kt5, Kt–B2; 20 P–Q5, B–R3; (a
preventive measure directed against P–R5, for now the reply
could be P–Kt4;) 21 K–B2, Q–B2; 22 QR–Q1, (22 Q–R6,
fails because of the combinative reply: Kt×P; P×Kt,
B×B; K×B, Q×P; Kt–B1, Kt–R4; with permanent
imprisonment of White's Q: Black would win with a
general pawn advance); 22 ...., K–R1; and 23 ....,
Kt–R4; Black will seek to prepare the break-through
P–KR3; by R–KKt1; K–Kt2–B1–K2–Q2. If one considers
that Black could have played P–QR4; before playing
20 ...., B–R3; (preventing thereby White's counter-

chance P–R5,) it is clear that the deadlock desired by White will, in practice, be very difficult to attain.

14 ....   P–KR4

The beginning of the tying-up process.

15 B–Q2   ....

Or 15 Q–R4, Kt–B4; 16 Q–Kt5, Kt–R2; 17 Q×P, Kt–Kt6.

15 ....   Q–B4

In order to wander on to KR2, the unusual point of the restrictive manœuvre.

16 K–R2   Q–R2
17 P–QR4   Kt–B4

Threatening Kt–Kt5ch.; P×Kt, P×P, dis. ch.; K–Kt1, P–Kt6; etc.

18 P–Kt3   P–R4

The QKtP is easily covered.

19 R–KKt1   Kt–R3
20 B–KB1   B–Q2
21 B–B1   QR–B1

Now the position has changed from that occurring after tht 14th move. Black no longer has to fear the closing up of the Q side by P–Q5, he has enough play on the K side.

22 P–Q5   K–R1
23 Kt–Q2   R–KKt1
24 B–KKt2   P–KKt4
25 Kt–B1   R–Kt2
26 R–R2   Kt–B4
27 B–R1   QR–KKt1
28 Q–Q1   P×P
29 KP×P   B–B1
30 Q–Kt3   B–R3
31 R–K2   ....

He takes advantage of his opportunity; the KP is in need of cover. Had White played a purely defensive game as for instance by 31 B–Q2, Black would have won by a beautiful combination, as follows: 31 B–Q2, R–Kt3; 32 B–K1, Kt–Kt5ch.; 33 P × Kt, P × P dis.ch.; 34 K–Kt2, B × P; 35 Q × B, and now comes the waiting move P–K6; and the mate at KR3 can only be parried by Kt × P, upon which the Q is lost.

| 31 | .... | Kt–R5 |
| 32 R–K3 | | .... |

Here Black had expected Kt–Q2, as a matter of course, for the weakness of the KP is White's only chance. There would have been a delightful sacrifice in that case: 32 Kt–Q2, B–B1; 33 Kt × P, Q–B4; 34 Kt–B2, Q × Pch.; 35 Kt × Q, Kt–Kt5; mate. It is noteworthy that the order of the moves ...., B–B1; and ...., Q–B4; cannot be inverted, e.g.: 32 Kt–Q2, Q–B4; (instead of B–B1;) 33 Q–Q1, B–B1; 34 Q–B1, and everything is protected whereas if after 32 ...., B–B1; White were to play 33 Q–Q1, Black would reply with 33 ...., B × P; and the corner stone of the White building would be swept away (34 K × B, Q–B4ch.; etc.)

32	....	B–B1
33 Q–B2		B × P
34 B × P		....

If 34 K × B, Q–B4ch; 35 K–R2, Black mates in three.

| 34 | .... | B–B4 |

Best now for P–R5; can no longer be prevented. The fall of the KRP has left White defenceless.

35 B × B	Kt × B
36 R–K2	P–R5
37 KR–Kt2	P × P dbl. ch.
38 K–Kt1	Q–R6
39 Kt–K3	Kt–R5
40 K–B1	R–K1 and wins.

A very exact finish, for the threat now is:—41 ...., Kt × R; 42 R × Kt, Q–R8ch.; 43 K–K2, Q × Rch.; against which White has no defence. If 41 K–K1, there would even be a mate by ...., Kt–Bch.; 42 K–B1 (or Q1,) Q–R8ch.

One of our best blockade games.

Game No. 35.—Carlsbad, 1907.

Black: Dr. Vidmar.

1 Kt–KB3	P–Q4
2 P–Q3	Kt–QB3
3 P–Q4	Kt–B3
4 P–QR3	....

In order to force Black to declare his intentions: if 4 ...., P–K3; the QB remains shut in, if 4 ...., B–B4; White plays P K3, then P–B4, and eventually Q–Kt3, if 4 ...., B–Kt5; 5 Kt–K5, is the intended reply.

4	B–Kt5
5 Kt–K5	B–R4
6 P–QB4	....

The following surprising combination underlies this move: 6 P–QB4, P × P; 7 Q–R4, Q × P; 8 Kt × Kt, Q–Q2; 9 P–KKt4, Kt × P; 10 B–Kt2, Kt–K4; 11 Q–Kt5, and maintains the extra piece. It is curious that no one has thought of 9 ...., B–Kt3; (instead of Kt × P;) after 10 Kt–QB3, Q × Kt; 11 Q × Q, P × Q; 12 B–Kt2, K–Q2; 13 P–Kt5, Kt–K1; Black would have the advantage. White, however, had a simpler and better line of play in: 6 P–QB4, P × P; 7 Kt × Kt, P × Kt; 8 Q–R4, Q Q2; 9 P–K3, with a good game. Therefore, the play for Zugzwang on the 4th move seems to be sound after all, an uncommon occurrence at so early a stage of the game.

6	P–K3
7 Q–R4	B–Q3

Plays into the opponent's hands, as now the restrictive P–B5 can be played with the gain of a tempo.

However, after 7 ...., B–K2; there follows 8 Kt–QB3, and Black, after 8 ...., Castles; 9 Kt × Kt, P × Kt; 10 Q × P, will probably be unable to exploit his advantage in time and so the pawn plus would become a deciding factor.

8 Kt × Kt	Q–Q2
9 P–B5	B–K2
10 B–B4	....

To prevent Q × Kt; the blockader must, as a rule, try to avoid exchanges.

10	P × Kt
11 P–K3	Castles KR

He could not play 11 ...., P–R4; because of
P–QKt4, but now the Black QRP will be immobilised.

12 B–R6   ....

This blockade must be very unpleasant for Black, as it
counteracts a plan, the execution of which was to him of the
utmost moment; this plan was to get rid of his QRP by
pushing it on. That this blockading B at QR6 also commands the square at QKt7 cannot be surprising to us, as we
know : " Blockade squares, almost without exception, prove
to be strong squares in every respect."

12 ....   KR–Kt1
13 P–QKt4   Kt–K1

Black plans a break-through in the centre by means of
P–B3; and P–K4 eventually. This is the only resource.

14 Castles   ....

The gain of the exchange by Kt–Q2–Kt3–R5 was
" on," but White aims at bigger game.

14 ....   P–B3
15 Kt–Q2   P–Kt4
16 B–Kt3   Kt–Kt2
17 P–R3   ....

To preserve the QB.

17 ....   B–K1
18 B–R2   B–Q1

19 P–Kt4   ....

To restrain the Kt. But this is only the point tactically ;
the strategical reason lies deeper ; Black will have to
challenge this troublesome pawn (........., P–KR4;) and
inevitably files will be opened, which, as matters stand,
will only benefit the White Rooks. The play ranges from
wing to wing. In view of his precarious position on the Q
side, Black feels the necessity of counter-action on the other

flank, and for a well-defined reason this counter-action must from the first, appear hopeless. We perceive this reason in the poor means of communications, a consequence of the pitiful state of affairs on the Q side (there is no fast service between the two wings).

19	....	P–R4
20	Q–Q1	B–Kt3
21	Kt–Kt3	P × P
22	P × P	P–B4
23	B–K5	P × P
24	Q × P	Kt–B4
25	Kt–R5	Q–R2
26	B–K2	....

Note that White did not withdraw the B sooner; it was essential that the reserve troops should be on the spot first (Kt–R5,) and Black's possible liberation by P–QR4; had to be kept in mind the whole time (compare note to Move 12).

26	....	Q Q2
27	Q–R3	....

To-day I should have played 27 P–B4, for I never willingly release a blockaded pawn (here the KtP). After 27 P–B4, the continuation could be: 27 ...., K–B2; (27 ...., Kt × KP?; 28 Q–R3;) 28 P × P, B–K2; 29 P–K4, P × P; 30 B–QB4, K–K1; (R × Kt, was threatened); 31 QR–Q1, and wins easily as Black is tied up, e.g.: 31 ...., Kt–K6; 32 Q–R3, Kt × KR; 33 B × P, Q–Q1; 34 Kt × P.

27	....	K–B2
28	P–B4	P–Kt5

Black avoids the opening up of the KB file, which he could not have done had White played 27 P–B4. Of course the game is lost either way.

29	B × P	B–K2
30	R–R2	R–Kt1
31	R–KKt2	Kt–R5
32	R–Kt3	QR–KB1

Comparatively the best. 32 ...., Kt–B4; would be inadequate: 33 B × Kt, B × B; 34 Q–R5ch., B–Kt3; 35 Q–R6, and White will very soon enforce the win with K–B2, and QR–KKt1.

33	K–B2	R–KR1

Desperation. But a waiting policy spells destruction; e.g., 33 ...., R–QR1; 34 QR–KKt1, QR–KB1; 35 B–Q1, etc.

34 B × R	R × B
35 KR–KKt1	R–R3

36 B–R5	....

Marco says: " A splendid and decisive combination."
But four moves later White makes a bad mistake and the
decision misses fire.

36	B × B
37 R–Kt7ch.	K–K1
38 R–Kt8ch.	B–B1
39 Q × Kt	Q–R2
40 R × Bch. ?	....

A painful hallucination. 40 R(Kt1)–Kt7, Q × R ; (if
Q–B7ch.; K–Kt3,) 41 R × Q, B × R ; 42 Q–Kt5, B–B1 ;
43 Kt × P, would have won easily.

40	K × R
41 P–B5	....

In playing 40 R × Bch., White had intended to follow
up with Q–Q8ch., but he had entirely overlooked the obvious
reply B–K1.

41	P × P

The correct answer was ...., Q × P ch.

42 R–KR1	....

Now White has again a winning position.

42	P–B5
43 Q–Q8ch.	B–K1
44 Q–B6ch.	R × Q
45 R × Q	B–B2

Draw.

Instead of this drawing combination White had an easy
win by 43 Q × Pch., K–K1 ; 44 P–K4, but he was still under
the disturbing influence of his terrible blunder. Nevertheless
a very interesting game.

Game No. 36.—New York, 1927.

White: Marshall.

1	P–K4	P–K3
2	P–Q4	P–Q4
3	Kt–QB3	B–Kt5
4	P × P	P × P
5	Kt–B3	Kt–K2
6	B–Q3	QKt–B3
7	P–KR3	B–K3
8	Castles	Q–Q2
9	B–KB4	B × Kt
10	P × B	P–B3

In order to safeguard the B against a possible Kt–KKt5
—the prophylactic meaning of 7 ...., B–K3; is thus clear.
White now tried an attack on the open QKt file, but it is not
surprising that it failed, on account of the dynamic weakness
of the double complex.

11	R–Kt1	P–KKt4
12	B–Kt3	Castles QR

Looks risky, but is part of the plan initiated on the 9th
move.

13	Q–K2	QR–K1

Not QR–Kt1; because a flank attack is best undermined
by a concentration in the centre and not by a counter-attack
on a wing.

14	KR–K1	Kt–B4
15	B × Kt	....

The move 15 B–R6, proves insufficient after ....,
P × B.

15	....	B × B
16	Q–Kt5	Kt–Q1
17	Q–B5	P–Kt3
18	Q–R3	K–Kt2
19	Q–Kt3	Kt–B3

Already a blockader makes for QB5 where it will demonstrate the weakness of the doubled pawn.

20	Kt–Q2	Kt–R4
21	Q–Kt2	R × Rch.
22	R × R	R–K1
23	R × R	Q × R
24	Q–Kt1	K–B1

Here ...., Q–K7; was also good.

25 Q–Q1	Q–K3
26 Kt–Kt3	Kt–B5
27 Kt–Q2	Kt–R6
28 Kt–B1	Kt × P

Now Black has an ending with a pawn plus but Bishops of opposite colours, and many of the onlookers prognosticated a draw.

| 29 Q–R5 | B–Q6 |
| 30 Q–Q1 | Q–K5 |

Not ...., Q–K7; at once because of Q × Q, and Kt–K3.

| 31 Kt–Q2 | .... |

If 31 P–B3, then Q–K7; is sound.

31	Q–K7
32 Q × Q	B × Q
33 P–KB4	Kt–R6
34 P × P	P × P
35 K–B2	B–R4
36 B–K5	P–Kt5
37 P × P	B × P
38 K–K3	B–B4
39 B–Kt7	B–K3
40 B–B8	Kt–Kt4
41 Kt–Kt1	....

| 41 .... | P–QR4 |

Here 41 ...., B–B4; was also playable: 42 P–R4, B × Kt; 43 P × Kt, B–R7; 44 K–B4, B–B5; 45 K–K5, K–Q2; 46 B–Kt4, P–B3; 47 P × Pch., K × P; and the King migrates to QKt6.

| 42 K–Q2 | .... |

A winning line, not unlike that shown in the preceding note would be: 42 K–B4, B–B2; 43 P–R4, B–Kt3; 44 P × Kt, B × Kt; 45 K–K5, B–R7; 46 K–K6, B–B5; with ...., K–Kt2; and ...., P–B3; etc.

42	B–B4
43 Kt–R3	Kt × Kt
44 B × Kt	B–Kt8
45 B–B8	B × P
46 B–Kt7	B–Kt8
47 K–K3	K–Kt2
48 B–B6	K–R3
49 K–Q2	....

If 49 B–Q8, Black has a win, the K penetrating to QKt6, e.g.: 49 B–Q8, K Kt4; 50 B × P, K–B5; 51 B × P, P–R5; with K–Kt6; and wins as the QRP cannot be stopped.

This variation shows the enduring weakness of the dead and gone double complex. For in the passed QRP is mirrored the weakness of the defunct White QRP, and in the blocked long Diagonal KB6–QR1 is manifested. in memoriam, the obstructive effect of the pawn formation QB3 and Q4. White might have resigned here.

49	B–K5
50 P–Kt3	K–Kt4
51 K–B1	K–B5
52 K–Kt2	P–B4
53 B–K5	P × P
54 B × P	P–Kt4
55 B–Kt6	P–R5
56 B–R5	P–Q5
57 P × P	P–Kt5
58 B–Kt6	P–R6ch.
59 K–R2	K–Kt4
60 B–B5	K–R5
Resigns.	

FROM THE WORKSHOP OF THE BLOCKADE.

(a) Spreading the Blockade Net.
(b) The formation of gaps is prevented by prophylactic means.
(c) The Blockade Net in action.
(d) Blockade by sacrifice.

Two armies of pawns are face to face; there are no open lines; can the interlocking of the pawns be forced in these circumstances? We have, on several occasions, noted how effective an open line can be as a restrictive instrument; an open line can prevent the hostile mass of pawns from advancing and to this evil of stagnation there easily can be added the further evils of restriction and blockade.

But what is to be done in the absence of open lines? Answer: the greatest care is called for, for all violent attempts to enforce the interlocking of the pawn-formations are doomed to failure.

Compare how the following two games began:—

I.—(Black: Morrison, London, 1923): 1 P–QKt3, P–KKt3; 2 B–Kt2, Kt–KB3; 3 P–KKt3, B–Kt2; 4 B–Kt2, P–Q3; 5 P–Q4, Castles; 6 P–QB4, Kt–B3; (a violent attempt; Black foregoes two tempi only to get White to advance P–Q5, and so to obtain a stiffening of the pawn skeleton; much sounder would be: 6 ...., QKt–Q2); 7 P–Q5, Kt–Kt1; 8 Kt–QB3, QKt–Q2; (in order to play P–QR4; and Kt–B4; Burn's idea); 9 Kt–B3, P–QR4; and now White could have obtained a finely centralised game with: 10 Castles, Kt–B4; 11 Kt–Q4, P–K4; 12 P × P e.p., P × P; when Black's loss of tempi would have weighed heavily in the balance. But in the game the continuation actually was: 10 QKt–R4, (instead of Castles,) and here also White obtained an excellent game with: 10 ...., P–K4; 11 P × P e.p., P × P; 12 Castles, Q–K2; 13 Kt–K1, P–K4; when the best continuation would have been: 14 Kt–B2, and 15 Kt–K3.

II.—(White: Fairhurst, London, 1927): 1 P–Q4, P–K3; 2 P–QB4, Kt–KB3; 3 Kt–KB3, B–Kt5ch.; 4 B–Q2, Q–K2; 5 P–KKt3, B × Bch.; 6 QKt × B, P–Q3; 7 B–Kt2, Castles; 8 Castles, P–KR3; (Black is in no hurry, for P–K4; can be played at any time, and if at once 8 ...., P–K4; the reply 9 P × P, P × P; 10 Q–B2, with, eventually, Kt–Kt5–K4, would open the game in a manner not quite to Black's liking); 9 Q–B2, R–K1; 10 P–K4, P–K4; (only now, as White's K4 is no longer available for his pieces, is this blockading move of value); 11 P–Q5 (better would certainly be: 11 KR–K1, Kt–B3; 12 Q–B3, although Black has a good position in this case also); 11 ...., P–QR4; with the square at QB4 (Kt–R3–B4;) as the basis of blockading operations.

Carefully handled strategy can rightly be expected to make use of preventive tactics, and indeed, prophylaxis is here of great moment. If, in Games 38 and 39, Black contrives to keep his as yet unfinished blockading frame secure against severe shocks, he has, in the first place, to thank the stratagem of the prophylaxis.

In Games 40 and 41 also, the blockade structure could not have been maintained without preventive measures, even though this structure, to all appearances, was completed and fully set.

We can, therefore, say : whether completed or otherwise, the blockade lay-out, at all times, is, logically, in a state of dependence upon the stratagem of the prophylaxis.

We should particularly recommend to the student the game v. Colle (41), for this game shows how difficult it is to guard an extensive blockading net against disruption. That it can be done is proved as convincingly as could be desired in Games 42–45 to which I would add many further examples.

Game No. 37.—Carlsbad, 1923.

Black: Réti.

This is a negative example : Master Réti does not succeed in enforcing the interlocking of the pawn formations. (When we say negative, we refer merely to the theoretical and didactic value of the play, and we do not mean to infer that the game was badly played).

1 Kt–KB3	Kt–KB3
2 P–B4	P–KKt3
3 P–QKt4	....

One of the author's innovations which Réti himself adopted upon occasion as in Réti-Capablanca (New York, 1924).

3	P–QR4

Of doubtful value.

4 P–Kt5	B–Kt2
5 B–Kt2	Castles
6 P–K3	P–Q3
7 P–Q4	QKt–Q2
8 B–K2	P–K4

This move would only be sound if Black were in a position to enforce P–Q5, or at least P × P, for he would then gain the excellent blockade square at his QB4, e.g., 9 P × P ? Kt–Kt5 ; etc.

9 Castles   P × P

And as soon as started the blockading manœuvre is already demolished. Theoretically and strategically the only course was : 9 ...., R–K1 ; and if 10 QKt–Q2, then P–B3 ; and, according to circumstances Q–B2 ; or P–K5 ; and P–Q4 ; establishing a chain of pawns.

10 P × P   R–K1
11 QKt–Q2   ....

It is not easy for White to take advantage of his superior pawn position. This move takes too little account of Black's advance P–Q4 ; and with 11 Kt–B3, he would have drawn considerably nearer to his goal.

11 ....   Kt–B1
12 R–K1   Kt–K3
13 P–Kt3   P–R3
14 B–KB1   Kt–Kt4
15 Kt × Kt   P × Kt
16 B–Kt2   ....

With the Kt at QB3 instead of Q2, the pressure brought to bear by White's forces would give winning chances. As it is Black can equalise approximately.

16 ....   P–Q4
17 R × Rch.   ....

The only chance to maintain the fleeting advantage lay in 17 P–B5. With this move White would have obtained a clearly superior position at least on the Q side; it is, however, very doubtful whether anything could be made of the position after : 17 ...., B–B4 ; 18 Q–R4, P–Kt3 ; etc. It seems that move 11 Kt–Q2, which must be deprecated from the point of view of centralised development, can no longer be remedied.

17 ....   Q × R
18 P × P   Q × P
19 Q–Kt3   B–Q2
20 Q × Q   ....

Or 20 R–QB1, Kt–K1 ; 21 Q × Q, B × Q ; 22 Kt–K4, P–Kt5 ; and eventually ...., R–Q1.

20 ....   B × Q
21 R–QB1   R–K1

Playable would also be the simple 21 ...., Kt–K1;
e.g., 22 Kt–K4, P–Kt5; 23 P–KR3, P×P; 24 B×P, R–Q1;
etc.

22	R×P	R–K8ch.
23	Kt–B1	B×Kt
24	B×B	Kt×P
25	R×KtP	R–Kt8
26	R–Kt8ch.	K–R2
27	R–Kt5	Kt–B2
28	R–Kt7	Kt–K3
29	K–Kt2	B×P
30	R×Pch.	K–Kt1
31	R–K7	R×QB
32	B–B4	R×Pch.
33	K–R3	R–B3
34	B×Ktch.	K–B1
35	R–Q7	R×B
36	R×B	....

After the interesting skirmishing of the last four-
teen moves, a Rook-ending is reached in which White has
some advantage without being able to force the win, though
the game went on to the 90th move before being drawn.

Game No. 38.—Berlin, 1927.

White: Ahues.

In contrast with the preceding example, the blockader
here succeeds in spreading his net *secumdum artem*. To this
end he makes extensive use of the stratagem of the prophylaxis.

1	P–Q4	Kt–KB3
2	P–QB4	P–K3
3	Kt–QB3	B–Kt5
4	B–Q2	Castles
5	Kt–B3	P–QKt3
6	P–K3	B×Kt

If 6 ...., B–Kt2; White could prevent the threatened
occupation of K4 as follows: 7 B–Q3, B×QKt; 8 B×B,
Kt–K5; 9 B×Kt, B×B; 10 Kt–Q2, B×P; 11 R–KKt1, with
a promising attack.

7	B×B	Kt–K5
8	Q–B2	B–Kt2
9	Castles	P–KB4
10	Kt–K5	....

After 10 B–Q3, Black intended a preventive manœuvre against a possible break-through by P–Q5, namely:—
10 B–Q3, Q–B3; if then 11 P–Q5, Kt×B; 12 Q×Kt, Q×Q; 13 P×Q, Kt–R3; and ...., Kt–B4; with a winning position for Black.

10 ....   Q–K2

There is no urgency to play P–Q3; the square at K3 must first be strengthened against Kt–Q3–B4, (in the variation beginning with P–Q3).

11	P–B3	Kt×B
12	Q×Kt	P–Q3
13	Kt–Q3	Kt–Q2
14	K–Kt1	....

14 ....   QR–Q1

A preventive manœuvre. Black forestalls the ingenious threat of P–B5. Had Black played QR–K1; this threat would have made itself felt most disagreeably by: 15 Q–R3, P–QR4; 16 P–B5, QP×P; 17 P×P, Kt×P; 18 Kt×Kt, Q×Kt; 19 Q×Q, P×Q; 20 R–B1.

15 P–KR4   ....

It is correct to say that 15 Q–R3, with 16 P–B5, no longer suffices because of: 15 Q–R3, P–QR4; 16 P–B5, QP×P; 17 P×P, Kt–K4; (stronger than 17 ...., Kt×P; 18 R–B1,) with the double threat: 18 ...., Kt–B5; and 18 ...., Kt×P; on the other hand the move in the text cuts both ways. To be considered was: 15 B–K2, P–K4; 16 Kt–B1, (not 16 P–Q5, because of ...., Q–Kt4).

15 ....   Q–B3

In order to strengthen the effect of the intended ...., P–K4.

16	Q–R3	P–QR4
17	B–K2	P–K4
18	P–Q5	....

The slow development on prophylactic lines has proved its worth. White is compelled to play P–Q5, and the blockade net is already spread over the centre and Q side. In the next move the K side also will be drawn in.

    18 ....   P–B5

    19 P–K4   ....

Compulsory because 19 P × P, P × P; would yield the K file to Black as well as important central squares.

    19 ....   Q–Kt3

Now White's KKt2, KKt3 and KR4 are obviously weak.

    20 QR–Kt1   Kt–B3

With the intention of bringing the Kt to KKt6, e.g., 21 P–B5 (not a bad counter-attack), Kt–R4; 22 P–KKt4, P × P e.p.; 23 P × KtP, P × P; 24 Q–Kt3, B–R3; 25 Kt × P, P × Kt; 26 B × B, P–Kt7; and wins.

    21 P–KKt3   P × P

    22 P–B5   ....

An ingenious attempt to save the situation which, however, is foiled by a counter sacrifice.

    22 ....   Kt × KP

A beautiful combination ! It runs as follows : 23 P × Kt, Q × P; 24 B–Q1, (24 B–B1, R × Bch.; with P–Kt7;) P–Kt7; 25 R–R2, B–R3; 26 B–B2, R–B8ch.; or 23 P × Kt, Q × P; 24 R–K1, P–Kt7; 25 KR–Kt1, QP × P; 26 QP × P, and wins.

    23 P × KtP   Kt–Q7ch.

    24 K–R1   ....

Had the King moved otherwise, there would have been attractive evolutions by the Kt with the gain of tempi at the expense, alternatively, of the King or the Queen as follows : 24 K–B2, Kt–B5; 25 Q–B3, Kt–K6ch.; with Kt × P; attacking the Queen or 25 Q–Kt3, (instead of B3)

Kt–K6ch.; with 26 ...., B × P, gaining a tempo, or 24 K–B1, Q–R3.

24	P × P
25 R–R3	P–Kt7
26 Q–B3	....

If 26 R–R2, Black's intention was to sacrifice the Q : Kt × P; 27 KR × P, Kt × R; 28 R × Q, P × R.

26	Q–R3
27 R × P	R–B1
28 Q–R3	Kt × P
29 R–R1	B × P

More ruthless than ...., P–K4; for all the White pieces are "hanging."
White resigns.

Game No. 39.—Kecskemet, 1927.

White: Ahues.

The phase in the struggle, which is of interest to us here, can be characterised as follows : with White's 13th move, P–Q5, Black has enforced the interlocking of the pawn formations, but cannot derive any benefit from the fact, because the blockading continuation Kt–QB4; would fail as it makes a break-through possible. But he anticipates this counter-chance and so enables the blockading action to develop smoothly, intensifying its effect by a simultaneous attack.

1 Kt–KB3	P–QKt3
2 P–K3	....

After 2 P–K4, there follows : B–Kt2; 3 Kt–QB3, P–K3; 4 P–Q4, B–Kt5; with P–Q3; and Black has a cramped but not a bad position.

2	B–Kt2
3 P–QKt3	P–KB4
4 B–Kt2	P–K3

Not good would be : 4 ...., Kt–KB3; because of 5 B × Kt, KP × B; 6 Kt–R4, P–Kt3; and now perhaps 7 B–B4, (provoking P–Q4;) P–Q4; 8 B–K2, and we should feel inclined to give White the preference.

5 Kt–K5	....

To imitate Black's Dutch development. Better would have been : 5 P–B4, with Kt–B3, to follow.

5	Kt–KB3
6 P–KB4	P–Kt3
7 P–B4	B–Kt2
8 Kt–QB3	Castles
9 Q–K2	P–Q3

Black has prepared this advance effectively, for he is ready to follow it up with ...., P–K4.

10 Kt–B3	QKt–Q2
11 P–Q4	Q K2
12 Castles	P–K4

Consummatum est.

| 13 P–Q5 | P–QR4 |
| 14 Q–Q2 | .... |

White is now about to complete his development.   His position appears to be quite secure, for in answer to Kt–B4; he has P × P, P × P; P–Q6, with a not unfavourable break-through.

| 14 .... | Kt–R4 ! |

A preventive combination which anticipates the possibility of the break-through alluded to above; in the first place P–Kt3, is to be provoked.

| 15 P–Kt3 | Kt–B4 |

Now 16 P × P, P × P; 17 P–Q6, would not be possible because after ...., P × P; etc., the White KKt would be *en prise*.

16 B–K2	P–R5
17 P–QKt4	P–R6
18 B–R1	....

Black's success consists in the fact that the White QB is now unprotected.

| 18 .... | Kt–K5 |
| 19 Kt × Kt | .... |

If 19 Q–K1, P×P; 20 KP×P, Kt×Kt; 21 B×Kt, B×B; 22 Q×B, Q×B.

	19	P×Kt
	20 Kt–Kt5	P×P

After the exchange of Bishops on White's KKt7, mate in two is threatened by Black.

	21 B×B	Q×B
	22 Q–Q4	P–B6

Black's far-seeing combinative play has borne fruit; it is now a question of holding on to what he has gained.

	23 B–B1	KR–K1
	24 B–R3	....

Clearly not 24 Kt×KP, because of R×Kt.

| | 24 .... | B–B1 |

24 ...., R–R5; would be questionable on account of 25 B–K6ch., K–B1; 26 Q×Qch., with B–Q7; though in this case with ...., R×P; Black would obtain sufficient compensation for the exchange.

	25 B×B	QR×B
	26 P–Kt5	R–K4
	27 Kt–K6	Q–K2
	28 K–Kt1	Kt–Kt2
	29 Kt–B4	Q–Q2
	30 P–R4	....

Because P–Kt4; was threatened.

	30	Kt–B4
	31 Q–B3	Kt×KtP
	32 KR–Kt1	Kt–R4
	33 Kt–K6	Kt–Kt2
	34 Kt–Q4	R–B1

Resigns.

For if 35 Q×P, there follows R–R4; 36 R–R1, Q–Kt5; 37 QR–Kt1, R×RP; 38 R×Q, R×Rch.; with P–B7; and wins.

The value of the strategy decided upon by Black on the 14th move (see Diagram 47) is demonstrated clearly in the following variation : White foregoes 15 P–Kt3, and plays 15 B–K2, instead. 15 ...., Kt–B4; 16 P×P, P×P; 17 P–Q6, P×P; 18 Q×P, Q×Q; 19 R×Q, B–KR3; 20 Kt×P, B×Pch.; 21 K–B2, B×P; 22 KR–Q1, Kt–B5; and Black ought to win.

Game No. 40.—Berlin, 1927.

White: Schweinburg.

1	P–K4	Kt–QB3
2	Kt–KB3	P–K3
3	P–Q4	P–Q4
4	P×P	P×P
5	B–Q3	B–Kt5
6	B–K3	B–Q3
7	P–B3	KKt–K2
8	QKt–Q2	Q–Q2
9	Kt–Kt3	Castles QR
10	P–KR3	B–R4
11	Q–B2	P–B4
12	Castles QR	....

An exchange variation of the French defence with an unusual development of the Bishops.

12	....	P–B5
13	B–Q2	B×Kt
14	P×B	Q–K3

Only this move explains the exchange. Otherwise (with 14 ...., P–KKt3;) White would set about to roll up the K side (P–KR4–R5,). Referring back to Game No. 33, the text move will be understood as a preventive measure, which it pre-eminently is.

15	QR–Kt1	....

If 15 B×RP, P–KKt3.

15	....	Q–R3
16	K–Kt1	QR–B1
17	Kt–B1	Kt–KKt1

Again a preventive manœuvre. As ...., P–KKt3; will have to be played, the attack shown in Note 14 is to be met by ...., Kt–B3–R4.

18	P–Kt4	P–KKt3
19	Q–R4	K–Kt1
20	Kt–Kt3	Q–R4
21	B–K2	Kt–B3
22	Kt–B5	Kt–Q1
23	K–Kt2	R–K1
24	B–Q1	Q–R5

With this move Black proceeds at leisure to take advantage of the weakness of the "complex." Without the exercise of prophylaxis on moves 14 and 15 he would not

have been able to do this.   A clear proof of our contention
that blockading without prophylaxis is an impossibility.

25 R–B1	R–K2
26 Q–Kt5	KR–K1
27 P–R4	P–Kt3

Because his position is preferable in every respect, Black
now proceeds to eliminate the advanced White Kt, without
giving a thought to any weaknesses this may create in his
own camp.   But violent measures are seldom good and,
moreover, White's position, though deficient in mobility, is
not actually weak.   Black's strategy, therefore, should be
deliberate, namely :   27 ...., P–B3; 28 Q–Q3, Kt–Q2;
(threatening Kt–Kt3–B5;) 29 P–R5, P–QR3.   The march
forward of the White pawns appears to be held up, and Black
would have time and leisure for elaborate manœuvres such
as : 30 ...., K–R2; 31 .... B–B2; with Kt–B2–Q3–B5;
after which White could hardly withstand the ever increasing
pressure.

28 Kt–Kt3	K–R1
29 Kt–B1	....

Preferable was : 29 Q–R6, Kt–Kt2; with a complicated
game only slightly in Black's favour.

29	P–B3
30 Q–Q3	P–B4

If at once 29 ...., P–B4; then 30 P–R5.

31 QP × P	....

White failed on his 29th move to show up the weakness
of Black's QR3, and now it would be too late to do so,
although the attempt would be difficult to refute, e.g. :
31 Q–R6, (instead of 31 QP × P,) P × QP; 32 P–R5,
(suggested by Dr. Lasker) P × Pch.; 33 B × P, P–Q5;
34 B × P, Kt–B3; 35 P × P, Kt × B; 36 P–Kt7ch., R × P;

37 Q×B, and now simple liquidation by: 37 ....,
R×Pch.; 38 Q×R, R–QKt1; 39 Q×Rch., K×Q;
40 Kt–Q3, Kt–Q4; and is difficult to see why Black's extra
pawn in conjunction with his centralised position should not
be sufficient to win. After the move in the text, Black's
attack becomes overpowering.

31	P×P
32 B–Kt3	Kt–Kt2

A decisive pawn sacrifice. Insufficient would be the
continuation: 32 ...., P–B5; 33 B×QBP, P×B;
34 Q×B, R–Q2; because of 35 Q×P, P–Kt4; 36 Q×KtP.

33 B×QP	Kt×B
34 Q×Kt	P×P
35 P–R5	....

A last ingenious attempt! If 35 P×P, R–Q1; is decisive.

35 .... R–Q1

The threat P–R6 can safely be ignored.

36 P–R6	P×Pch.
37 K–B2	B–Kt5
38 Q–B6	R×Bch.
39 K–Kt1	K–Kt1

Resigns.

Game No. 41.—Baden-Baden, 1925.

White: Colle.

1	P–Q4	P–KB4
2	P–K3	Kt–KB3
3	B–Q3	P–Q3
4	Kt–K2	P–K4
5	P–QB4	P–B4

Black feels that he has stored up sufficient mobility in
his pawns at KB4 and K4, and so he has no objection to
blocking up the centre and the other wing; he now tries to
bring this about.

6	Castles	Kt–B3
7	QKt–B3	P–KKt4

Bold play for, as yet, the deadlock for which Black
is playing has not been accomplished; rather is White in a
position to open up in the centre. Will Black, in that case,
be equal to the two-fold task of safeguarding the Q file
against inroads and the K side pawns against loss?

	8 P×BP	P×P
	9 Kt–Kt3	P–K5
	10 B–K2	B–Q3

Consolidation.

	11 Kt–Kt5	B–K4
	12 Q×Qch.	K×Q
	13 R–Q1ch.	K–K2
	14 R–Kt1	P–KR4
	15 B–Q2	P–R5

The following line of play deserved the preference:
15 ...., P–B5; 16 Kt–B1, B–Kt5; e.g.: 17 B×B, P×B;
18 P×P, P×P; 19 R–K1, K–K3; with a strongly centralised formation. Or: 15 ...., P–B5; 16 Kt–B1, B–Kt5;
17 B×B, P×B; 18 R–K1, P–B6; 19 P–KKt3, P–R3;
20 Kt–R3, KR–Q1; 21 P–Kt4, R–Q6; 22 Kt–B2, QR–Q1;
and wins.

	16 Kt–B1	B–K3
	17 B–QB3	B×B
	18 Kt×B	Kt–K4
	19 P–QKt3	KR–KKt1

Here and on the next move, Black neglects an important
prophylactic measure, namely ...., P–Kt3; which would
render P–QKt4, purposeless, and this neglect leads to the
loss of the whole of his advantage.

	20 R–Kt2	P–B5
	21 Kt–Q2	B–B4
	22 P–QKt4	....

Splits the blockade-net, spread at the cost of so much
trouble.

| 22 .... | Kt (K4)–Q2 |
| 23 P × KBP | .... |

It would have been advisable to continue the break-through initiated with 22 P–QKt4, by 23 P × QBP, Kt × P; 24 Kt–Kt3; Kt × Kt; 25 R × Kt, P–Kt3; 26 R–Kt5, etc.

| 23 .... | P × BP |
| 24 R–K1 | K–B2 |

He should have played K–B1.

25 Kt(Q2) × P	Kt × Kt
26 B–R5ch.	K–Kt2
27 Kt × Kt	K–R3

Black, in a bad plight, discovers a way to save himself by an interesting manoeuvre.

| 28 B–B7 | .... |

If 28 B–B3, Kt–K4.

28	P–B6
29 B × R	R × B
30 Kt–Q6	....

If 30 P–Kt3, R–K1.

30	R × Pch.
31 K–R1	B–R6
32 R–KKt1	....

He should be content with a draw, obtainable by: 32 Kt–B7ch., K–Kt2; 33 Kt–K5, R–Kt4; 34 Kt × Kt, B–Kt7ch., etc.

| 32 .... | Kt–K4 |

Now White cannot exchange Rooks because of mate in two. On the other hand Kt–Q6; is threatened.

| 33 P × P | .... |

An interesting win after 33 R–Q2, is as follows: Kt–Kt5; R × R, P × Rch.; K–Kt1, Kt–K4!!; (Echo theme)

33	Kt–Q6
34 R–Q2	R × Rch.
35 K × R	Kt–B5

Bad mating troubles considering the paucity of material.

36 Kt–B7ch.	K–Kt2
37 Kt–K5	Kt–K7ch.
38 R × Kt	P × R
39 Kt–Q3	B–K3

The End-Game is better for Black as the King can take a hand.

40	P–QR3	B × P
41	Kt–K1	K–B3
42	P–B3	K–K4
43	K–B2	K–Q5
44	Kt–Kt2	K × P
45	Kt × P	P–Kt4
46	P–B4	P–R4
47	Kt–B3	P–R5
48	P–B5	P–Kt5
49	P × Pch.	K × P
50	P–B6	P–R6
51	Kt–Q4	P–R7
52	Kt–B2ch.	K–B6

Resigns.

Game No. 42.

From a Simultaneous Exhibition, Arnstadt, 1926.

White: Hage.

A companion game to No. 41. We see here how a blockade, undisturbed by any sins of omission, could have been worked out in the preceding game.

1	P–Q4	P–KB4
2	P–K3	P–Q3
3	B–Q3	P–K4
4	P × P	P × P
5	B–Kt5ch.	P–B3
6	Q × Qch.	K × Q
7	B–B4	B–Q3
8	Kt–KB3	Kt–B3
9	Kt–B3	....

A better line of play would be P–QR4, with P–QKt3, and B–Kt2, or B–R3.

9	....	K–K2
10	P–QR3	R–Q1
11	B–Q2	P–QKt4
12	B–R2	P–QR4
13	Castles KR	P–Kt5
14	Kt–Kt1	P–B4
15	B–B4	P–K5
16	Kt–Kt5	B–R3
17	B × B	R × B
18	P × P	RP × P
19	R × R	Kt × R

Black's blockade shows the same component parts as in the preceding game, namely the Q file, the central square at his K4 and the qualitative majority on the K side. Added to this there is the Q side, which is threatening in a blockading sense.

20	P–QB3	P–R3
21	Kt–KR3	Kt–Kt5
22	P–KKt3	Kt–K4
23	K–Kt2	P–Kt4
24	B–B1	P–Kt6
25	Kt–Q2	P–QB5

26	Kt–KKt1	Kt–B4
27	Kt–K2	R–KKt1
28	Kt–Q4	P–B5

If now 29 KP×P, P×P; 30 R–K1, then P–K6; 31 P×KP, P×KtP.

29	Kt–B5ch.	K–K3
30	Kt×B	P–B6ch.
31	K–Kt1	K×Kt

The White position now looks hopeless.

32	R–Q1	K–K3
33	Kt–Kt1	Kt(B4)–Q6
34	Kt–R3	K–Q4
35	Kt–Kt5	R–QKt1
36	Kt–R3	R–QR1
37	P–R3	K–B4

| 38 K–B1 | Kt × B |

This leads to an immediate win.

39 R × Kt	Kt–Q6
40 R–Kt1	Kt × KtP
41 R × Kt	R × Kt
42 R–Kt1	P–Kt7

Resigns.

A genuine blockade-game with a blockading net covering both wings as well as the centre. Without belittling the operations on the wings, we feel inclined to attach greater importance to the central manœuvres round Black's K4 and Q6 : the blockade no doubt originated in the centre.

Game No. 43.—Breslau, 1926.

White: Blümich.

This game is recommended to our readers not only as an example of the blockade, but also because from beginning to end it illustrates the value of lines.

The glossary on the events in these open lines has been, for that reason, the object of particular care.

1 Kt–KB3	P–K3
2 P–KKt3	P–QKt3
3 B–Kt2	B–Kt2
4 Castles	P–QB4
5 P–Q3	Kt–KB3
6 P–K4	B–K2
7 Kt–B3	Castles
8 B–Q2	Kt–B3
9 P–K5	....

This puts life into the game, but he would be less committed by : 9 K–R1, with Kt–KKt1, and P–B4.

| 9 .... | Kt–K1 |
| 10 Kt–K4 | R–B1 |

A preventive measure against the possibility of P–B3, and P–Q4, which might occur later.

| 11 B–B3 | P–QKt4 |

Luring him on to play P–Kt3 : the reason will soon be seen.

12 P–Kt3	P–B4
13 P × P e.p.	Kt × P
14 Q–K2	Kt–Q4
15 B–Kt2	P–Kt5

Now Black has an inexpugnable Kt in the centre, as well as White, and it is difficult to determine how matters will develop.

| 16 QR–K1 | P–QR4 |
| 17 P–QR4 | .... |

Not good; KKt–Q2, and P KB4, were the right moves.

| 17 .... | Q–K1 |

There is no reason why he should not simply have opened the game by 17 ...., P × P e.p.; 18 B × RP, Kt–Q5; 19 Kt × Kt, (he must not go in for 19 Q–Q1, because of 19 ...., Kt–B6; 20 Kt(K4) × Kt, B × Kt; 21 Q–B1, Q K1; and 22 ...., Q–R4;) 19 ...., P × Kt; and the QB file, together with the preventive 10 ...., R–B1, would have come into its own. After the move in the text the threatened mummification is difficult to avoid.

| 18 QKt–Q2 | .... |

The other Kt would be preferable, e.g.: 18 KKt–Q2, Kt–Q5; 19 Q–Q1, with P–KB4, and Kt–KB3.

| 18 .... | B–B3 |
| 19 B × B | P × B |

The Black position becomes steadily more compact and the White K file proportionately of less value; Black's K3 remains firm as a rock and he already controls his K4 and K5.

20 Kt–B4	Q–R4
21 Kt–Q4	Q × Q
22 Kt × Q	QR–B2
23 P–B4	B–R3
24 B × Kt	P × B
25 Kt–Q6	P–B4

The plucky White Kt, in order to secure the K file for his side, has ventured into a blind alley, and it remains to be seen whether the K file was worth it.

26	R–B2	Kt–Q1
27	Kt–B1	R–QB3
28	Kt–Kt5	B × Kt
29	P × B	R–K3

The crucial point: R–QKt3; must be eschewed for the sake of the K file.

30	KR–K2	K–B2

31 K–B2 ....

Play on the K file by the occupation of the outpost at K5 was of urgent necessity. Black would then have had to solve an extremely difficult problem. 31 R–K5, K–B3; 32 K–B2, P–Q3; 33 R × Rch., (not 33 R × QP, because of K–K3; after the exchange of Rooks) Kt × R; 34 Kt–K2, R–QKt1; 35 R–QR1, R × P; 36 P–B4, P × P e.p.; 37 Kt × P, R × P; 38 Kt × Pch., K–B2; 39 R × P, R × P; 40 R–R7ch., K–K1; 41 Kt–B6ch., K–Q1; 42 Kt × P, P–B5; 43 Kt–Kt5, Kt–B4; 44 K–K2, K–K1; (Position: White: K at K2, RQR7, KtKKt5, Pawns KR2, KKt3, KB4. Black: KK1, KtQB4, RQ6, Pawns QB5, Q3, KB4). Now the advance of the QBP is threatened, whereas on the 44th move it would have been a mistake owing to Kt–K6ch., the continuation would be: 45 R–QB7, P–B6; 46 Kt–B7 (if now 46 ...., P–B7; 47 Kt × Pch., etc. But if 46 ...., R–Q4; in order, after 47 Kt × Pch., to play the K to B1—not Q1 on account of R × Kt—there follows 48 Kt–Kt7, P–B7; 49 Kt × Kt, P–B8Q; 50 Kt–K6ch., and wins); 46 ...., R–Q7ch.; 47 K–K3, R–Q4; 48 Kt × Pch., K–B1; and the QBP walks in with check.

In the position after the 44th move, White could not save the position by other moves, e.g. : 45 P–R4, P–B6; 46 P–R5, P–B7; 47 R–R1, R–R6; 48 R–QB1, Kt–Kt3; 49 R × P, Kt–Q5ch. and wins.   This is the solution, long-winded but interesting throughout, of the problem set on move 31.   There may be another solution by 44 ...., K–B1 (intending K–Kt1; when occasion arises), which, however detracts but little from the beauty of the solution given here.   Therefore : the evil of Knight's " blind alley " out-weighs the advantage of the " K file."

| 31 .... | K–B3 |
| 32 K–B3 | .... |

Even now White can conjure up the problem sketched out above by 32 R–K5.   In any event the technique of line-play should not break down suddenly! Exploitation of a line and, in particular, the occupation of an outpost, should be a matter of course.   Compare the disquisitions about open lines in " My System " (Chap. I.)

| 32 .... | Kt–B2 |

Secures K4 against invasion.   The QKtP must fall.

| 33 Kt–R2 | P–Q5 |
| 34 R–QR1 | R–QKt1 |

At last the time has come to bring home the spoils. Already from this point a marked blockade effect can be observed.   The moves and manœuvres of the White pieces are effected clumsily and with increasing internal friction, whilst the light-footed Black pieces control the board.

35 Kt–B1	R × P
36 R–Q2	Kt–Q1
37 Kt–K2	Kt–B3
38 Kt–Kt1	P–Q4

The QP waited until the 38th move before moving.

| 39 Kt–K2 | R–Kt1 |
| 40 R–R4 | R(Kt1)–K1 |

Now Black is master of the K file.

41 R–R1	P–R4
42 Kt–Kt1	R–K6ch.
43 K–B2	....

At long last the position is ripe for a break-through.

| 43 .... | P–B5 |

44 QR–Q1 ....
Or 44 QP × P, P × P; 45 P × P, R–B6.

44 .... P–B6

A sacrificial combination crowns the edifice of the Blockade.

45 R–K2 P–QR5
46 P × P P–Kt6
47 P × P Kt–Kt5

and wins.

(48 R × R, R × R; 49 Kt–K2, P–B7; 50 R–QR1, Kt × Pch.; 51 K–B1, R × Kt; 52 K × R, P–B8 (Q); 53 R × Q, Kt × Rch.; 54 K–B3, Kt × P; 55 P–R3, P–Q6).

Game No. 44.—Dresden, 1926.

White: v. Holzhausen.

1 P–K4 P–QB4
2 Kt–KB3 Kt–QB3
3 P–Q4 P × P
4 Kt × P P–Q4

An innovation first tried by the author v. Rubinstein, Carlsbad, 1923.

5 B–QKt5 ....

Better seems 5 Kt × Kt, P × Kt; 6 P × P, Q × P; 7 Kt–B3, Q × Qch.; 8 Kt × Q, and White has a more compact position although the games may be even.

5 .... P × P
6 Kt × Kt Q × Qch.
7 K × Q P–QR3
8 Kt–Q4 dis ch. P × B
9 Kt × P B–Kt5ch.
10 K–K1 R–Q1

Black thought the position after 10 ...., Castles; somewhat unstable, e.g., 10 ...., Castles; 11 QKt–B3, P–K4; 12 P–KR3, B–R4; 13 P–KKt4, B–Kt3; 14 P–QR4, with 15 P–R5, and 16 P–R6, or 12 ...., B–Q2; (instead of B–R4;) 13 B–K3, B–QKt5; 14 K–K2, in both cases the Black King's position appears to be open to attack.

11 QKt–B3   P–K4

This move, strong though it may look, does in no way answer the strict requirements which blockading strategy demands of its protagonists. The basis of blockading operations here was to be found in the diagonal from White's KKt4 to Q1 and therefore this diagonal had to be protected and over-protected. This is specially the case as White already intends to destroy this basis in no gentle manner by means of: 12 P–KR3, B–R4; 13 P–KKt4. The proper procedure, from a blockading point of view, was: 11 ...., P–B4; (instead of P–K4;). If then 12 P–KR3, B–R4; 13, P–KKt4, P × P; 14 Kt × P, P × P; White certainly could avoid serious loss by: 15 B–B4, B–B6; 16 Kt–Kt5, B × R; 17 Kt–B7ch., K–Q2; 18 Kt–B7, but his game could not be held for more than a few moves: 18 ...., B–B6; 19 Kt × KR, P–K4; 20 B × P, B–Q3; 21 B × B, K × B.

Should White give up all attempts to break up the position forcibly and decide quietly to continue his development, he would obtain no componsation for the KR being out of play, e.g.: 11 ...., P–B4; 12 B–B4, Kt–B3; with P–K3; and K–B2; to follow. After the move in the text, however, the situation is doubtful.

12 P–KR3   B–R4

Black could not make up his mind to continue: 12 ...., B–Q2; 13 Kt–B7ch., K–K2; 14 QKt–Q5ch., K–Q3; 15 B–K3.

13 P–KKt4   B–Kt3
14 Kt–B7ch.   ....

The continuation indicated here was: 14 B–K3, P–B4; 15 K–K2, and the KR could get into play. Strategically it would then be Black's duty to play for the recapture of the proud diagonal from his KR4–Q8, perhaps as follows:— 15 ...., P × P; 16 P × P, Kt–B3; 17 P–Kt5, B–R4ch.; 18 K–B1, B–B6; 19 R–R4, Kt–Kt5; 20 Kt × P, B × Kt; 21 R × Kt, B × P; 22 Kt–B3, with approximately even chances. This variation impresses one as being built up on strictly logical lines.

14	K–Q2
15 KKt–Q5	K–B3
16 Kt–K3	....

Tempting was 16 B–K3, but after R × Kt; 17 Kt × R, K × Kt; 18 R–Q1ch., K–B3; 19 R–Q8, there would be 19 ...., Kt–B3; 20 K–K2, R–Kt1; and B–K2; unpinning the R could not be prevented.

| 16 .... | B–Kt5 |

The logical trend of the game required an immediate 16 ...., P–R4; (17 P–Kt5, P–B4; or .... P–R5; with advantage to Black). Black develops on mechanical lines and so pays a tribute to the false teaching of the old school, that " all the puppets " must be in the play before anything is undertaken. How ridiculous and out-of-date is such a dogma in our time.

| 17 B–Q2 | Kt–K2 |
| 18 P–KR4 | .... |

Better would be 18 P–R3, with some chances of counter-play.

| 18 .... | P–R4 |

The recapture of the diagonal is initiated herewith. The next eight moves are taken up in a bitter struggle, a struggle full of tension. But after these eight moves the real fight is over and White lies prone, blockaded and gagged, waiting resignedly for the end.

19 P–Kt5	Kt–B4
20 Kt × Kt	B × Kt
21 R–KKt1	R–Q5

Threatens P–K6; B × P, R × P; and Black has a passed pawn.

22 P–R3	KR–Q1
23 P × B	R × B
24 R–Q1	R × Rch.
25 Kt × R	B–Kt5
26 Kt–K3	B–B6
27 P–B4	....

White is practically helpless.

27	P–Kt4
28 P–Kt3	R–Q6
29 R–Kt3	P–Kt3

30 R–Kt1   ....

The White R is restricted to the squares KKt1 and Kt3. For if 30 R–R3, there follows: R × P; 31 K–Q2, R–Q6ch.; 32 K–B2, P × P; and 33 Kt × P, is not feasible because of B–Q8ch., and R × R.

30 ....   K–Kt2
31 P × P   ....

Simplifies matters for Black. If 31 R–Kt3, the Black K would first migrate to K3. Then, with the White R at Kt3, would come liquidation by R × P; K–Q2, P × P; Kt × P, R × P; Kt–K3, and the Black R occupies the opponent's first rank. The position then is naturally untenable for White. If nothing else, with the White R at his KR3, Black could force the exchange of Rooks by R–KR8; and follow up with P–B3; and a simple win. The rest is pure garotting.

31 ....   K–Kt3
32 R–Kt3   K × P
33 R–R3   K × P
34 K–B1   R × P
35 K–Kt1   R–Kt7
36 Kt–Q5ch.   K–B5
37 Kt–K3ch.   K–Q6
38 Kt–Kt2   R–Kt8ch.
39 K–R2   K–K7

The Black K follows up in an amusing manner.

40 K–Kt3   R–Kt8
41 R–R2   K–B8
42 K–R3   B × Ktch

Resigns.

Game No. 45.—Hanover, 1926.

Black: Duhm.

A short but edifying blockade game. The pawn formations resemble those in Games 41 and 42, but the manner of the blockade, based, as it is, on a Diagonal is reminiscent of Game 44. Be that as it may, the blockading net here acts with certainty and dispatch.

1 P–QB4	P–K3
2 P–K4	P–QB4

Better is: 2 ...., P–Q4; 3 BP×P, P×P; 4 P×P, Kt–KB3.

3 Kt–QB3	Kt–QB3
4 P–B4	P–Q3

Better Kt–B3.

5 Kt–B3	P–KKt3
6 P–Q4	B–Kt2
7 P×P	....

This clearly establishes White's advantage.

7	P×P

If 7 ...., B×Ktch.; first, then 8 P×B, P×P; 9 Q×Qch., followed if ...., K×Q; by Kt–K5, with advantage to White. But if the Kt recaptures 9 ...., Kt×Q; there follows 10 P–QR4, 11 B–K3, and if 11 ...., P–QKt3; 12 P–R5, comfortably rolling up the Q side.

8 Q×Qch.	K×Q
9 P–K5	P–KR4

Unquestionably Black should have played 9 ...., P–B3; in order to eliminate the blockading KP which also commands Black's Q3. Black's counter-plan to establish a Knight at his KB4 and so to set up a blockade of his own— for there the Kt would hold up the opposing qualitative majority—is found to be impracticable: an immediate attack by White leaves him no time for lengthy manœuvres.

10 B–K3	P–Kt3
11 Castles ch.	K–K2
12 B–B2	....

The all important long diagonal is to be occupied with decisive results. See next note.

12	Kt–R3
13 B–R4 ch.	K–B1
14 B–Q3	B–Kt2
15 B–K4	....

The decisive effect of this B on the long Diagonal is due to the fact that now Black is robbed of the possibility of opposing a R on the Q file : he has to abandon this file to his opponent and so, particularly with the KR out of play, his game becomes hopeless.

15	Kt–R4
16 B × B	Kt × B
17 R–Q7	R–QKt1
18 KR–Q1	K–Kt1
19 B–K7	....

So as to play Kt–KKt5, without shutting out the Bishop.

19	Kt–B4
20 Kt–KKt5	R–K1
21 B–B6	B × B
22 P × B	Kt–R4
23 R–Q8	....

Initiating a mating attack.

23	K–B1
24 KR–Q7	Kt–R3
25 QKt–K4	Kt–B3

26 R × P ch.	Kt × R
27 Kt × P ch.	K–Kt1
28 R × R ch.	K–R2
29 Kt(K4)–Kt5 ch.	and mate in two.

Game No. 46.

Match, Kolding (Denmark), 1922.

White: Brinkmann.

This game is an illustration of the " Blockade sacrifice," which stratagem was supposed to have originated with the author's games v. Spielmann and v. Leonhardt, San Sebastian, 1912. Since then it was established that another of his games, that v. John, Hamburg, 1910, contains a pawn sacrifice with the same tendency, and this game, which we give in extenso, must therefore be held to be the parent game : White : John. 1 P–Q4, P–Q4; 2 Kt–KB3, P–K3; 3 P–K3, P–QB4; 4 P–QKt3, Kt–KB3; 5 B–Kt2, Kt–B3; 6 B–Q3, B–Q3; 7 QKt–Q2, Castles; 8 Castles, Q–K2; 9 P–B4, P–QKt3; 10 Kt–K5, B–Kt2; 11 R–B1, KR–Q1; 12 Kt × Kt, (the Kt could not very well be maintained on K5. With the text-move White plays for " hanging pawns,") 12 ...., B × Kt; 13 BP × P, KP × P; 14 Q–B2, (P × P, which is part of the plan reserved for a more favourable occasion). 14 ...., P–KR3; 15 KR–Q1, QR–B1; 16 B–B5, R–B2; 17 Q–B3, P–B5 !! 18 P × P, P × P; 19 Kt × P, Kt–K5; (19 ...., B–R5; is also a move, but it would not be in harmony with the sacrifice and its blockading tendencies) 20 Q–K1, (the idea underlying Black's play would have appeared clearly if White had played 20 B × Kt, e.g., B × B; 21 Q–Q2, Q–Kt4; 22 P–B4, Q–Q4; as Black for the pawn minus would have compensation in the block position. The move in the text is faulty) 20 ...., B–Kt5; 21 Q–K2, B–Kt4; 22 B × Kt, (a little better would be 22 Q–B3,) Q × B; 23 Kt–Q6, (there is nothing better) B × Q; 24 Kt × Q, R–K2; 25 Kt–Kt3, B × R ; and won after a hard fight. After this introduction, which illustrates the characteristics of the " blockade sacrifice," let us turn to Game No. 46 which sets out this stratagem most plastically and which, for that reason, is one of the author's favourite games.

1 P–Q4	P–K3
2 P–QB4	Kt–KB3
3 Kt–QB3	B–Kt5
4 B–Q2	Castles

P–QKt3; at once can be played.

5	Kt–B3	P–Q3
6	P–K3	P–QKt3
7	B–Q3	B–Kt2
8	Q–B2	B × KKt

A very dangerous undertaking.

9	P × B	QKt–Q2
10	P–QR3	B × Kt
11	B × B	P–B3

As Black, whilst exploiting the dynamic weakness of the double complex, tries at the same time to block the two Bishops, he avoids any premature opening up of the game as a matter of course. For instance: 11 ...., P–Q4; 12 P × P, P × P; 13 Castles QR, with K–Kt1, and R–QB1. White has now scope on both the QB and the KKt files, whereas Black's only counter chance, ..., P–B4; would call up the answer P × P, liberating the Bishops.

12	Castles QR	P–Q4
13	P–K4	....

Such an advance, though it produces chances of attack, also weakens, as we know, the double complex to an appreciable extent.

13	....	P–Kt3

Compulsory. But not as bad as it looks. The Kt at B3 counteracts a rolling up policy by P–KR4–R5.

14	BP × P	....

It would be better to play P–KR4, or K–Kt1. But White wishes to play P–K5, which would be unfavourable, if played at once, because of P × BP; B × P, Kt–Q4; etc.

14	....	BP × P
15	P–K5	Kt–R4

Now Black gloats over his opponent's paralysed double complex.

16	P–KR4	P–R4

In order to restrain White's QB; the re-grouping of forces by Q–K2; KR–B1; and Kt–B1; can now be undertaken.

17	QR–Kt1	Q–K2
18	Q–Q2	KR–B1
19	P–B4	....

19 ....   P-QKt4 !!

The "Blockade sacrifice": a pawn is given up so that the KB can be exchanged; White is then weak on the White squares and must lose.

20 B × QKtP   QR-Kt1
21 B-K2   Kt-Kt3

The sacrifice of a piece is sound; but more correct and also more stylish was 21 ...., Kt-Kt2; 22 P-R5, Kt-KB4; followed by Kt-Kt3-B5, with the superior game.

22 K-Q1   ....

He should have accepted the sacrifice, e.g.: 22 B × Kt, Kt-B5; 23 Q-B2, Kt × RP; 24 Q-Q2, Kt-B5; with a drawn conclusion.

22 ....   Kt-B5
23 B × QKt   R × B
24 R-Kt5   Kt-Kt2
25 P-R5   Kt-B4
26 P × P   BP × P

Examine the position after Black has solved the problem indicated in the note to move 11; the doubled pawn is hopelessly blockaded and White has manifold weaknesses.

27 R × Kt   ....

A desperate attempt which is refuted energetically.

27 ....   KP × R
28 B × P   R-Kt6
29 K-K2   Q-QKt2
30 B-Kt4   Q-R3

Resigns.

31 K-K1, fails on account of : QR × B × B; 32 P × R, Q-R8ch.; 33 Q-Q1, R-B8.

Game No. 47.—San Sebastian (1912).

Black: Leonhardt.

The parent game to the stratagem "Sacrifice for Blockade." (See, however, introductory note to No. 46).

1	P–K4	P–K3
2	P–Q4	P–Q4
3	P–K5	P–QB4
4	Kt–KB3	Q–Kt3

After 4 ...., P×P; could follow 5 B–Q3, in Gambit style or 5 Q×P, Kt–QB3; 6 Q–KB4, with sound pressure.

5	B–Q3	P×P
6	Castles	Kt–QB3
7	P–QR3	....

We have now reached a position typical of our stratagem; White's KP appears to be ample compensation for the small sacrifice, because it assists in restricting Black's position.

7	....	KKt–K2

After the game my opponent was curious to know what I would have played in reply to 7 ...., P–QR4? I mentioned the variation: 8 B–KB4, Q×P; 9 QKt–Q2. "You would never have dared to play this," said Leonhardt. But I would have done it: this second "Sacrifice for Blockade" is a logical complement of the first. After 7 ...., P–QR4; 8 B–KB4, Q×P; 9 QKt–Q2, Q–Kt3; (if 9 ...., B×P; White could already secure the draw by 10 Kt–Kt3, followed by B–QB1, and B–Q2,) 10 R–K1, it is not easy to decide whether White has sufficient compensation. Black's extra pawns are certainly not mobile and his development is fraught with difficulties. Besides 8 B–KB4, which is based on my novel stratagem, 8 P–QR4, has also to be considered, e.g.: 7 ...., P–QR4; 8 P–QR4, B–B4; 9 Kt–R3, with chances for both sides. Finally it can be noted that, Lasker, in a similar situation, played 7 ...., P–B4; upon which we would recommend 8 P–QKt4, P–QR3; 9 P–B4, P×P e.p.; 10 Kt×P, and White threatens to occupy QKt6 by means of B–K3, and Kt–QR4.

8	P–QKt4	Kt–Kt3
9	R–K1	B–K2
10	B–Kt2	P–QR4

A little better would be ...., P–QR3.

11	P–Kt5	P–R5
12	QKt–Q2	....

Threatens P × Kt, Q × B; R–Kt1, followed by P × P.

12	....	Kt–R2
13	B × P	B–B4
14	B × B !	....

The QRP could have been won by P–B3.

14	....	Q × B
15	P–B4	P × P
16	Kt–K4	Q–Q4
17	Kt–Q6ch.	K–K2
18	Kt × QBP	Q–B4

Preventing Kt–Kt6.

19	B × Kt	RP × B

Or 19 ...., Q × Kt; 20 Q–Q6ch., K–K1; 21 QR–Q1,
BP × B; 22 Q–Q8ch., with Kt–Kt5, mate.

20	Q–Q6ch.	Q × Q
21	P × Qch.	Resigns.

For if ...., K–K1; there follows 22 Kt–Kt6, R–QKt1;
23 Kt–K5, and there is no reply to the threat P–Q7ch.

Game No. 48.—Niendorf, 1927.

Black: Ahues.

The sacrifice brought here on Move 25 is a blockade
sacrifice only in appearance. In reality it is a case of an
attacking raid, the blockade already existed before the
sacrifice was made.   But, as everything has to have a
name, we should describe the play as follows : a blockade
game crowned by a sacrifice.

1	P–QB4	Kt–KB3
2	Kt–QB3	P–Q3
3	P–Q4	QKt–Q2
4	P–K3	P–K4
5	B–Q3	B–K2

All this has been done before. Now, at this stage, it
is customary for White to continue with KKt–K2, Castles,
and P–B4, undoubtedly a strategically sound continuation.
White, however, attempts to employ a more incisive method
of development.

6	P–B4	Castles
7	Kt–B3	P × QP !
8	P × P	P–Q4

Black has parried well and the games are approximately equal.

9 P–QB5   P–B3

Now there is a constant threat of rolling up by ...., P–QKt3; on the part of Black.

10 Castles   ....

He eschews 10 P–QR3, because of P–QKt3; 11 P–QKt4, P×P; 12 KtP×P, Kt×P; 13 P×Kt, B×P; with a strong attack.

10 ....   P–QR4

There was no reason for delaying the liberating move P–QKt3; e.g., 10 ...., P–QKt3; 11 Kt–K5, Q–B2; 12 P×P, (best) P×P; 13 B–Q2, followed by R–B1, with equal prospects. After the text-move, Black drifts into an inferior position.

11 Kt–K5   Q–B2
12 Q–R4   ....

Now ...., P–QKt4; is rendered difficult if not made impossible. At the time, to be sure, I was under the impression that the move, in connection with combinative subtleties, could still be played, e.g., 12 ...., P–QKt4; 13 P×P e.p., Q×P; 14 Kt×QBP, B–Q3; and this impression was so strong that even subsequently I could not get rid of it. For instance in the " K. N. Nachrichten " I recommended against 12 ...., P–QKt4; the continuation : Q–B2, and Black's intention to occupy his K5 would be frustrated as follows : 13 ...., P–Kt5; 14 Kt–R4, B–R3; 15 B×B, R×B; (now ...., Kt–K5; is threatened); 16 Q–K2, and wins because of the indirect threat to Black's KB.

To-day I cannot see why the offer of a pawn should not be accepted; after 12 ...., P–QKt4; 13 P×P e.p., Q×P; 14 Kt×QBP, B–Q3; White could simply have played 15 K–R1, and 16 Kt–K5, and Black would not have had any compensation.

12 ....   R–K1
13 K–R1   Kt–B1

Again in the " K. N. Nachrichten " I attempted to parry 13 ...., P–QKt4; in the most complicated manner, instead of leading with P×P e.p. into the variation shown previously, e.g., 13 ...., P–QKt4; 14 P×P e.p., Q×P;

15 Kt×QBP, (in " K.N.N." I only gave Q×BP,) B–Kt2;
(B–Q3; Kt–K5,) 16 Kt–K5, Kt×Kt; 17 BP×Kt, Kt–K5;
18 Kt×Kt, P×Kt; 19 B–QB4, R–KB1; 20 Q–Kt3, etc. It
seems therefore proven that, with his 10th move, Black committed a sin of omission which cannot be redeemed.

| 14 Q–Kt3 | .... |

Now the moves P–QKt3; or P–QKt4; are to be
prevented positively.

| 14 .... | Kt–K3! |

Very good! B–K3, is to be answered by B×P; etc.

| 15 Kt–K2 | Kt–Q2 |

Black has succeeded in keeping the White QKt off the
route QB3–R4–Kt6, but for this success he has paid a heavy
price in that his Kt at K3, as will soon be seen, is badly
placed. The blockade operations now begin.

| 16 Kt×Kt | B×Kt |

Recapture by the Q was preferable, as then the KB
could have reached KB3 which is not the case now.

17 P–B5	Kt–B1
18 B–KB4	Q–B1
19 B–K5	P–B3

See preceding note.

| 20 B–Kt3 | P–R5 |
| 21 Q–Kt4 | .... |

The only move to prevent the blockade ring from being
shattered, e.g.: 21 Q–B3, P–QKt3; 22 P×P, B–Q1; and
eventually ...., Q–Kt2, etc.

| 21 .... | P–QKt4 |
| 22 Q–Q2 | .... |

Now White has a free hand on the K wing; the Q side
is locked and barred.

| 22 .... | B–Q1 |

Here R–Q1, deserved serious consideration in order to
bring the QB to KB2 as speedily as possible.

| 23 R–B3 | B–B2 |
| 24 QR–KB1 | R–K2 |

This permits an interesting sally by the enemy. A little
better seems 24 ...., B×B; 25 Kt×B, Q–B2; 26 Kt–R5,
R–K2; 27 P–KKt4, P–R3; 28 P–R4, Kt–R2. But in this
case also, after 29 Kt–B4, and 30 Kt–R3, White would seem
to be ready for the assault.

25 B–Q6 ....

A pawn sacrifice many moves deep. There will be a derelict pawn at Q6, but as soon as Black sets about capturing it, his K position will be shattered by the sacrifice of the Knight.

25 ....   B × B
26 P × B   R–K1
27 Kt–Kt3   Q–Q1
28 Q–B1   ....

Another waiting move; whereby B–B1; is prevented, (........., B–B1; Q × P).

28 ....   Q–Kt1
29 Q–KB4   R–Q1
30 Kt–R5   R–R2

If 30 ...., B–K1; there follows 31 Kt × Pch., a smashing blow. E.g., 30 ...., B–K1; 31 Kt × Pch, P × Kt; 32 R–Kt3ch, K any; 33 Q–R6, and wins.

31 Kt × Pch.   Resigns.

After 31 ...., K–R1; White had thought of 32 Kt × RP, and demonstrated the following continuation immediately after the game: 31 ...., K–R1; 32 Kt × RP, Kt × Kt; 33 Q–R4, K–Kt1; 34 P–B6, Kt × P; 35 R × Kt, etc., or 31 ...., K–R1; 32 Kt × RP, K × Kt; 33 P–B6 dis. ch., P–Kt3; 34 Q–R4ch., K–Kt1; 35 P–B7ch., K–Kt2; 36 Q–B6ch., K–R2; 37 R–B4, etc. Not so strong after 31 ...., K–R1; would be the continuation 32 Q–R4, because of 32 ...., P–R3; 33 Kt–Kt4, Kt–R2; 34 P–B6, B × Kt; and White must make another effort, namely, 35 Q × B, Kt × P; 36 Q–Kt6, and White's attack should win through.

6.—MY NEW TREATMENT OF THE PROBLEM OF THE PAWN-CHAIN.

THE DRESDEN VARIATION.

In games 49-51 Black foregoes an early challenge of the White chain of pawns, in order to substitute for the attacking values thus lost, positional play on the White squares, i.e., the White KB is exchanged and Black proceeds to operate against the White squares which have become weak. Logically an essential condition for the success of this mode of procedure is the safeguarding of the home K side, and in this lies the chief difficulty of this mode of play.

Let us consider any kind of chain, say the chain which occurs after 1 P–K4, P–K3; 2 P–Q4, P–Q4; 3 P–K5. The White K side would be hemmed in by P–KR4; and P–KKt3. In this case the black squares in Black's position at his KKt4 and KB3 would become weak. See game No. 50. Compare also the following beginning: White: Steiner, Berlin, 1928. 1 P–K4, P–K3; 2 P–Q4, P–Q4; 3 Kt–QB3, B–Kt5; 4 P–K5, P–QB4; (This challenge, as will soon be seen, is not meant seriously and the pawn presently passes on in peace.) 5 B–Q2, Kt–K2; 6 P–QR3, B × Kt; 7 P × B, P–B5?; 8 P–KR4, P–KR4; 9 B–K2, Kt–B4; 10 P–Kt3, P–KKt3; 11 B–Kt5, Q–R4; 12 Q–Q2, (the White QB's Diagonal has a crippling effect and Black's counter-blockade by the Kt at KB4 soon proves untenable). 12 ...., Kt–B3; 13 B–B6, R–KKt1; 14 Kt–R3, K–Q2; 15 Kt–Kt5, Kt–R3; 16 P–B3, K–B2; 17 P–Kt4, R–K1; 18 B–Kt7, Kt–Kt1; and Black is repulsed all along the line. After 19 P × P, P × P; 20 P–B4, Black's position can no longer be held. And what is the moral?—Black's KB must only be exchanged against the opposing QB otherwise the White QB obtains the upper hand (game 50). Furthermore, it is advisable to protect the P at Black's KR4 without calling on the KKtP for the purpose (game 51). Compare also game 13. The Dresden variation is illustrated by game 52. The idea here is an enduring stabilisation of the centre.

Game No. 49.—Kecskemet, 1927.

White: Dr. Vajda.

1 P–K4	Kt–QB3
2 P–Q4	P–Q4
3 Kt–QB3	P–K3
4 P–K5	KKt–K2

Not B–Kt5; because of 5 Q–Kt4.

5 Kt–B3	....

For now, if Q–Kt4, P–KR4; etc.

5	P–QKt3
6 Kt–K2	....

" Both soliloquised alternately and imagined they were conversing," once said an author in a melancholy mood. This talking past one another is happening here. Black tries to secure points on white squares, whilst White tries for the black squares—he plans Kt–Kt3–R5, with pressure against black's KKt2 and KB3—and the only link between the two is that they move by turns.

6	B–R3
7 P–B3	....

Worthy of consideration was: 7 Kt–Kt3, at once, e.g.: ...., B×B; 8 K×B, P–KR4; (or else Kt–R5;) 9 P–KR4, followed by Kt–Kt5.

7	Q–Q2
8 Kt–Kt3	B×B
9 Kt×B	P–KR4
10 B–Kt5	Kt–R4

The play against the " white " points at Black's QKt4, QB5, and KB4 now becomes apparent.

11 Q–K2	P–R3
12 Kt–K3	Q–Kt4
13 P–QKt4	Q×Qch.
14 K×Q	QKt–B3.

Both 14 ...., Kt–B5; and 14 ...., Kt–Kt2; would be bad, the former because of 14 ...., Kt–B5; 15 Kt×Kt, P×Kt; 16 Kt–Q2, and if then P–QKt4; 17 P–QR4, and the latter because 14 ...., Kt–Kt2; 15 Kt–K1, P–QB4; would only help White, e.g.: 16 KtP×P, P×P; 17 QR–Kt1, etc.

15 Kt–K1	Kt–Kt3
16 Kt–Q3	B–K2

The end of the monologues; the deadly altercation can now begin.

17 B × B	QKt × B
18 P–KB4	Kt–R5

This secures the point KB4. If White, on the preceding move, had prevented this by playing 18 P–Kt3, there would have followed: 18 ...., Kt–B1; with Kt–Q2; Castles KR; KR–B1; and finally P–QB4; with full play for Black.

19 P–Kt3	KKt–B4
20 Kt × Kt	Kt × Kt
21 K–B3	....

A plot is hatched against the Black Knight, namely, P–KR3, and P–Kt4. How can this be circumvented?

21	P–R4

At the right moment.

22 P–QR3	....

White would not commit himself to 22 P–Kt5, P–QB3; 23 P × P, R–QB1; the pressure on the QB file would have become unpleasant, nor would the QKt file have been an equivalent.

22	K–Q2
23 P–R3	....

He overlooks his opponent's combination. He could have played KR–QKt1 and then Kt–K1–B2–K3. But Black has some advantage even then.

23	P × P
24 Kt × P	....

A bitter necessity. If 24 RP × P, there follows: P–R5; 25 P–Kt4, Kt–Kt6; 26 KR–QB1, Kt–K5; and wins the QBP, or secures the QR file.

24 .... R–R5

Here also the manœuvre indicated came into strong consideration. But the text-move should be good enough.

25 P–Kt4 Kt–K2
26 K–K3 P–QB4

Black is not content with the variation : 26 ...., P × P ; 27 P × P, R × R ; 28 R × R, R × P ; as it concedes the KR file to the enemy.

27 Kt–B2 Kt–B3
28 QR–QKt1 R–QB1

There was a winning line by : 28 ...., P × Pch. ; 29 P × P, (if Kt × P, R × P ;) R–B5 ; 30 K–Q3, R–QB1 ; 31 R × P, Kt × KPch. ; 32 BP × Kt, R–B6ch. ; 33 K–Q2, R × Ktch. ; 34 K–K3, P–Kt4 ; with an easy win for Black.

29 R × P P × Pch.
30 P × P Kt × KP
31 BP × Kt R × Kt
32 R–Kt3 ....

Black's advantage has more or less evaporated.

32 .... P × P
33 P × P ....

A most attractive combination was available, securing the draw, namely : 33 R–KB1, R–KR7 ; 34 R × Pch., K–K1 ; 35 R(Kt3)–Kt7, (looks like a bad blunder !) R(R5) × Pch. ; 36 K–B4, R–B7ch. ; 37 K × P, R × R ; and now it is White's turn. He plays : 38 R–Kt8ch., and draws.

33 .... R–KKt7
34 R–Kt7ch. ....

Here K–B3, would have drawn, e.g. : 34 ...., R–QR7 ; 35 R–R7, or 34 ...., R–Q7 ; 35 R–R7, etc.

34 .... K–B3
35 R(R1)–QKt1 R × Pch.
36 K–B4 R–R3
37 K–Kt5 ....

If 37 K–B3, R–Kt8 ; etc.

37 .... P–B3ch.

Not 37 ...., P–B4 ; because of 38 R × P, R × Pch. ; 39 K–B6, etc.

38 P × P P × Pch.
39 K × P R × P
40 R–K7 ....

There is nothing better. The White King is too badly
situated for the end-game, and his forces are not sufficient
for a mating attack.

40	R–B5ch.
41 K×P	R×P
42 K–B5	R(R3)–R5
43 R–K6ch.	K–B4
44 K–B6	R–B5ch.
45 K–K7	R–R2ch.
46 K–K8	R–K5

Resigns.

Notwithstanding the omission on the 28th move, this is,
strategically, of importance.   Few would have dared to
defer until the 26th move, that soul-saving advance
........., P–QB4; without which Dr. Tarrasch could not
imagine any sort of fight against, or any kind of defence from,
a pawn-chain! Surely this game has shown us unexplored
land.

Game No. 50.—Niendorf, 1927.

White: Kmoch.

1 P–K4	Kt–QB3
2 Kt–QB3	P–K3
3 P–Q4	B–Kt5

Safer would be P–Q4.

4 KKt–K2	P–Q4
5 P–K5	P–KR4

Black selects our preventive formation.   But better
would be 5 ...., KKt–K2; 6 Kt–B4, Kt–Kt3; 7 Kt–R5,
R–KKt1; followed by B–K2; after which Black proceeds to
Castle on the Q side.

6 Kt–B4	P–KKt3
7 B–K3	B×Ktch.

Very risky, for the weakness of White's double complex
is more than balanced by his command of the diagonal
Kt5–Q8. Correct would be KKt–K2; or even B–B1.

8 P×B	Kt–R4
9 B–Q3	Kt–K2
10 Kt–R3	P–QB4
11 B–Kt5	P–B5
12 B–K2	QKt–B3
13 B–B6	....

White should now win with little trouble.   Compare
Steiner's game in the preliminary note.

13 ....   KR–Kt1
14 Castles   ....

Not a strong continuation; correct would be: 14 Kt–Kt5,
with P–B3, and P–Kt4, or else 14 Kt–Kt5, with 15 P–Kt4.
After 15 ...., P × P; 16 B × KtP, a decision would be
reached by P–KR4–R5.

14 ....   Q–R4
the slender counter-chance.

15 Q–Q2   Kt–B4
16 KR–Q1   ....

A more economical way of using the Rooks was available in 16 QR–Q1, the QRP would of course be taboo.

16 ....   K–Q2
A weighty decision; the K abandons the KBP to its
fate. And yet this line of play appears to be justified, being
in keeping with the stratagem shown in games 29 and 30,
"the King's Flight as a palliative measure."

17 Kt–Kt5   R–B1
It is open to question whether the straightforward
17 ...., K–B2; is not more in the spirit of the said stratagem. It is not a question of the KBP qua pawn, but
rather of preventing White, after Kt × BP, from using KB7
as a base for further attacks. The continued flight of the
King would have opposed White's plans in this direction,
e.g.: 17 ...., K–B2; 18 Kt × BP, B–Q2; 19 P–B3,
QR–KB1; 20 Kt–Kt5, and now either 20 ...., Kt–Kt2;
with Kt–K1; or 20 ...., K–Kt1, with a waiting policy,
and it is doubtful whether White can win.

18 P–KR3   ....
The wrong method: he should have played P–B3.

18 ....   K–B2
19 P–Kt4   P × P
20 P × P   KKt–K2
21 K–Kt2   Kt–KKt1

A bad mistake, but White fails to take advantage of it.
With 21 ...., B–Q2; 22 R–R1, QR–K1; 22 R–R7,
Kt–Q1; Black could curl up like a hedgehog.

22 B–Kt7   R–K1
23 R–R1   ....

Here Kt × BP; would capture not only the pawn but also
the crucial point Q6. If 23 Kt × BP, R–K2; 24 Kt–Q6,

B–Q2; (........., R×B; Kt–K8ch., K–Q1; Kt×R, Q–B2; Q–Kt5ch.,) 25 B–R6, and White has a good game.

23	B–Q2
24 R–R3	Kt–Q1
25 R–B3	R–QB1
26 R–R1	....

An unjustified sacrifice of a pawn, for it soon becomes clear that the intended doubling of rooks means only beating the air. 26 Kt×BP, or 26 Q–B1, with Q–Kt2, deserved consideration. If 26 Kt×BP, then Kt×Kt; 27 R×Kt, R–K2; 28 R×R, Kt×R. If 26 Q–B1, on the other hand, the continuation would be: K–Kt1; 27 Q–Kt2, R–B3; 28 Q–Kt4, K–R1; 29 B–B8, R–Kt3; 30 B–Q6. From this exposition arise two points. Firstly the soundness of the prophylactic method 26 Q–B1, 27 Q–Kt2. Secondly the affinity between White's minor pieces and the point Q6. Without any regard for man's sometimes dizzy plans, the pieces develop a logic of their own, which frequently, as here, is full of beauty as well as being convincing.

26	Q×RP

Considering the slenderness of his counter-attack, Black can be well satisfied with this result.

27 R–R7	K–Kt1
28 Kt×BP	Kt×Kt
29 R×Kt	B–B3

Now the doubled Rooks are actually out of play.

30 B–B6	P–R4

To be preferred was Q–Kt7; in order to anticipate the preventive move 31 Q–B1. But White has no thought of preventive manœuvres.

31 R–R1	Q–Kt7
32 B–Kt5	R–B1
33 R(B7)–R7	R–QB2
34 R×R	....

Or 34 R(R7)–R3, R(B2)–B2.

34	K×R
35 Q–B1	....

If White did not shine whilst playing for a win, he certainly makes most of the few chances he has of drawing the game. The ensuing attempts to save the situation are of a high order—one is forcibly reminded of Schlechter.

35	Q × P(B6)
36 Q–R1	Q × Q
37 R × Q	R–R1
38 B–Q2	P–Kt3
39 K–Kt3	....

The King threatens to advance to KKt5.

39	Kt–K2
40 B–Q1	B–Q2

Black could win—if at all—only by B–Kt2.

41 B–Kt4	Kt–B3
42 B–Q6ch.	K–Kt2
43 P–QB3	P–QKt4
44 R–Kt1	P–Kt5
45 B–R4	....

Not 45 P × P, P × P; 46 B × P, Kt × QP; 47 B–B5, Kt–Kt4; etc.

45	P–Kt6

This looks good, but it allows a deadlock to be reached. The alternative, however, cuts both ways, e.g.: 45 ...., Kt × QP; 46 B × B, Kt–K7ch.; 47 K–B3, Kt × P; 48 B × P, K–B3; etc.

46 B × Ktch.	K × B
47 P–Kt5	....

Debars the Black B from coming out via his KKt3.

47	R–R2
48 R–Kt2	R–Kt2
49 K B4	....

Now Black has a break-through reminiscent of a study. 49 B–R3, would have drawn.

49	B–B1
50 K–Kt3	....

50	R–Kt5 !

The winning move.

          51 P × R   ....

Compulsory, or else R–R5; etc.

          51 ....   P–R5
          52 P–Kt5ch.   K × P
          53 B–R3   P–B6
          54 R–Kt1   K–B5

As White's R and B are immobilised—otherwise P–Kt7; with K–Kt6; is immediately decisive—the Black K can at leisure feast upon the QP and return to QB5. This is the deciding factor.

          55 P–B4   K × P
          56 K–B2   K–B5
          57 K–K1   P–Q5
          58 K–K2   K–Q4
          59 K–B3   ....

If K–Q3, B–R3; mate.

          59 ....   B–Kt2
          60 R–K1   K–B5 dis. ch.
          61 K–B2   P–Kt7
          62 P–B5   KP × P
          63 P–K6   B–B3

Resigns.

Game No. 51.—Niendorf, 1927.

White: Brinckmann.

          1 P–K4   Kt–QB3
          2 Kt–QB3   P–K3
          3 P–Q4   P–Q4
          4 P–K5   KKt–K2
          5 Kt–B3   P–QKt3
          6 Kt–K2   B–R3

We have already discussed these moves in the notes to game 49.

          7 Kt–Kt3   B × B
          8 K × B   P–KR4
          9 B–Kt5   ....

Now White threatens to capture points on Black squares as follows: Kt–R4, P–KKt3; B–B6, together with Kt–B3–Kt5. How can the KRP be covered without having recourse to P–KKt3?

9 .... Q-B1

If now 10 Kt-R4, there follows: Q-R3ch.; K-Kt1, Q-R5; P-QB3, Q×Q; and the RP is sufficiently protected without the aid of the KKtP.

10 Q Q3 Kt-Kt3
11 P-B3 P-R5

This, a weakening move in itself, is meant as a preventive measure against White's intended P-KR4, e.g., 11 ...., B-K2; (instead of P-R5;) 12 P-KR4. But 11 ...., B-K2; would also be thoroughly sound.

12 Kt-K2 B-K2

Here the following came into serious consideration: 12 ...., P-R6; 13 P×P, B-K2; or 13 P-KKt3, P-R4; followed by Q-R3.

13 P-KR3 B×B

Here R-R4; was playable.

14 Kt×B QKt-K2

At this point too R-R4; had to be considered.

15 K-Kt1 ....

This affords Black time for a comprehensive attack in the centre. Brinckmann therefore thinks that a counter-attack by 15 Q-B3, would have been in order. But in that case also Black's position was decidedly preferable after: 15 ...., Kt-B4; 16 P-KKt4, P×P e.p.; 17 P×P, (or Kt×KtP, Kt(Kt3)-R5;) Q-Q2; 18 P-KR4, Castles QR; 19 P-R5, Kt(Kt3)-K2; 20 P-KKt4, Kt-R3.

15 .... P-KB3
16 Kt-B3 Q-Q2

After this move White has an opportunity, which he neglects, of saving the game by a most cunning manœuvre. Therefore 16 ...., P-QB4; at once, with eventually Q-B2; would be better fitted to maintain the advantage.

17 K–R2	P–QB4
18 P–B4	....

Plucky and ingenious; it is a pity that, on the 24th move, he did not find the right continuation which, however, was far from obvious.

18	Q–B2
19 P × QP	P–B5

If 19 ...., P × KP; there would follow: 20 Q–Kt5ch., K–B1; 21 Kt–Kt5, P × P dis. ch.; 22 P–B4, Kt(Kt3) × P; 23 KR–KB1, Kt × QP?; 24 Kt × Pch., and wins.

20 Q–B2	P × QP
21 KR–K1	Castles KR

Black did not quite like the continuation: 21 ...., P × P; 22 P × P, Kt × P; 23 Kt × Kt, Q × Ktch.; 24 P–B4, Q–Q3; with possibly 25 QR–Q1, threatening Q × P.

22 Kt–B3	P × P
23 Kt × KP	....

Not 23 P × P, because of R × Kt; and Kt × P; with a decisive attack.

23	Kt × Kt

24 P × Kt	....

The correct continuation was: 24 R × Kt, e.g.: 24 ...., Kt–B3; 25 Kt × P, Q–Q3; 26 Q × P, Kt × R; 27 P × Kt, Q × Pch.; 28 P–B4, Q–K3; 29 P–B5, Q–K4ch.; 30 K–R1, R–B2; 31 QR–Q1, White is unable to improve his position and the game would therefore be drawn.

24	P–Q5
25 Kt–Kt5	Q–B4
26 Kt–Q6	P–Q6

Not 26 ...., P–QKt4; because of Q–K4, and White is centralised.

27 Q × Pch.   Q × Q
28 Kt × Q   R × P

The sequel is a classic example of play on the 7th and 8th ranks.

29 QR–Q1   R–QB1
30 Kt–K3   R–Q1
31 Kt–B4   Kt–B4

Preventing Kt–Q6.

32 P–R4   ....

32 P–K6, would be answered by R–K7; e.g.: 32 P–K6, R–K7; 33 R × P, (33 R × R, P × R; 34 R × Rch., K–R2; and wins) R × KR; 34 R × Rch., K–R2; and the threat Kt–Kt6; is decisive. Should White, after 32 P–K6, R–K7; seek to gain a valuable tempo by 33 P–K7, (e.g.: 33 P–K7, Kt × P; 34 R × P, R × KR; 35 R × Rch., K–B2; 36 Kt–Q6ch., K–K3; 37 Kt–B8, with a drawn conclusion,) Black simply plays 33 ...., R–K1; and wins the pawn.

32 ....   K–B2

This move is entirely sound, as may be seen in the following analysis: 33 P–K6ch., K–K1; 34 Kt–K5, P–Q7; 35 R–K4, R–Q5; (on no account the joke 35 ...., R–B8; instead of 35 ...., R–Q5; for there would follow R × R, Kt–Kt6; and the joke would be turned against the joker by: R–B8ch., K × R; Kt–Kt6ch., with R × P, and mate on R8), 36 R × R, Kt × R; 37 Kt–B4, Kt–Kt6; 38 K–Kt1, R–B5; 39 Kt–K3, R × P; and White is lost. It may be added that Black could quite well have played R–K7; instead of the move in the text, but it is always better to play for blockade.

33 R–K4   R–K7
34 R–B4   K–K3

Black has achieved his ambition, the R on the 7th, the blockade at his K6. Now it only remains to drive the White Kt from Black's QB5.

35	R–Kt4	P–Q7
36	R–Kt6ch.	K–B2
37	R–Kt4	P–R3
38	R–B4	K–K3
39	Kt–Q6	Kt–K6

Resigns.

Game No. 52.—Dresden, 1926.

White: L. Steiner.

1	P–K4	P–QB4
2	Kt–KB3	Kt–QB3
3	Kt–B3	P–K4

A move of this type requires courage—and faith in the inner meaning of the blockade. The move gives up a tempo (non-development of a piece) and creates a hole at Q4, all this to prevent White's P–Q4, and so to obstruct his opponent.

4	B–B4	P–Q3
5	P–KR3	B–K3
6	P–Q3	B–K2
7	Castles	P–KR3

Black is taking his time.   His opponent is short of effective moves.

8	Kt–Q5	………

With the object of emphasising the strength of Q5; but, as soon becomes clear, this can be achieved only with the help of sacrifices in material or in position.

8	………	Kt–B3

Now White's Q5 is under fire,

9	Kt–R4	………

whilst White seeks to maintain it by combinative means.

9	………	Kt × Kt

Bad would be 9 ………, Kt × P; 10 P × Kt, B × KKt; because of 11 P–B4.

10	P × Kt	B × QP
11	Kt–B5	………

The sacrificial operation mentioned in the note to move 8. White wins back his pawn but remains with doubled pawns : the sacrifice therefore turns out to be positional. He had the option of a sacrifice in material by 11 B × B, B × Kt; 12 P–KB4, with attacking chances. All things being equal, either sacrifice should suffice to secure a draw.

11	....	B × B
12	P × B	P–KKt3

If 12 ...., Castles; 13 Q–Kt4, B–Kt4; 14 P–KR4, etc.

13	Kt × RP	Q–Q2
14	Q–Q5	Kt–Q1
15	B–K3	....

If 15 Kt–Kt4, P–B4; 16 Kt–K3, Kt–K3; followed by Castles QR; and the position would be summed up as follows: Black has opportunities in the KR file, whilst any attack attempted by White would break down against Black's compact pawn-formation.

15	....	P–B4
16	Kt–Kt8	B–R5
17	P–KKt3	Q–K3

18	QR–Q1	....

The losing move; 18 P × B, R × Kt; (not 18 ...., Q × Q; because of Kt–B6ch.,) 19 B–Kt5, should be enough for a draw, e.g.: 19 ...., Q × Q; 20 P × Q, R–R1; 21 P–KB4, P–K5; 22 QR–K1, followed by R–K3.

18	....	R × Kt
19	P × B	P–B5

Now the B cannot get to Kt5.

20 B x KBP   ....

Or 20 B–B1, Q x Q; 21 R x Q, Kt–B2; with Castles; and R–R1; and an easy win for Black.

20	Q x Q
21 R x Q	P x B
22 R x QP	K–K2
23 KR–Q1	P–Kt3
24 R–Q7ch.	K–B3

and White resigned after a few unimportant moves.

One gains the impression that the line of play, P–QB4; in connection with P–K4; which weakens Black's Q4, still is sound, for White could only maintain himself at his Q5 with difficulty and should, at the most, have attained a draw.

PART III.

OVER-PROTECTION AND OTHER FORMS OF PROPHYLAXIS.

" Strategically important points should be over-protected," is a principle discovered by the author. " For the pieces concerned there is a reward waiting in that they, who help to protect strategically important points, will also be posted favourably in every respect; and so the importance of the strategic point covers them with its own glamour."

This can be stated more simply by saying: the contact to be established between the strong point and the over-protectors should benefit both; the strong point, because the prophylaxis thus employed provides the utmost possible security against all and any attacks; the over-protectors, because the strong point becomes to them a constant source of energy from which they are able to draw new strength.

The author himself has almost invariably derived excellent results from over-protection.

From time to time, it is true, some unfriendly critic has tried to cast ridicule on the idea, but an objective summing up will prove him to be wrong. The following difficulties, for instance, are alleged to be due to over-protection: I. Black: Capablanca, New York, 1927. 1 P–K4, P–QB3; 2 P–Q4, P–Q4; 3 P–K5, B–B4; 4 B–Q3, B×B; 5 Q×B, P–K3; 6 Kt–QB3, Q–Kt3; 7 KKt–K2, P–QB4; 8 P×P, B×P; 9 Castles, Kt–K2; 10 Kt–R4, Q–B3; 11 Kt×B, Q×Kt; 12 B–K3, Q–B2; 13 P–KB4, (13 Kt–Q4, anticipating Kt–B4; was also good.) Kt–B4; 14 P–B3, (with this move begins the over-protection of the point Q4, which fully deserves this concentrated attention; for this is a centrally situated blockade square and, be it noted, a pawn stood there once, which formed the basis of a proud chain of pawns. And even if the P at Q4 has disappeared long ago, and furthermore, if the pawn chain is now based on KB4, nevertheless the glamour and the immense importance of Q4 are practically unchanged. From this it is clear that the grouping of pieces around Q4 must be of the utmost import-ance from the point of view of consolidation. Granted that other lines of play are available, e.g.: 14 QR–B1, (instead of P–B3,) followed by P–B4, but what does that prove? Merely that over-protection is not the one and only

stratagem.)   14 ...., Kt–B3; 15 QR–Q1, P–KKt3; 16
P–KKt4, (only here does a mistake occur. After 16 B–B2,
P–KR4; 17 P–KKt3, Black would have found it difficult
to hit upon a satisfactory continuation.)   16 ...., Kt × B;
17 Q × Kt, P–KR4; 18 P–Kt5, Castles KR; 19 Kt–Q4,
Q–Kt3; and Black obtained the advantage through play on
the QB file and the occupation of his KB4.   Instead of
19 Kt–Q4, White should have played Q–B5, e.g.: 19 Q–B5,
KR–B1; 20 Kt–Q4, Kt–K2; 21 Q × Q, followed by
K–B2–K3–Q3, with a safe game. Or 19 Q–B5, KR–B1;
20 Kt–Q4, Q–Q1; 21 Q–Kt5.

II.   White: Spielmann, from the same Tournament.
1 P–K4, Kt–QB3; 2 Kt–KB3, P–K3; 3 P–Q4, P–Q4; 4
P–K5, P–QKt3; 5 P–B3, QKt–K2; 6 B–Q3, P–QR4;
7 Q–K2, Kt–B4; (the prototype of my game v. Sämisch,
Berlin, 1928, see No. 13). 8 P–KR4, P–R4; 9 Kt–Kt5,
P–Kt3; (the wrong over-protecting move; correct was
KKt–K2; at once. Then White could not have executed the
manœuvre Kt–Q2–B1, with P–B3, and P–KKt4, e.g.:
9 ...., KKt–K2; 10 Kt–Q2, P–B4; and the basis of the
chain at White's Q4 is shaky.)   10 Kt–Q2, KKt–K2;
(B–K2; would have been better, for the over-protection has
now no object, as White's P–B3, and P–KKt4, can no longer
be prevented.) 11 Kt–B1, P–B4; 12 P–B3, P–B5; 13 B–B2,
P–Kt4; 14 P–KKt4, Kt–Kt2; and White had the better
position, although he lost in the end by an over-hasty attack.
It can be seen that, in this game also, over-protection, if
correctly carried out, would have been beneficial.

On the subject of over-protection, we have to add that only
strong points which are positionally important, and not weak
points, are to be over-protected. Furthermore, it is desirable
that the points concerned should be, to an extent, an object of
contention. Instructive examples are shown in games 20 and
44. Prophylaxis is shown in games 53–56. We are particularly
concerned to show the affinity between waiting moves and
preventive measures.   In game 53 v. Behting, 8 ....,
P–QR3; would seem to have achieved nothing after the reply
9 P–R4, and yet White's chance in the end-game would have
been less.   A move which counteracts some sharp threat by
the opponent need not, for all that, be devoid of deeper
prophylactic meaning: we perceive this in move 6 of game 55.
In avoiding the restriction of his own playing chances, a
player has certainly exercised prophylaxis (see game 55).

But it happens but infrequently that prophylaxis is combined with threats; it does occur, however, and is, in fact, a notable species of prophylaxis (see move 24, game 54). We must raise one more point : what are the unpleasant contingencies, which deserve the attention of systematic preventive measures? They are the " positional " threats, which the opponent desires to execute. In this respect game 53 is particularly instructive : the difficult and extremely complicated manœuvre (Black's 21st move) is intended to help in the prevention of the threatened centralisation. Modern Tournament praxis is very rich in prophylactic manœuvres : we would single out games 7, 13, 20, 21, 32, 33, 38, 39 and 43.

Game No. 53.

Informal Game, Riga, 1910.

White: K. Behtling.

1	P–K4	P–Q3
2	Kt–QB3	Kt–KB3
3	P–B4	P–K4

This leads to the P–Q3, defence of the K gambit.

4	Kt–B3	QKt–Q2
5	P–Q4	....

There is no fault to find with this move, as K4 can easily be held, see note to move 8.

5	....	P × QP
6	Kt × P	B–K2
7	B–B4	Castles
8	Castles	P–QR3

One of those mystery moves, for which the pseudo-classic school of the year dot only found words of scorn. The point is that the closed formation of P–QKt4; and P–QB4; is only a side issue. The main object is to wait for White's Q–B3, and then to go in for the prophylactic structure R–K1; and B–B1. For an immediate 8 ...., R–K1; would fail on account of 9 Kt–B3, with a double threat of 10 P–K5, and 10 Kt–KKt5. Therefore 8 ...., P–QR3; represents the sacrifice of a tempo in order to make the prophylactic R–K1; etc. possible. This line of play would have appeared to the strategists of former times as, intellectually, an outrageous claim, for they dismissed the subject of the prophylaxis with a contemptuous shrug; but to go to the length of preparing

for it by means of a sacrifice, that was " bizarre," " crazy,"
etc. . . . . . ! In truth 8 ...., P–QR3; can be termed
a very fine move, for White's KP is statically as well as
dynamically full of life, and so restrictive operations require
care and patience—in other words, waiting and preventive
moves.   Direct action such as: 8 ...., Kt–Kt3; (instead
of 8 ...., P–QR3;) 9 B–K2, P–Q4; 10 P–K5, Kt–K5;
11 P–B5, would have been only to Black's disadvantage.

| | 9 Kt–B5 | .... |

A possibility was 9 P–QR4, which would have
re-established the status quo.   A probable continuation
would have been: 9 ...., P–B3; 10 B–R2, (P–Q5; and
Kt–K3; were threatened) R–K1. If then 11 Kt–B3, P–R3;
and the thrust 12 P–K5, would be unsound because of:
P × P; 13 P × P, Kt × P; 14 Kt × Kt, Q × Q; 15 B × Pch.,
K–B1; 16 R × Q, B–B4ch; followed by R × Kt.

| 9 .... | Kt–B4 |
| 10 Kt–Kt3 | .... |

If 10 Kt × Bch., Q × Kt; 11 R–K1, P–QKt4; (not
Kt × P; because of B–Q5, after the exchange of Knights)
12 B–Q5, Kt × B; 13 Kt × Kt, Q–Q1 or Q2; and Black
obtains some play against the KP by R–K1; with B–Kt2.
The move in the text, whilst thoroughly protecting this pawn,
does mean a measure of decentralisation, (Kt–B5–Kt3).

10	P–QKt4
11 B–Q3	P–Kt5
12 Kt–Q5	Kt × Kt
13 P × Kt	....

Black has scored a success in that White's centre—
thanks to 13 P × Kt,—has become dynamically useless; on
the other hand he is facing the difficult problem of having to

take preventive measures on two sides at the same time: for White plans a rolling up process with P-QR3, as well as P-B5, with a gain in space. With 13 ...., P-QR4; both threats could have been answered (because of Kt×B; Q×Kt, B-R3; etc.).

	13	P-B4

Prevents White's P-B5, but prepares at the same time for play on the K file by B-R5; B×Kt; R-K1; and the Kt settles on K5.

14	P-QR3	P×P
15	R×P	R-Kt1
16	P-B3	B-R5
17	Q-B3	B×Kt
18	Q×B	R-K1
19	B-B2	Q-B3
20	P-Kt4	Kt-K5
21	Q-Q3	....

As we see, Black has managed to get on without preventive measures on the Q side, for the weakness of the QRP is balanced by strength in the K file. But now he cannot carry on without them, because White aims at centralisation via B-K3-Q4, and Black, if anything, would have the worst of it. How can the intended manœuvre be frustrated?

21	....	Q-B2
22	B-K3	Kt-B3
23	B-Kt3	B-Kt2
24	R-Q1	....

This is not good; Black had expected 24 P-B4, as a matter of course, intending to restore the original position by: ...., B-B1; 25 B-Q2, Kt-K5; 26 B-K1, Q-B3; but then the long diagonal would be irretrievably lost for White. This preventive combination, containing as it does a six-move return-variation, should help to impress the reader with the richness and variety of the combinative possibilities inherent in prophylactic practice. One of the author's favourite combinations.

24	B × P
25 B × B	Q × B
26 Q × Q	Kt × Q
27 B–R7	....

A dangerous move, which, however, Black had not overlooked, when he ventured on the exchanges. The continuation 27 R × Kt, R × B; 28 R × BP, QR–K1; is better for Black.

27	Kt–K6
28 R–Q3	Kt–Kt5
29 R–Q1	R–R1
30 B–Q4	....

If 30 R × RP, Black would obtain the advantage by: ...., R–K5; 31 P–Kt3, R–K7; or 31 R–KB1, Kt–K6–Q4.

30	R–K5
31 P–R3	Kt–K6
32 B × Kt	....

Now compulsory on account of ...., Kt–B5 or Q4.

32	R × B
33 K–B2	R–K5
34 P–Kt3	K–B2

Black abandons the QRP, so that the King can penetrate decisively into the game.

35 R(Q1)–QR1	K–K3
36 R × P	R × R
37 R × R	K–Q4
38 R–R5ch.	....

Black threatened R–B5; followed by K–K5–Q6.

| 38 .... | K–B5 |
| 39 R × P | R–K2 |

The White K is cut off, and Black threatens to obtain two united passed pawns.

| 40 P–Kt5 | K × P |
| 41 P–Kt6 | P × P |

Not 41 ...., P–B3; because of: 42 R–QR5, R–Kt2; 43 R–R7, R × P; 44 R × P, and the issue is in doubt.

42	R–Q5	R–Q2
43	R–QKt5	R–Kt2
44	R–Q5	P–QKt4
45	R × QP	P–Kt5
46	K–K2	P–Kt6
47	R–B6ch.	K–Kt7
48	P–B5	K–Kt8
49	P–Kt4	P–Kt7
50	P–Kt5	K–R2

and Black won.

Game No. 54.—Carlsbad, 1907.

White: Schlechter.

1	P–K4	P–K4
2	Kt–KB3	Kt–QB3
3	B–Kt5	P–QR3
4	B–R4	Kt–B3
5	Kt–B3	B–Kt5
6	Kt–Q5	B–K2
7	Castles	Castles
8	R–K1	P–Q3
9	Kt × Ktch.	B × Kt
10	P–B3	P–R3

Black decides on a waiting policy.   His position—one of watchful defence—cannot be changed to any great extent. The waiting-move emphasises the fact.

11	P–KR3	Kt–K2
12	P–Q4	Kt–Kt3
13	B–K3	K–R2

Black still marks time.

14	Q–Q2	B–K3
15	B–B2	Q–K2
16	P–Q5	....

White had done better to mark time also; the text move would have a meaning only if it were introducing an attack against the Q side, (P–B4, and P–QKt4).   But he intends to operate on the K wing, and for this P–Q5, is a bad preparation.

16	....	B–Q2
17	K–R2	Kt–R1

A preventive move directed against White's plan of Kt–Kt1, and P–KB4.

18	Kt–Kt1	P–KKt4
19	P–KKt3	Kt–Kt3
20	Q–Q1	B–Kt2
21	Q–B3	P–QR4

Again preventive play. This time the possibility of P–B4, and P–QKt4, is to be anticipated.

22	Kt–K2	B–Kt4
23	P–QR4	B–Q2

It is achieved; the White Q side has lost all momentum and the action just mentioned, to be initiated by P–B4, and P–QKt4, is a thing of the past.

24	R–R1	………

With this move White plans to break through eventually with P–R4, e.g.: 24 ………, P–Kt3; 25 P–R4, P × P; 26 P × P, Kt × P; 27 Q–R5, P–KB4; 28 K–Kt1, etc.   But Black discovers a move, which not only has a high preventive value, but which also has the attribute of driving the opponent into quick action.

24	………	Q–K1 !

The threat is: Q–B1; e.g.: Q–B1; P–R4, B–Kt5; winning a Knight. White, therefore, has no further time for preparations and opens the battle for a break-through.

25	P–R4	Q–B1

Threatening B–Kt5; etc.

26	B–Q3	B–Kt5
27	Q–Kt2	P × P
28	P–B3	P–R6
29	Q–B1	………

The break-through looks like succeeding, for if now B–Q2; then 30 P–KKt4, followed by Q × P, with a winning attack.

$$29 \quad \ldots\ldots\ldots \qquad\qquad \text{P–KB4}$$

The counter-stroke, long since prepared, which decides the battle for Black.

$$30 \quad \text{P} \times \text{B} \qquad\qquad \text{P} \times \text{KP}$$

Only now can the full effect of 28 ...., P–R6; be discerned. By this move the White Q was forced from KKt2 to B1, into the range of the Black Rook.

$$31 \quad \text{Q} \times \text{P} \qquad\qquad \text{P} \times \text{B}$$
$$32 \quad \text{B} \times \text{P} \qquad\qquad \text{R–R1}$$

Resigns.

This game is noteworthy on account of the comprehensive prophylaxis employed; preventive measures were taken against P–QB4, and P–QKt4, as well as against P–KB4, and later on P–KR4. A few words about the characteristics of the preventive moves selected: the waiting policy by 10 ...., P–R3; is typical of this style of play, for waiting moves form the beginning of all prophylactic manœuvres.

The fact that the preventive move 24 ...., Q–K1; contains a threat at the same time by no means detracts from its purity in a prophylactic sense. It illustrates a very definite form of prophylaxis, in which part of the plan is to drive the opponent to accelerated action.

Game No. 55.—Stockholm, 1921.

White: Wendel.

1 P–K4	Kt–QB3
2 P–Q4	P–Q4
3 Kt–QB3	P × P
4 P–Q5	Kt–K4
5 B–KB4	Kt–Kt3
6 B–Kt3	P–QR3

This move requires understanding. The threat of Kt–Kt5, could apparently be prevented more simply by P–KB4; especially as this advance is made after all, but White refrains from showing his hand too soon, and that also lies in the nature of the prophylaxis. On 6 ...., P–KB4; would follow 7 P–KR4, and Black would be in a quandary, e.g.: 6 ...., P–KB4; 7 P–KR4, P–B5; 8 P–R5, P×B; 9 P×Kt, P×Pch.; 10 K×P, and now, after all this, the accessibility of White's QKt5 has become of moment.

| | 7 P–B3 | P–KB4 |
| | 8 P×P | .... |

If now 8 P–KR4, then P–K4; 9 P–R5, Q–Kt4; and Black has the advantage.

	8	P–B5
	9 B–B2	P–K4
	10 Kt–B3	B–Q3

Dictated by the requirements of the Blockade. (Passed and semi-passed pawns must be restricted.) The position is approximately even; White should now bring his majority into the fray by P–QB4–B5, but there are great difficulties in the way.

| | 11 P–KR4 | .... |

Here, in White's opinion, B–Q3, Castles, Kt–K2, P–B4, would have been better.

| | 11 .... | P–Kt4 |

A diversion derived originally from the preventive move 6 ...., P–QR3.

| | 12 P–R5 | Kt–B1 |
| | 13 B–R4 | Q–Q2 |

Threatening ...., Q–Kt5.

| | 14 B–K2 | P–Kt5 |
| | 15 Kt–QKt1 | Kt–B3 |

This is the point. As White's K4 and R5 are attacked simultaneously, B×Kt, is compulsory and the Black pieces, at one stroke, obtain space.

	16 B×Kt	P×B
	17 QKt–Q2	Q–Kt2
	18 K–B1	Kt–Q2
	19 P–R6	Q–Kt6

In order to provoke R–R3, by which White loses a tempo on the 22nd move.

	20 R–R3	Q–Kt1
	21 Kt–R4	Kt–B4
	22 R–R1	R–Kt1
	23 P–B3	....

The opening of the QKt file is advantageous for Black, but he has the better game in any event.

23	P × P
24 P × P	Q-Kt6
25 Q-B2	R-Kt1
26 Kt-B4	B-Q2
27 Kt × Bch.	P × Kt
28 B-B3	....

White has consolidated his position fairly satisfactorily, and Black has to reckon with freeing manœuvres such as 29 Q-B2, or even 29 Kt-B5, B × Kt; 30 P × B, with the comical drawing threat of R-R3, Q-Kt4; R-R5, etc. A prophylactic tour by the Black K (........., K-Q1; ...., K-B2;) would now be very good. The doubling of Rooks on the QKt file would then be threatened. If after 28 ...., K-Q1; White plays 29 Q-B2, according to plan, then follows: ...., Q × Qch.; 30 K × Q, R-Kt7ch.; 31 K-Kt1, P-B4; 32 R-K1, R × P; 33 P × P, K-K2. If 28 ...., K-Q1; 29 Kt-B5, there follows 29 ...., B × Kt; 30 P × B, and the Black Rook occupies the correct file at once, 30 ...., R-K1; 31 R-R3, and the Black Q retires via Kt1 with an excellent game for Black. It is clear that 28 ...., K-Q1; is an excellent preventive move, which would anticipate any attack, even in the distant future, on the K or Q. However, there is, instead of 28 ...., K-Q1; a deep-laid combination which leads more quickly to the goal, and Black gives it the preference.

28	B-Kt4ch.
29 P-B4	B × Pch.
30 Q × B	R-Kt7
31 B-K2	R-KKt5
32 Q-B1	....

Black had expected this parry. If instead: **32 R–R3,** R × Kt; 33 R × Q, R–R8ch.; 34 K–B2, P × Rch.; 35 K × P, R × R; and Black wins by a direct attack by the Rooks with a passed pawn hovering in the rear.

32 ………	R × Kt
33 R × R	R × B
34 K × R	Q × Pch.

The point of the combination; the capture of the Rook can wait whilst Black gains a decisive preponderance in pawns.

35 K–Q1	Q–B8ch.
36 K–Q2	………

36 K–B2, better in other ways, would be refuted by a problem-mate, Q–Q6ch.; and Kt–R5 mate.

36 ………	Q–Q6ch.
37 K–K1	Q–Kt6ch.
38 K–B1	Q × R

White is lost.

39 K–Kt1	Q–Kt6ch.
40 K–R1	Q–R6ch.
41 K–Kt1	Kt × P
42 Q–B6ch.	………

With the assistance of a few checks the Q returns to the defence at KKt2.

42 ………	K–B2
43 Q–B7ch.	K–Kt3
44 Q–Kt7ch.	K–R4
45 Q–Kt2	Q–K6ch.
46 K–R2	Kt–B7
47 R–KB1	………

If R–KKt1, then simply ………, Q–Kt7; as White has no checks.

47 ………	Kt–Kt5ch.
48 K–R1	P–K5
49 R–KKt1	P–B4
50 P–R4	K × P
51 P–R5	K–Kt4
52 R–Kt1	P–B6
53 Q–Kt2	P–B7

Resigns.

One of my best games.

Game No. 56.—London, 1927.

(Double Round Tournament)

White: Yates.

1	P–K4	P–QB4
2	Kt–KB3	Kt–KB3
3	P–K5	Kt–Q4
4	Kt–B3	Kt × Kt
5	KtP × Kt	Q–R4

A conscious exaggeration of the prophylactic principle; a minor piece can be employed to this end but not the Queen. However, Black wished at all cost to set new problems.

6	B–B4	P–K3
7	Q–K2	B–K2
8	Castles	Kt–B3

More consistent would have been the complete shutting out of the Queen by P–QKt3; Black had then the option of ...., B–R3; or ...., B–Kt2.

9	R–Q1	Castles
10	R–Kt1	P–QR3
11	P–Q4	....

White has now solved the problem set on Black's fifth move excellently; if now ...., Q × BP; he intended: 12 B–Kt2, Q–R4; 13 P–Q5, Kt–Kt1 (or R2); 14 P–Q6, B–Q1; and Black is in jeopardy.

11	....	P–QKt4
12	B–Q3	P–B5
13	B–K4	P–B4

Or else 14 P–Q5, follows.

14	P × P e.p.	B × P
15	Kt–K5	B × Kt

Compulsory.

16	P × B	R–B2
17	Q–R5	....

A terrifying onslaught!

17	....	P–Kt3
18	B × P	P × B
19	Q × Pch.	R–Kt2
20	Q–K8ch.	K–R2
21	Q–R5ch.	K–Kt1
22	B–R6	Q × RP

In his unhappy situation Black finds the only move which promises salvation. After 22 ...., Q × BP; he loses immediately: 23 Q–K8ch., K–R2; 24 B × R, K × B; 25 R × Pch., B × R; 26 Q × Bch., K–R1; 27 Q × Kt, and wins.

23	B × R	....

Conserving the B was strongly to be considered, e.g.: 23 QR–B1, (instead of B × R,) Q–R6; 24 R–Q6.

23	....	K × B
24	Q–Kt5ch.	K–B2
25	QR–B1	Q–R6
26	R–K1	K–K1

The King leaves the bombarded region. Now White should have remembered that he has a passed KRP, but No, he still plays for a mate.

27	R–K4	Q–K2
28	Q–R6	K–Q1
29	R–Q1	K–B2
30	R–Kt4	Q–B4

31	R–K4	....

If 31 P–R4, there is a possibility of a wonderful combination. Observe: 31 P–R4, P–R4; 32 Q–Kt7, P–R5; 33 P–R5, P–R6; 34 P–R6, P–R7; 35 P–R7, P–R8(Q); 36

R × Q, R × Rch.; 37 K–R2, and Black wins as follows:
37 ...., Q × BP; 38 P–R8(Q), Q–Kt8ch.; 39 K–Kt3,
Q–K6ch.; 40 K–R2, R–KB8; (threat: Q–K8; and mate.)
41 Q–R4, Q–B8; 42 Q(R4)–B6, Q–K8; (not R × Q; because
of P × R, and wins); 43 Q × R, Q × Q; and Black must win.
In spite of this 31 P–R4, is good.   Only, in answer to
31 ...., P–R4; White must not play Q–Kt7.   Correct
would be 32 P–R5, P–R5; 33 Q–Q2. Having regard to
these various points, the following line of play appears to be
the best in answer to 31 P–R4, namely: 31 P–R4, P–R4;
32 P–R5, Q × P; 33 Q–B4, Q × Q; 34 R × Q, B–Kt2; 35
R–B7, Kt K4; 36 R–Kt7, B–Q4; 37 P–B4, R–R1; 38
P × Kt, R × P; 39 R–K1, R–B4; and Black has the superior
position.

| 31 .... | Kt–K2 |
| 32 Q–Q2 | .... |

It was essential to play Q–K3.   The passed pawns could
become dangerous only after the exchange of Queens,
although even then Black's position should remain superior,
as follows: 32 Q–K3, Q × Q; 33 R × Q, B–Kt2; 34 P Kt4,
Kt–Kt3; 35 P–R3, R–KB1; 36 R–KB1, Kt–B5; threatening
........., B–Kt7; or 36 ...., P–R4; 37 K–R2, P–R5; 38
K–Kt3, Kt–B5; threatening Kt Kt7; R–K2, R–B6ch.

32	Kt–Q4
33 P–R4	B–Kt2
34 R–Q4	R–R1
35 Q–K1	B–B3
36 P–Kt3	Q–B1
37 P–B4	Q–B4

With telling effect.

38 Q–B2	Q–R6
39 Q–R2	Q–Kt5
40 Q–B2	R × P

    41 P–B5   Kt–B3
Not ...., Kt–B5; because of R × Pch.
    42 Q–K3   Q × Rch.
Elegant and decisive.
    43 R × Q   R–R8ch.
    44 K–B2   Kt–Kt5ch.
    45 K–K2   R–R7ch.
    46 K–K1   Kt × Q
Resigns.

Game No. 57.—London, 1927.
(Double Round Tournament).
White: Morrison.

This and the following games are examples of over-protection.

    1 P–K4   P–K3
    2 P–KKt3   ....
Tartakower's interesting suggestion.
    2 ....   P–Q4
    3 Kt–QB3   ....

More obvious was B–Kt2, with P–Q3. At QB3 the Knight is subject to molestation.

    3 ....   Kt–QB3
    4 P × P   ....

P–Q3, and B–Kt2 would still have been better.

    4 ....   P × P
    5 P–Q4   B–KB4
    6 P–QR3   Q–Q2
    7 B–Kt2   Castles

The QP is covered indirectly, e.g.: 8 Kt × P, Q–K3ch.; 9 Kt–K3, Kt × P; or 8 B × P, Kt–B3; 9 B × Kt, Q × B; with a superior attacking game.

    8 KKt–K2   ....

8 ....   QKt–K2

The following are the component parts of this strange-looking line of play: (1) Black's K5 clearly must be looked upon as a strategically important point (=an outpost on the K file), (2) consequently the QP which supports this point is valuable. Over-protection of this valuable pawn is therefore in keeping with our stratagem of over-protection. The question arises (3) will the Kt which is to occupy Black's K5 be able to maintain itself there? It must be recognised already that such is the case (compare Black's 12th move). Much weaker at this stage would be the " natural " defensive move 8 ...., Kt–B3; because of 9 B–Kt5.

9 Kt–B4   Kt–KB3

Now B–Kt5, can no longer be played.

10 P–KR3   P–KR4
11 Kt–Q3   Kt–K5
12 B–K3   ....

Now White threatens exchanges followed by Kt–B5. The prospects of the Knight on outpost duty appear to have shrunk alarmingly, in fact, the whole system 8 ...., QKt–K2; appears to be practically refuted. But No, it is not so.

12 ....   Kt × Kt

The Knight inflicts a gaping wound, namely, the doubled pawns at QB2 and B3; White's open file is more or less of no value and he will be slowly crushed to death. The Knight at Black's K5 has succeeded in maintaining his position, though not in a literal sense (compare note to move 8).

13 P × Kt   Kt–B3
14 Kt–Kt4   B–K3
15 Q–K2   Kt–R4
16 P–KR4   P–QB3
17 Castles KR   B–Q3
18 Kt–Q3   B–KKt5

In control of a tremendously powerful point at his QB5, and with an excellent development, Black now opens the attack on his opponent's weakened K side.

19 B–B3   ....

There is scarcely anything better.

19 ....   QR–K1
20 B × B   P × B
21 Q–Q1   Kt–B5

Avoiding the trap 21 ...., B x P; 22 Kt–B5, and wins.

22 B–B4	B x B
23 Kt x B	P–KKt4
24 P x P	Q–B4
25 Kt–Kt2	Q x KtP
26 P–B4	....

If 26 Kt–R4, R x Kt; 27 P x R, Q x P; 28 R–K1, R–R1; 29 K–B1, Q–R8ch.; 30 K–K2, Q–B6ch.; etc. Note the effect of the Kt at Black's QB5.

26	Q–R4
27 K–B2	....

Black had expected 27 R–K1, and had prepared the pretty reply 27 ...., R–K6; e.g.: 28 Kt x R, Q–R8ch.; and R–R7ch.

27	Kt–Q3

Abandons his outpost for an even stronger one at K5.

28 Kt–R4	Kt–K5ch.

Resigns.

If K–Kt2, Kt x KtP; is immediately decisive.

Game No. 58.—Match, Kristianstad, 1922.

Black: A. Hakansson.

1 P–K4	P–K3
2 P–Q4	P–Q4
3 P–K5	....

Since 1911 the author has upheld this continuation, but it has taken 17 years to convince the chess-world of the correctness of his view.

3	P–QB4
4 Q–Kt4	....

White's innovation, played here for the first time. As will be seen, the basis of the idea is over-protection.

4	P x P
5 Kt–KB3	Kt–QB3
6 B–Q3	P–B4

White, minus a pawn, plays for a Blockade and so employs the stratagem known to us from games 46 and 47, " sacrifice for Blockade." So that the plan can function, the P at K5, the bearer of the Blockade idea, has to be over-protected. The over-protectors should then win laurels, almost without doing anything, so ordains the stratagem of over-protection.

7	Q–Kt3	KKt–K2
8	Castles	Kt–Kt3
9	P–KR4	………

Poor Knight!

9	………	Q–B2
10	R–K1	B–Q2

Here 10 ………, B–B4; 11 P–R5, Kt–B1; should have been played.

11	P–R3	Castles
12	P–Kt4	………

Here White could already have won the exchange: 12 P–R5, KKt–K2; 13 Kt–Kt5, R–K1; 14 Kt–B7, R–Kt1; 15 Kt–Q6ch., but would then have had some difficulties to overcome. (White's KRP is unprotected, and he is undeveloped). The move in the text is the logical complement of White's dispositions.

12	………	P–QR3

A little better was: 12 ………, K–Kt1; 13 P–B3, P × P; 14 Kt × P, Kt × KtP; 15 P × Kt, Q × Kt; 16 B–K3, Q × B; 17 B × Pch., K–B1; 18 KR–B1ch., B–B3; 19 P–Kt5, Q × P; 20 Kt–Q4, with complications. Of course, after 12 ………, K–Kt1; White could have continued with 13 B–Kt2.

13	P–R5	KKt–K2
14	B–Q2	P–R3
15	P–R4	P–KKt4
16	P–Kt5	P–B5
17	Q–Kt4	………

A very good square for the Queen.

17	………	Kt–QKt1
18	P–B3	………

Without having done anything at all, the over-protecting Rook now obtains control of the QB file and with it a big field of action : a small actor has a big part thrust upon him. Why and how? The producer willed it so. Who, in our illustration, was the all-powerful producer, who can distribute parts? Answer : the Stratagem of Over-Protection!

18	………	R–K1

There is nothing better. Black has to undertake a remarkable re-grouping in order to save his material.

19	P × QP	K–Q1
20	R–QB1	Q–Kt3
21	P–R5	Q–R2
22	P–Kt6	Q–R1

A Q position which one expects to find only in problems.

23	R–B7	Kt–B4
24	Kt–B3	B–K2
25	Kt×QP	Kt×P

If 25 ...., P×Kt, 26 B×Kt, etc.

| 26 | Kt×Kt | P×Kt |
| 27 | Q×Bch | |

and mate next move.

Game No. 59.—Kecskemet, 1927.

Black: Székely.

1	P–K4	P–K3
2	P–Q4	P–Q4
3	P–K5	P–QB4
4	Q–Kt4	....

This line of play would appeal only to the few; it is not everybody's fancy to give up a pawn and, afterwards—not to play for an attack.

4	....	P×P
5	Kt–KB3	Kt–QB3
6	B–Q3	KKt–K2
7	Castles	Kt–Kt3
8	R–K1	Q–B2
9	Q–Kt3	....

It may be asked: what has White really achieved after giving up a pawn? The answer is simple, he has given thorough protection to his K5, which is the key to all future blockading operations, and thus he has given his own game a spearhead. The idea of White's formation stands out clearly: the loss of the QP, the position arrived at tells us, need not be deplored, for its principal function is apparently carried out by pieces. In other words, the P at K5, the key to the entire restrictive strategy, no longer requires the support of the QP, as it is splendidly protected by Rook, Knight and Queen. Therefore White, although a pawn down, has for it ample opportunities, with K5 the life and soul of all future operations. (Compare note to move 6 in the preceding game). Incidentally, we think that Black's 8th move is none too strong; correct was 8 ...., B–K2; which also would have militated against P–KR4–R5, by White.

          9 ....   B–B4
       10 P–KR4   ....

Less an attacking move than an attempt to relieve the KP.

      10 ....   K–B1

10 ...., B–Q2; certainly looks better, e.g.: 11 P–R5, KKt–K2; 12 Q×P, Castles QR; although 13 B–KKt5, would have been awkward enough.

      11 P–R5   KKt–K2
      12 P–R6   P–KKt3
      13 P–R3   ....

In order to provoke ...., P–R4; a further weakness.

      13 ....   P–R4

Now White's QKt5 has become accessible to the White pieces, but to allow P–QKt4, would have been still more hazardous.

      14 B–KKt5   Kt–KKt1

Compulsory because of B–B6, and Kt–Kt5.

      15 QKt–Q2   P–B3

It is open to question whether this violent attempt to free his game should not have been renounced in favour of a waiting policy, but it is in the nature of things that the besieged should attempt sorties. The desire for an active defence is understandable, and against passivity White, inter alia, had considered Kt–B1–R2–Kt4–B6.

16 Kt–Kt3   ....

This incidental move is intended to call forth P–Kt3; and so to cause a weakening in the QKt's position. After an immediate 16 P × P, White feared B–Q3; (though not the exchange of Queens, e.g. 16 P × P, Q × Q; 17 P × Q, B–Q3; 18 R–K2, B × KtP; 19 R–KB1, and Black would be fairly helpless, for the KKt is dead and the opening of lines eventually is threatened by P–B7,) 16 P × P, B–Q3; 17 Q–R4, P–K4; 18 B–Kt5, B–Q2; and it is not clear how to sacrifice, though it is clear that with the opponent for practical purposes without a Rook and Knight, more or less any sacrifice would be sound, but where and how? White came to the conclusion that, as a first step, the Black QKt had to be dislodged, and only then would the basis be provided for a break-through, by means of a sacrifice either at Q4 or at K⁵

16 ....   P–Kt3
17 P × P   Q × Q

If instead 17 ...., B–Q3; 18 Q–R4, P–K4; 19 B–Kt5, (with the Black QKtP at his third, his move is far more effective than before) B–Q2; 20 B × Kt, B × B; 21 B–B4, P × B; 22 QKt × P, B–Q2; 23 Kt–KKt5, and wins.

18 P × Q   B–Q3

If 18 ...., P–R5; White would have decided for the sacrificial continuation: 19 Kt × B, P × Kt; 20 P–B7, K × P; 21 B–Kt5, KKt–K2; 22 Kt–K5ch, Kt × Kt; 23 R × Kt, and wins.

19 B–Kt5   Kt–R2
20 KKt × P   K–B2
21 P–B4   P–K4
22 P × P   P × Kt
23 B–K8ch.   K–B1
24 P–B7   ....

The rest is silence (Kt–K2; QB–B6,).

24 ....   B–KB4
25 Kt × QP   B–B4
26 QR–Q1   Kt–Kt4
27 P × Kt(Q)ch.   R × Q
28 B × Kt   K–B2
29 P–Q6   Resigns.

In this game also, the over-protectors have come off with flying colours.

Game No. 60.

Russian Masters' Tournament, 1913.

White: Bogoljubow.

1	P–K4	P–K3
2	P–Q4	P–Q4
3	Kt–QB3	Kt–KB3
4	P–K5	KKt–Q2
5	Q–Kt4	....

The Gledhill variation.

5	....	P–QB4
6	Kt–B3	P–QR3

Black wisely avoids the following variation with which he was unfamiliar: 6 ...., P×P; 7 KKt×P, Kt×P; 8 Q–Kt3.

7	P×P	Q–B2
8	Q–Kt3	Kt×BP
9	B–Q3	P–KKt3
10	B–KB4	....

He plays—sub-consciously, for this principle had not been discovered at the time—for over-protection.

10	....	Kt–B3
11	Castles KR	Kt–K2

Tacking about. If 11 ...., B–Kt2; with Castles; the over-protectors would have become effective for an attack, for instance by: R–K1, Q–R4, B–R6.

12	QR–B1	....

An ingenious preventive measure against the intended ...., Kt×B; followed by Kt–B4.

12	....	B–Kt2
13	P–QKt4	....

In order to safeguard the B once and for all; but it slightly weakens the Q side.

13	....	Kt–Q2
14	Kt–K2	Castles
15	Kt (K2)–Q4	Kt–QB3
16	Kt×Kt	P×Kt
17	P–B4	....

If now the obvious-looking ...., Q–Kt1; then 18
P × P, BP × P; 19 P–QR3, and White has a free
hand on the K wing. 19 ...., B–Kt2; 20 P–KR4,
P–KR4; 21 QR–K1, (over-protection) and White threatens
22 Kt–Q4, with Kt × P, as well as 22 Q–R3, with P–Kt4.
Observe the easy grace with which the over-protectors
suddenly got into action. But now the following question
arises : was the manœuvre which started with 17 P–B4, with
the object of safeguarding and freeing the Q side—and after
17 P–B4, Q–Kt1 ; 18 P × P, etc., the Q side was in fact freed
—absolutely necessary? Might not White have considered
burning his boats by 17 KR–K1? There could
have followed : 17 ...., P–QR4; 18 P–B3, P × P; 19
P × P, Q–Kt3; (19 ...., R × P; 20 Kt–Q4,), 20 P–KR4,
Q × P; 21 P–R5. If now 21 ...., R × P; 22 P × P, BP × P;
23 B–K3. But after the sacrifice of the exchange by 23
........., R × Kt; 24 P × R, Kt × P; 25 B–QB5, Q–KR5 ; Black
should be able to win after all. Bogoljubow was therefore
well advised to eschew a ruthless prosecution of the K side
attack.

17 ....   P × P !

An heroic remedy which culminates in a pawn-sacrifice.
What follows is a mighty duel between. . . the two players?
No, between centralisation and over-protection. On this
occasion over-protection gets the worst of it.

18 B × P   Q–Kt1
19 R–Kt1   Kt–Kt3
20 Kt–Q2   ....

This move is not in accordance with over-protection.

20 ....   R–Q1
21 KR–B1   Kt–Q4

Centralisation! If 22 B × Kt, the R is to recapture, e.g.: 22 ...., R × B; 23 R × P, B–Kt2; 24 R–Q6, Q–B2; threatening Q–B7; and the game would be approximately even; another possible continuation would have been: 23 ...., B × P; (instead of B–Kt2;) e.g.: 24 B × B, (if 24 R × Bch, then Q–B7; later on). 24 ...., Q × B; 25 Q × Q, R × Q; 26 Kt–B4, R–K7; 27 Kt–Kt6, B–Kt2; 28 R–B7, R–Kt1; 29 Kt–Q7, R–Q1; 30 R × B, R–Q7; with an equalised game.

22 R–K1 ....

Correct was B × Kt, as shown in the preceding note. After the move in the text, White's fortunes decline mightily.

22	Kt × B
23 Q × Kt	B × P
24 R × B	R × Kt
25 Q–Kt5	....

White could still have resisted with Q × R, Q × R; Q Q8ch.

25	Q–Q3
26 QR–K1	Q Q5

Still centralising.

27 B–B1	Q × Pch.
28 K–R1	P–B3
29 Q–K3	P × R

Resigns.

PART IV.

THE ISOLATED QP.   THE TWO HANGING PAWNS. THE TWO BISHOPS.

Let us consider the following frame-work: White pawns at QR2, QKt2, Q4, KB2, KKt2, KR2; and Black pawns at QR2, QKt2, K3, KB2, KKt2, KR2. The isolated QP, in spite of static weakness, possesses a certain amount of dynamic strength. It is now essential to differentiate statics from dynamics with the utmost precision, if the subject is to be understood.

Static weaknesses become manifest in the end-game, and that in two ways: firstly, the QP requires support, secondly, weaknesses of adjacent squares become of moment (e.g. the Black King seeks to penetrate via his Q4 to his QB5 or K5.) To the credit of dynamic strength can be placed, besides the urge to expand (P–Q5,), the following line of play: White allows his isolated pawn to stay where it is, but occupies the squares which the P at Q4 makes dynamically particularly valuable, namely QB5 and K5.

There are engines of war which even twenty years ago were the terror of all belligerents, and yet, to-day, they are no more than harmless playthings. Defensive technique has progressed, that is the reason. To-day, the dynamic power of this isolated QP has become to us just such a plaything, and we find it difficult to understand how anyone could take to flight before such a weapon.

The following opening moves will demonstrate how innocuous the said dynamic power really is:

I. White: Erich Cohn, Carlsbad, 1911: P–Q4, P–Q4; 2 Kt–KB3, P–K3; 3 P–B4, P–QB4; 4 P–K3, Kt–KB3; 5 B–Q3, B–Q3; 6 Castles, Castles; 7 P–QR3, P×QP; 8 KP×P, P×P; 9 B×P, Kt–B3; 10 Kt–B3, P–QKt3; 11 B–KKt5, B–Kt2; 12 Q–K2, P–KR3; 13 B–K3, Kt–K2; 14 Kt–K5, (an attempt to make use of the dynamic power of the isolated pawn, which procedure is easily refuted). QKt–Q4; 15 Kt×Kt, Kt×Kt; 16 Q–R5, B×Kt; 17 Q×B, Kt–B3; 18 KR–K1, B–Q4; 19 B–Q3, R–B1; 20 QR–B1, Kt–Kt5; 21 Q–Kt3, Kt×B; 22 P×Kt, Q–Q2; 23 B–R6, R×R; 24 R×R, Q–R5; 25 B–B1, Q–Kt6; 26 Q–B2, P–B4; 27 Q–Q2, R–B2; 28 Q–B3, Q–R5; 29 P–KKt3, K–R2; 30 B–Kt2, Q–Kt4; 31 B×B, P×B; and Black for 70 moves concentrated his attack on the KP and later on the KKtP as well, after White was compelled to play P–KR4. The end phase of the game is given under the heading of " the technique of alternation."

II. Black: Gemsöe, Copenhagen, 1922: 1 P–K3, P–Q4; 2 P–QB4, P–K3; 3 Kt–KB3, Kt–KB3; 4 P–Q4, P–B4; 5 Kt–B3, Kt–B3; 6 B–K2, B–K2; 7 Castles, Castles; 8 P × BP, B × P; 9 P × P, P × P; 10 P–QKt3, B–K3; 11 B–Kt2, R–B1; 12 R–B1, Q–K2; 13 Kt–QKt5, KR–Q1 ; 14 KKt–Q4, P–QR3; 15 Kt × Kt, R × Kt; 16 Kt–Q4, R–B2; 17 Q–Q3, KR–QB1; 18 Kt–B5, Q–Q1; 19 KR–Q1, B–B1; 20 R × R, R × R; 21 Kt–Kt3, (notice the small value of the " dynamic trumps," namely, the open QB file; but there is, dominating all happenings, the static weakness of the isolated P. The slow manœuvring of the White Kt emphasises still more the situation just described). 21 ......, B–K2; 22 B–KB3, R–Q2; 23 Kt–K2, Kt–K5; (this dynamic joy-ride is short-lived). 24 Kt–B4, B–B3; (what else is there?) 25 Kt × B, P × Kt; 26 B × Kt, B × B; 27 B × Pch., and White won after a long-drawn ending.

We shall now examine the next weapon on the agenda, the two hanging pawns. White: pawns at QR2, QKt2, K3, KB2, KKt2, KR2. Black: pawns at QR2, QB4, Q4, KB2, KKt2, KR2. Unlike the isolated pawn, this weapon is by no means out-of-date. Only it is necessary not to lay over-much stress on its dynamic value; many a tournament game has gone to pieces through an all-too-violent advance (= P–Q5; with a hankering after the break-through). Equally ill-advised would be to forsake any initiative in favour of the quest for a safe position; we are thinking of P–B5; whereby the hanging pawns Q4 and QB5 appear to be protected, but have lost all driving power. (I call this: to retire into blockaded security.) The true course would lie in a blending of statics and dynamics with a dash of initiative, (as for instance in game 65 the play against White's P at his QB2); that should be the correct strategy.

Compare my disquisition on the subject in " My System." The great "infant mortality" of the hanging pawns must not tempt us to hasty—a little sceptical—judgment. This high death-rate can be considerably reduced by the exercise of a little care; look, for instance, at my discomfiture against Rubinstein at Gothenburg: White: Rubinstein: 1 P–Q4, P–K3; 2 P–QB4, P–QKt3; 3 Kt–KB3,

B–Kt2; 4 P–KKt3, B–Kt5ch.; 5 B–Q2, B × Bch; 6 Q × B,
Kt–K2; 7 Kt–B3, P–Q4; 8 P × P, P × P; 9 B–Kt2, P–QB4;
10 P × P, P × P; 11 Castles KR, Kt–Q2; 12 QR–Q1, Castles;
13 Kt–K1, Kt–QKt3; 14 Kt–Q3, Q–Q3; 15 Kt–B4, Q–KB3;
(the stumble; he should have played ...., Q–K4; the next
note will explain why.) 16 P–Kt3, (now R–Q1; is no longer
feasible because of P–K4, P–Q5; P–K5, and Black loses his
Bishop.) 16 ...., P–B5; 17 P × P, Kt × P; 18 Q–Q4,
Q × Q; 19 R × Q, Kt–QKt3; 20 Kt × P, and after the exchange
of the minor pieces Rubenstein won a R end-game in classic
style.

The power of the two Bishops is shown in two games
of which that against Goldstein is particularly salient. A
third game, No. 63, provides an example of the two Bishops.

Game No. 61.—Copenhagen, 1923.

Black: Eigil Jacobsen.

1	P–Q4	P–Q4
2	Kt–KB3	Kt–KB3
3	P–B4	P–K3
4	Kt–B3	B–K2
5	B–Kt5	Castles
6	Q–B2	QKt–Q2
7	Castles	....

The last two moves of White are well known and yet,
White's plan, taken as a whole, contains a new " nuance,"
see note to move 9.

7	....	P–B4
8	P × BP	Kt × P
9	P–K3	....

The gain of a pawn, which is possible here, would be
bad. But one would now expect 9 ...., Q–R4; with a
fairly easy attacking development against White's Castled
position, which gives the impression of heedlessness. This
attack has often led to a win for instance in the
famous game Rotlevi-Teichmann, 1911: 1 P–Q4, P–Q4;
2 Kt–KB3, Kt–KB3; 3 P–B4, P–K3; 4 Kt–B3, B–K2;
5 B–Kt5, QKt–Q2; 6 P–K3, Castles; 7 Q–B2, P–B4;
8 Castles, Q–R4; 9 P × QP, KP × P; 10 P × P, Kt × P;
11 Kt–Q4, B–K3; 12 K–Kt1, QR–B1; 13 B–Q3, P–KR3;

14 B × Kt, B × B; 15 B–B5, KR–Q1; and Black had the easier game. However the transposition of moves selected by White makes it possible to delay P × QP, which move is comfortable only for Black, and by this subtlety White's chances are appreciably increased.

| | 9 .... | B–Q2 |

If 9 ...., Q–R4; White plays 10 K–Kt1.

| | 10 K–Kt1 | QKt–K5 |
| | 11 Kt × Kt | Kt × Kt |

Correct was P × Kt.

	12 B × B	Q × B
	13 B–Q3	Kt–B3
	14 P × P	P × P

Here comes the isolated pawn.

	15 Kt–Q4	KR–B1
	16 Q–Kt3	P–QKt4
	17 P–B3	....

In order to play P–Kt4. White's centralised structure can afford the small weakness at K3.

| | 17 .... | P–Kt3 |
| | 18 KR–K1 | P–Kt5 |

This permits a rally by which the enemy temporarily seizes the QB file; therefore ...., QR–Kt1; was undoubtedly better.

	19 B–R6	KR–Kt1
	20 P–Kt4	R–Kt3
	21 B–B1	B–K3

This is acceptable to White, for the line of attack K7–K3 is interrupted, but the isolated pawn was already in need of direct protection.

	22 R–B1	P–QR4
	23 P–QR4	Kt–Q2
	24 B–Kt5	Kt–B4
	25 Q–B2	R–QB1
	26 P–R4	R (Kt3)–Kt1
	27 Q–R2	....

Here Kt–B6, would have won the exchange at once.

| | 27 .... | Q–B2 |

28 Q × Q ?   ....

White was stronger on the Diagonals: the occupation of the diagonal outpost KB4 would have won easily, e.g., 28 Q–B4, Q × Q; 29 P × Q, and P–B5, cannot be prevented.

          28 ....   R × Q
          29 Kt–B6   R × B ?

A serious error. R × Kt; was indicated. After 29 B × R, Kt–Q6; 30 B–Kt5, Kt × KR; 31 R × Kt, P–B4; 32 P–Kt5, R–B1; 33 R–QB1, K–B2; 34 R × R, B × R; 35 K–B2, K–K3; 36 K–Q3, K–K4; 37 P–B4ch., K–Q3; 38 K–Q4, White cannot achieve anything. With his KBP at its third instead of its fourth White could still have made some attempt which, however, would fail on account of the weakness of his QRP. That the position of Black's King at his Q3 does not necessarily neutralise White's K position at his Q4 is shown in the following Bishop's ending, which is very similar to the present position: White: K at Q4, B at K8, Pawns at QKt4, K3, KB3, KKt5, KR4. Black: K at Q3, B at K3; Pawns at QKt3, Q4, KB4, KKt3, KR2. There followed: 1 P–R5, P × P; 2 B × P, B–Kt1; 3 B–K8, B–K3; 4 B–Kt5, B–B2; 5 B–Q3, B–K3; 6 P–K4, BP × P; 7 P × P, P × P; 8 B × P, B–Kt1; 9 B–Q3, and the Black King must give way. This confirms what we said in our preliminary notes concerning the weak complex of the adjacent squares of the isolated pawn (here at Black's QB4 and especially K4).

          30 P × R   Kt–Q6
          31 Kt × RP   R–R2
          32 Kt–B6   R–Kt2
          33 Kt–Q4   Kt × KR

After 33 ...., B–Q2; 34 KR–Q1, leads to the same position.

34	R × Kt	B–Q2
35	R–QB1	B × QKtP
36	R–B5	B–Q2

A pawn is lost in any event.

37	R × P	K–B1
38	K–B2	P–Kt6ch.
39	K–B3	K–K2
40	P–R5	B–K3
41	R–QB5	K–Q3
42	R–B6ch.	K–Q2
43	P × P	RP × P
44	Kt × B	P × Kt
45	R–B5	K–Q3
46	R–KKt5	R–Kt2
47	P–B4 and White won.	

Game No. 62.—Dorpat, 1910.

Played simultaneously with three other consultation games.

Black: Prof. Kudrjawzew and Dr. Landau.

1	P–Q4	P–Q4
2	Kt–KB3	Kt–KB3
3	P–B4	P–K3
4	Kt–B3	P–B4
5	P × QP	KP × P

Kt × P ; is much better.

6	B–Kt5	P × P
7	KKt × P	B–K2
8	P–K3	Castles
9	B–K2	Kt–B3
10	Kt × Kt	………

The " isolated pair of pawns " at Black's QB3 and Q4 soon turns out to be a weakness.

10	………	P × Kt
11	Castles	B–K3

This development of the B can pass muster only as a preparation for a prospective advance of P–QB4; otherwise B–Q2 at once should have been played.

12	R–B1	R–Kt1
13	Q–B2	B–Q2

Was P-B4; really not to be thought of? Let us examine: 13 ...., P-B4; 14 KR-Q1, Q-R4; 15 B-B3, KR-Q1; 16 P-QKt3, P-B5; or 16 B×Kt, (instead of P-QKt3,) B×B; 17 B×P, B×Kt; 18 B×B, B×P; with an even game. Black must be held to have committed a serious error in neglecting to obtain the hanging pawns (QB4 and Q4) instead of letting his game die of inanition over the helpless pair at QB3 and Q4.

14	KR-Q1	Kt-K1
15	B×B	Q×B
16	Kt-R4	Kt-B3

Kt-B2; would have provided a better defence, e.g.: 17 Kt-B5, B-K1; followed by Kt-K3.

17	Kt-B5	R-Kt3
18	R-Q4	....

The blockade proceeds apace. Incidentally, Black's QRP is difficult to defend.

18	....	KR-Kt1
19	P-QKt3	B-K1
20	B-Q3	P-KR3
21	Q-B3	....

Over-protection of White's Q4.

21	....	B-Q2
22	R-QR4	R-R1
23	Q-Q4	Kt-K1
24	R-R5	Kt-B2
25	Q-QR4	Kt-Kt4
26	B×Kt	P×B
27	Q-Q4	....

Now the QP is again isolated.

27	....	B-B3
28	P-QKt4	R(R1)-Kt1
29	Kt-Kt3	P-B3
30	Q-B5	Q×Q
31	Kt×Q	R-R1
32	R-B3	....

The RP is lost.

32	....	R-K1

Best; he seeks the open play which he has missed for so long.

33	R × RP	P–Q5
34	R–Q3	P × P
35	R × P	R × R
36	P × R	B–Q4
37	P–QR3	B–B5
38	K–B2	R–Q3
39	R–Q7	....

The pressure, carried over from the period of the blockade, even now, on an open board, exerts its laming influence.

39	....	R × R
40	Kt × R	K–B2

Now only, the strong points have their say; White, as it seems, can no longer prevent the Black King from occupying a central position at K5 or Q5; but that would mean a victory of the opening-up idea over the principles of the blockade.

41	Kt–Kt6	....

At the risk of losing the Kt. But White had thought out the move carefully.

41	....	B–Kt6
42	K–B3	K–K3
43	K–K4	K–Q3
44	K–Q4	....

If now 44 ...., K–B3; White plays Kt–B8, and as the Kt has two flight squares (R7 and K7), there is no danger.

44	....	B–K3
45	P–QR4	K–B3
46	P–R5	P–R4
47	P–K4	P–B4
48	P × P	....

Anything wins here—even K–K5, e.g.: 48 K–K5, P × P; 49 K × B, P–K6; 50 Kt–Q7, P–K7; 51 Kt–K5ch.; etc.

48	....	B × P
49	Kt–Q5	K–Kt2
50	K–B5 and White won in a few moves.	

The isolated pair did not acquit themselves to advantage; the White Blockade held out until the end, even after the opening up of the game. The isolated pawn played rather a poor rôle.

Game No. 63.

Played by Correspondence, 1924—1925.

White: Dr. O. H. Krause.

1	P–K4	P–QB3
2	P–Q4	P–Q4
3	P × P	P × P
4	P–QB4	Kt–KB3
5	Kt–QB3	Kt–B3
6	Kt–B3	B–Kt5

Worthy of consideration was P–KKt3.

7	P × P	Kt × P
8	B–QKt5	R–B1
9	P–KR3	B × Kt
10	Q × B	P–K3
11	Castles	B–K2
12	Kt × Kt	………

Very strong at this point, and Black has to find the finest counter-play even only to hold the balance. And yet, from the point of view of strategy and theory, there can only be one interpretation to this move: it is a confession that all this talk about the dynamic strength which is alleged to be vested in the isolated pawn is—just talk. No, the sombre reality discloses a different picture; the player with the isolated pawn must be satisfied if he succeeds in concealing its weakness:

12	………	Q × Kt
13	Q × Q	P × Q
14	B–K3	P–QR3
15	B–R4	B–Q3

After this move, Black's difficulties become acute; Castles; (but who thinks of Castles in an end-game?—would definitely have led to an easier game, e.g.: 15 ………, Castles; 16 B–Kt3, QR–Q1; 17 QR–B1, Kt–R4; 18 R–B2, Kt × B; 19 P × Kt, B–Q3; 20 KR–B1, and Black can view the White QB file with equanimity.)

16	B–Kt3	Kt–K2
17	B–Q2	………

Now the doubling of Rooks on the K file is threatened. The necessity to keep the QP covered has a paralysing effect on Black's game, and White, with two Bishops, has a nice easy game.

   17 ………   P–QKt3

The beginning of a deep-laid defensive manœuvre.

   18 QR–K1   K–Q2
   19 R–K2   P–R3
   20 KR–K1   KR–Q1
   21 P–R3   ………

Now B–Kt4, is already threatened.

   21 ………   R–B2

Black's plan of defence has become clear; he wishes to have his Rooks on Q1 and QB2, and 17 ………, P–Kt3; was essential in order to prevent B–R5. But, P–KR3; also was necessary, as otherwise White's B–Kt5, would force P–B3; disarranging Black's K side: he could not have stood the hole at his K3.

   22 P–Kt4   ………

If 22 B–Kt4, B × B; with K–Q3.

   22 ………   K–B1

With the defensive threat: Kt–B3; B–K3, B–B1; and Black's game is freed.

   23 B–K3   Kt–Kt3

Black must not delay the liberating process; the strengthening of White's game by P–B4–B5, must be avoided by prophylactic means.

   24 KB × P   Kt–B5

Compelling equalisation.

25	B × Kt	B × B
26	R–K8	R–B8
27	R × R(Q8)ch.	K × R
28	K–B1	R × Rch
29	K × R	B–B8
30	P–Kt3	B × P
31	B × P	B–Kt7
32	P–Q5	K–K2
33	B–K6	K–Q3

Draw.

The isolated pawn scored a partial success in this game but only in the generally accepted sense. Theoretically speaking, the course of this game is tantamount to a declaration of insolvency on the part of the isolated pawn: instead of the alleged dynamic strength, we see a timid concealment of its static weakness. Dr. Krause, it must be admitted, has planned and conducted the game excellently; that no advantage can be obtained from an isolated pawn is clearly not his fault.

Game 64.—Carlsbad, 1907.

Black: Janowski.

1	P–K4	P–K4
2	Kt–KB3	Kt–QB3
3	P–Q4	P × P
4	Kt × P	Kt–B3
5	Kt–QB3	B–Kt5
6	Kt × Kt	KtP × Kt.
7	B–Q3	P–Q4
8	P × P	P × P
9	Castles	Castles
10	B–KKt5	P–B3
11	Kt–K2	B–QB4
12	Kt–Kt3	P–KR3
13	B–KB4	R–K1
14	P–KR3	B–K3
15	Q–B3	....

An opening easy to understand; the position is approximately even, White has greater potentialities in the centre, against which Black has a stronger pawn-centre.

15	....	B–Q3
16	QR–Q1	....

The other Rook should have been played to Q1.

16	B × B
17 Q × B	Q–Kt1
18 Q–QR4	....

Youthful enthusiasm; the pawn sacrifice can scarcely be correct.

| 18 .... | Q–B2 |

Better would have been Q × P; Q × BP, Q × RP; etc.

19 P–QB4	QR–Kt1
20 P–Kt3	P–QR4
21 P × P	B × P

The isolated QP gives itself airs for a while before putting in an appearance.

22 KR–K1	KR–Q1
23 Q–R3	R–Kt5
24 Q–Kt2	P–R5
25 Kt–B5	....

Threatening Kt × Pch.

25	Q–B5
26 Kt–K7ch	K–R1
27 Kt × B	P × Kt

Here comes the isolated QP ! Better late than never.

28 Q–B3	P × P
29 P × P	Q–Kt1
30 B–B2	R–QB1
31 Q–Q2	....

White's isolated pawn is troublesome in so far as the B has the unwelcome task of covering it.   This, however, is easily remedied.

31	....	Q–Q3
32	R–R1	R–Kt2
33	R–R4	R(Kt2)–B2
34	B–B5	R–Kt1
35	R–Q4	R–K2

If 35 ...., R × P; 36 R × P.

36	R × R	Q × R
37	P–QKt4	....

Now White has at least as good a game as his opponent.

37	....	Q–K4
38	B–Kt4	R–R1

Disdaining the draw which he would obtain by Kt × B.

39	P–B4	R–R8ch.
40	K–R2	Q–B2

Better would be 40 ...., Q–Kt1; e.g.: 41 B–B3, R–QKt8.

41	B–B3	..,......

Blockade followed by annihilation, that was the fate of the isolated QP in the present game.

41	....	Q–Q3
42	B × P	....

With this capture the pedagogical interest in the struggle is by no means exhausted. We must, on the contrary, observe how White's manœuvres continue to proceed over Q4, the important blockade square during the lifetime of the isolated pawn.

42	....	Q–K2
43	B–B3	P–Kt3
44	Q–B3	R–QKt8
45	R–B4	K–Kt2
46	Q–K5	R–K8
47	Q × Q	R × Q
48	P–Kt5	R–K3
49	R–B6	Kt–Q2
50	B–Q5	R–B3
51	K–Kt3	Kt–Kt3
52	B–Kt3	Kt–Q2
53	R × R	K × R

The result of White's line of play is now clearly shown; Black could not avoid the simplifying exchange.

54 K–B3	K–K2
55 K–K3	P–B3
56 K–Q4	K–Q3

How strange! If we imagine the isolated pawn at Black's Q4 still with us, the respective position of the Kings could be termed the typical position in cases of isolated pawns, the position in which the object is the conquest, respectively defence, of the adjacent squares (here White's QB5 and K5). What matter if the isolated pawn has vanished? It still has its say; indeed, its shadow controls the whole game, and the pieces—its own as well as the opponent's—gather round it and seek to attack or to protect it, just as if it were still in existence. We have had an opportunity, in the last phase of game 36, to observe a very similar picture, in which a no longer present unit manifested itself quite clearly even after its capture.

57 B–Q1	Kt–Kt3
58 B–B3	Kt–B1
59 P–R4	Kt–K2
60 B–K4	P–Kt4

Now White captures the "adjacent" square K5 as if a real, and not an imaginary isolated pawn position were in question.

What do we learn from this transcendental case? Well, that the question is not only one of a weak pawn, but also one of a weak square. With the capture of the QP, play against the point Q5 is by no means at an end; matters proceed unconcernedly on the same lines. The rest needs no comments.

61 BP × P	BP × P
62 P × P	P × P
63 P–Kt6	P–Kt5
64 P–Kt7	K–B2
65 K–K5	P–Kt6
66 K–B4	Kt–Kt1
67 K × P	Kt–B3
68 B–B3	Kt–Q2
69 K–B4	K–Q3
70 K–B5	K–K2
71 B–B6	Kt–Kt1
72 B–Kt5	Resigns.

Game No. 65.—Carlsbad, 1907.

White: Rubinstein.

1	P–Q4	P–Q4
2	Kt–KB3	P–K3
3	P–QB4	P–QB4
4	BP × P	KP × P
5	Kt–B3	Kt–QB3
6	B–B4	....

In those days the refutation—6 P–KKt3,—was not yet known.

6	....	P × P
7	Kt × P	B–QKt5
8	P–K3	Kt–B3
9	Kt × Kt	P × Kt
10	B–Q3	Castles
11	Castles	B–Q3

Black does not intend to allow himself to be encircled in the style of game 62; he prepares P–B4.

12	B–Kt3	....

The reply B–KKt5, would have been rendered purposeless by a centralising action as follows: 12 B–KKt5, R–Kt1; 13 P–QKt3, (Q–B2, B × Pch;) B–K4; 14 R–B1, Q–Q3.

12	....	B × B
13	RP × B	P–B4
14	R–B1	B–K3
15	Q–R4	....

An attempt to dislocate Black's game by 15 P–K4, would at most lead to equalisation: P × P; 16 Kt × P, P–B5; 17 Kt × Ktch., Q × Kt; 18 B × P, Q × P.

15	....	Q–Kt3

Black saw clearly that P–B5; and not P–Q5; was the correct plan, for P–Q5; craving to break through would be overstraining the "dynamics" and therefore uncommendable. Less dynamic is here: P–B5; which provides a certain amount of security (our "blocked security") and gives occasion to a limited but sensible offensive. Compare preliminary note.

16	Q–R3	....

He "compels" P–B5; which at that time was still thought to be compromising.

16	....	P–B5
17	B–K2	P–QR4
18	KR–Q1	Q–Kt5

The initiative on a small scale.

19	R–Q4	....

White need not apprehend the doubling of his RP.

19	....	KR–Q1

If 19 ...., Q×Q; 20 P×Q, QR–Kt1; (otherwise 21 R–Kt1,) 21 B–B3, KR–Q1; 22 QR–Q1.

20	QR–Q1	R–Q2
21	B–B3	QR–Q1

This well-knit position with its extraordinary economy and ideally posted forces is akin to a Greek work of art. Nothing should have been changed in this position seeped in perfection. 22 K–B1, K–B1; 23 K–Kt1, K–Kt1; etc., with a draw would have been a fit conclusion to the game.

22	Kt–Kt1	....

This upsets the balance and leads to the disruption of White's game.

22	....	R–Kt1
23	R(Q1)–Q2	Q×Q

Stronger than: 23 ...., R(Q2)–Kt2; 24 Q–B3, Q × Q; 25 Kt × Q, R × P; 26 R × R, R × R; 27 B × P, Kt × B; 28 Kt × Kt, R × P; 29 R × P, with equalisation.

	24 Kt × Q	K–B1

Not 24 ...., R(Q2)–Kt2; because of Kt × P.

25 P–K4	P × P
26 R × R	Kt × R
27 B × P	Kt–B4
28 R–Q4	....

The weakness of White's KtP would have been apparent even in the best continuation, e.g.: 28 B–B6, R–Kt5; 29 B–Q5, Kt–R5. After the text-move the win is easy.

28	....	Kt × B
29	R × Kt	R × P
30	Kt × P	R–Kt5
31	Kt–Q6	R × R
32	Kt × R	B × P

and Black won.

In the following game the hanging pawns are maintained for a considerable space of time on their location at QB4 and Q4. To this static security is built on a " limited initiative " on the extreme Q wing and on the long white diagonal.

Game No. 66.—New York, 1927.

Black: Dr. Vidmar.

1	P–K4	P–QB4
2	Kt–KB3	P–K3
3	P–B3	....

A draw was sufficient for White, whilst Black had to play for a win.

3	....	Kt–KB3
4	P–K5	Kt–Q4
5	P–Q4	P × P
6	P × P	B–K2

Here 6 ...., P–QKt3; would please us more.

7	Kt–B3	Kt × Kt
8	P × Kt	P–Q4

Here also we should have preferred P–QKt3.

9	P × P e.p.	....

A possible continuation was 9 B–Q3, Castles; 10 Q–B2, P–KKt3; 11 P–KR4, etc.

9	Q × P
10 B–K2	....

With hanging pawns the B must be played to K2 and not to Q3.

10	Castles
11 Castles	Kt–Q2
12 P–QR4	....

The "limited" initiative directed against the pawn, which will presently be posted at Black's QKt3.

12	Q–B2
13 Q–Kt3	P–QKt3
14 P–B4	B–Kt2
15 P–R5	B–KB3

On 15 ...., P × RP; the sequel would have been: 16 B–B4, Q–Kt3; 17 Q–R4, with a double attack on R5 and Q7.

16 P × P	P × P
17 B–K3	P–R3
18 P–R3	KR–B1

19 KR–B1 !	....

This move, in effect, gains a whole tempo. Black cannot accept the pawn-sacrifice which this move involves without foregoing all his chances, e.g.: 19 ...., R × R; 20 R × R, B × Kt; 21 B × B, Q × P; 22 Q × Q, R × Q; 23 R–R8ch., Kt–B1; 24 P–Q5, and White has full command of the game.

19	KR–Kt1
20 R × R	R × R

The two moves by the Rook (........., R–B1; and ...., R × R;) gave White the tempo mentioned above.

21	Kt–Q2	B–K2
22	B–B3	R–R6
23	Q–Kt2	B × B
24	Kt × B	R–R4
25	Q–Q2	B–R6
26	R–B2	B–Q3
27	R–B1	B–R6
28	R–B2	B–Q3
29	R–B1	Q–R2
30	Q–Q3	R–R6
31	Q–K4	....

The central hegemony established herewith is in full logical agreement with the course of the game. It will not have escaped the thoughtful reader that the wing attack initiated by White, (P–QR4–R5 × KtP.) has only resulted in Black assuming the offensive himself in that quarter. The attack thus passing over to the enemy could be explained only by mistakes on the part of White, or else by the fact that White's attack had no justification. But in reality neither is the case and White played the attack correctly and had good reasons for attacking. Only in this way could the stability of the White hanging pawns be preserved.

Therefore Black—*sit venia verbo*—must have usurped the attack on the extreme wing, which would only be done by giving up other important territory, namely, the centre. On this basis, White's hegemony in the centre can be understood. The conclusion is logically convincing.

31	....	Kt–B3
32	Q–B6	R × B
33	Q × B	....

Draw.

Black's operations on the Q wing were conducted with the utmost energy but were parried by cool-headed play in the centre: wing operations and central manœuvres kept the balance. Concerning the acceptance of the sacrifice, the following variation is informative: 33 P × R, Q–R6; 34 R–K1, B–Kt6; 35 R–KB1, Q × Pch.; 36 K–R1, Kt–K5; with the main threat of B–B5. A game very soundly played by both sides.

Game No. 67.—Hamburg, 1910.

White: Dr. Tarrasch.

1	P–Q4	P–Q4
2	Kt–KB3	P–K3
3	P–B4	P–QB4
4	P–K3	Kt–KB3
5	Kt–B3	Kt–B3
6	B–Q3	B–Q3
7	Castles	Castles
8	P–QKt3	P–QKt3
9	B–Kt2	B–Kt2
10	Q–K2	QP × P
11	KtP × P	P × P
12	P × P	....

The pros and cons of the hanging pawns appear to be approximately balanced in this position.

12	....	R–B1

13	QR–Q1	....

A feeble move: a possible onset against the KB, the mainstay of the hanging pawns had to be prevented by 13 P–QR3, e.g.: 13 P–QR3, Kt–QR4; 14 Kt–K5, B–R3; (not 14 ...., Kt–Kt6; 15 QR–Q1, Kt × P; because of 16 ...., B × Pch; etc.) 15 QR–Q1, B × Kt; (15 ...., Q–K2; would lose a piece because of: 16 P–B5, etc., but 15 ...., Q–B2; should be considered, e.g., 16 Kt–Kt5, B × QKt; etc.) 16 P × B, Kt–Q2; and now White has the choice of two lines of play: 17 Kt–Kt5, or 17 P–B5. I.—17 P–B5, B × B; 18 R × B, Q–K2; 19 Kt–K4, (threatening Kt–B6ch,) KR–Q1; 20 P × P, Kt × KtP; 21 Kt–Q6, White

could venture on this line as cheerfully as on the more
positional II.—17 Kt–Kt5, B × Kt; 18 P × B, R–B2;
19 Q–K4, P–Kt3; 20 Q–QKt4, with a secure position (the
weakness of the "White squares" is well covered) and one not
devoid of initiative: 20 ...., Q–B1; 21 KR–K1, Kt–B4;
22 B–KB1, R–Q1; 23 B–B1, threatening B–Kt5. The
keen student should study the variations here shown. The
various aspects of the " hanging pawns " are demonstrated
in a clear light.

13	....	Kt–QKt5
14	B–Kt1	B × Kt
15	P × B	B–Kt1

Kt–R4; was also strong.

16	P–QR3	Q–B2
17	P–B4	Q × KBP
18	P–B3	Kt–B3

White has forfeited a pawn, but the two Bishops, the
KKt file and, last but not least, the two hanging pawns
promise him some attacking chances.

19	Kt–K4	KR–Q1
20	K–R1	Kt–K2
21	B–B1	Q–B2
22	Kt × Ktch.	P × Kt
23	Q–Kt2ch.	Kt–Kt3
24	B–R2	K–R1
25	P–B4	Kt–R5
26	Q–R3	Kt–B4
27	P–Q5	....

In order to exploit the long black diagonal for attacking
purposes. The advance of pawns for the purpose of opening
lines for the pieces in the rear must be classified entirely
under the heading " Dynamics." We should have given
preference to "Statics," therefore the scheme: 27 B–Kt2,
with Q–B3, and posting the Rooks at Q1 and K1 respectively.

Observe now how Black answers "Dynamics" with
" Statics "; he hems in and blockades the pawns at White's
QB4 and Q5 to the utmost.

27	....	R–Kt1
28	B–Kt2	R–Kt3
29	R–KKt1	QR–Kt1
30	R × R	R × R
31	R–KB1	Q–B4
32	Q–KB3	B–Q3

The Blockade.

	33 Q–B2	Q × Q

The Blockade squares at Black's QB4 and particularly Q3 provide a starting point for various inroads; for instance Q–K6; was threatened.

34	R × Q	B–B4
35	R–Kt2	K–Kt2
36	R × Rch.	RP × R

Now it is no longer difficult.

37	K–Kt2	B–Q5
38	B–B1	B–K6

The neat manœuvre by the Bishop forces the exchange.

39	B × B	Kt × Bch.
40	K–B3	Kt–B4
41	B–Kt1	Kt–Q3
42	B–Q3	P–K4
43	K–Kt4	P–B4ch.
44	K–Kt3	P–B3
45	P–KR4	K–B2
46	B–K2	Kt–K1
47	K–B3	K–K2
48	K–K3	Kt–Kt2
49	B–B3	K–Q3

The Knight makes for KR4 in order to undouble the pawns. In the meantime the K deputises in the Blockade field.

50	B–Q1	Kt–R4
51	P × P	………

The pawn ending after 51 B × Kt, would be hopeless for White because of the break-through by P–QKt4; etc.

51	………	P × P
52	K–Q3	K–B4
53	P–R4	Kt–B3
54	B–K2	Kt–K1
55	K–B3	Kt–Q3
56	B–B1	P–K5
57	K–Q2	P–B5
58	K–B3	P–B6

Resigns.

Game No. 68.—Oslo, 1921.

(Informal Game with Clocks).

White: Brekke.

The hanging pawns appear only as a latent threat, as ghosts, in this game, which is as protracted as it is interesting; the ending is particularly racy.

1	P–Q4	P–Q4
2	Kt–KB3	Kt–KB3
3	P–K3	P–KKt3
4	B–K2	B–Kt2
5	Castles	Castles
6	P–QKt3	P–B4
7	B–Kt2	P × P
8	P × P	....

Now Black has it in mind to create hanging pawns with P × P; should White play P–B4.

8	....	B–Kt5
9	Kt–K5	B × B
10	Q × B	QKt–Q2
11	P–KB4	R–B1
12	Kt–R3	....

Original and by no means bad.

12	....	Kt–Kt3
13	QR–B1	P–QR3
14	P–B5	....

If 14 P–B4, P × P; 15 P × P, and P–QB5, without delay, after which QKt–B4, would have brought about the situation we have pronounced desirable, namely: security by Blockade combined with some measure of initiative. 14 P–B5, must therefore be held to be a departure from the straight path, albeit a pardonable one.

14	....	P × P
15	R × P	Kt–K5
16	QR–B1	P–B3
17	Kt–Kt4	P–K3
18	R–R5	....

A Rook astray! Its absence will soon be felt. KR–B3, looks better.

18	P–B4
19 Kt–K5	R–QB2
20 Q–K3	Kt–Q2
21 P–B4	....

At last White, a player of undoubted master-strength, decides on this advance. But now different pawn formations result from it and the hanging pawns do not occur.

21	Kt × Kt
22 P × Kt	R–Q2

Note this Rook's freedom on its own 2nd rank.

23 P × P	R × P

The Q file is now tremendously effective, see note to move 18.

24 Kt–B4	P–Kt4
25 Kt–Q6	....

Comparatively best.

25	R × Kt
26 P × R	B × B
27 Q–R6	B–Q5ch.
28 K–R1	R–B2
29 Q × P	Q × P
30 R–Kt5ch.	B–Kt2
31 Q × Q	Kt × Q
32 R–Q1	....

The ending is clearly not an easy one to win.

32	R–B3
33 K–Kt1	K–B2
34 P–QR4	P–Kt5
35 R–Q5	R–K3
36 R–QR5	R–K6
37 R × QRP	B–Q5
38 K–B1	B–K4
39 P–R5	R × P
40 R–R5	R–Kt8ch.
41 K–K2	P–Kt6

He could quite well have played K–Kt3.

42 R × RPch.	K–K3
43 R–R3	P–Kt7
44 R–QKt3	R–QR8
45 R(R6)–Kt6	R × P
46 R × P	....

There was no urgency for this.

46	B × R
47 R × B	Kt–B5
48 R–B2	K–Q4
49 K–B3	R–R5
50 R–K2	Kt–K4ch
51 K–B2	P–B5
52 P–R3	R–R6
53 R–Q2ch.	K–K5
54 R–B2	R–K6
55 R–R2	Kt–Q6ch.
56 K–Kt1	R–K8ch.
57 K–R2	K–K6
58 R–R3	R–K7
59 K–Kt1	R–Kt7
60 R–R1	R–QB7
61 R–R3	K–K7
62 R–R4	R–B8ch.
63 K–R2	K–K6
64 R–R3	R–QKt8
65 R–B3	R–Kt7
66 K–Kt1	....

66	K–Q5
67 R–R3	Kt–K8
68 R–R4ch.	....

Then follows an interesting duel between King and Rook.

68	K–K4
69 R–R5ch.	K–B3
70 R–R6ch.	K–Kt4

Simpler would be to escape via Kt2, R3, R4, to R5, but Black sees a captivating turn, which he does not wish to miss.

71	R–R8	K–R3
72	R–KKt8	K–R2
73	R–Kt4	P–B6
74	K–B1	………

Obviously if 74 P × P, Kt × Pch.; with mate or winning the Rook.

74	………	P × Pch.

More elegant as well as quicker was 74 ………, Kt × P; 75 R–K4, etc.

75	K × Kt	K–R3

and Black won by Zugzwang (76 P–R4, K–R4; 77 R–Kt5ch, K × P; etc.).

Game No. 69.—Ostend, 1907.

Black, Leonhardt.

1	P–K4	P–K4
2	KKt–KB3	Kt–QB3
3	Kt–B3	Kt–B3
4	P–Q4	B–Kt5
5	Kt × P	………

An innovation first tried on this occasion.

5	………	Q–K2

Best; unfavourable would be 5 ………, Kt × Kt; 6 P × Kt, Kt × P; on account of 7 Q–Kt4.

6	Kt × Kt	………

If the sacrifice of a pawn does not appeal, the following line of play, recommended by Dr. Krause, will serve: 6 Q–Q3, Kt × Kt; 7 P × Kt, Q × P; 8 B–Q2.

6	………	Q × Pch.
7	B–K2	Q × Kt
8	Castles	B × Kt
9	P × B	Q × P
10	R–Kt1	Castles
11	P–Q5	………

With this move the White Bishops become jointly active.

11	………	Q–K4
12	P–QB4	………

At this stage the following continuation is also playable: 12 P–Q6, Q × P; 13 Q × Q, P × Q; 14 B–R3, etc.

12	R–K1
13 B–Q3	P–Q3
14 B–Kt2	Q–R4
15 Q–Q2	Kt–K5

It is clear that Black under-estimates the hostile Bishops or he would have played 15 ...., Kt–Kt5; if then 16 P–KR3, Kt–K4; and Black threatens to benefit materially (Kt×B;) and theoretically (P–KB3; closing the long diagonal). The Bishops are made innocuous. But then the prophylactic style appeals only to the few.

16 QR–K1	B–B4
17 Q–B4	Q–Kt3
18 R–K3	....

The violent move 18 P–Kt4, would be refuted by 18 ...., Kt×P; etc.

| 18 .... | K–B1 |

In order to hold the R more securely covered.

| 19 P–KR3 | .... |

Not 19 KR–K1, because of Kt–Kt6; etc. The move in the text is a preliminary to the decisive attack by R–B3, which now would fail on account of B–Kt5.

19	P–KR4
20 R–B3	B–Q2
21 R–K1	Resigns.

The impression is gained that two Bishops have to be taken seriously. But prophylactic measures based on the elimination—in fact or in effect—of one of the Bishops (see note to move 15) do appear to present a notable specific.

Game No. 70.—London, 1927.

(Double Round Tournament).

White: M. E. Goldstein.

1 P–Q4	P–Q4
2 Kt–KB3	P–K3
3 P–B4	Kt–Q2
4 Kt–B3	KKt–B3
5 B–Kt5	B–Kt5

Spielmann's ingenious variation.

| 6 P×P | P×P |
| 7 P–K3 | .... |

If 7 Q–R4, P–B4; can be played at once, e.g.: 7 Q–R4, P–B4; 8 P × P, B × Ktch.; 9 P × B, Castles; 10 P–B6, Q–B2.

7 ………   P–KR3

A possibility: 7 ………, P–B4; 8 P × P, Q–R4; etc.

8 B × Kt   Q × B

Very sound, instead of this move, would be 8 ………, B × Ktch; with 9 ………, Kt × B; if then 10 P–QB4, the counterstroke P–B4; is available.

9 Q–Kt3   Q–QKt3

With the object of complicating the game; otherwise he could have played 9 ………, Q–Q3; with 10 B–K2, P–B4; 11 P × P, Kt × P; 12 Q–B2, Kt–K5; 13 Castles KR, B × Kt.

10 B–Q3   ………

Accepting the sacrifice of the pawn leads to an unclear situation after: 10 Q × P, B × Ktch.; 11 P × B, Q–Kt7; 12 Q–K4ch, K–Q1; 13 R–Q1, Q × QBPch.; 14 Kt–Q2, R–K1; 15 Q–Kt1, Kt–Kt3; (risky would be 15 ………, Q × P;) 16 B–K2, B–Q2.

10 ………   Kt–B3
11 Castles KR   Castles

A pawn sacrifice relying solely on the superiority of the two Bishops.

12 Kt × P   Kt × Kt
13 Q × Kt   B–K3
14 Q–QKt5   ………

Not 14 Q–K4, because of P–KB4; 15 Q–K5, QR–K1.

14 ………   B–K2
15 KR–B1   P–QB3
16 Q × Q   P × Q
17 P–QR3   P–QKt4

18 Kt–K5	B–Q3
19 P–B4	....

He advances his central majority all too quickly.
Observe now that the two Bishops hinder and obstruct.

19	P–B3
20 Kt–B3	B–Q4
21 P–K4	B–KB2
22 P–K5	B–Kt1

The QP now looks very weak.

23 R–K1	P × P

If 23 ...., B–R2; there could have followed, *inter alia*,
24 P × P, and R–K7.

24 BP × P	....

If 24 QP × P, B K3; 25 P–KKt3, P–Kt4; etc.

24	B–K3

Hemming in the QP. See note to move 19.

25 K–B2	B R2
26 K–Kt3	....

K–K3, would be no better.

26	QR–Q1
27 QR–Q1	R–Q2
28 R–Q2	KR–Q1

There is much to be said for: 28 ...., P–Kt4;
29 P–R3, R–Kt2; with threats which could not be
disregarded.

29 B–B2	P–Kt4
30 P–R3	K–B2

There is no hurry to recover the lost pawn. (30 ....,
B × QP; 31 Kt × B, R × Kt; 32 R × R, R × R; 33 R–Q1, with
an even game). The K move is intended, *inter alia*, as a
preventive measure directed against the passed KP. The
King could act as a reserve blockader at K2.

31 KR–Q1	K–K2
32 B–K4	P–R4
33 P–Q5	....

The British Master defends the difficult position
excellently.

33	P × P
34 B–Q3	R–KKt1
35 B × P	P–Kt5
36 P × P	R × Pch.
37 K–R2	R–B2
38 B–Q3	....

With 38 Kt–Q4, the game could have been held.

38	B–K6
39 R–QB2	R × R
40 B × R	P–Q5
41 P–Kt4	P–R5
42 B–Q3	P–R6
43 B–B1	....

If 43 P × P, B–B5ch.; 44 K–R1, B–Q4; But if 43 K × P, R–Kt1 dis. ch.; 44 K–R2, B–B7; 45 Kt–Kt1, B–Q4; 46 B–B1, B–Kt6ch; 47 K–R1, R–R1ch.; 48 Kt–R3, R × Ktch.; and wins.

| 43 .... | P × P |
| 44 B × P | .... |

The march forward of the RP has not only led to a reduction to the ranks of White's B (now acting as a pawn), but also to the freeing of Black's passed pawn. Therein lies the meaning of Black's manœuvre.

44	B–Kt6
45 R–K1	B–B5ch.
46 K–R1	....

If 46 K–Kt1, B–Q4; 47 R–KB1, P–Q6.

46	B–Q4
47 R–Q1	R–Kt1
48 R × P	R–R1ch.

and Black won.

The achievements of the two Bishops in this game have been many-sided. They have lured on and hemmed in the pawns, until the hostile majority became valueless. Then the hostile King was bombarded on all possible Diagonals. Finally, they gave the insignificant little passed pawn at their Q5 their high patronage, and this passed pawn became a giant.

PART V.

ALTERNATING MANŒUVRES AGAINST ENEMY WEAKNESSES WHEN POSSESSING ADVANTAGES IN SPACE.

In the strategic combination of enemy weaknesses with the attacker's own advantage in territory, the latter is the dominating factor.

These weaknesses frequently occur, so to speak, as a consequence of territorial pressure from the other side, as in games 71 and 73.

The course of manœuvres directed alternately against two weaknesses in the opposing camp could be analysed as follows: two weaknesses which could very well be defended, if treated singly, will be placed under fire turn and turn about, during which process the attacker will rely on the existing superiority of his lines of communications: the loss of the game ensues because the defender at a given moment cannot keep pace with his opponent in the rapid re-grouping of his forces.

The point of the stratagem under discussion clearly seems to lie in the proper use of lines of communications. Of what do these consist?

Almost without exception such lines of communication lead over one particular square, which therefore forms the axis of the alternating operations.

The relation between the point itself and the pieces which make for the enemy camp via this point, corresponds to the contact existing between a "strong point" and its "over-protectors."

In the game v. Schlage (71) (White: KKt1, KtQKt2, KtQ2, pawns at QKt4, QB3, KB3, KKt2, KR3. Black: KQB3, B–Q4, KtK4, pawns at QKt4, K3, KB4, KKt4, KR4,) Black's Q4 formed he axis; by threats on the K side Black managed to deflect the White keepers of the gate (the Knights), and then broke through with B–B5; Kt–Q6; and Kt–Kt7. It is to be noted that White's Q4, QB5 and Q6 were all weaknesses on White squares.

In the Q ending against Antze (75) White's Q4 (together with the points connected with it K5 and KB6) acted as the axis. The curve described by the Queen was: Q4–KB6–KB7–K8–KB7–KB6–Q4.

In the game against von Gottschall we see a Zugzwang taking part as *deus ex machina*; the defender had to destroy a defensive position, built up with much trouble, as it were, with his own hands.

In No. 74 the alternating manœuvres are carried out within the inner line, whilst No. 76 is remarkable because here the axis, comprises two squares (K6 and later K5), one white and one black, whereas it is usual for the square-complex to be of one colour only, e.g., 71, 75, etc.

Alternating manœuvres can also be aimed at one weakness only. In this case the variety of the attacks (such as frontal-, flank-, rear-attacks) takes the place of the variety of points to be attacked.

Any further information will be found by the interested reader in games 71-77, which have been treated with particular care.

Game No. 71.—Berlin, 1928.

White: Schlage.

1	P–K4	P–QB4
2	Kt–KB3	Kt–KB3
3	Kt–B3	P–Q4
4	P × P	Kt × P
5	B–Kt5ch.	....

Here 5 Kt–K5, was worth considering.

5	....	B–Q2
6	B–B4	Kt–Kt3
7	B–K2	Kt–B3
8	Castles	....

He rightly rejects 8 P–Q4, e.g., P × P; 9 Kt × P, Kt × Kt; 10 Q × Kt, B–B3.

8	....	B–B4

In order to control the centre squares as far as possible, (here White's K4 and Q4). However, the old classical move 8 ...., P–K4; is by no means to be despised.

9	R–K1	P–QR3

In order to protect the control square at K4 indirectly.

10	P–Q3	P–K3
11	Kt–K4	Q–B2
12	P–B3	R–Q1
13	Q–B2	Kt–Q4

Each player now has a Kt in the centre, and the games are approximately even.

	14 B–Kt5	B–K2
	15 B × B	Q × B
	16 P–KR3	Castles
	17 QR–Q1	R–Q2
	18 B–B1	KR–Q1
	19 Q–B1	P–R3
	20 K–R2	P–KKt4

In view of his strong centre Black can afford this slight
loosening, but 20 ...., B–R2; certainly was sounder,
e.g.: 21 P–Q4, B × Kt; with Kt–B3; etc.

	21 Kt–Kt3	....

Complications after 21 P–KR4, P–Kt5; 22 Q × P,
P × Kt; 23 P–B4, turn out well for Black because of
23 ...., Kt–K1; 24 P × P, Kt × Pch.; and ...., Kt × R.
With the move in the text White obtains a clear-cut, even
position.

	21	B–Kt3
	22 P–Q4	Kt–Kt3

With a view to a possible diversion by Kt R5.

	23 P × P	Q × P
	24 R × R	R × R
	25 K–Kt1	Q–K2

A well-grounded retreat. The Queen had no longer
much scope at B4 and was even a little exposed in the event
of P–Kt4, with P–R3, and P–B4.

	26 R–Q1	R × R
	27 Q × R	Q–Q1
	28 Q–B1	K–Kt2
	29 Q–K3	Kt–Q4
	30 Q–Q2	Kt–B5
	31 Q × Q	....

The play tends to the end-game stage, for which Black,
because of the greater mobility of his King, is the better
equipped.

	31	Kt × Q
	32 Kt–K5	B–Kt8
	33 P–R3	P–B3
	34 Kt–Q7	K–B2
	35 Kt–QB5	....

An excellent position for a Knight.

	35	K–K2
	36 B–B4	P–B4
	37 Kt–K2	....

This gives Black the opportunity of eliminating the beautiful White Bishop.   But 37 Kt–B1, K–Q3; 38 P–QKt4, P–Kt4; 39 B–Kt3, Kt–K7ch.; 40 K–R2, P–QR4; would have been still less favourable.

	37	K–Q3
38	P–QKt4	B–R7
39	Kt × Kt	B × B
40	Kt–R5	P–Kt3
41	Kt–R4	B–Kt6
42	Kt–Kt2	....

If 42 Kt × P, K–B2; 43 Kt–R8ch., K–Kt2.

	42	Kt–B2
43	Kt–Kt3	Kt–K4
44	Kt–B1	P–Kt4

Black clearly has the superior position, but it is difficult for him to make headway, for here the White Knights are good gate-keepers.

45	Kt–Q2	B–Q4
46	P–QR4	P–KR4
47	P × P	P × P
48	P–B3	K–B3

The beginning of complicated alternating play.   The required two weaknesses in the White position stand out clearly.   On the K side the threat: P–Kt5; or P–K4–K5; on the Q side the threatened entry ultimately of Black's King via his QB5. The axis will be Black's Q4 in the first place and the whole surrounding territory, as, for instance, Black's QB5 and the squares becoming available after its occupation. The K move enables the Black Kt to move, for if P–QB4, (after Kt–B2;) Black would win a pawn by P × P; Kt × P, B × Kt; Kt × B, K–Kt4.

| | 49 K–B1 | .... |

White already feels the effects of compulsion.   If 49 K–B2, (instead of B1,) there follows P–Kt5; RP × P, RP × P; P × P, Kt × Pch.; K–Kt1, Kt–K6; with unpleasant consequences for White.

| | 49 .... | P–R5 |
| 50 | Kt–Q1 | B–B5ch. |

See note to move 48.

| | 51 K–Kt1 | .... |

If 51 Kt × B, Kt × Kt; 52 K–K2, K–Q4; 53 K–Q3, P–K4; and Black has the advantage.

| | 51 .... | Kt–Q6 |
| 52 | Kt–K3 | .... |

At this stage also, Kt × B, would be very questionable,
e.g.: 52 Kt × B, P × Kt; 53 Kt–K3, K–Kt4; 54 Kt–B2,
K–R5; 55 Kt–Q4, P–K4; 56 Kt × P, K–Kt6; 57 P–Kt5,
K × P; etc.

52	B–Q4
53 Kt–B2	Kt–Kt7
54 Kt–Q4ch.	K–Kt3
55 K–R2	Kt–Q8
56 Kt–K2	P–K4

The Black Knight has utilised his QB5 as a spring-
board, and White, in the last few moves, has lost territory.

57 K–Kt1	....

If 57, P–Kt3, then simply P–B5; etc.

57	K–B3
58 K–B1	B–R7
59 K–Kt1	Kt–K6
60 K–B2	Kt–Q4
61 P–Kt4	....

There threatened already Kt–B5; e.g.: 61 K–B1,
(instead of P–Kt4,) Kt–B5; 62 Kt × Kt, KtP × Kt; 63 K–K2,
K–Q4; followed by P–K5–K6; and wins.

Note the full use made of the axis at Black's Q4, (both
by the Kt and the B).

61	P × P e.p. ch.
62 K × P	Kt–B3
63 K–B2	....

The intended P–R4, would fail against P–B5ch.; K–R3,
B–K3ch.; Now the weakness on the K side has become
tangible (the RP soon will be the sick child of the family).
When weaknesses are clearcut, alternating manœuvres are
easier to carry out.

63	K–Q3
64 Kt–KKt3	K–K3
65 Kt–K2	Kt–Q4
66 K–Kt3	Kt–B3
67 Kt–QB1	B–Q4
68 Kt–Q3	Kt–R4ch.
69 K–R2	P–K5

At last the pawn majority gets under way; as the White
King is tied to the weak point KR3 and cannot help to
localise the hostile break-through, it becomes catastrophic.

70 P × P	P × P
71 Kt–K1	Kt–B5
72 Kt–B2	Kt–K7

For the second time, the Kt penetrates into the game.

73 Kt–Kt1 ....

If 73 Kt–Q4ch., Kt × Kt; 74 P × Kt, P–K6; and White loses forthwith.

73	B–B5
74 K–Kt2	B–Q6
75 Kt(B2)–R3	Kt–B5ch.
76 K–B2 !	....

He offers something but—

76 .... Kt–Q4

the opponent says, No. For now both Knights are stalemated.

77 K–Kt3 ....

If 77 Kt–Q2, P–K6ch.

77	P–K6
78 K–B3	K–K4

79 P–B4 ....

Compulsory, for if 79 K–Kt3, Kt–B5; 80 K–B3, P–K7; 81 K–B2, Kt–Kt7; all is over.

79	P × P
80 P–Kt5	K–Q3
81 P–Kt6	K–B3
82 P–Kt7	K × P
83 Kt–Kt5	....

Zugzwang. He has no moves.

83	B × Kt
84 Kt–Q6ch.	K–B2
85 Kt × P	B–B4

Resigns.

This game lasted twelve hours. One of my best endgames. Schlage played the defence excellently.

Game No. 72.—Hanover, 1926.

White: von Gottschall.

1	P–K4	P–K3
2	P–Q4	P–Q4
3	B–Q3	P–QB4
4	P–QB3	P×KP
5	B×P	Kt–KB3
6	B–B3	....

Denies the KKt its natural developing square and permits subsequently P–K4; freeing Black's game.

6	....	QKt–Q2
7	Kt–K2	B–K2
8	Castles	Castles

Without apparent reason Black gives up the intended fighting course—P–K4;—and in consequence gets into difficulties.

9	B–K3	P×P
10	P×P	Kt–Kt3
11	QKt–B3	Q–Q2

In order to consolidate the position as rapidly as possible by R–Q1; and KKt–Q4.

12	R–B1	....

He should have given preference to Q–Kt3, followed by Kt–B4–Q3, in consequence of which he would have been able to utilise his isolated pawn.

12	....	R–Q1
13	Q–Kt3	KKt–Q4
14	Kt×Kt	....

White plays for a draw.

14	....	Kt×Kt
15	B×Kt	Q×B
16	Q×Q	R×Q
17	Kt–B3	R–QR4
18	KR–Q1	B–Kt5

To forestall P–Q5.

19	P–QR3	B×Kt
20	R×B	B–Q2

A dead draw!? The game is over!? No, there is still a great deal in the position, and the play has still to begin. The great discussion about the pros and cons of the isolated pawns occurs only in the " third act."

21 R–B5   R × R
22 P × R   B–B3

The isolated pawn is not only a pawn—but also a square—weakness: the neighbouring squares Q5, QB4 and K4 are difficult to protect and even the elimination of the isolated pawn cannot alter that fact. Compare the preliminary notes to Part IV.

23 P–B3   P–B3
24 K–B2   K–B2
25 R–Q4   P–QR4
26 P–KKt3   ………

Better seems 26 P–QKt3, B–Q4; 27 R–Q3.   After 28 P–R3, White's position would have been difficult to get at.

26 ………   P–R5
27 P–B4   P–R4
28 P–R3   R–R1

A preventive measure against White's intended P–KKt4.

29 R–Q1   K–Kt3
30 R–Q4   K–B4
31 B–Q2   R–KB1
32 B–K1   P–K4
33 P × P   P × P
34 R–R4   P–KKt4
35 R–QKt4   ………

If R × KRP, K–Kt3 dis. ch.; and wins.

35 ………   K–K3 dis. ch.
36 K–K2   P–K5
37 B–B2   R–B6

Now the basis obtains for systematic alternating operations, as both White's QB5 and KR3 are inclined to

be weak: after ...., P–R5; P×P, P×P; B×P, White's
QB5 is left uncovered for a moment. But in what manner
can this trifling circumstance be utilised?

38	R–Kt6	K–K4
39	R–Kt4	K–Q4

Now a Zugzwang-position of great piquancy is reached.
For White has no reasonable move. If 40 R–Kt6, P–R5;
41 P×P, P×P; 42 B×P, and now Black plays K×P;
attacking the Rook. (For which reason the Rook was lured
to Kt6). If, on the other hand, 40 R–Q4ch., K×P; and
the reply 41 R×KP dis. ch., would be inadmissible because
of R×Bch.

40	P–R4	....

He refused to play his R to Kt6; but now Black's King
obtains a place on the K wing.

40	....	P×P
41	P×P	R–R6
42	R–Q4ch.	K–K4
43	R–Q8	B–Q4

The win is not too difficult now; in spite of disturbing
checks, the Black army, now welded into a homogeneous
whole, creeps ever nearer. The alternating manœuvres have
now well-defined objectives and dispose of excellent territory
for the purpose, with the axis at Black's KKt5, etc. The
rest requires few commentaries.

44	R–K8ch.	B–K3
45	R–Q8	....

The threat was R–QKt6; etc.

45	....	K–B5
46	R–B8ch.	B–B4
47	R–B7	R–R7

Not ...., P–K6; because of B–Kt1.

48	R–K7	B–Kt5ch.
49	K–K1	....

If 49 K–B1, R–R8ch.; 50 B–Kt1, K–Kt6; etc.

49	....	K–B6
50	R–B7ch.	K–Kt7
51	K–Q2	K–B8
52	K–K3	B–B6
53	B–Kt3	R×KtP
54	B–Q6	R–Kt6ch.
55	K–Q4	K–B7
56	R–Kt7	P–K6

57	B–Kt3ch.	**K–B8**
58	R–KB7	**P–K7**
59	R–K7	**B--B3**

Resigns.

This game, which I think is one of my best, is also significant as to the weakness of an isolated pawn in the end-game.

Game No. 73.—Hanover, 1926.

White: von Holzhausen.

1	P–K4	Kt–QB3
2	Kt–KB3	P–K3
3	P–Q4	P–Q4
4	P × P	P × P
5	B–KKt5	B–K2
6	B × B	Q × Bch.
7	Q–K2	....

Playing for a draw, otherwise 7 B–K2, was quite playable, e.g.: 7 ...., Q–Kt5ch.; 8 Kt–B3.

7	....	B–B4
8	P–B3	B–K5

With the occupation of this outpost Black begins to operate on the K file.

9	QKt–Q2	Castles
10	Castles	Kt–R3

Directed against the freeing move Kt–K5, which would have been good had Black played 10 ...., Kt–B3; instead.

11	Kt–K5	....

Here we would have given preference to 11 P–KR3, e.g.: ...., P–R3; (otherwise Q–Kt5,) 12 Q–K3.

11	....	Kt × Kt
12	P × Kt	B–Kt3

Alternating play is in course of preparation. The White weaknesses are his KP and his badly protected Diagonal QKt1–KKt6; the axis will be the fortified diagonal point at Black's K5.

13	Kt–B3	KR–K1
14	Q–K3	K–Kt1
15	Q–B4	B–K5

See preceding note.

16	R–K1	....

For 16 B–Kt5, would lose a pawn as follows: ...., B × Kt; 17 P × B, Q × P.

16	....	Q–B4
17	Kt–Q2	B–Kt3
18	Kt–Kt3	Q–Kt3
19	Q–Q4	P–KB3
20	P–KB4	P × P
21	P × P	....

Or 21 R × P, R × R ; 22 Q × R, R–K1 ; etc.

21	....	B–K5
22	Kt–Q2	P–B4
23	Q–K3	R × P

If 23 Q–R4, R × P ; 24 Kt × B, P × Kt ; 25 R × P, Q–K3 ;
26 R × R, Q × R ; and wins.

24	Q–Kt3	Q–B2
25	B–Q3	QR–K1
26	B × B	P × B
27	Kt–B4	R(K4)–K3
28	Q × Qch.	K × Q
29	Kt K3	....

Now White has built up an excellent Blockade position ;
a win for Black is still in the dim and distant future.

29	....	Kt–B2

To centralise the badly placed Kt at Q3. The alternative
would be 29 ...., R–KB1 ; (in order to take up the contest
on the KB file), e.g.: 30 KR–B1, R(K3)–K1 ; 31 P–B4,
K–B3 ; 32 K–B2, and now P–KKt3 ; intending Kt–B4 ;
if then 33 P–KKt4, R–B6 ; could follow. It is hard to say
which continuation is preferable.

30	K–B2	Kt–Q3
31	P–B4	K–B3
32	KR–B1	....

32	....	R–R3

This move is born of an exact knowledge of the laws of alternation. Black will have to act on the flank by means of P–QR3; and P–QKt4; and, as the antagonist's forces are fully occupied in keeping the KP under observation, he should have an opportunity of penetrating into the game, by opening up the QR or QKt file.   Thereby the axis necessary for alternating manœuvres would be created; but there is still lacking the second of the two weaknesses in the adversary's position, the first being his commitment to keep the KP under control. The R move to KR3 has the object of clearing this second weakness, which will subsequently prove of decisive importance in the ensuing Rook ending.

	White	Black
33	P–KR3	R–Kt3
34	R–K2	P–QR3
35	R–B4	P–Kt4
36	P–QKt3	R–Kt4
37	P–KKt4	R(Kt4)—K4
38	K–B3	P–QR4

Intending a double exchange of pawns, after which nothing would stand in the way of the Rooks penetrating into the game, for instance, by R(K4)–K2–R2–R6 or R8.

| 39 | R(K2)–KB2 | P–R5 |
| 40 | P × RP | P × BP |

In deciding on this move, Black had to give due consideration to the Rook ending which obtains after the 44th move.

| 41 | R–B8 | R(K4)–K2 |

Not R × R; as the White Rook would penetrate into Black's position.

42	R × R	R × R
43	Kt × P	Kt × Kt
44	K × Kt	R–QR1
45	R–B7	....

Or 45 K–Kt3, K–Q4; etc.

45	....	R × Pch.
46	K–Kt3	R–Kt5ch.
47	K–B3	R–Kt2

In this ending the loosened K side, (pawns at White's KR3 and KKt4) is a decisive weakness, as will soon be seen.

48	R–B5	R–R2
49	K–B4	R–R5ch.
50	K–Kt3	R–Q5

51 R–K5	K–Q3
52 R–K8	R–Q6ch.
53 K–B4	R × P

Compare notes to moves 47 and 32.

| 54 R × P | R–R6 |
| 55 R–K2 | R–R5ch. |

and Black won.

In this game the logical connection between " alternation " and the " two weaknesses " stands out boldly and clearly.

Game No. 74.—London, 1927.

Black: Buerger.

The striking feature of the alternating manœuvres in the following game is that they are carried out on inner lines, as it were, in the attacker's own camp. The opening seemingly went in White's favour.

1 P–QB4	Kt–KB3
2 Kt–QB3	P–Q4
3 P × P	Kt × P
4 P–KKt3	Kt × Kt
5 KtP × Kt	P–KKt3
6 B–KKt2	B–Kt2
7 Q–Kt3	....

Had Black played 6 ...., P–QB4; instead of B–Kt2; he could now have had an easy defence by Q–B2.

7	P–QB3
8 P–Q4	Castles
9 B–QR3	Kt–Q2

And now White is suddenly in a state of the utmost perplexity, for Black threatens, with Kt–Kt3; B–K3; to occupy the central square at White's QB4. What can he invent against that?

| 10 B–R3 | .... |

A drastic preventive measure. White intends to eliminate the troublesome Bishop at all cost.

10	R–K1
11 P–KB4	Q–B2
12 Kt–B3	Kt–B3
13 B × B	....

Another version would be 13 Kt–Kt5.

13	....	QR×B
14	Castles KR	P–K3
15	QR–Q1	....

The massing on the Q file is meant as a prophylactic measure against P–QB4; see the next note.

15	....	P–Kt3
16	P–B4	KR–Q1
17	R–Q3	....

Now P–B4; is to be answered by P × P, and if P × P; KR–Q1.

17	....	B–B1
18	B–Kt2	B–Kt2
19	B–R3	B–B1
20	B × B	R × B
21	Q–Kt2	Q–K2
22	Kt–K5	KR–Q1
23	KR–Q1	Kt–K5

Now that the liberating P–B4; has lost almost all its appeal, the talented English master tries another way: a central obstructive action is launched.

24	Q–B2	P–B3
25	Kt–B3	P–QKt4
26	P–B5	....

Also worthy of consideration was 26 Kt–Q2.

26	....	P–B4

Consolidation in the centre is now achieved.

27	R–K3	....

Coming to grips at once by 27 Kt–Q2, would be repulsed as follows: 27 Kt–Q2, Kt×Kt; 28 R(Q3)×Kt, R–Q4; 29 P–K4, P×P; 30 R–K2, (the Rooks in front with the Queen behind them seems to be the best disposition of forces) 30 ...., Q–B3; 31 R × P, and with the preventive move 31 ...., P–KR4; (directed against P–Kt4,) Black's position would be satisfactory.

27	....	P–QR4
28	Kt–K5	R–B2
29	P–QR3	K–Kt2
30	K–Kt2	....

Intending to play P–Kt4–Kt5, with P–KR4–R5, etc.

30	....	P–R4

31 R × Kt   ....

Was this sacrifice of the exchange obvious? Certainly;
but a defensive plan had to be visualised already now
against the hostile majority on the Q side, and that was not
easy. It was also essential for White to feel certain that,
having obstructed the said majority, he would have a won
game on the grounds that the essentials, known to him, of
successful "alternation," would obtain in the fullest
measure. How this is to be understood will soon become
clear.

31	....	P × R
32	Q × P	Q–B3
33	Kt × BP	R–Q4

The counter sacrifice by 33 ...., R × Kt; 34 Q × R,
R × P; would not pass muster because of the intervening
move 35 Q–B7ch., for if the K move ...., K–R3; White
exchanges Rooks and plays Q–Q6. And after K–Kt1;
White wins by 36 R–QKt1, P–Kt5; 37 Q × P.

34 Kt–K5   ....

If 34 Kt × P, R(B2) × P; etc.

34	....	Q–B4
35	Q–Q3	Q × Q

A fork was threatened. E.g.: 35 ...., R(B2) × P;
36 P–K4.

36	R × Q	R–Q1
37	K–B3	R–QKt1
38	R–Kt3	....

The Blockader, equipped for the *coup-de-grâce*.

38	....	P–Kt5
39	P–QR4	R–Q1
40	K–K4	R(B2)–B1

White's main and final threat is to obtain two united passed pawns by posting his King at QB4 and following this up with P–K4, and P–Q5. But there are difficulties in the way of getting the K to QB4. For instance, 41 K–Q3, at once would be a bad blunder on account of ...., R × P. It is therefore a question of attaining this K position by slow alternating manœuvres.

41 Kt–B4	R–QR1
42 R–K3	K–B3
43 Kt–Q2	K–K2
44 Kt–Kt3	....

Reveals the alternating tactics; the blockade square QKt3 is to be occupied in turn by Kt and R, whilst the piece remaining mobile at any time will undertake various attacks. On move 55 the same position obtains as on move 40 with the important difference that the White King occupies the much-desired position at QB4.

44	R–R3
45 K–Q3	R–Q4
46 P–R4	R–R1
47 K–B4	K–Q2
48 R–Q3	K–B2
49 R–Q1	R–Q2
50 R–KKt1	R–B2
51 R–Kt1	....

The sealed move: the changing of the guard.

51	K–Kt2

The attempt to break through by 51 ...., P–Kt4; would not be adequate. Note moreover the exceptionally fine parry 51 ...., P–Kt4; 52 R–Kt1.

52	Kt–Q2	K–B3
53	Kt–B3	K–B2
54	Kt–K5	R–Kt2
55	R–Kt3	R–QKt1
56	P–K4	....

Clear the decks for the fight !

56	....	R(Kt2)–Kt1
57	P–Q5	P × Pch.
58	P × P	R(QKt1)–QB1
59	P–Q6ch.	K–Q1
60	P–B6	Resigns.

Game No. 75.—Hanover, 1926.

Black: Dr. Antze.

Here again the weaknesses, on which the alternating manœuvres are based, bear the stamp of originality. The " alternator "—White—threatened to carry out a defensive manœuvre which would have ruled out any kind of counter-play. In an attempt to counteract this operation, Black went to pieces on the " second weakness."

1	P–Q4	Kt–KB3
2	P–QB4	P–KKt3
3	P–KKt3	B–Kt2
4	B–Kt2	Castles
5	P–B4	P–Q3
6	Kt–KB3	P–B3
7	Castles	P–Q4
8	P × P	P × P
9	Kt–K5	Q–Kt3
10	Kt–QB3	R–Q1
11	P–Kt3	Kt–R3

If 11 ...., Kt–B3; the following combination arises: 12 B–QR3, Kt × P; 13 Kt–R4, Kt × P dbl. ch.; 14 K–R1, Q–R3; 15 B–B3.

12	B–QR3	B–B1
13	Kt–R4	Q–Kt4
14	Q–Q3	Q–R4

The exchange of Queens would be simpler.

15	KR–B1	B–B4
16	Q–QB3	Q–Kt4
17	B–B1	Kt–K5
18	Q–K1	Q–K1
19	P–K3	....

The first player has succeeded in warning off the Black
Queen from the triangle at Black's QKt3, QKt4, and QR4,
but Black might have played for P–K4; with 19 ....,
P–B3; 20 Kt–B3, B–Kt5. He fails to do so, and instead
makes a mistake which should have brought about a fairly
quick decision.

19	....	P–QKt4?
20	Kt–B6	KR–B1
21	B × KtP	B–Q2
22	B × Kt	R × Kt
23	B–Kt7	R × R
24	R × R	R–Q1

If 24 ...., R–Kt1; 25 B × QP, Kt–B3; 26 B–B3,
B × Kt; 27 P × B, Q × P; 28 Q–B3, and eventually B–B6,
with an easily won game.

25	Kt–B5	....

Here also 25 B × QP, would have been strong, e.g.:
25 ...., Kt × P; 26 P × Kt, B × Kt; 27 B × Pch., Q × B;
28 P × B, Q × RP; 29 Q–B3, exchanging Queens eventually
after which the end-game would be an easy win for White.

25	....	B–B1
26	B × B	....

Again B × QP, was worth considering.

26	....	R × B
27	Q–R5	P–K3
28	Kt × Kt	P × Kt
29	R × R	Q × R
30	B–B5	B × B
31	Q × B	....

With this bad mistake, due to weariness, White nearly
gives away the whole game. 31 P × B, would have enforced
surrender in a few moves. If then 31 .... Q–Q2; which
seems to be awkward, the sequel would be: 32 Q–B3,
Q–Q8ch.; 33 K–B2, Q–B6ch.; 34 K–K1, with an easy escape
to QR3 and an immediate decision. After this blunder,
White has to win the game a second time.

31	....	Q–R3
32	Q–B2	Q–R4

33	K–B2	Q–R4
34	Q × P	Q × Pch.
35	Q–Kt2	Q–R4
36	P–KKt4	Q–R4
37	K–Kt3	P–KR3

Better would be Q–B6.

38	Q–KB2	Q–B2
39	K–R3	P–B4
40	P × P	KtP × P
41	P–Q5	P × P
42	Q–Kt2ch.	K–B2
43	Q × Pch.	K–B3

Now begins most protracted alternating play. The weaknesses in Black's position are: (a) the Q side where White threatens to obtain a passed pawn; (b) the K side where the White King threatens to break in via R5; checks by White from the rear will necessitate awkward covering moves on account of the isolated pawns.

Furthermore, the White Q will occupy a centralised position, say at Q4, with subsequent flight of the White

King into safety (see note to move 65). Black's counter-chances are repeated checks and his passed KR pawn.

44	Q–Q4ch.	K–Kt3
45	Q–Q2	K–B3
46	Q–Kt2ch.	K–Kt3
47	P–Kt4	Q–B5
48	Q–Q2	K–R5
49	P–R4	P–R3
50	K–Kt3	Q–Kt1ch.

Only one modest little K move (50 K–Kt3,), and already Black sees himself compelled to adopt defensive measure on the K wing as well. This compulsory reaction at the slightest sign of a threat is typical of the present situation.

51	K–R2	Q–B5
52	Q–QKt2 ·	Q–Q6
53	Q–Kt2	Q–B5

If 53 ...., Q × P ; 54 Q–R3ch.

54	K–Kt3	Q–Kt1ch.

We should prefer Q–Q6.

55	K–R3	Q–B5
56	Q–B3ch.	K–Kt3
57	K–R4	K–Kt2

If 57 ...., Q × P ; 58 Q–B6ch., with K–R5.

58	Q–Kt7ch.	K–Kt3
59	Q–Kt6ch.	K–R2
60	Q–KB6	....

The occupation of this valuable point marks an important step forward.

60	....	Q–Q4
61	K–Kt3	Q–Kt1ch.
62	K–R2	Q–R7ch.
63	K–R3	Q–Q4
64	Q–K7ch.	K–Kt3
65	Q–K8ch.	....

This square is here of even greater importance than KB6.

65	....	K–R2

After this White will be able to make the winning move P–R5, without danger. But also after 65 ...., K–B3 ; 66 K–Kt3, Q–Q6 ; (relatively best) 67 P–R5, the position is reasonably safe, e.g. : 67 ...., Q–B8 ; (if Q–Kt8 ; Q–B6ch., followed by Q–Kt7ch., and Q × P, as in the actual game), 68 Q–K5ch., K–Kt3 ; 69 Q–K6ch., K–Kt2 ; 70 Q × BP, Q–Kt8ch. ; 71 K–B3, Q–B8ch. ; 72 K–K4, Q–B5ch. ;

73 K–K5, Q–Kt4ch.; 74 K–K6, and wins.   This illustrates
the defensive threats of the second player referred to before.

66 K–Kt3	Q–Kt6	
67 P–R5	....	

Best, for the threat P–Kt5, now has a weighty effect.
Another likely variation is as follows : 67 Q–Q7ch., K–Kt3;
68 Q–B6ch., K–R2; 69 Q–Kt7ch., K–Kt1; 70 Q–Kt8ch.,
K–R2; 71 Q R7ch., K–Kt1; and again 72 K–R4.

67	Q–Kt8

A better move is 67 ...., Q–Q6; after which the
winning line would be none too simple, namely : 68 Q–B7ch.,
K–R1; 69 Q–B6ch., K–R2; 70 Q–Q4, and there are now
two variations according to whether Black plays the Queen
to Kt8 or B8. In both cases there follows 71 Q Q7ch., and
White will win either the QRP or the BP, which ever is
unprotected : 70 ...., Q–Kt8; 71 Q–Q7ch., K–Kt3;
72 Q–B6ch., K–Kt2; 73 Q Kt7ch., K–B1; 74 Q×P, as in
the game, or 70 ...., Q–B8; 71 Q–Q7ch., K–Kt3;
72 Q K6ch., K–Kt2; 73 Q×BP, with the escape of the
White King as shown in the note to Black's 65th move.
And so, after alternating for a sufficiently long time we
see the Black pawn-weaknesses break down alternatively,
a triumph for the logic of alternation.

68 Q–Q7ch.	K–Kt3
69 Q–B6ch.	K–Kt2
70 Q–Kt7ch.	K–B1
71 Q×P	Q K8ch.
72 K–B3	Q–Q8ch.
73 Q–K2	Q Q4ch.
74 K–B2 and White won.	

The defensive threat of White—escape of the King after
establishing security in the centre—has had an enduring
influence on the course of events.

A typical position would be : White : K at KKt3, Q at
Q4, pawns at QR5, K3, KB4.   Black : K at his KKt3,
Q at KR8, pawns at KB4 and KR3.   White plays K–B2,
and the King escapes to the Q side.

It remains to determine the axis of the alternating
manœuvres : it must be taken to be the diagonal Q4–KB6;
the main variation is convincing on this point, in which
(after 67 ...., Q–Q6; instead of the obviously weaker
Q–Kt8;) the Q returns from K8 to KB6 to Q4.   A most
instructive example of alternating strategy. We conclude
this chapter by giving two Game-Endings.

Game (Ending) No. 76.—Copenhagen, 1928.

Black: Strange Petersen.

1	P–QKt3	P–Q4
2	B–Kt2	B–B4
3	P–K3	P–K3
4	P–KB4	Kt–KB3
5	Kt–KB3	QKt–Q2
6	P–Kt3	B–Q3
7	B–Kt2	Q–K2
8	Castles	P–K4

My youthful antagonist plays with delightful unconcern.

9	P × P	Kt × P
10	Kt × Kt	B × Kt
11	P–Q4	B–Kt5
12	Q–Q3	B–Q3
13	P–B4	P–B3
14	P × P	P × P
15	Kt–B3	B–K3
16	Q–Kt5ch.	Q–Q2
17	P–K4	....

It would have been better to exchange Queens before playing this move.

17	....	P × P
18	Q × Qch.	B × Q

Now the King need not be troubled.

19	Kt × P	Kt × Kt
20	B × Kt	R–QKt1
21	B–Q5	Castles
22	K–Kt2	....

A preventive measure against B–R6; and restriction.

22	....	P–QKt3
23	QR–B1	QR–B1

Play on the K file seems more appropriate, e.g.: 23 ...., QR–K1; with ...., B–K3; and ......, R–K2

24	R × R	B × R
25	B–B6	....

To be followed by P–Q5, when the B and the P will make a nice picture.

25	R–Q1
26 R–B1	K–B1
27 P–Q5	B–R3
28 R–K1	P–B3
29 R–K4	B–B1
30 R–QR4	P–QR3
31 B–B3	K–B2
32 B–K1	P–R3
33 P–QKt4	B–B2
34 P–Kt5	P–QR4

Now the Bishop, firm as a rock, is on the other hand, somewhat shut in.

35 B–B2	K–B1
36 R–K4	K–B2
37 R QB4	B–B4
38 P–Kt4	B–Kt8
39 P–QR3	B–R7
40 R–Q4	B–QKt6
41 R–Q2	P–R5
42 K–B3	P Kt3
43 K–K4	....

The weaknesses in Black's position relate to squares rather than pawns. They are situated almost without exception in the K file, and White could attempt to assume control of either his K6 or K5, e.g.: B–Kt3, with an exchange of Bishops followed by K–Q4, and finally by R–K2–K6. Or P–R4, and P–Kt5. After ...., RP × P; P × P, P–B4ch.; follows K–B3, with B–K3–B4, with the exchange of Bishops and the White K will go to K5.

43 ········   P–R4

He fails to find the right plan; he should have played P–Kt4; after which the attempt on White's K5 is nipped in the bud. The attack on K6 would be warded off as follows: 43 ...., P–Kt4; 44 B–Kt3, B–Q3; 45 B × B, R × B; 46 K–Q4, K–B1; 47 R–K2, K–B2; and White can make no headway. (R–K8, R × B;). If White, after 43 ...., P–Kt4; tries 44 B–Q4, the continuation is simply ...., B–QB5; 45 R–KB2, R–Q3; (46 B–K5, R × B;). There simply is no win for White after 43 ...., P–Kt4; he has one B less in play and his QP requires protection. He certainly is strong on the K file, but this is scarcely sufficient to win.

44 P × P   P–B4ch.

After 44 ...., P × P; the method outlined above would now lead more quickly to the goal, for now the Black KRP would be the " second weakness," e.g.: 44 ...., P × P; 45 B–Kt3, B–Q3; 46 B × B, R × B; 47 K–Q4, K–B1; 48 R–K2, K–B2; and now 49 R–K3. 49 ...., B–Q8; 50 B–K8ch., K–B1; 51 B–Kt6, B–Kt6; 52 R–K8ch., followed by B–K4, with a winning game.

45 K–B3   P–Kt4

Or ...., P × P; 46 B–R4, R–Q3; 47 B–Kt3, P–B5; 48 B × P, R–B3; 49 P–Q6.

46 B–Kt3   B–Q3

If 46 ...., P–B5; obviously 47 B–B2, with P–R4, etc.

47 B × B	R × B
48 K–Kt3	K–Kt2
49 P–R4	K–R3
50 P × Pch.	K × KtP
51 K–B3	K × P
52 K–B4	K–Kt3
53 K–K5	R–Q1
54 P–Q6	K–B2
55 R–KB2	B–K3
56 R–B4 and White won.	

Game (Ending) No. 77.—Carlsbad, 1911.

White: E. Cohn.

| 63 .... | P–QR4 |

In order to provide the K with a secure retreat at QR2.

64	P–KR4	K–Kt3
65	K–R2	P–R4
66	K–Kt2	K–R3
67	R–B2	P–Kt3
68	R–B1	K–Kt2

He begins his pilgrimage to QR2.

69	R–B2	K–B2
70	K–R2	K–K2
71	R–K2	Q–B8
72	Q–B2	K–Q2
73	R–K1	Q–B3
74	K–Kt2	R–Kt5

Concentrating in turn on enemy weaknesses is one of the most effective weapons of the strategy of alternation or else ...., K–B2; could have been played at once.

| 75 R–KB1 | .... |

If 75 R–K2, (to make ...., K–B2; more difficult) then perhaps: R–K5; 76 K–R2, Q–B8; 77 K–Kt2, Q–Q8; 78 K–R2, Q–Q6; and Black's K gets to his QR2, after which matters take their course.

75	....	Q–B2
76	Q–B3	K–B1
77	Q–B2	K–Kt1
78	K–R3	K–R2
79	R–KKt1	....

White must consider the possibility of ...., P–KKt4 ;
he must allow for many threats. No wonder if matters go
awry for him in the end.

79	....	Q–Q2
80	K–R2	Q–Q3
81	K–R3	Q–QB3
82	R–K1	Q–K3
83	K–R2	Q–K5
84	K–R3	Q–K3

This manœuvring backwards and forwards has not only
a psychological value, but must be understood as a testing-
out of the terrain for elastic lines of communications.   The
idea is : will the adversary be able to keep up with the speed
of the regrouping of Black's forces ?

85	K–R2	Q–K2
86	K–R3	Q–K5
87	R–KKt1	Q–K3
88	K–R2	R–K5
89	R–QB1	....

White was afraid after 89 R–K1, of a break through by
89 ...., P–KKt4 ; 90 P × P, P–KR5 ; 91 P × P, P–B5 ;
92 P–Kt6, P–B6 ; with dangerous complications. Let the
reader examine whether this fear was well grounded.

89	....	R × KP
90	Q–B4	R–K7ch.
91	K–R3	K–R3
92	P–QKt4	P × P
93	P × P	K–Kt4
94	R–B7	Q–K5
95	Q × Q	R × Q
96	R–KKt7	R–K3
97	R–Q7	K–B5
98	K–Kt2	K × QP
99	K–B3	K–B5
100	P–Kt5	P–Q5

Resigns.

It may be that the "logos" of the win does not stand
out with the desirable clearness, but one thing is certain : the
difficulties with which the defender had to contend were such
that the question of the draw which has been suggested
simply could not arise.

This concludes the fifth part.

PART VI.

EXCURSIONS THROUGH OLD AND NEW TERRITORY OF HYPER-MODERN CHESS.

The reading of this part may lead the reader astray in making him believe that it is hyper-modern in contrast with the previous parts. No, the first five fully deserve the same appellation.

Thus "restriction" and particularly "over-protection," which can almost be called the vanguard of hyper-modern chess, are still awaiting recognition and are, as yet, not even accepted.

Thus it was with my doctrine of the centre and other canons of my system : some considerable time had to elapse before they were incorporated in hyper-modern theory.

There can be no question of any sort of contrast. The idea underlying this Part VI is partly to provide an incentive in various minor ways, but particularly to probe the value of the first revolutionary achievements at our leisure.

We look upon the pseudo-classic school (Tarrasch period) now as before as the symbol of conventionalism in Chess, whilst we are inclined to see in the hyper-modern school an earnest tendency to seek out the uttermost truth.

Frequently only a small divergence is in question, but it suffices to show us events in a warm and true light instead of the unreal and cold glare of the period of formalism.

One example will be enough. My tenet, which we give under par. 3 of this chapter, says that a solid central formation justifies a diversion on a flank, be its object ever so shadowy.

If now this "solid central formation" had to be understood in the sense of the orthodox school (therefore at least an equal number of centre pawns as the opponent's and equally far advanced), the whole precept would be wrong and unreal.

Equally so if we omit the nuance "shadowy object."

The point is, in fact, that, in this particular case, we advocate in all seriousness a haphazard attack.

Having said this, we shall now proceed to analyse the various components of Part VI.

I.—CONCERNING THE THESIS OF THE COMPARATIVE INEFFICACY OF THE MASSED PAWNS' ADVANCE.

This stratagem, first used by the author of this book in 1911, soon proved itself most productive.

Out of the original game, with the opening moves: 1 P–K4, P–QB4; 2 Kt–KB3, Kt–KB3; (Spielmann-Niemzowitsch, San Sebastian, 1911) there grew, *inter alia*, the lines of play 1 P–Q4, Kt–QB3; (Bogoljubow) and 1 P–K4, Kt–KB3; (Alekhin). To-day, provoking an advance by pawns is one of the most favoured and best-known methods of play, with which almost every player in a minor tournament is as familiar as the discoverer himself. In short, the idea, still unknown ground in 1911, to-day already belongs to the surveyed land of hyper-modernism.

Game No. 78.—Marienbad, 1925.

White: Michell.

1 P–K4	P–QB4
2 Kt–KB3	Kt–KB3
3 P–K5	Kt–Q4
4 Kt–B3	Kt × Kt

Safer is 4 ...., P–K3; 4 ...., Kt–Kt3; is also worth considering.

5 QP × Kt	P–QKt3

A conception of hyper-modern boldness: he tries artificially to retard his own development so that his opponent should commit himself prematurely, a most hazardous procedure. More correct would be 5 ...., P–Q4; e.g.: 6 P × P e.p., P × P; and the QP can be held.

6 B–Q3	....

More energetic would be 6 B–QB4, P–K3; 7 B–B4, with Q–Q2, R–Q1, or Castles QR.

6	B–Kt2
7 B–KB4	Q–B2

He still holds his hand (see note to move 5), keeps Castling on either side in reserve, as well as all possible pawn formations, hoping besides for lapses on his opponent's part.

8 B–Kt3	....

We should prefer 8 Q–K2.

8	P–K3
9 Castles	B–K2
10 Kt–Q2	....

An excellent centralising idea; the threat is now
Kt–B4–Q6, impeding Black's development.

| 10 .... | P–KR4 |

A decidedly questionable parry; a diversion on the wing
is seldom strong enough to neutralise an attack in the centre;
therefore 10 ...., Kt–B3; or 10 ...., P–Q4; deserved
the preference.

| 11 P–KR3 | P–KKt4 |
| 12 B–K4 | .... |

Why does he defer Kt–B4, and Kt–Q6ch? Let us
examine: 12 Kt–B4, P–Kt4; 13 Kt–Q6ch, B × Kt; 14 P × B,
Q–B3; 15 P–B3, P–B4; 16 B–K5, R–Kt1; 17 Q–K2, and
wins (17 ...., P QB5; 18 B × KBP, P × B;
19 B–B6 dis. ch., K–B2; 20 Q–K7ch., K–Kt3; 21 B × P,
with a winning attack), or 12 Kt–B4, Kt–B3; 13 Kt–Q6ch.,
B × Kt; 14 P × B, Q–Q1; 15 Q–K2, Q–B3; 16 B–K4, with
the superior position in the centre. Or finally 12 Kt–B4,
Kt–R3; 13 Q–K2, Castles QR; 14 Kt–R5, and White
eliminates Black's aggressive QB and preserves the better
pawn-formation. 12 Kt–B4, would therefore have been
strong.

12	Kt–B3
13 R–K1	Castles QR
14 Kt–B4	....

Now this attack dies away ineffectually.

| 14 .... | P–Kt4 |

Vacates the square QKt3 for the Queen.

15 Kt–Q6ch.	B × Kt
16 P × B	Q–Kt3
17 B–B3	....

With this he foregoes the last remains of his superiority
in the centre. 17 B–K5, was the correct move, though Black
could have fished in troubled waters with 17 ...., P–B4;
18 B × R, R × B; 19 B–Q3, P–KKt5; (e.g.: 20 P–KR4,
P–Kt6; and 21 P × P, would lose a piece because of ....,
P–B5 dis. ch.;) But after 19 B × Kt, (instead of 19 B–Q3,)
Q × B; 20 P–B3, P–Kt5; 21 R–K3 or K5, we should feel
inclined to prefer White's game. After the weaker move in
the text, the wing attack dominates the board.

17	P–KKt5
18 P × P	P × P
19 B × P	P–B4
20 B–B3	R–R2
21 K–B1	P–K4
22 B × Kt	....

There is nothing else against the double threat of P–K5;
and P–KB5.

22	Q × B
23 P–B3	P–K5
24 P × P	R–Kt1
25 B–B2	P × P
26 Q–Q2	....

Threatening the blockade by Q–K3.

26	P–K6
27 Q × P	Q × Pch.
28 K–K2	R–B2

With the pretty threat R × Bch.; Q × R, R–K1ch; K–Q1,
and then first B–B6ch.; and wins, (not at once Q × Q;
because of R–K8, mate).

| 29 K–Q1 | .... |

Threatens mate at K8.

| 29 .... | K–Kt1 |
| 30 R–KKt1 | .... |

| 30 .... | R × B |

A decisive Q sacrifice.

| 31 R × Q | R(B7) × R |

Stronger than R(Kt1) × R.

| 32 P–Kt3 | R–Kt8ch. |

and won easily.

(33 K–Q2, R(Kt1)–Kt7ch.; 34 K–Q3, R × R; etc.)

Game No. 79.—Copenhagen, 1928.

White: Werner Nielsen.

1 P–K4	P–QB4
2 Kt–KB3	Kt–KB3
3 P–K5	Kt–Q4
4 P–Q4	P × P
5 Q × P	P–K3
6 B–Q3	....

Schlechter played here 6 B–QB4, (San Sebastian, 1912) and there followed: 6 ...., Kt–QB3; 7 Q–K4, P–Q3; 8 P × P, Kt–B3; 9 Q–R4, B × P; 10 Kt–B3, Kt–K4; (emphasising White's inferiority in the centre brought about by the untimely diversion by the White Queen) 11 Kt × Kt, B × Kt; 12 Castles, Castles; 13 B–Q3, Q–Q5; (intending to reply to 14 Q–R3, with a correct pawn sacrifice, namely : 14 Q–R3, Q–KKt5; 15 B × Pch., K–R1; 16 B–B5 dis. ch., Q × Q; 17 B × Q, B × Kt; 18 P × B, P–K4; with the better game.) 14 Q × Q, B × Q; (Black's game appears to be far better centralised,) 15 Kt–Kt5, B–B4; 16 B–KB4, B–Q2; 17 QR–Q1, P–QR3; 18 B–Q6, (better 18 Kt–B3,) KR–B1; 19 B × B, B × Kt; 20 B–Q4, B × B; 21 R × B, (Schlechter's admirable chess sense is here manifest; he prefers to lose a pawn rather than to permit the Knight to be posted centrally at Black's Q4.) 21 ...., R × P; 22 R–QKt3, P–QKt4; 23 B × Kt, P × B; 24 R–Q1, QR–QB1; 25 K–B1, P–B4; (25 ...., QR–B4; 26 K–Kt1, R–B5; 27 R–KB1, and the win is just as difficult.) 26 K–K1, QR–B5; 27 R–Q2, and Schlechter obtained a draw on the 79th move, a creditable performance in view of the pawn minus.

6	Kt–B3
7 Q–K4	P–B4

Striving for hyper-modern pawn-formation, or else he could have played 7 ...., P–Q3; or 7 ...., KKt–Kt5.

8 Q–K2	....

With 8 P × P, e.p., Kt × P; 9 Q–K2, " hanging " pawns could have come about.

8	B–B4

Already the position is being explored for central points (Q5;) the more heedful ...., B–K2; would have appealed to us less.

9 Castles	Castles
10 P–QR3	Q–B2

Not 10 ...., P– QR4; which would needlessly weaken Black's QKt4.

11	P–B4	KKt–K2
12	P–QKt4	Kt–Q5

See note to Black's 8th move.

13	Kt × Kt	B × Kt
14	B–Kt2	B × B
15	Q × B	Kt–Kt3
16	R–K1	P–Kt3
17	Kt–B3	P–QR3
18	Kt–Q1	B–Kt2
19	Q–Q4	....

Better opportunities for consolidation provided: 19 P–B3, with B–B1, and Kt–B2.

19	....	QR–Q1
20	Q–Q6	....

Overlooking Black's 24th move.   The balance could have been maintained with 20 P–B5.

20	....	Q × Q
21	P × Q	B × P
22	K × B	Kt–B5ch.
23	K–B3	Kt × B
24	R–K3	P–K4

Black has a clearly won ending, but the continuation has much interest.

25	K–Kt2	Kt–B5ch.
26	K–B1	P–K5
27	P–B3	P × P
28	R × P	Kt–Kt3
29	R–B1	Kt–K4

The interesting feature is the excellent co-ordination of Knight and passed pawn: at one time the formation P at KB4 and Kt at KKt5 obtains, at another, P at KB5 and Kt at K6; at all times the Kt succeeds in laying stress on the territory gained by the pawn's advance.

30	R–K3	Kt–Kt5
31	R–K2	P–B5
32	R–KKt2	Kt–R3
33	R–B3	R–B1
34	Kt–Kt2	Kt–B4
35	R–KB2	Kt × P
36	R(B2)–B3	P–KKt4
37	R(QB3)–Q3	Kt–B4

38 R × QP	Kt–K6ch.
39 K–K1	P–Kt5
40 R–B2	P–Kt6
41 R–B3	QR–K1
Resigns.	

2. THE " ELASTIC " TREATMENT OF THE OPENING. (TRANSPOSING FROM ONE OPENING TO ANOTHER.)

This stratagem, introduced at the time by the author, was looked upon as a product of decadence. For example an amateur who played a weak enough game to enable him to conduct an important chess-column, maintained that to mask one's intentions in the opening showed a lack of pluck! In reality it is only an introduction into the opening of the principles of alternation. Although employed on several occasions as early as 1907, 1910 and 1911, (see games 4, 53 and 19), this stratagem is, as yet, not fully explored. Little known, for instance, is the following method tried by the author: (I.) White: Grünfeld, Breslau, 1925. 1 P–Q4, Kt–KB3; 2 P–QB4, P–K3; 3 Kt–KB3, P–QKt3; 4 P–KKt3, and now B–R3; the idea is as follows: 3 ...., P–QKt3; aimed at centralisation by B–Kt2; in order to weaken the effect of this move White played 4 P–KKt3, intending B–Kt2, but at the same time left his QBP uncovered. This was a signal for the second player to start an attack against his QB5. 5 Q–R4, P–B3; 6 B–Kt2, P–QKt4; 7 P × P, P × P; 8 Q–Q1, B–Kt2; and Black, having eliminated White's QBP has at least an equal game.

(II.) White: Grünfeld, Semmering, 1926. 1 P–Q4, Kt–KB3; 2 P–QB4, P–K3; 3 Kt–KB3, P–QKt3; 4 P–KKt3, B–K2; 5 B–Kt2, Castles; 6 Castles, B–R3; 7 QKt–Q2, P–B3; 8 P–Kt3, P–Q4; 9 B–Kt2, QKt–Q2; 10 R–B1, R–B1; 11 Q–B2, P–B4; with a completed development.

If we examine both the above examples from the point of view of their strategical features, we realise that the essential component parts of alternating play, namely the two weak points and the axis, are present. The central threat by B–QKt2; represent one weakness, the prospective attack on White's QBP the other. The axis is the "White" square complex QB4–Q5 and QR6–QKt7. As illustrations of the stratagem which interests us here, we give the games 80 to 83, all of which show a blending of the Indian and the Dutch openings. It is to be noted that this fusion relates not only to the opening phase, but comprises also various middle-game themes. The Indo-Dutch combination (parent game Bernstein-Nimzowitsch, St. Petersburg 1914), was at the time the first of its kind and, so to speak, opened the door to the new method of play.

Game No. 80.—New York, 1927.

White: Dr. Vidmar.

1	P–Q4	Kt–KB3
2	Kt–KB3	P–K3
3	P–B4	B–Kt5ch.
4	B–Q2	Q–K2

This innovation, introduced by the author, does not in any way indicate an early commitment to a particular line of opening: the Queen is well-placed at K2 in any case—Indian or Dutch.

5	Kt–B3	....

Slightly better would be 5 P–KKt3.

5	....	Castles
6	P–K3	P–Q3

Black is still at the crossroads between Dutch (P–QKt3; and B–Kt2;) and Indian (P–B4; or P–K4; with Kt–B3;) the decision is taken on the next move.

7	B–K2	....

He foregoes 7 B–Q3, which must count as a success for Black's alternating policy. If 7 B–Q3, P–K4.

7	....	P–QKt3
8	Castles	B–Kt2
9	Q–B2	QKt–Q2
10	QR–Q1	B × QKt
11	B × B	Kt–K5
12	B–K1	P–KB4

He turns completely Dutch.

13	Q–Kt3	....

The idea of this slightly puzzling move is to keep his KP covered, e.g., after Kt–Q2, Kt × Kt; R × Kt, Q–Kt4; P–B3, and the KP is covered.

13	....	P–B4

With this move the Dutch formation is completed: point K5, and the pawn at QB4 for attack or defence, (stopping White's P–B5).

14	Kt–Q2	Kt × Kt
15	R × Kt	P–K4
16	P × KP	P × P
17	P–B3	P–KKt4

Black's task is now to manage his wing attack in such a way that his opponent cannot in the meantime break through on the Q file.

18	B–B2	Kt–B3
19	KR–Q1	QR–K1
20	Q–R4	B–R1
21	R–Q6	………

Insufficient would be the sacrifice of the exchange by 21 R–Q7, Kt × R; 22 R × Kt, because of ………, Q–B3; 23 Q × P, and now simply ………, P–R3.

21	………	Q–KKt2
22	B–B1	………

A better defence is available by 22 B–K1, e.g.: 22 ………, P–K5; 23 B–B3, or if 22 ………, P–Kt5; 23 P × P, Kt × P; 24 R–Q7, Q–Kt4; 25 B × Kt, Q × B; 26 Q–B2.

22	………	P–K5
23	B–K1	P × P
24	B–B3	………

Now this digression comes too late, as the pretty reply demonstrates.

24	………	Q–K2

Now 25 B × Kt, would lead to a mate: 25 ………, Q × Pch.; 26 K–R1, P × Pch.; with ………, Q–K8ch.

25	R(Q6)–Q3	P × P
26	B × P	B × B
27	B × Kt	………

If 27 K × B, Q–K5ch; with a short and decisive attack.

27	Q–K5
28 R(Q1)–Q2	B–R6
29 B–B3	Q–Kt5ch.

and mate in two.

Game No. 81.—Kecskemet, 1927.

White: Przepiorka.

1 P–Q4	Kt–KB3
2 Kt–KB3	P–K3
3 P–B4	P–QKt3
4 Kt–B3	B–Kt2
5 Q–B2	B–Kt5
6 P–QR3	....

This move looks very much like the loss of a tempo. Why not 6 P–KKt3?

| 6 .... | B × Ktch. |
| 7 Q × B | P–Q3 |

Better than 7 ...., Kt–K5; at once, e.g.: 8 Q–B2, P–Q3; 9 P–KKt3, Kt–Q2; 10 B–Kt2, and, in view of the threatened Kt–Kt5, Black would be forced to play the defensive and uninviting 10 ...., R–QKt1; the transition to the second phase of the opening must not be too sudden.

8 P–KKt3	QKt–Q2
9 B–Kt2	Q–K2
10 Castles	Castles KR
11 P–QKt4	Kt–K5

Only now is the proper time!

12 Q–B2	P–KB4
13 Kt–Kt5	QKt–B3
14 Kt × Kt	....

Preferable would be 14 P–B3, Kt × Kt; 15 B × Kt, P–K4; 16 P–K3, with drawing chances.

14	B × Kt
15 B × B	Kt × B
16 P–B3	Kt–B3
17 B–Kt2	R–B2

But not 17 ...., P–QR4; 18 B–B3, and Black would only have committed himself needlessly.

| 18 QR–B1 | .... |

Correct was R–B2.

18	QR–KB1
19 Q–Q3	P–KR4
20 P–K4	....

If this were feasible, Black's preventive scheme
(R–B2; and QR–KB1;) would have been useless. But the
move is not playable, and the KB file which he opens so
light-heartedly makes short work of his chances. A little
better would be 20 P–K3, though White would still be at a
disadvantage after 20 ...., P–R5; 21 K–Kt2, Kt–R4.

| 20 .... | P × P |
| 21 P × P | Kt–Kt5 |

The execution so kindly predicted in the preceding note
now begins.

22 P–R3	Kt–B7
23 Q–K2	Kt × Pch.
24 K–R1	Q–Kt4
25 R × R	R × R
26 Q–Kt2	Kt–B7ch.
27 K–Kt1	Q–K6

Resigns.

In order to understand this game as a whole, it is
necessary to grasp the connection between Black's waiting
and attacking strategy: all the Black waiting moves (7, 17
and 18) were made, so to speak, only so that the powerful
19 ...., P–R5; should gain in effect. Viewed in this
light, the enormous power of this move becomes clear.   A
victory of alternating strategy applied to the opening.

Game No. 82.—New York, 1927.

Black: Spielmann.

1 Kt–KB3	P–Q4
2 P–QKt3	P–QB4
3 B–Kt2	Kt–QB3
4 P–K3	Kt–B3
5 B–Kt5	B–Q2
6 Castles	P–K3
7 P–Q3	B–K2
8 QKt–Q2	Castles
9 B × QKt	B × B
10 Kt–K5	....

Arriving at the Dutch formation.

| 10 .... | R–B1 |

H. Wolf, Carlsbad, 1923, played here ...., Kt–Q2;
and there followed 11 QKt–B3, R–B1; 12 Q–K2, Kt×Kt;
13 Kt×Kt, B–K1; 14 Q–Kt4, P–B4; 15 Q–K2, B–B3;
16 P–QB4, Q–K2; 17 P–B4. In the sequel White initiated
a strong attack with P–KR3, K–R2, R–B2, R–KKt1,
P–KKt4, and won.

11 P–KB4	Kt–Q2
12 Q–Kt4	Kt×Kt

If 12 ...., P–B4; 13 Q × Pch., K × Q; 14 Kt × Bdis.ch.,
B–B3; 15 Kt×Q, B×B; 16 Kt×Pch., and wins.

13 B×Kt	....

The alternative 13 P × Kt, could also be played, e.g.:
13 ...., B–Q2; 14 R–B3, P–B4; 15 P×P e.p., B×P;
16 B×B, R×B; 17 R×R, Q×R; 18 R–KB1, Q–K4;
19 Q–KB4, Q×Q; 20 P×Q, with a slight superiority in the
centre, (Kt–B3–K5,). Or 13 P × Kt, Q–R4; 14 R–B2, and
White has to choose between P–K4, followed by P × P, (the
Black B must now recapture) equalising the game or the
manœuvre 15 Kt–B1, followed by Kt–Kt3, and Kt–R5.
Compare notes to the Diagram in the following game.

13	B–B3
14 R–B3	B × B
15 P × B	Q–B2

Now 15 ...., Q–R4; would be useless because of
R–Kt3, and Kt–B3.

16 Q–R5	P–KR3

The liberating move ...., P–B4; is not yet possible,
(e.g.: 16 ...., P–B4; 17 P×P e.p., R×P; 18 R×R,
P×R; 19 Q–Kt4ch.,) but Black should have prepared for it
by 16 ...., B–K1; 17 R–R3, P–KR3; 18 Kt–B3, P–B4;
and White's attack would have been difficult to carry out.

17 QR–KB1	P–KKt3

A clear superiority in the centre could have been attained
by White against 17 ...., B–K1; (instead of P–KKt3;)
e.g.: 17 ......, B–K1; 18 R–Kt3, P–B4; 19 Q×KRP, Q×P;
(threatening ...., Q×R;) 20 Q–B4, Q–B3; 21 Kt–B3.
Less clear, after 17 ...., B–K1; would be the sacrificial
continuation 18 R–B6, Q–R4; (always the same sortie by
the Queen!) 19 R×RP, P×R; etc.

18 Q×P	Q×P
19 R–B6	Q–R4

White threatened to become unpleasant after P–KKt4,
and R(B1)–B3–R3. The move costs a pawn and Black
struggles on for a long time, but without avail.

20	Q × Q	P × Q
21	Kt–B3	R–B2
22	R–R6	P–B3
23	Kt–R4	B–K1
24	R(R6) × BP	R × R
25	R × R	R–K2
26	K–B2	....

White must manœuvre on the Black squares, as required by the " logos " of the game. The fact that White preferred to win the KBP rather than the KRP seems to indicate that the first player did not misjudge the situation. A weak move at a later stage, however, unnecessarily prolonged Black's resistance.

26	....	K–Kt2
27	R–B4	B–Q2
28	K–K2	....

This is the mistake. He should have played K–K1. The inherent strength of the Black squares manifests itself most impressively. (" Play on Black squares " would incline one to think only of K5 or KKt5.)

28	....	P–K4
29	R–B5	R–K1

The position of the White King now precludes 30 R × RP.

30	R–B2	P–K5
31	R–B4	....

Slowly but surely he creates again a foundation on Black squares.

31	....	R–K4
32	K–Q2	P–Kt4
33	P–Kt3	B–R6

The Knight is now temporarily a prisoner.

34	P–Q4	P × P
35	P × P	R–Kt4
36	P–B3	P–R4
37	R–B2	P–R5
38	K–K3	P–R6

39	R–B2	B–B8
40	R–B1	B–Q6
41	Kt–Kt2	....

The position is reversed. Now the Bishop is the prisoner and the Knight dances around swinging the cudgel.

41	....	R–B4
42	Kt–B4	K–B2
43	R–Q1	....

Now Kt × B, is threatened which was inadmissible before because of ...., R–B6ch.

43	....	K–K2
44	Kt × B	P × Kt
45	P–QKt4	....

Frees the square QKt3 for his King. The QP can wait.

45	....	K–Q3
46	K × P	R–B7
47	R–Q2	R–B6ch.
48	K–B2	K–K3
49	R–K2ch.	K–Q3
50	K–Kt3	R–Q6
51	R–K5	P–R5
52	P × P	R–R6
53	R–R5	K–B3
54	R–R6ch.	K–B2
55	P–R5	Resigns.

Game No. 83.—Semmering, 1926.

Black: Rubinstein.

The first nine moves as in the preceding game.

| 10 | Kt–K5 | B–K1 |
| 11 | P–KB4 | Kt–Q2 |

It will repay the trouble to spend some time on the possible continuation 12 Q–Kt4, Kt × Kt; 13 P × Kt, Q–R4; (more aggressive than ...., B–Q2; and ...., P–B4;) 14 R–B2, (the manœuvre Kt–B1–Kt3, is projected,) 14 ...., Q–Kt5; 15 P–K4, B QB3; (best; only centralisation can lead to anything.) 16 P–QR3, Q–R4; 17 P × P, B × P; (17 ...., P × P; appears to be bad because of 18 P–K6, P–B3; 19 Kt B3, threatening Kt–R4–B5,) 18 Kt–B1, (the preventive 18 P–QR4, directed against ...., P–QKt4; would, on the other hand, let in ...., Q–Kt5;) 18 ...., Q–B2; (not 18........., P–QKt4; because of 19 P–QR4, and the Black Q side is crippled,) 19 Kt–K3, P–QKt4; (the typical counter-chance ...., P–B5; is to be made possible at all cost—even by a pawn sacrifice!) 20 Kt × B, P × Kt; 21 P–K6, P–B3; 22 QR–KB1, and White gets there first, e.g.: 22 ...., K–R1; 23 R–B3, followed by R–R3.   This analysis seems to show that 12 Q–Kt4, would have been promising.

12 Kt × Kt	Q × Kt
13 P–K4	P–B3
14 Q–B3	....

The formation is now more of an Indian character.

| 14 .... | B–B2 |
| 15 P–QR4 | .... |

There is no preventive measure enduringly effective against ...., P–QB5.

| 15 .... | P–QKt3 |

Not 15 ...., P–QR3; because of 16 P–R5, with paralysing effect.

| 16 QR–K1 | P–QR3 |

Instead of 16 QR–K1, the serried advance P–KKt4, P–R4, and P–Kt5, would have been possible. Whether 16 R–R2, with 17 KR–R1, came in question as a preventive

manœuvre against Black's threat of ...., P–QR3; and
........., P–QKt4; is an open question   How could Black
make headway in that case?

   17 P–B5   P×KP

  Bad would be 17 ...., P×BP; 18 P×QP, B×P;
19 R×B.

   18 Q×P   P–K4
   19 R–K3   ....

In order to open fire against the hostile K side which
looks cramped; but the attack is not easy to conduct,
especially on account of the White Queen being out of place,
(K4 would be a far more suitable square for the Kt). Instead
of 19 R–K3, we should suggest therefore the following
re-grouping: 19 Q–R4, P–QKt4; 20 Kt–K4, P–B5;
21 KtP×P, P×BP; 22 R–K3, and threatens to continue
with R–R3, P–R3; R–Kt3, etc.   This re-grouping would
combine attack with just a sufficient defence of his own
Q side.

   19 ....   P–QKt4
   20 R–Kt3   ....

Threatens to win a piece by Q–KKt4, P–Kt3; P×P,
Q×Q; P×Bch, and R×Q.

   20 ....   K–R1
   21 Kt–B3   ....

It would still have been expedient to play Q–KKt4, and
Kt–K4.

   21 ....   P×P

A mistake; he should have played ...., B–Q3.

   22 Kt×P   Q–K1

  If 22 ...., P×Kt; 23 Q×P, B–B3; 24 Q×B, P×Q;
25 B×P, mate.

23 Q–KKt4	R–KKt1
24 Kt × B ch.	Q × Kt
25 Q × RP	....

Now White has an extra pawn and the pleasant choice between a mating attack and a winning end-game, (Black's QRP and QBP are bad weaknesses) : in short, White's game is as good as won.

25	Q–Q4
26 Q–KKt4	B–Q1
27 Q–Kt6	P–R3
28 R–K1	Q–Q2
29 R–K6	....

Simpler would be 29 R–K4, with complete command of the board. The text move, intending R × KBP, should win still more quickly.

29	P–B5
30 KtP × P	....

Partly in vexation at having allowed this break-through, (when prophylaxis by 29 R–K4, was so palpable), and partly through the strong belief in the potency, proved by past chess history, of ...., P–B5 ; White has not the courage to carry out the intended winning manœuvre.   He was, besides, short of time.   The game could have been won by : 30 R × KBP, B × R ; 31 B × B, P × B ; 32 Q × RP ch., Q–R2 ; 33 Q × P ch., R–Kt2 ; 34 R–Kt6, P × Kt P ; 35 P × P, K–Kt1 ; 36 R–R6, R–B2 ; 37 Q–Kt5 ch., R–Kt2 ; 38 Q B4, and wins.

30	R–Kt1
31 B–B3	R–Kt8 ch.
32 R–K1	B–Kt3 ch.

It is extraordinary that this plausible check should throw away the draw which could have been obtained here by 32 ...., R × R ; 33 B × R, Q–R5 ; etc.

33 K–B1	R × R ch.
34 B × R	....

The resourceful Bishop steers for, *inter alia*, B2 and Kt4.

34	Q–R5

If 34 ...., R–K1 ; 35 B–Kt4, and ...., Q–K2 ; is prevented.

35 R–R3   R–KB1

Against any other move by the R, the sacrifice at R6 is decisive, e.g.: 35 ...., R–K1; 36 R × Pch., P × R; 37 Q × RPch., K–Kt1; 38 Q–Kt6ch., K–R1; 39 Q × Pch., followed by Q × B.

36 B–B3   B–Q1

The final error. Black had still a small chance of a draw by 36 ...., Q × P(B7); 37 R × Pch., P × R; 38 Q × RPch., K–Kt1; 39 Q–Kt6ch., K–R1; 40 B × Pch., R × B; 41 Q × Rch., K–Kt1; 42 Q × B, Q × QPch.; and the Q ending is not without certain difficulties for White.

37 B–Q2   Q × P(B7)

And now we have an ending in which one expects a banal manœuvre with a discovery, only to be most agreeably surprised.

38 B × P   Q–Kt8ch.
39 K–K2   Q–B7ch.
40 K–K3   ....

The point. Not so good would be 40 B–Q2 dis. ch., because of 40 ...., K–Kt1; 41 R–R7, R–B2; threatening R–K2ch.; etc.

40 ....   B–Kt3ch.

Or 40 ...., Q–B8ch.; 41 K–K4, Q–K8ch; 42 R–K3, Q–R5ch.; 43 K–Q5, P × B; 44 R–R3, and wins.

41 K–K4   Q–K7ch.
42 R–K3   Resigns

3.—WING PLAY AND THE CENTRE.

Which is better (in the American sense of the word, therefore of great practical importance for achieving the desired end), attack in the centre or diversion on the wing? This is a moot point. It is fairly obvious that flank-attacks can be undertaken only when the position in the centre is sufficiently strong; but the question is: what constitutes a sufficiently strong centre?

The assumption that, in positions characterised by the pawn formations: White, pawns at Q4, QB4, K3; Black, pawns at Q4, QB3, K3, the advance P–B5, is refuted by the counter-thrust ...., P–K4; has been proved by the author, as early as 1913, as by no means unassailable (see My System, p. 314). The move ...., P–K4; (or ...., P–KB4; in the position: White, pawns at K4, Q5, KB2; Black, pawns at Q3, K4, KB2,) must be regarded as a normal re-action, but there can hardly be a question of refutation. The respective prospects of the pawn-chains (and in both examples the closing-up achieved by P–B5 and P–Q5 respectively) leads automatically to chain formations) must be deemed to be approximately equal. This, my contention, has long been accepted. I myself had been converted to this view as long ago as 1907. Examine the opening of my game v. Tschigorin, Carlsbad, 1907. 1 P–Q4, P–Q4; 2 Kt–KB3, B–Kt5; 3 Kt–K5, B–B4; 4 P–QB4, P–K3; 5 Kt–QB3, (if 5 Q–Kt3, Kt–QB3;) P–QB3; 6 Q–Kt3, Q–Kt3; 7 B–B4, Kt–B3; 8 P–B5, Q × Q; 9 P × Q, QKt–Q2; 10 P–QKt4, Kt–R4; 11 Kt × Kt, K × Kt; 12 B–Q2, (White gives no thought to the prevention of .... P–K4;) B–K2; 13 P–Kt5, Kt–B3; 14 P–K3, P–K4; (what boots it?) 15 B–K2, Kt–K1; now Black even loses a pawn. The attack begun with ...., P–K4; might have continued with ...., P–K5; or ...., P × QP (instead of ...., Kt–K1;) but could not in any way shake White's central position. After 15 ...., Kt–K1; the continuation was 16 P × Pch., P × P; 17 P × P, and 17 ...., B × P; is not playable, as it would lose the exchange by 18 Kt–R4, and Kt–Kt6ch.

The modern view is clearly to look upon any sound central position as defensible, be it ever so cramped. A conspicuous example is Game 85, in which I follow my maxim "a solid central formation justifies a diversion on the wing, be its object ever so shadowy," by undertaking on a flank a most peculiar, some would say bizarre, attack.

A further pioneering postulate will be found by the reader in Game 88. It runs as follows: "An eye on the flank, the mind on the centre, that is the deepest meaning of positional play."

We shall now pass on to the following games which the modern-minded reader should play over with care.

Game No. 84.—Copenhagen, 1924.

Black: Allan Nilsson.

1	Kt–KB3	Kt–KB3
2	P–B4	P–B3
3	P–K3	P–Q4
4	B–K2	B–B4
5	Kt–B3	P–K3
6	P–Q4	....

By devious ways a very well-known formation has arisen.

6	....	B–Q3

Better would be first ...., QKt–Q2.

7	Q–Kt3	Q–Kt3

Preferable would be ...., Q–B1.

8	P–B5	Q×Q
9	P×Q	B–B2
10	P–QKt4	....

White ignores the coming counter-attack (........, P–K4;) with an easy conscience about his own centre, for even if Black "achieves" ...., P–K4; nothing is yet achieved. The further advance ...., P–K5; (........, P×P; is certainly harmless) would only lead to a mummification which might be terminated by the KBP (........, P–KB4–B5;) but only at the cost of far too much time. Thus ...., P–K4; is revealed as harmless and White can ruthlessly prosecute his flank attack.

10	....	QKt–Q2
11	P–Kt5	K–K2
12	P–QKt4	P–QR4

An ingenious attempt to open up the game. With any other continuation White's game is clearly superior.

13	P×P e.p.	P×P

14 Kt–KR4 ....

Taking the RP is hardly to be recommended, e.g., 14 R×P, R×R; 15 B×R, R–QKt1; 16 P–Kt5, Kt–K5; 17 B–Q2, Kt×Kt; 18 B×Kt, B–Q6. On the other hand R–R4, to cover the KtP must be deemed inferior as, in some variations, White must be able to reply to ...., P–QR4; with P–Kt5. The R file must therefore be given up in order to secure the base QKt1 instead.

14	KR–QKt1
15 Kt×Bch.	P×Kt
16 R–QKt1	Kt–K5
17 Kt×Kt	BP×Kt

It now looks as if ...., P–K4–K5; had actually been played.

18 K–Q2 ....

Making for QB2 in order to protect the QR thoroughly.

18 .... R–Kt2

If 18 ...., P–QR4; 19 P–Kt5, P×P; 20 R×P, R×R; 21 B×R, R–QKt1; 22 B R4, R–Kt5; 23 B–B2, threatening B–K3, and White's game is preferable.

19 K–B2 Kt–B3

In order to play the Kt to QKt4 via K1 and B2. The initiative by means of 19 ...., R(R1)–KKt1; 20 B–Q2, P–QR4; would fail against 21 P×P, (this shows how sound it was to protect the QR adequately).

| 20 B–Q2 | Kt–K1 |
| 21 R–R1 | .... |

First consolidation, then attack!

| 21 .... | R(Kt2)–R2 |
| 22 P–B3 | .... |

This opens not only the KB file for his Rooks, but also the diagonal K1–KR4 for his QB.

22	P–B4
23 P×P	BP×P
24 R–R2	B–Q1
25 KR–R1	Kt–B2
26 B–K1	....

This wrecks Black's pretty defensive play.

26	Kt–Kt4
27 B–R4ch.	K–K1
28 B×B	K×B
29 B×Kt	BP×B
30 K–Q2	....

The point of the exchanges. The King hastens to the
K side in order to support the Rook which is to break into
the KB file. Later on the KRP will lend a hand (see note
to White's 37th move), whilst, against this, the Black pieces
do not succeed in getting into concerted action.

30	………	K–K2
31	K–K2	K–K3
32	K–B2	K–Q2
33	R–R5	………

A blockading move with a prospective threat of R × KtP.

33	………	K–B3
34	K–Kt3	K–Kt2
35	R–KB1	K–B3
36	R–B5	R–K2
37	P–R4	………

Threatening P–R5–R6, with R–B6ch., to follow.

37	………	R(R1)–R2

He gives up his first rank, but if ………, R–Q2; R–K5.

38	P–R5	R–K3

If 38 ……… P–R3; either 39 K–R4, with P–Kt4–Kt5, or
39 R–B8, K–Kt2; 40 R–Q8, would win. Black has too many
weaknesses.

39	R–B8	………

The rest is a question of technique.

39	………	P–Kt3
40	P–R6	P–Kt4
41	R–QKt8	K–B2
42	R(Kt8) × P	R × P
43	R–R4	R–KB3

Or 43 ………, R–Kt2; 44 R(Kt5)–R5.

44	R(Kt5)–R5	K–B1
45	K–Kt4	………

To lure the pawn on to KR3.

45	………	P–R3
46	R–R2	R(R2)–KB2

If 46 ………, R–QKt2; 47 R × P, R × R; 48 R × R,
R × P; 49 R × P, (compare note to move 45) R–Kt6;
50 R–R3, and wins.

47	R × P	R × R
48	R × R	R–B7
49	P–Kt3	R–QKt7
50	R × P	R–Kt6

Or 50 ………, R × P; 51 K × P, R–Kt6; 52 K–B4.

51	R–Q6	R × KP
52	R × P	R–Q6
53	P–Kt5	P–Q6
54	K–B3	Resigns.

Game No. 85.—Carlsbad, 1923.

White: Yates.

1	Kt–KB3	P–K3
2	P–KKt3	P–Q4
3	B–Kt2	P–QB3

Black tries to anticipate White's P–QB4.

| 4 | P–Q3 | .... |

After 4 P–Q4, B–Q3; could be played with 5 B–B4, B × B; 6 P × B, Kt–KR3; with Kt–B4; and Black has a sound position.

4	....	B–Q3
5	Kt–B3	Kt–K2
6	Castles	Castles
7	P–K4	....

| 7 | .... | P–QKt4 |

Black appreciates that his central position is sound and well-knit and feels justified thereby in launching forth a flank-attack. Unsettling the Knight by ...., P–Kt5; when occasion arises is the first step.

| 8 | Kt–K1 | P–KB4 |

He could have afforded some such move as ...., P–QR4; as the operations planned by his opponent in the centre are evidently of little moment.

| 9 | P × QP | .... |

A bad mistake would be 9 P–B4, because of QP × P;
10 P × P, P–Kt5; with ...., B–B4ch.; (it can be seen
that the " threat " ...., P–Kt5; has already taken effect).

| 9 .... | KP × P |

Black now has a good game.

| 10 Kt–K2 | .... |

To stop ...., P–B5.

| 10 .... | Kt–Q2 |
| 11 B–B4 | .... |

The play against the " Black squares " is soon seen to
be ill-advised.   The correct continuation was 11 P–QB4,
Kt–QKt3; with fairly even chances.

| 11 .... | Kt–QKt3 |

The continuation of a flank attack begun with 7 ....,
P–QKt4; incidentally it anticipates a possible P–QB4, by
White.

12 Q–Q2	Kt–Kt3
13 P–KR4	Kt × B
14 Kt × Kt	Q–B3

The play against White's Q side begins at last to take
tangible form; a loosening (P–QB3) is to be brought on.

| 15 P–QB3 | .... |

Or 15 R–Kt1, B–Q2; with ...., QR–K1; and Black
has a good game.

| 15 .... | B × Kt ? |

Instead of this exchange which serves only to weaken
his K4, Black should have selected the continuation
........., B–Q2; and ...., QR–K1.   Later on he could have
considered ...., P–QR4; and ...., P–Kt5.

| 16 Q × B | Kt–R5 |
| 17 R–Kt1 | .... |

Now White's Knight threatens to settle at K5, (P–Q4,
Kt–B3, Kt–K5).

17 ....   Kt–B4

Black's mistake on the 15th move has altered the whole situation to such an extent that the flank-attack, which only a short while ago, with a solid central formation, had to be taken seriously, now appears only as a shattered body of troops helplessly beating the air—a better move would have been : 17 ...., B–R3 ; e.g. : 17 ...., B–R3 ; 18 Kt–B3, QR–K1 ; 19 KR–K1, (19 P–Q4 ?, P–Kt5 ; 20 KR–B1, B–Q6 ; with ...., Kt × KtP ;) 19 ...., R × Rch. ; 20 Kt × R, R–K1 ; 21 Kt–B3, Kt–B4 ; 22 R–Q1, B–Kt2 ; and the games would be nearly equalised, although the weakness of the Black squares at White's K5, Q6, QB7, and Q4, would still weigh in the balance, e.g. : 23 Q–B7, Q–Q1 ; (or 23 ...., Q–K2 ; 24 Q–R5, with continued molestation) 24 Q × Q, R × Q ; 25 Kt–Q4, (25 Kt–K5, Kt–Q2 ;) P–Kt3 ; 26 P–QKt4, Kt–R5 ; 27 R–QB1, K–B2 ; 28 Kt–Kt3, and Black would be beset with difficulties, as both P–QB4, and Kt–R5, are threatened. Nevertheless, we feel inclined to look upon 17 ...., B–R3 ; as relatively the best defence.

18 Q–K3   ....

He entirely misapprehends the significance of the Black Diagonal KB4 to QB7. At all hazards he should have played 18 R–Q1. If then 18 ...., Kt–K3 ; then 19 Q–Q6.

18 ....   Q–Q3

Very good. The variation 18 ...., Kt–K3 ; would also have led to equalisation ; e.g. : 19 P–KB4, P–Q5 ; 20 P × P, Q × P ; 21 Q × Q, Kt × Q ; 22 Kt–B3, Kt × Ktch. ; 23 B × Kt, B–Kt2 ; although White may be better by a shade. With the text-move a complete retrieval of the threatened Black squares could have been achieved.

19 P–KB4   B–R3

Interesting but not the right line ! 19 ...., Kt–Q2 ; should have been played ; e.g. : 20 Kt–B3, Kt–B3 ; 21 Kt–K5, Kt–Kt5 ; 22 Q–K2, B–Q2 ; 23 P–Q4, (otherwise ...., P–Q5 ;) P–QR4 ; 24 QR–K1, KR–K1 ; 25 Q–Q3, P–R5 ; (secures the Q side against P–Kt3, and P–B4, eventually,) and Black's position appears to be fully consolidated.

20 Kt–B3	P–Kt5
21 KR–Q1	P × P
22 P × P	Kt–R5
23 Q–Q4	Q–R6

Black's attack looks promising, but it lacks a sound basis: his central formation is not solid enough. From which the moral can be drawn: after the mistake 15 ...., B × Kt; which weakened his centre, Black should no longer have played for the flank-attack; he should have been exclusively bent on consolidation, (with the help of a strategic retreat, see note to move 18).

As played, White should have obtained the advantage.

24 Kt–K5 ....

The correct continuation was 24 R–Q2, Kt × P; 25 R–Kt3, Q–B8ch.; 26 K–R2, Kt–Kt4; 27 Q–Kt4, threatening P–R4, and R–Kt1. This would have given White the advantage. The ingenious move in the text prepares a "*coup de main*" which is to secure for the Knight his long-desired Siegfried line (K5).

24	Kt × P
25 R–K1	Kt × R
26 R × Kt	....

The tempting 26 B × Pch., P × B; 27 Q × Pch., K–R1; 28 Kt–B7ch., R × Kt; 29 Q × Rch., R–B1; 30 R–K8, fails because of 30 ...., Q–B4ch.; followed by ...., K–Kt1.

26	K–R1
27 P–R5	Q–Q3
28 K–B2	....

Here the blockade system, beginning with R–QB1, and R–B5, is far better than the attempted attack begun with the text-move.

| 28 .... | QR–K1 |

A covert sacrificial combination.

29	P–R6	Q × P
30	R–KR1	Q–B3
31	Q × RP	R × Kt
32	P × R	Q × P
33	Q × B	Q–Q5ch.

Against an immediate ...., P–B5; White could have defended himself better, namely: P × P, R × Pch.; B–B3, or P × P, Q × Pch.; K–Kt1.

34	K–B1	P–B5
35	Q–R3	K–Kt1
36	R–R4	....

An ingenious thought. If ...., P × P dis. ch.; Q × Rch., wins.

36	....	P–Kt4
37	R–Kt4	Q–R8ch.
38	K–B2	P × P dbl. ch.
39	K × P	Q K4ch.
40	K–R3	P–R4
41	R QR4	P–Kt5ch.
42	K R4	R–B4

The Black King can look after himself.

43	R–R8ch.	K–Kt2
44	Q–R7ch.	K–R3
45	Q–Kt1	Q–B3ch.

And mate by ...., R–B6ch.; B × R, Q × Bch.; K–R2, Q–R6; mate.

This game was awarded a first brilliancy prize.

Game No. 86.—Copenhagen, 1928.

Black: Gemsöe.

1	P–K3	P–KKt3
2	P–QB3	Kt–KB3
3	P–Q4	B–Kt2
4	B–B4	....

To provoke ...., P–Q4; but ...., P–Q3; which White seems to fear, would have been quite bearable, e.g.: 4 B–Q3, P–Q3; 5 Kt–K2, with a formation similar to that in the preceding game.

4	....	P–Q4
5	B–K2	QKt–Q2

Here 5 ...., Kt–B3; could be entertained.

6 Kt–B3	Castles
7 Castles	R–K1
8 P–QKt4	………

The same stratagem as in No. 85. He deems himself secure against ………, P–K4; or ………, Kt–K5; (he would not contest his K5,) and therefore he sounds the attack.

8 ………	Kt–K5
9 P–QR4	P–KB4
10 P–R5	………

This controls Black's QKt3, but, as will soon be seen, it also creates a point of inertia at White's QKt5. 10 P–B4, would therefore have been preferable.

10 ………	P–QR3
11 B–Kt2	P–B3
12 Kt–K1	Kt–Q3

If 12 ………, P–K4; 13 Kt–Q3, and 14 P–KB4, with Kt–K5, and consolidation.

13 P–QB4	Kt × P
14 B × Kt	P × B
15 Q–B2	Kt–B3

Not good; compare the following note. Correct was P–K4; to make room for both Bishops. The following is also playable: 15 ………, P–QKt4; 16 P × P, e.p., Kt × P; 17 Kt–R3, B–K3; 18 Kt–B3, K–R1; 19 Kt–Q2, R–QKt1; for the transaction 20 Kt(R3) × P, Kt × Kt; 21 Kt × Kt, R × P; 22 Kt–K5, would be quite pleasing for Black after 22 ………, B × Kt; with 23 R–B5.

16 Kt–Q2	B–K3
17 Kt × P	………

We should prefer Kt(K1)–B3.

17 ………	Q–B2

The attempt to capture the White squares with 17 ………, B × Kt; 18 Q × B, Kt–Q4; would probably fail because of 19 Kt–Q3, with QR–K1, P–B3, and P–K4. Therefore 15 ………, Kt–B3; appears to be refuted.

18 Kt–Q3	QR–Q1
19 Kt–B4	B–Q4
20 Kt–K5	………

White's threat lies in the sequence QR–K1, P–B3, and P–K4; it is difficult to find an antidote.

20 ………	B–R3
21 QR–K1	………

More careful would be 21 Kt(B4)–Q3.

| 21   .... | R–KB1 |

B × Kt; and P–K3; would have made a strong resistance possible.

| 22   P–B3 | .... |

First Kt(B4)–Q3, would have been better.

| 22   .... | K–Kt2 |

Here again B × Kt; was better.

| 23   Kt(B4)–Q3 | B–Kt1 |
| 24   P–K4 | .... |

Now White has the better game.

| 24   .... | Q–B1 |
| 25   Kt–B5 | .... |

Reviving memories of the by-gone flank-attack. But 25 Q–K2, and 26 P–Kt4, would also have been very strong, e.g.: 25 Q–K2, K–R1; 26 P–Kt4, B–Kt2; 27 KP × P, P × P; 28 P–Kt5, Kt–Q4; 29 P–B4, and White has a K side attack.

25	K–R1
26 Q B2	K–Kt2
27 P × P	....

Now that the second player has lost all hold on the White squares, White should win without difficulty, especially as he practically dominates the Black square. For instance, 27 P–Q5, would be decisive, e.g.: 27 P × QP; 28 P × BP, P × P; 29 B–Q4, and Black is defenceless against P–B4, and R–K3–KR3. Or 28 ...., Q × P; (instead of ...., P × P;) 29 P–Kt4, Q–B1; (........., Q–B5; 30 Kt(K5)–Q3, or B–B1,) 30 P–B4. But the text-move should decide the game more quickly.

| 27   .... | P × P |
| 28   P–B4 | .... |

White would have won easily with 28 Q–Kt3ch., K–R1; 29 Q–R4, K–Kt2; 30 P–Kt4, B–KB5; 31 P–KKt5, Kt–Q4; 32 Q–R6ch., K–R1; 33 Kt–Kt6 mate. After the perfunctory move in the text Black saves the situation through a most attractive concerted action of the defending pieces.

28	Kt–Q4
29 Q–R4	R–Q3
30 R–B3	K–R1
31 QR–KB1	B–Kt2
32 R–KKt3	KR–B3
33 QR–B3	R–R3
34 Q–Kt5	KR–Kt3
35 Kt × R	R × Kt

Draw! The Q cannot escape the " perpetual check."

The following game illustrates our stratagem in an instance typical of modern tournament practice. Central security on which Black bases his flank attack is here by no means apparent; the pre-modern school would in fact deny its existence altogether. And yet the modern-minded second player succeeds in making it the basis of a long drawn-out flank attack. Let the game speak for itself.

Game No. 87.—Berlin, 1928.

White: P. Johner.

1	P–Q4	Kt–KB3
2	P–QB4	P–K3
3	Kt–KB3	P–QKt3
4	P–KKt3	B–Kt2
5	B–Kt2	B–Kt5ch.
6	B–Q2	B × Bch.
7	QKt × B	P–B4

Black looks upon his position in the centre after 8 P × P, P × P; as entirely sound.

8	Castles	....

In our game, Berlin, 1927, Bogoljubow continued: 8 P × P, P × P; 9 Castles, Q–B2; 10 Q–B2, Castles; 11 QR–Q1, P–KR3; (to prevent the re-grouping Kt–Kt5, and later Kt(Kt5)–K4,) 12 P–QR3, Kt–B3; 13 KR–K1, QR–Kt1; 14 R–Kt1, P–QR4; but he already had to attend with 15 P–Kt3, to the weaknesses in his Q side.

8	....	Castles
9	Q–Kt3	Q–B2
10	KR–Q1	P–KR3

He is in no hurry.

11	Q–K3	P–Q3
12	P × P	KtP × P

In spite of being backward, the QP is obviously as sound as a bell.

13	Kt–K1	B × B
14	Kt × B	Q–B3
15	Q–KB3	....

He contests the beautiful long Diagonal, but after the exchange of Queens, the Black King can participate in the defence.

15	....	Q × Q
16	Kt × Q	R–Q1
17	R–Q3	Kt–B3
18	QR–Q1	Kt–K1

This Knight will soon be relieved by the King.

19	R–R3	....

He only pretends to attack; there already threatened ...., QR–Kt1; and if P–Kt3, P–QR4; etc. Therefore the text-move represents a fine preventive manœuvre against the threat indicated.

19	....	P–R3

To preclude " R–R6," once and for all.

20	Kt–B4	KR–Kt1
21	R–Q2	R–Kt5
22	R–B2	K–B1
23	P–K3	K–K2
24	P–R4	Kt–B2
25	Kt–Q3	R–Kt2
26	Kt–Q2	P–QR4
27	P–B3	Kt–Kt5
28	Kt × Kt	R × Kt

It is difficult to shape the course of the attack as White consistently refused to play the weakening P–Kt3. On the other hand, in course of time certain weaknesses have developed on the other wing.

29	K–B2	P–R5
30	K–K2	K–Q2
31	K–Q1	K–B3
32	Kt–K4	P–B4
33	Kt–B2	P–K4
34	R–Q3	QR–QKt1
35	K–B1	....

White has defended himself skilfully.

35	....	Kt–K3
36	P–R3	R–Kt6
37	R(B2)–Q2	R × R
38	R × R	Kt–B2
39	K–B2	Kt–R1

Intending .... Kt–Kt3; and ...., P–Q4; eventually.

40	P–K4	Kt–Kt3
41	P–Kt3	P × Pch.
42	R × P	R–KB1
43	R–B3	Kt–R5
44	R–Q3	Kt–Kt3
45	R–B3	Kt–R5
46	R–Q3	Kt–Kt3
47	R–B3	....

Draw.

It was far from the second player's intention to play for a draw; but he overlooked that the position had recurred three times. He should have played ...., P–Kt3; on the 45th move with a threat of ...., P–R4; and ...., P–B5; if White replies 46 K–Kt3, R–QKt1 ; 47 R–Q3, there would follow ...., P × P; 48 Kt × P, P–Q4; 49 P × Pch., Kt × P dis. ch. ; 50 K–B4, (or 50 K–B2, P–B5 ;) Kt–Kt3ch.; 51 K–B3, Kt–R5ch.; but probably there is not more than a draw in it. Throughout the game Black had the attack and the more compact pawn formation : our stratagem has proved its worth.

Game No. 88.—Eskilstuna, 1921.

One of 34 Simultaneous Games.

White: Carl Nilsson.

1	P–K4	Kt–QB3
2	P–Q4	P–Q4
3	P–K5	B–B4
4	P–QR3	....

To be able to play Kt–QB3.

| 4 | .... | P–K3 |
| 5 | Kt–QB3 | P–KR4 |

Early preventive play against White's advance P–KB4, and P–KKt4.

6	B–K3	P–KKt3
7	P–B4	Kt–R3
8	Kt–B3	Kt–KKt5

In order to provoke P–KR3, subsequently.

9	B–Kt1	P–R5
10	P–R3	Kt–R3
11	B–K3	B–K2
12	Q–Q2	P–R3

Making a show of preparing for ...., P–QKt4;
should White Castle on the Q side.

13 Castles   R–QKt1

The reply 13 ...., P–QKt4; would only have led to
obstupefaction after 14 Kt–QR2, (not 14 Kt × KtP, because
of ...., Castles; and ...., R–QKt1;) R–QKt1;
15 P–QKt4, and Black's QB4 would have remained weak.
The discreetly threatening play in the text has an immediate
effect.

14 Kt–QR2   B–K5

Your eye on the wings, your mind on the centre, that
is the deepest meaning of positional play.

15 Kt–K1   Kt–B4
16 K–Kt1   Kt–Kt6
17 R–Kt1   Kt × B
18 R × Kt   R–Kt1

With the object of exerting pressure against the backward KKtP by opening the KKt file.

19 K R1   K Q2

In order to establish communication between the major
pieces.

20 R–KKt1   K–B1

The King makes for QKt2.

21 Kt–B1   P–Kt3

Now there threatens also ...., Kt–R4–B5; the
White-squared points are clearly difficult to defend.

22 P–QKt4   P–R4
23 P–B3   P × P
24 BP × P   R–QR1
25 K–Kt2   K–Kt2

He could have played 25 ...., R × P; but he wants to
see all his positional chances mature (........., P–KKt4;)
before hitting out. Now ...., R × P, is a powerful
threat.

26 Kt–R2   P–KKt4
27 P × P   KB × KKtP
28 P–Kt4   P × P e.p.
29 R × P   B × B
30 R × B   Q–R5

Black has captured the KKt file; White is weak at Q4
and KR3.

31 Q–B3   Kt–R2
32 R–B1   ....

Here 32 P–R4, is better, but Black has the superior game in any event.

32	Q–B7ch.
33 K–Kt3	Kt–Kt4
34 Q–B6ch.	K–Kt1
35 Q × Kt	Q × Rch.

Resigns.

In this game the process of reasoning is disclosed by the moves 12 ......, P–R3; 13 ...., R–QKt1; and 14 Kt–QR2, with 14 ...., B–K5.

With 12 ...., P–R3; and 13 ...., R–QKt1; Black adopted a threatening attitude; upon this White felt induced to take counter-measures (14 Kt–QR2,) which, however, had a decentralising effect. With 14 ...., B–K5; White's decentralisation was duly registered and the ball set in motion. The far-reaching effect of the sober threat of a flank attack must cause surprise. The explanation seems to us to be that the balance was already disturbed (therefore previously to 12 ...., P–R3;) in favour of the second player! he was clearly strong on White-squared points. The sequence of moves 12 ...., P–R3; etc., only brought out a latent situation into actuality.

A simultaneous game played logically from beginning to end.

We would refer to move 20 ...., P–KKt4; in Game 71 and to the excellent game Sämisch-Alekhin, Dresden, 1926.

4.—THE SMALL BUT SECURE CENTRE.

As we know, the possession of a firm, if restricted, centre justifies the launching of flank attack, which, in a way, rests on the firmness of this centre.

In games 85 and 86 the geographical distances between the centre and the scene of action on the wing were considerable; logically both actions were entirely separate.

Matters are different in those "Paulsen positions," which are in fashion to-day, and which occur frequently for instance, in Sämisch's games: here the flank attack is only to help the freeing of the somewhat cramped centre and is therefore meant as a subordinate action. Geographically, too, the distance between both fields is inconsiderable. It is of importance for the student to study the strategy here indicated.

The two main requirements of a good "Paulsen" player consist of : (a) prophylaxis, (b) the art of manœuvring on inner lines. Both can be observed in the following two openings—

I.—White: Dr. Vidmar, Semmering, 1926. 1 P–Q4, Kt–KB3; 2 P–QB4, P–K3; Kt–KB3, B–Kt5ch.; 4 B–Q2, QK2; 5 P–K3, B × Bch.; 6 QKt × B, P–Q3; 7 Q–B2, P–B4; 8 P–KKt3, P–QKt3; 9 B–Kt2, B–Kt2; 10 Castles KR, Kt–B3; (although White's P–K4, is not to be feared because there could always follow ...., P × P; Kt × P, with a Paulsen position, Black prefers preventive play); 11 P–QKt3, Castles KR; 12 QR–Q1, KR–Q1; 13 KR–K1, QR–B1; 14 Kt–Kt3, P × P; 15 P × P, Kt–Kt1; (the beginning of manœuvres on inner lines) 16 KKt–Q2, B × B; 17 K × B, Q–Kt2ch.; 18 K–Kt1, R–B2; (bad would be 18 ...., P–Q4; or 18 ...., P–QKt4; because of the reply P–B5,) 19 Q–Q3, QKt–Q2; 20 P–B4, P–Kt3; 21 R–QB1, KR–QB1; 22 P–R3, P–KR4; (preventive play against P–KKt4,) 23 R–B3, P–Q4; and Black obtained the slightly superior game: 24 P × P, R × R; 25 P × R, Q × P; 26 P–B4, Q–Q3; and White's hanging pawns do not inspire confidence.

II.—White: Rubinstein. Black: Sämisch, Berlin, 1926. 1 P–Q4, Kt–KB3; 2 P–QB4, P–K3; 3 Kt–QB3, B–Kt5; 4 Q–B2, P–B4; 5 P × P, B × P; 6 Kt–B3, Kt–B3; 7 B–Kt5, P–QKt3; 8 P–K3, B–K2; (for the intended formation with pawns at Q3 and K3 a Bishop is wanted at K2) 9 R–Q1, P–QR3; 10 B–K2, B–Kt2; 11 Castles, P–Q3; 12 R–Q2, Castles; 13 KR–Q1, R–B1; (the " small centre " K3 and Q3 appears to be entirely tenable also against an eventual 14 B × Kt, P × B; 15 Kt–K4, Kt–Kt5; the text move 13 ...., R–B1; is therefore opportune) 14 B–B4, Kt–K1; 15 Q–Kt1, Kt–R4; (he fights against the encircling of his small centre, therefore he attacks the QBP) 16 P–QKt3, P–QKt4; 17 Kt–K4, B × Kt; 18 Q × B, P × P; 19 P × P, Q–B2; 20 Q–Kt1, R–Kt1; 21 Q–B2, Kt–Kt2; (over-protecting the QP; as we shall see, this procedure is fully justified. Q3 is a strong point, and only strong points are worthy of over protection) 22 P–K4, B–B3; 23 B–K3, Kt–B4; 24 Kt–Q4, B–K2; 25 Kt–Kt3, Kt–B3; 26 P–B3, KR–B1; 27 P–Kt4, (there is no sufficient motive for this attack) 27 ...., P–R3; 28 K–Kt2, KKt–Q2; (the point at Black's KB3 was extensively used in these manœuvres) 29 Kt–Q4, R–Kt3; and Black obtained the advantage in the QKt file.

The foregoing shows clearly that the "small centre " belongs to the hyper-modern repertoire. A player of the so-called classical school, which requires much terrain for their rather unimaginative manœuvres, would simply have been suffocated. Or alternatively, he would have been unable to keep out the hostile thrusts in the long run, the preventive technique of those days not being sufficient for the purpose.

During the twenty years of my activities in the field of chess pedagogy, it has been my experience that the study of this type of game (with restricted centre) engenders a healthy aversion from the loose formation so beloved in the widest chess circles. We ourselves have felt this wholesome re-action, for instance, at the end of a tour of simultaneous exhibitions, which, as is well-known, are not exactly beneficial to one's tournament style.

We now give two games illustrating the small (restricted) centre and one dealing with loose formation.

Game No. 89.—New York, 1927.

White: Capablanca.

1 P–Q4	Kt–KB3
2 Kt–KB3	P–K3
3 B–Kt5	P–KR3

Of questionable value : on balance the increase in possible resources resulting from this move is less than the danger of the loosening it occasions. Generally speaking, an overburdening of the restricted centre should be avoided. A wide and active centre could more easily absorb some weakness on the wings. The restricted centre is too passive in this respect.

4 B–R4	P–QKt3
5 QKt–Q2	B–Kt2
6 P–K3	B–K2
7 B–Q3	P–Q3
8 P–B3	Castles
9 P–KR3	....

In order to be able to play B–Kt3, without being exposed to an exchange by ...., Kt–R4; but 9 Q–K2, and Castles QR, with a K side attack looks much more natural. The following opening is instructive on this point: Black, Dr. Vidmar. 1 P–K3, P–Q4; 2 Kt–KB3, Kt–KB3; 3 P–QKt3, B–Kt5; 4 B–Kt2, QKt–Q2; 5 P–KR3, (the present game, with

colours reversed, has now come about,) 5 ...., B–R4;
6 B–K2, P–K3; 7 Kt–K5, B×B; 8 Q×B, B–Q3; 9 Kt×Kt,
Q×Kt; 10 P–QB4, P–B3; 11 Castles, Castles QR; 12 Kt–B3,
B–B2; 13 P–Q4, P–KR4; 14 P–B5, P–KKt4; 15 P–QKt4,
P–R5; 16 P–Kt5, QR–Kt1, and Vidmar won by a direct K
side attack.

9	....	P–B4
10	Castles	Kt–B3
11	Q–K2	Kt–KR4
12	B×B	Q×B
13	B–R6	Kt–B3
14	KR–Q1	KR–Q1
15	P–K4	....

15	....	B×B

Because he has at his disposal a manœuvre which is to
prove the weakness on the White squares to be illusory.
Much weaker would be 15 ...., P–K4; because of
16 P–Q5, with possibilities on either flank.

16	Q×B	Q–B2
17	QR–B1	R–Q2
18	P–QKt4	QR–Q1
19	Q–K2	....

The Queen retires voluntarily.

19	....	Kt–K2
20	R–K1	Kt–Kt3
21	P–Kt3	R–QB1
22	KtP×P	QP×P
23	Kt–Kt3	P×P
24	P×P	Q–Kt2

White has achieved nothing at all.

25 R × Rch.	Q × R
26 R–QB1	R–B2
27 R × R	Q × R
28 KKt–Q2	Q–B6
29 Q–R6	Q–B2
30 Q–K2	………

Draw.

Typical of the restricted centre were the slow evolutions of the major pieces on inner lines (moves 16, 17, 18, 21 and 26 by Black).

Game No. 90.—Copenhagen, 1923.

White: Egil Jacobsen.

1 P–Q4	Kt–KB3
2 Kt–KB3	P–QKt3
3 P–B4	B–Kt2
4 Kt–B3	P–K3
5 B–Kt5	P–KR3

Here this move is more to the point.

6 B–R4	B–K2
7 P–K3	P–Q3
8 R–B1	QKt–Q2
9 B–Kt3	Castles
10 B–Q3	P–R3

It is to be noted that Black, who occupies only three ranks, appears to be quite comfortable in his incapacious quarters, as, for the present, he is obviously contemplating neither ………, P–K4; nor P–B4. He invents instead a singular manœuvre on inner lines, as a consequence of which ………, P–B4; will acquire real attacking value. In White's lay-out the move 8 R–QB1, is difficult to understand. It appears to be directed against ………, P–Q4; which thrust does not at all conform with the second player's plans.

11 Castles	Kt–R4
12 B–Kt1	P–Kt3
13 Kt–K2	QKt–B3
14 Kt–Q2	P–B4

By which he at least secures a " Paulsen " position, (………, P × P; and ……… R–B1;) but he is trying for more.

15 Kt–B4   Kt–Kt2

In comparing this position with that obtaining after
White's 11th move, the impression is given that Black's
QKt has wandered from Q2 to KKt2, whereas it is really the
KKt which is on KKt2: a real "manœuvre on inner lines"
with interchange of rôles and places.

16 Q–K2   Kt–B4
17 B × Kt   ....

Or 17 P × P, KtP × P; 18 B × Kt, KP × B; with ....,
R–K1; and ...., B–KB1; followed by a Q side attack,
and Black would have ample play.

17 ....   KP × B
18 P–Q5   P–QKt4
19 P–Kt3   R–K1
20 Q–Q3   Kt–Kt5

He tries to obtain points in the K file, whilst opposing
White's intentions (Kt–K2, and P–K4,) by preventive means

21 Q–B2   B–R5

Preventive play as mentioned in the preceding note!
A similar result but—as we think—with lesser effect would
be achieved by 21 ...., B–QB1; e.g.: 22 Kt–K2, B–B3;
23 P–K4, P × KP; 24 Kt × P, B–B4; 25 Kt × Bch., etc.

22 P–K4   ....

After this move Black obtains distinctly the better game.
Better would be: 22 B × B, Q × B; 23 P–KR3, Kt–K4;
24 Kt–Q3.

22 ....   B × B
23 RP × B   P × KP
24 Kt × KP   B–B1
25 P–B3   Kt–B3

Not 25 ...., Kt–K6; because of 26 Q–B3, and
Kt–B6ch., eventually.

        26 Kt × Ktch.   ....
Better Kt–B3.

        26 ....   Q × Kt
        27 Q–Q2   R–R2
        28 QR–K1   R(R2)–K2
        29 R × R   Q × R
        30 K–B2   P × P

White has succeeded in safeguarding the K file in a
measure, but the weak QBP which he now obtains is more
than the position can stand.

        31 P × P   P–QR4
        32 Kt–Q3   Q–B3

Alternating manœuvres; the weaknesses in White's
camp are his QBP, the K file, and the long Black Diagonal.

        33 Q–Kt2   Q × Q
        34 Kt × Q   B–B4

The exchange of Queens has not improved matters for
White.   Although the long Black Diagonal is secure, the
QBP is more difficult to defend.

        35 R–B1   P–R4

Not 35 ...., R–Kt1 ; 36 Kt–Q1, because the White
King is to be kept out as long as possible.   The text move
prepares the subsequent storming by pawns.

        36 R–B3   P–QR5
        37 Kt–Q1   ....

If 37 Kt × P, R–R1 ; 38 Kt–Kt2, (38 Kt–Kt6, R × Pch. ;
with ...., R–R3 ; and the King makes for the invested
Knight) 38 ...., R × P ; 39 R–Kt3, and ...., P–Kt4 ;
with the superior end-game.   But if 37 R–R3, R–Kt1 ;
38 Kt × P ?, R–R1 ; and wins.

        37 ....   P–Kt4
        38 Kt–K3   B–Q2
        39 K–K2   P–B4

40 K–Q2 ....

After this move the K side becomes weak, but 40 P–B4, also, although better, would hardly have been adequate, e.g.: 40 P–B4, P × P; 41 P × P, P–R5; or 40 ...., K–B2; 41 P × P, K–Kt3; and in either case White would be in difficulties.

40	P–B5
41 P × P	P × P
42 Kt–Q1 ?	....

The correct move obviously would be 42 Kt–B2, and eventually Kt–K1, although in this case Black would have obtained a strong end-game attack, e.g.: 42 Kt–B2, K–B2; 43 Kt–K1, K–B3; 44 R B2, R–QKt1; 45 K–B3, R–Kt8; 46 R–K2, R–B8ch.; 47 Kt–B2, B–B4; with a general exchange and a won end-game, as the Black K penetrates to KKt6.

42 ....   K–B2

and Black wins easily.

43 Kt–B2	R–KKt1
44 K–K2	R × P
45 R–B1	B–B4
46 P–R3	P–R5
47 R–B1	K–B3
48 K–Q1	P–R6
49 K–K2	P–R7
50 R–QR1	B–Q6ch.
51 K × B	R × Kt
52 K–K4	K–Kt4
53 R–QKt1	R–K7ch.
54 K–Q3	R–K6ch.

Resigns.

In this ending the reflex weakness of White's K side was noteworthy: the weakness of his Q side was communicated, so to speak, to the other wing, so that Black's K side pawns could be looked upon as a qualitative majority; in consequence they advanced, not without success. The game itself is indicative of the modern tendency to carry out difficult manœuvres even in difficult terrain circumstances. The manner in which Black, from a terribly cramped position, slowly but surely gained ground and finally obtained a strong attack in the end-game, lends instructive interest as well as enjoyment to the game. The restricted centre has once more acquitted itself well.

Game No. 91.—Copenhagen, 1928.

White: Eigil Hansen.

1 P–QB4   P–QB4
2 P–B4   ....

This move makes a puzzling impression, but as will soon be seen, it is not the move that is wrong, but the impression! How trivial it is to judge a move by appearances, a procedure still in favour not so very long ago.

2 ....   Kt–KB3
3 P–Q3   P–Q4

Otherwise 4 P–K4, follows with a solid formation.

4 P × P   Kt × P
5 P–K4   ....

Compare the following opening: 1 P–QB4, P–QB4; 2 Kt–QB3, Kt–KB3; 3 Kt–B3, P–Q4; 4 P × P, Kt × P; 5 P–K4, (the so-called Dresden Variation, introduced by the author). The position obtained by Hansen resembles that just shown in principle (White's pawn at Q3 on an open file), but shows an improvement in detail in that Black's resource ...., Kt × Kt; with ...., P–KKt3; is now cut out.

Herr Hansen deserves recognition.

5 ....   Kt–KB3
6 B–K3   P–K3
7 Kt–QB3   Kt–B3
8 Kt–B3   B–Q2

To induce 9 P–Q4!

9 P–Q4?   ....

Much sounder would be 9 P–KR3, with B–K2, e.g.: 9 P–KR3, Kt–KR4; 10 K–B2, with 11 P–KKt4. The text move shows that the first player does not possess the feeling for the solid formation. The move 9 P–Q4, would not even have occurred to a player, for instance, of Sämisch's type.

9 ....   P × P
10 Kt × P   B–Kt5

Everything is already hanging loose in the White camp.

11 Kt × Kt   B × Kt
12 Q × Qch.   R × Q
13 P–K5   ....

White was compelled to make concessions in the centre. He now labours under weaknesses on White-squared points.

13 ....   Kt–K5
14 P–QR3   ....

An ingenious expedient; he plays for Bishops of opposite colours.

14	B × Ktch.
15 P × B	Kt × P
16 B–B4	....

Here 16 B × P, is inadmissible because of ...., Kt–Q4; and the KBP cannot be covered (17 P–Kt3, Kt × P; 18 P × Kt, B × R;).

| 16 .... | R–QB1 |

The proper strategy when the opponent's formation is loose! Let everything go on being loose, and create further tension.

17 R–QB1	B × P
18 R–KKt1	R × B
19 R × B	P–QKt4
20 R(Kt2)–QB2	....

Or 20 R × P, K–K2; followed by ...., KR–QB1; with serious threats.

| 20 .... | Kt–Q4 |

A very sound Knight!

21 R × R	P × R
22 R × P	K–Q2
23 B × P	....

| 23 .... | R–QB1 |

Triumph of the firm formation! The resourceful first player has regained all that could be regained, namely, the whole of the lost material. But here he is with a butterfly at KB4, the greyhound at QR7 and the two mangy sheep at QR3 and KR2, whilst the King sits at a befitting distance on his throne—there ensues a conclusion full of terror.

24 R–K4   ....
If 24 R × R, K × R; our butterfly would be no more.
24 ....   R–B8ch.
25 K–B2   ....
If 25 K–Q2, there follows: ...., R–KR8; 26 R–K2, R–R8; (not at once 26 ...., Kt × P; because of 27 R–B2, P–Kt4; 28 B–K3,) 27 B–B5, Kt × P; etc.
25 ....   R–B7ch.
26 K–Kt3   ....
Or 26 K–Kt1, R–B6; 27 P–QR4, R–B6; etc.
26 ....   R–B6ch.
27 K–Kt4   ....
A mistake under time pressure, but there was no saving clause.
27 ....   P–B4ch.
Resigns.
For if 28 P × P e.p., Kt × Pch.; and the Rook is lost.
The weakness of an extended centre advancing all too impulsively is shown here with the greatest possible clearness.

5.—ASYMMETRIC TREATMENT OF SYMMETRICAL VARIATIONS.

Followers of the so-called classic school had a marked preference, which is to-day difficult to understand, for symmetrical variations. Not only that, but they managed to surround this unpleasing circumstance with a scientific cloak. The belief gained ground that many positions and openings had a natural tendency towards symmetry, and that it would be sacrificing the intellect to wish to avoid this heaven-sent gift, and that, therefore, any such attempts were bound to be incorrect and to lead to a loss against sound opposition.

Let us examine the question more closely in the light of the following example: 1 P–Q4, P–Q4; (what objection could there be to the asymmetrical move 1 ...., Kt–KB3;?) 2 P–QB4, P–K3; 3 Kt–QB3, P–QB4; (In quest of symmetry or levelled position. The only continuation is the asymmetric 3 ...., Kt–KB3; followed by ...., QKt–Q2; etc.) 4 P–K3, (generally thought at the time to be the correct reply. The right way is of course Kt–B3, with P–KKt3, commonly known as the Schlechter-Rubinstein variation) 4 ...., Kt–QB3; 5 Kt–B3, Kt–B3; 6 B–Q3, B–Q3; if any one in those days had hit upon the idea of playing 6 ...., B–K2; the pundits would have shaken their heads, and yet this departure from symmetrical development is the only logical continuation. The weakness of 6 ...., B–Q3; lies in the fact that as a consequence the QP remains in need of protection. With 6 ...., B–K2; by which the Queen remains effective on the line Q1–Q5; this fact is taken into consideration, e.g.: 6 ...., B–K2; 7 Castles, Castles; 8 Q–K2, (each player lays stress on his own chances, Black on his play against the QP, White on the K side attack based on his B at Q3.)   8 ...., P × QP; 9 KP × P, P × P; 10 B × P, Kt × P; 11 Kt × Kt, Q × Kt; and it is difficult to predict the outcome. And so, even a superficial examination creates the impression that each game of chess is full of problems, of which symmetrical chess, tremulous and unimaginative, would fight shy! This impression gains strength if other symmetrical variations are drawn upon for the purpose of comparison. In the exchange variation of the French Defence, after the moves: 1 P–K4, P–K3; 2 P–Q4, P–Q4; 3 P × P, P × P; 4 B–Q3, B–Q3; the K Knights can be developed centrally (Kt–KB3) or with diversional tendencies (Kt–K2). In the second case (Kt–K2) defence in the centre, say with P–KB3 would have to be carried out concurrently, or else the development would be strategically wrong. (Diversions on the flanks, without adequate security in the centre, have been shown on several occasions in this book, to be a "*reductio ad absurdum*."

From which follows with compelling logic (though many players will feel disinclined to admit the compulsion), that Kt–KB3, must be answered by ...., Kt–K2; and conversely ...., Kt–KB3; is the necessary answer to Kt–K2! This asymmetric treatment, advocated by Svenonius, is, in the logic of its strategy, far superior to the symmetrical system.

Note how clearly this contrast in fighting ideals stands out: Aalesund 1925, Simultaneous Performance, White: Strande: 1 P–K4, P–K3; 2 P–Q4, P–Q4; 3 P × P, P × P; 4 B–Q3, B–Q3; 5 Kt–KB3, Kt–K2; 6 Castles, QKt–B3; 7 B–K3, (to weaken the effect of ...., B–KKt5;) 7 ...., B–KB4; 8 Kt–B3, Castles; 9 R–K1, B × B; (this move introduces a Kt manœuvre which is to set the centre to rights and is at the same time to strengthen aspirations on the flank), 10 Q × B, Kt–Kt5; 11 Q–Q2, P–QB3; 12 P–QR3, Kt–R3; 13 R–K2, (he quite rightly realises that his chance is in the centre; but may not B–Kt5, be technically preferable?)

13 ...., Kt–B2; 14 QR–K1, Kt–K3; 15 Q–Q3, (15 Kt–KKt5, would be harmless because of the possible reply 15 ...., Kt–Kt3; e.g.: 16 Kt×Kt, P×Kt; 17 B–Kt5, Q–B2;) 15 .... Kt–Kt3; (seeking to check the adversary's aspirations in the centre) 16 P–KKt3, R–K1; 17 B–B1, (the centre file clear for the attack! But Black has already made preparations) 17 ...., Q–Q2; 18 Kt–Q1, (for better or for worse he should have played 18 Kt–K5, the occupation of the outpost K5 provides the only continuation of the initiative in the centre.) 18 ...., R–K2; 19 Kt–K3?, Kt(K3)–B5; (The diversion now sets in with weighty effect. 19 Kt–K5, was still the right move. If then 19 ...., B×Kt; 20 P×B, there would follow ...., QR–K1; and the thrust 21 P–KB4, could be held up by the promising pawn sacrifice 21 ...., Kt–B4; 22 Q–Q4, Kt—K5; 23 Q×RP, P–B3; 24 P×P, P×P. We would then have an interesting case in which persistent defence in the centre has led to centralisation, to which favourable issue the latent effect of Black's intended diversion has, *inter alia*, contributed. After a faulty text-move 19 Kt–K3, all is over. 20 P×Kt, Kt×P; 21 Q–Q2, Q–R6; and White resigns.

In this game Black indirectly protected his K4 by allowing a White Knight to settle there, but at the same time minimising its effect, should it do so. It could also be presented directly (by ...., P–KB3;).

We shall now pass on to the games and only wish to repeat that we are convinced that the quest of symmetry in development can in these unimaginative times, be assessed only as a " *testimonium paupertatis*."

The next two games are devoted to the co-ordination of centralised defence and wing attack.

Game No. 92.

Friendly Game with Clocks, Copenhagen, 1922.

White: J. Möller.

1 P–K4	P–K3
2 P–Q4	P–Q4
3 Kt–QB3	B–Kt5
4 P×P	P×P
5 Kt–B3	Kt–QB3
6 P–QR3	B–R4

If 6 ...., B × Ktch.; 7 P × B, B–B4; 8 B–Q3,
KKt–K2; 9 Castles, Castles; 10 B–KB4, and White, with
satisfactory central action, has the not to be under-rated
advantage that, of the two Bishops at Q3 and KB5, his own
is the better protected.

7	B–QKt5	Kt–K2
8	Castles	Castles
9	Kt–QR4	B–Kt3
10	Kt × B	RP × Kt
11	B–Q3	B–B4

Black is not only better developed, but he has also the
firmer formation; White's Kt manœuvre cost too much time.

12	R–K1	....

The central operation, which—*a priori*—will not be
judged too optimistically (see preceding note).

12	....	Q–Q2

Why does Black, at this stage, omit the obvious ....,
P–B3; by which the action in the centre, which his adversary
has begun, would be nipped in the bud? For without
Kt–K5, or, in other words, the occupation of the outpost in
the centre file, White can apparently make no progress on
the file in question! The answer is of moment for the correct
appraisement of those positions which are characterised by
Kt at KB3 v. Kt at K2. For the moment Kt–K5, is not an
actual threat and would only impair White's position, e.g.:
Kt–K5, Kt × Kt; P × Kt, and White's majority on the K
side would have little mobility. On the other hand ....,
P–B3; would be the very move to give White new
possibilities on the K file, for Black's K3 would become
vulnerable.

And the inference? Well, if ...., P–B3; can be deferred at all, Black's K3 must first be strengthened; once this is done ...., P–B3; can be played without misgivings. A thorough analysis of the variation arising from ...., P–B3, would prove most instructive. 12 ...., P–B3; 13 Kt–R4, (an interesting experiment) 13 ...., Kt × P; (another line, 13 ...., B × B; 14 Q × B, Q–Q2; 15 B–Q2, P–KKt4; with 16 ...., Q–B4; would also be a sound and comfortable continuation.) 14 Kt × B (or A), Kt (Q5) × Kt; 15 Q–Kt4, Kt–Q3; if (15 ......, Q–B1; 16 Q–R3, threatening P–KKt4,) 16 B–KB4, P–KB4; 17 Q–R3, Q–Q2; 18 R–K2, Kt–Kt3; 19 B × Kt, P × B; 20 P–KKt3, Kt–K4; and Black has slightly the better position. It is to be noted that Black could only with difficulty repel White's attack. Or (A) 12 ...., P–B3; 13 Kt–R4, Kt × P; 14 R × Kt, B × B; 15 R–K3, Kt × P; 16 R × B, Kt × R; 17 B–K3, looks strong, but there follows: Q–K1; 18 Q × Kt, Q–K5; 19 R–Q4, Q–K3; 20 Q–R2, QR–Q1; 21 Kt–B3, P–QB4; 22 R–Q1, and now perhaps ...., K–R1; with ...., Q–B3; and the pawn phalanx is ready to march on. In this case also Black has a definite, if small, advantage, a position for Capa.). We are now in a position to sum up: 12 ...., P–B3; may be good enough but leads, in any event, to a temporary loosening of Black's well-knit formation. The text-move must be pronounced more in accord with the position, especially as, at this moment, Kt–K5, would only be beating the air.

13 Kt–K5	....

He beats the air. Much better is 13 B–KB4.

13	Kt × Kt
14 R × Kt	....

After 14 P × Kt, also, Black's position is preferable.

14	QR–K1
15 Q–K2	P–KB3

Only now can this be played with a clear conscience.

16 R–K3	P–B4
17 P–QB3	P–B5
18 B–B2	....

18 .... P–KKt4

Only after having successfully secured his centre does he feel justified in carrying out his projected diversion. The move in the text provides the Kt, eager for the fray, with a basis at his KR5.

19 P–QKt3   B × B
20 Q × B   Kt–B4
21 R × R   R × R

Now Black has even carried the K file: the action in the centre begun by White with the untimely 13 Kt–K5, must therefore be considered a complete failure.

22 B–Q2   Kt–R5

See note to move 18.

23 Q–Q1   P × P
24 Q × P   R–K7
25 B–K3   Q–B4

Even now Black has to consider the co-ordination of the defence in the centre with an attack on the flank; his Q4, for instance, must at no time be left undefended.

26 Q–Kt5   Q–K5

Instead of 26 Q–Kt5, White had to play 26 Q–Kt1, though, even so, the game could not be saved, e.g.: 26 Q–Kt1, Q–Kt5; 27 Q–KB1, P–R3; 28 P–R3, Q–K5; followed by ...., P–B4–B5; etc.

27 K–B1   R × B

Resigns.

Game No. 93.—Berlin, 1927.

White: Enoch.

1	P–K4	P–K3
2	P–Q4	P–Q4
3	P × P	P × P
4	Kt–KB3	B–Q3
5	B–Q3	Kt–QB3
6	P–B3	KKt–K2
7	Castles	B–KKt5
8	R–K1	Q–Q2
9	B–KKt5	P–B3

This move can now be played without apprehension as his K3 is strongly held.

10	B–R4	P–KR4

(A minor innovation! If now 11 B–Kt6ch., K–B1; 12 Q–B2, Kt × B; 13 Q × Kt, B–KB4; winning the Queen.)

11	QKt–Q2	P–KKt4
12	B–Kt3	B × B

Black has to put up with the weakness which this move creates at his QB4.

13	BP × B	Castles QR

14	P–Kt4	....

The position is extremely difficult to assess, especially on account of the numerous battlefields : these are found on both wings as well as in the centre (K file). But one fact already stands out clearly : the ardour for the flank-attack must on no account lead to a neglect of the centrally situated battlefield.

It seems to us to be of paramount necessity for both sides to keep the centre under observation, (White in an attacking sense, Black from the point of view of defence.) From these remarks it follows that the diversion 14 P–Kt4, does not quite appeal to us. A re-grouping by 14 R–K3, 15 Q–KB1, 16 QR–K1, is more deserving of consideration. Another continuation is possible and would lead to interesting play, namely: 14 Kt–Kt3, Q–Q3; (if 14 ...., P–Kt3; 15 Kt–B5,) 15 Kt–B5, and now 15 ...., P–R5; would be negatived by 16 Q–Kt3, Kt–R4; (........., P–Kt3; loses the exchange after 17 B–R6ch., K–Kt1; 18 Kt–Kt7, without any real compensation, e.g.: 18 ...., Q–Q2; 19 Kt × R, Kt × Kt; 20 Q–Kt5, Q–Q3; 21 Q–Kt4,) 17 Q–R4, P–Kt3; 18 P–Kt4, P × P; (now White's position looks doubtful). 19 P × Kt, (not 19 B–R6ch., because the B may be needed at Q3, to prevent ...., Kt–B4; eventually,) 19 ...., P × Kt; (P × QKtP, with annihilation was threatened) 20 P × BP, (a delightful winning line; bad would be 20 R × Kt, P–B5;) Q × Pch.; 21 K–R1, B × Kt; (he was helpless against the double threat of B–R6ch., and Q × B,) 22 B–R6ch., K–Kt1; 23 QR–Kt1ch., K–R1; 24 B–Kt7ch., K–Kt1; 25 B × P dis. ch., K–B1; 26 B–K6ch., and mate next move. It follows that after 14 Kt–Kt3, Q–Q3; 15 Kt–B5, Black must renounce ...., P–R5. Good and in keeping with the position would be 15 ...., QR–K1; the sequel would be 16 Q–Kt3, (16 Q–R4, P–R5; 17 P–Kt4, K–Kt1; 18 P–Kt5, Kt–Q1; and White is shaky.) 16 ...., Kt–Q1; 17 R–K3, Kt(K2)–B3; 18 QR–K1, R × R; 19 R × R, P–R5; 20 Kt–Q2, P × P; 21 P × P, with an approximately balanced position. In this variation we had an illustration of the way in which the required co-ordination between centre and wing play can be effected in practice. In the present game White gives only scant attention to the central idea, and so Black is enabled to obtain security in the centre with a minimum of forces, so that he can throw every available unit into the fray on the K side.

| 14 .... | QR–Kt1 |

This becomes clear on Black's next move. Of course 14 ...., QR–K1; would also be good and safe.

| 15 Q–K2 | R–Kt2 |

This provides just enough security for the K file. The QR is now the protagonist of the idea of co-ordination referred to several times.

16 P–QR4   ....

Initiative in the centre by 16 P–KR3, B–B4; 17 B × B, Kt × B; 18 Q–K6, would be rebutted by 18 ...., P–Kt5.

16	Q–Q3
17 P–R5	P–R5
18 P–Kt5	Kt–Q1
19 P–Kt6	K–Kt1
20 P × BPch.	....

Better seems 20 P–B4.

20	Q × P
21 P–B4	P × KtP
22 P × KtP	P × P

This provides the square Q4 for his Kt and also diverts the White QKt from the protection of the K side.

| 23 Kt × BP | .... |

If 23 B × P, Kt–B4; with a decisive attack.

23	Q × KtP
24 P–R6	Kt–Q4
25 B–K4	....

There is an interesting variation as follows: 25 P × P, Kt–B5; 26 Q–R2, P–R3; (not 26 ...., R × P; because of 27 KR–Kt1, threatening Q × Pch,) and Black wins.

25	Kt–B5
26 Q–Kt2	B × Kt
27 B × B	R (Kt2)–R2

Resigns.

On the 14th move White omitted to play a Kt to QB5: in consequence both central pressure and K side attack melted away. Black, on the contrary, succeeded with 15 ...., R–Kt2; in combining defence in the centre with his attacking plans on the flank. And, behold and see, not only did the execution of his plans, carried out whole-heartedly, succeed, but the R at Kt2 earned full marks as a defender: its defence took effect, past the centre, on the far wing at his QKt2 and QR2. A very instructive example of the asymmetric method of play.

Game No. 94.—New York, 1927.

White: Marshall.

1	P–K4	P–K3
2	P–Q4	P–Q4
3	Kt–QB3	B–Kt5
4	P × P	P × P
5	B–Q3	Kt–K2
6	Kt–K2	B–KB4
7	Castles	Castles
8	Kt–Kt3	B–Kt3
9	QKt–K2	B–Q3
10	B–KB4	QKt–B3
11	Q–Q2	Q–Q2
12	QR–K1	KR–K1

Both players have developed their KKt at K2 and the first part of the game has been rather monotonous. But now the dull game becomes lively.

13	P–B3	Kt–B1
14	B–K3	QKt–K2

The co-ordinated retreat of the united Knights is intended to create asymmetry. The Kt at B1, in making for his K5, gives the Black formation suddenly the character of the variation Kt at B3 v. Kt at K2.

Incidentally, this not unoriginal retreat was tried by the author against Spielmann, Copenhagen, 1923: on that occasion the play was ...., Kt(K2)–Kt1; ...., Kt(B3)–K2; and then Kt–KB3–K5.

15	Kt–B4	B × Kt
16	QB × B	B × B
17	Q × B	Kt–KKt3
18	Q–B3	....

If 18 B–Q2, Kt–Q3; but Black also obtains some play after the text-move.

18	....	P–KB4
19	B–Q2	R × R
20	R × R	P–B5
21	Kt–K2	Q–B4

The following would also be good: 21 ...., Kt–R5; 22 Q–R5, Kt × P; 23 K × Kt, P–B6ch; 24 K–R1, P × Kt; 25 R × P, followed perhaps by Kt–K2–B4; and play on White-squared points.

22 P–B4 ………

Parried adroitly : he seeks to make a breach in the hostile encircling wall.

22 ……… Kt–Kt3

Not 22 ………, Q–K5; because of Q × Q, and Kt–B3.

23 P × P	Kt × P
24 Kt–B3	Kt × Kt
25 B × Kt	P–B3
26 B–Kt4	R–Q1
27 Q–K4	Q–B2
28 P–QR3	P–KR3
29 P–KKt3	Q–B3
30 B–B3	R–Q4
31 Q–K8ch.	K–R2
32 Q–K4	Q–B4
33 K–Kt2	Q–Kt5

Black will not show his hand; the end-game did not seem advantageous enough to him after : 33 ………, Q × Q; 34 R × Q, P × P; 35 RP × P, K–Kt1 ; 36 R–K8ch., K–B2; 37 R–QR8, P–R3; 38 R–QKt8, R–Q2; 39 K–B3, Kt–K2; 40 K–K4, Kt–Q4.

34 P–B3	Q–Kt4
35 B–Q2	Q–B3

Simpler in any case would be 35 ………, Q–Q1; 36 B × P, R × P; 37 Q–B5, Q–Q2; 38 Q–B2, R–Q6; and the Bishop cannot occupy the important Diagonal QB3–KKt7.

36 B × P	R × P
37 Q–B2	R–-Q4

Overlooking the reply; he should have played ………, Q–Q1.

38 B–Q2	Q–Q1
39 B–B3	………

White has now an unembarrassed, buoyant Bishop, and therefore has the advantage.

39 ………	R–Q6
40 R–K4	Q–Q4
41 Q–K2	Q–Q2
42 P–KR4	P–KR4
43 R–K8	R–Q8
44 R–R8	P–R3
45 R–QKt8	………

Intending to lure the pawns forward (R × P, is threatened) after which the Queens are to be exchanged with a won R and B ending. But Black finds a most cunning counter. Incidentally, the correct move was 45 Q–K4, upon which Black would have tried to keep his head above water by ...., Q–KB2; with ...., R–Q4–KB4; the defence would have been far from easy.

45 ....   R–KR8
46 K × R   ....

. Marshall decided on this move after using up 70 (!) minutes of his time. The following defence would lose: 46 Q–K8, Kt–B5ch.; 47 P × Kt, Q–R6ch.; 48 K–B2, R–B8ch.; 49 K–K3, Q × Pch.; 50 K–Q4, Q–Q4ch.; 51 K–K3, R–B6ch.; 52 K–K2, Q–Q6ch.; 53 K–K1, R–B8 mate. Disastrous would also be 46 Q–B4, Kt × Pch.; 47 P × Kt, Q–R6ch; 48 K–B2, Q–R7ch.; with ...., Q × R. And so taking the R appears to be compulsory, and the changeful game is drawn.

46 ....   Q–R6ch
47 Q–R2   Draw

Of course not 47 K–Kt1, because of ...., Q × Pch.; 48 Q–Kt2, Q × R; 49 Q–Kt5, Q–B5; 50 Q × Pch., Q–R3; and Black has the advantage.

6.—THE BISHOP WITH AND WITHOUT AN OUTPOST.

In playing over the next three games, the gentle reader will have a definite impression, that the Bishops here have "*neo-romantic*" proclivities and cannot be mistaken for those of olden times. And yet the difference is inappreciable.

In 95 a B diagonal is treated according to the principles governing lineal play. In the following position:

White : R at Q1, Kt at QB3, pawn at K4. Black : Pawns at QB2 and Q3, (we follow here the lines of thought of " My System," from which we cull the scheme,) we find that our lineal play has at present no definite object, for the penetration of the seventh rank cannot be thought a real possibility in view of the firm hostile defensive position (QB2, Q3,). But there followed 1 Kt–Q5, whereby the vague lineal effect was enhanced by a very real outpost Knight. (The continuation was ...., P–B3; to drive off the unpleasant fellow, 2 Kt–B3, and the lineal play had now the definite point of attack, White's Q6.) The process sketched here, transferred to a Diagonal, that is the theme of our No. 95 !

Incidentally, compare in No. 61 the move 28 Q–B4, which was there recommended. The Q at KB4 represents the diagonal outpost. In No. 96 the Bishops are noteworthy for this boldness in attack and in No. 97, in defence. Taking it all in all, the " inappreciable difference " of which we spoke above, may originate in the fact that the modern generation of Masters may appraise constructive thought as such, a little more highly than did our forefathers. Courage and imagination appear in a different and better aspect. (See the precarious Bishops in No. 96, and note further the " courage of self-denial " shown by the Black B at QKt2 in No. 97.

Here are the games :—

Game No. 95.—Carlsbad, 1923.

Black: Dr. Tartakower.

1	Kt–KB3	P–KB4
2	P–QKt3	P–QKt3
3	B–Kt2	B–Kt2
4	P–Kt3	B × Kt

This exchange appears to be unfavourable, for, as will soon be seen, the Black pawn-formation will lack mobility.

5	P × B	P–K3
6	P–KB4	Kt–KB3
7	B–Kt2	P–B3
8	Castles	B–K2
9	Q–K2	Castles

The White Bishops are strongly posted but have, as yet, little effect.

10 Kt–R3   ....

This Knight is pressed into the service of the Bishops. In the sequel it will not only reconnoitre the ground but lure on the Black pawns.   Its most important function, however, will reveal itself only on the 13th move.

10 ....   P–QR4

The only way to develop the QKt.   ...., P–QKt4 fails against Kt × P, etc.

11 Kt–B4   P–R5
12 B–Q4   P–QKt4
13 Kt–K5   ....

If, in the course of play, I had looked upon this Knight as an outpost on the K file, there would have been no reason why I should publish this game here; but I saw in this Kt nothing but a diagonal outpost: a vague, up to now undefined diagonal effect acquires, through posting the Knight at K5, a definite aspect with clear-cut objects of attack, in other words : the diagonal action now obtains.

13 ....   Kt–Q4

After 13 ...., Kt–R3; the continuation would be, not sacrifices at QB6, but simple development by KR–K1, followed by P–B4.

14 P–B4   P × BP
15 P × BP   Kt–Kt5

With the understandable desire to take advantage of the Knight's short stay in the central position (Q4), according to the motto " via the centre into enemy land." The scheme, however, proves disastrous. But with passive play (Kt–B2;), an ultimate break-through by P–Q4–Q5, would have been decisive.

16 B–QB3   P–R6
17 P–Q4   QKt–R3
18 QR–Kt1   R–Kt1
19 P–B5   ....

Normally P–Q5, is the proper course, but the Knight's unfortunate position is more easily exploited by the text-move.

19 ....   B–B3
20 R–Kt3   B × Kt
21 BP × B   Q–R4

The only way to cover the QRP.

22	KR–Kt1	R–Kt2
23	Q–Q2	KR–Kt1
24	B–B1	Q–B2

There is no saving clause.

25	QB × Kt	Kt × B
26	R × Kt	Q–R4
27	R × R	Q × Q
28	R × Rch.	K–B2
29	B–B4	Q × QP
30	B–Kt3	Q × BP
31	R–Kt7	Q × P
32	R × Pch.	K–B3
33	R(Kt1)–Q1	P–B4
34	R(Q7)–Q6	Q–B6
35	R × Pch.	K–Kt4
36	R–K3	Q–Kt5
37	R–QB1	P–KB5
38	R–K5ch.	K–R3
39	R(K5) × P	and White won.

Game No. 96.—Oslo, 1922.

One of three Simultaneous Consultation Games.

White : Dalseg and Geelmuyden.

1	P–K3	P–KKt3
2	P–Q4	B–Kt2
3	Kt–KB3	P–Q3
4	B–K2	Kt–Q2
5	Castles	P–K4.
6	P × P	………

This sudden change over to the open game comes as a surprise; one would have thought rather of close development by P–B4, P–QKt3, and Kt–B3. If 6 P–B4, Black would hardly have adopted Tschigorin's device—P–KB4;—by which the resource ...., P × P; would be weakened unnecessarily: he would rather have played 6 ...., KKt–B3; e.g.: 6 P–B4, KKt–B3; 7 Kt–B3, Castles; 8 P–QKt3, and perhaps now ...., P × P; 9 P × P, P–Q4; 10 P–B5, Kt–K5; 11 Kt × P, QKt × P; etc.

| 6 .... | Kt × P |

The Bishop at Kt2 begins to show signs of life. If 6 ...., P × P; 7 P–K4, KKt–B3; 8 B–QB4, Castles; 9 Q–K2, Black would have a " Hanham " with two tempi thrown in—thanks to White's P–K3–K4, and B–K2–B4,— but it is questionable whether with the Fianchetto the best use would have been made of the gift. The diagonal (White's QR3–KB8) is likely to become weak, e.g.: 9 ...., P–B3; 10 P–QR4, Q–B2; 11 P–QKt3, Kt–Kt3; 12 B–R3, R–K1; 13 QKt–Q2.

7 Kt × Kt	B × Kt
8 P–KB4	B–Kt2
9 P–K4	Kt–K2
10 P–B3	....

The thrust 10 P–B5, can be answered in two ways: Accepting the sacrifice by 10 P–B5, (instead of 10 P–B3,) P × P; 11 P × P, B × BP; 12 B–Kt5, B × KtP; 13 R × B, B × R; or, if this line of play is thought to be too dangerous, declining it in quiet style by 10 ...., P × P; 11 P × P, B–B3; 12 Kt–B3, P–Q4; followed by ...., P–B3; ...., B–Q2; ...., Q–B2; or ...., P–Kt3; and ultimately ...., Castles QR.

| 10 .... | P–KB4 |
| 11 B–Q3 | .... |

Black clearly plans a clearance by ...., P × P; and ...., P–Q4. But on the other hand this could have led to the weakening of some central points, for instance, his K4. Therefore 11 Kt–Q2, should be given the preference. The reconnoitring expedition by the Knight cannot be undertaken too early. A plausible variation would be: 11 Kt–Q2, Castles; 12 B–B4ch., K–R1; 13 B–Kt3, P × P; 14 Kt × P, P–Q4; 15 Kt–Kt5, P–KR3; 16 Kt–B3, and White has control of the centre.

11	P × P
12 B × P	P–Q4
13 B–B2	P–Q5

With this and the next move Black seeks to oppose
White's attempt at consolidation, as outlined in the
preceding note. Decidedly weaker at this stage, would be
the unimaginative 13 ...., B–B4.

14 P × P	Q × Pch.
15 Q × Q	B × Qch.
16 K–R1	B–Kt5

This move has more than one point. First of all White's
dreaded manœuvre Kt–Q2–B3, is to be subverted
eventually by ...., B × Kt; secondly after 17 R–K1, the
answer ...., K–Q2; can follow, without White being able
to counter with 18 R–Q1, and thirdly if 17 P–KR3, the
Bishop is to stay with the utmost persistence at KKt5.

17 R–K1   ....

If 17 P–KR3, P–KR4; (much weaker would be
17 ...., B–KB4; 18 B–R4ch., P–B3; 19 Kt–Q2,
Castles QR; 20 Kt–B3, and White is not without prospects
of consolidation) 18 K–R2, Kt–B4; if now 19 B × Kt, B × B;
and Black has "two Bishops." But if 19 P–KKt3,—in order
to win the Bishop—then 19 ...., P–R5; and Black wins,
e.g.: 20 P × B, P × P dbl. ch.; 21 K–Kt2, R–R7 ch.;
22 K–B3, R × B; 23 Kt–R3, (or 23 P × Kt, P–Kt7;
24 R–K1ch., K–B2; 25 B–K3, B × B; 26 K × B, R–K1ch.;)
23 ...., R–B7ch.; 24 R × R, P × R; 25 B–Q2, B × P; and
Black has gained material.

Or 17 P–KR3, P–KR4; 18 K–R2, Kt–B4; 19 P–KKt3,
P–R5; 20 B–R4ch., (to safeguard this Bishop) K–B2;
21 P × B, P × P dbl. ch.; 22 K–Kt2, R–R7 ch.; 23 K–B3,
P–Kt7; 24 R–Q1, QR–KR1; 25 P × Kt, P × P; and White

is defenceless against the threat ...., R(R1)–R6ch.; K–K2, P–Kt8(Q) dis. ch.

It is clear that White would also obtain an inferior game after 17 Kt–Q2, (instead of P–KR3,) Castles QR ; 18 Kt–B3, B × Kt; 19 R × B, KR–K1 ; 20 R–Kt1, Kt–B4; we need only point out the variant 21 B × Ktch., P × B ; 22 B–Q2, B × P ; 23 R × B, R × B ; and wins.

| 17 .... | K–Q2 |

The King advances pluckily. The fact that, in doing so, he is supported by the Bishops which, so to speak, are in the air, reminds one of the most audacious acrobatic feats (we mean of course the human pyramid).

18 Kt–Q2	QR–K1
19 Kt–B4	Kt–Q4
20 B–Q2	....

A far stronger resistance results from 20 Kt–K5ch., (this opportunity of consolidating his position occurs at intervals throughout the game). It is true, Black would even then retain a small advantage, e.g.: 20 Kt–K5ch., K–B1 ; 21 R–QKt1, B–KB4; 22 B × B, P × B ; 23 B–Q2, B × Kt; 24 P × B, K–Q2 ; and ...., K–K3 ; and Black still has the superior ending.

| 20 .... | B–K7 |

Winning a pawn. The game should now turn to Black's advantage without much trouble.

21 B–Kt3	B × Kt
22 B × B	Kt–Kt3
23 B–Kt3	B × P
24 QR–Q1	R × Rch.

A mistake which lets in the opposing Bishops. After 24 ...., K–B1 ; White would have no sort of compensation for his lost pawn.

25 B × R dis. ch.	K–B1
26 B–K6ch.	K–Kt1
27 B–R4	....

Black is now in a critical position : it is difficult to find a sufficient parry against the exchange of Rooks (R–Q8ch.,), followed by a pawn-hunt (B–Kt8, etc.).

| 27 .... | Kt–B1 |

Sufficient for a draw would probably be 27 ...., P–B4; e.g.: 28 R–Q8ch., R × R ; 29 B × R, P–B5; 30 B × Kt, P × B ; 31 B × P, B–B8; 32 P–Kt3, P–KKt4; 33 P–B5, K–B2; 34 K–Kt2, K–Q3; 35 K–B3 (or A), K–K4;

36 K–Kt4, K–B3; 37 K–R5, K–Kt2.   Or A. 35 P–B6,
(instead of 35 K–B3,) K–K4; 36 P–B7, B–R6; 37 K–B3,
P–R4, etc.

	28 R–Q8	R × R
	29 B × R	B–R6

Black has relied on this counter.

	30 P–Kt4 ?	....

This loses.   Questionable is also 30 B–Kt8, because of
30 ...., B–K2; (30 ...., P–KR4; 31 B–B6, B–K2;
32 B–K5, P–R5; 33 B–R7, P–KKt4; 34 P–B5, Kt–Q3;
35 P–B6, B–B1; 36 P–Kt3, P × P; 37 P × P, P–B4;
38 K–Kt2, P–Kt4; 39 K–B3, threatening K–Kt4,).   After
30 ...., B–K2; 31 B × B, Kt × B; 32 B × P, K–B1;
33 P–Kt4, K–Q2; 34 P–KR4, P–QKt4; (not 34 ....,
K–K3; because of 35 B × P,) 35 P–R5, P × P; 36 P × P,
K–K3; 37 P–R6, K–B3; 38 K–Kt2, P–B4; 39 K–B3,
P–R4; 40 K–K4, P–R5; White would not be out of danger.
Against this 30 B–B6, appears to equalise entirely, e.g.:
........., Kt–K2; 31 P–Kt4, followed by K–Kt2, and the
threat B × Kt, P–Kt5, and B–Kt8.   Or 30 ...., B–K2;
31 B–Kt7, B–Q3; 32 P–B5, P × P; 33 B × P, P–KR4;
34 P–KR4, etc.   The premature exchange of Rooks
(24 ...., R × Rch.;) appears therefore to have thrown
away the win.

	30	B–K2

The winning move.

	31 B × Kt	B × B
	32 B–K6	P–KKt4.
	33 P–B5	P–Kt4

White has no hope in spite of Bishops of opposite
colours.

34	K–Kt2	P–B4
35	K–B3	K–B2
36	K–K4	K–Q3
37	B–Kt3	P–B5
38	B–B2	B–B3
39	B–Q1	P–QR4
40	B–B2	P–R5
41	B–Q1	P–R6

Resigns.

Game No. 97.—Berlin, 1928.

White: Stoltz.

1	P–K4	P–QB4
2	Kt–QB3	Kt–QB3
3	P–KKt3	P–KKt3
4	B–Kt2	B–Kt2
5	KKt–K2	P–K3

Black wishes to establish a diagonal outpost at his Q5 where it is to have the support of the KKt at QB3.

6	P–Q3	KKt–K2
7	B–K3	Kt–Q5
8	Q–Q2	KKt–B3

See preceding note.

9 Kt–Q1 ....

Kostich in our game at Niendorf played here 9 Castles KR. There followed 9 ...., P–Q3; 10 Kt–Q1, Q–R4; 11 Kt × Kt, Q × Q; 12 B × Q, P × Kt; 13 P–QB3, (P–QB4, at once is clearer) B–Q2; 14 P–KB4, P × P; 15 P × P, R–QB1; with some diagonal play.

9 .... Kt × Kt

There would be no fault to find with the straightforward 9 ...., P–Q4; e.g.: 10 Kt × Kt, P × Kt; with immediate pressure in the QB file and latent pressure on the long Black Diagonal which would come into its own when, sooner or later, White has to play P–QB3.

10	Q × Kt	Q–R4ch.
11	Q–Q2	....

If 11 P–B3, Kt–Q5; 12 Q–Q2, Kt–Kt6.

11	....	Q × Qch.
12	K × Q	P–Q3

Diagonal action, when still undefined, must be treated with the greatest circumspection, or it comes to nothing.

12 ...., P-Kt3; had possibilities: 13 P-QB3, B-Kt2;
14 P-KB4, P-Q4; 15 P×P, Kt-K2; 16 Kt-B2, and now
perhaps 16 ...., Kt-B4. It was of moment to reserve the
option of recapturing at Q4 with the KP eventually. After
the text-move, which unnecessarily diminishes the number
of possibilities, a win could no longer be proved.

13 P-KB4	P-Kt3
14 P-K5	B-Kt2
15 P×P	Castles QR
16 P-B3	R×P
17 Kt-B2	KR-Q1

Black position, though firmly knit, has altogether too
few possibilities of attack.

| 18 QR-Q1 | .... |

A clearly drawn position as White's Q3 is impregnable.
Steinitz has drawn a number of such positions in spite of
the most dogged perseverance. Examine, for instance,
18 ...., Kt-K2; 19 B×Bch., K×B; 20 K-B2, Kt-B4;
21 KR-K1, P-KR4; 22 Kt-K4, R(Q3)-Q2; 23 B-B1. Or
18 ...., Kt-K2; 19 B×Bch., K×B; 20 K-B2, Kt-Q4;
21 KR-K1, P-B4; 22 B-B1, and although Black plays his
King to KB2, (to secure the KP) White doubles his Rooks
on the K file and can await the coming onslaught (.........,
P-QKt4-Kt5;) with equanimity.

| 18 .... | P-K4 |

An "energetic" attempt, which the youthful adversary
parries without much trouble.

| 19 KR-K1 | P-B4 |
| 20 B×Kt | R×B |

If 20 ...., B×B; 21 P×P, B×P; 22 B×P.

21 P×P	B×P
22 B-Kt5	B-B3
23 B×B	R×B
24 R-K7	....

Now White has obtained a not inconsiderable degree
of initiative.

| 24 .... | R-Q2 |
| 25 QR-K1 | B-Q4 |

Black is not afraid to place his proud Bishop on the
defensive (at KB2). This kind of pluck, rather foreign to
the spirit of the so-called classic chess, appears to be typical
of the neo-romantic style.

26 Kt–R3	P–KR3
27 Kt–B4	B–B2
28 P–KR4	K–Q1
29 R × Rch.	....

The retreat 29 R(K7)–K5, would lead to liquidation after
29 ...., P–KKt4; 30 P × P, P × P; 31 Kt–R3, P–KB5;
32 R × KtP, P × P; 33 R × KtP, B × P; but after the move
in the text Black secures the advantage.

29	K × R
30 P–R3	P–KKt4
31 P × P	P × P
32 Kt–R3	R–Kt3
33 R–K5	B–K3

Now the Bishop, *inter alia*, forms a bridge for the
intended K–K2–B3.

34 K–K1	....

By 34 P–Q4, the bridge could be rendered useless, but
the continuation would be: 34 ...., P × P; 35 P × P, P–B5;
36 R × P, R × R; 37 Kt × R, P × P; and White would have
to deal with the " distant passed pawn."

34	K–K2
35 P–QKt4	K–B3
36 R–K3	R–Kt1
37 K–B2	B–Q4

Now the Bishop comes out of his shell.

38 P–B4	B–B2

Here the simple ...., B–Kt2; should be preferable.
After 39 K–Kt1, R–KR1; 40 Kt–B2, P–B5; would not be
ill-contrived, e.g.: 41 P × P, P × P; 42 R–K2, R–Kt1ch.;
43 K–B1, B–Kt7ch.; 44 K–K1, B–B6; 45 R–B2, R–Kt8ch.;
with advantage to Black. Or 42 R–K1, (instead of R–K2,)
R–Kt1ch.; 43 K–B1, B–Kt7ch.; 44 K–K2, R–K1ch.;
45 K–Q2, R × R; 46 K × R, K–K4; 47 K–Q2, K–Q5;
48 P × P, P × P; 49 K–K2, P–B6ch.; 50 K–Q2, B–B8; and
wins. Other lines of defence are even worse.

39 Kt–Kt1	R–KR1
40 Kt–B3	R–R8
41 Kt–K5	....

Better than 41 R–K1, R × R; etc.

41	B–K3
42 Kt–B6	....

White should no longer lose.

42	....	R–R7ch.
43	K–K1	R–R7
44	P × P	P × P
45	Kt × P	B–Q2

A last effort.

46	P–Q4	....

He could have drawn the game by 46 Kt–Kt5, e.g.:
........, B × Kt; 47 P × B, R × P; 48 R–K8, (the simplest)
R × P; (if ...., R–Kt6; 49 R–QKt8,) 49 P–Kt6, R–Kt6;
50 R–QKt8, K–K4; 51 P–Kt7, K–Q3; 52 R–Q8ch., K–B2;
53 R–B8ch., K × P; 54 R × P, R–KB6; 55 P–Kt4, etc.

46	....	P × P
47	R–Q3	K–K4
48	Kt–Kt5	B × Kt
49	P × B	R–QKt7

Initiating an interesting break-through.

50	P–R4	P–Kt5
51	R–Q2	....

Only 51 P–R5, R × P; 52 R–R3, would have afforded
the chance of a draw.

51	....	R × R
52	K × R	P–B5
53	P × Pch.	K–Q3

White is lost.

54	P–R5	P–Kt6
55	P–R6	K–B2
56	K–K2	P–Q6ch.
57	K × P	P–Kt7
58	K–K4	P–Kt8(Q)
59	K–B5	Q–Kt3
60	K–Kt5	K–Q2
61	P–B5	K–K2
	Resigns.	

7.—THE WEAK SQUARE-COMPLEX OF A SPECIFIED COLOUR.

A typical feature of modern master-play: one of the contestants persistently labours under a number of weaknesses, all of which are on squares of the same colour. The process of centralisation (No. 23), as well as that of restriction, is carried out with astonishing regularity on squares of one colour. Very much the same state of things obtains in alternating play (see Chapter 5); the needful two weaknesses are also either " Black " or " White," but practically never " mixed " (compare for example No. 71). Exceptional cases may occur: the defender of a line which is under control of his opponent (say the K file) has to watch two squares where a break-through might occur, perhaps K6 and K7 (compare No. 93); here we have a weak complex of squares of opposite colours.

What line has the defence to follow? (For the attack we have already given the necessary lead in Chapter 5.)

There are three possibilities:

1. It is possible to try for counter play on squares of the opposite colour. Such strategy (see No. 98) would only suit the attacking player; the positional player would hardly feel at home. For the type of position—in which one player has dug himself in on White squares, the other has occupied all Black-squared points—clearly lacks the tendency to gradual liquidation, of which the main feature—exchanges—hardly arises. (See note to move 9 in Game No. 98.)

2. It is possible to play for the re-capture of the territory lost on squares of one colour: a sound strategy which we would illustrate here by giving a pertinent example. White: Maroczy (Carlsbad, 1923). Position after Black's 22nd move: White: K at KB2, Q at Q2, R at QR1, R at QKt1, B at Q4; pawns at QR4, QB3, QB2, K5, KB3, KKt2, KR2.

Black: K at KKt1, Q at QB5, R at KB1, R at KB4, B at QR3, pawns at QR2, QKt3, Q4, K3, KB5, KKt2, KR2.

Play went as follows: 23 P–R5, P–QKt4; 24 B×P, R×P; 25 R–K1, (White now seeks to capture the Black-squared points in the centre). 25 ...., R×R; 26 Q×R, R–K1; 27 Q–K5, (he has apparently achieved his object). 27 ...., R–K2; 28 B–Q4, (28 B–Kt6, it is true, would be better in order to prevent ...., Q–B2; after 28 ....,

P–Kt5; 29 P×P, Q×P; 30 K–Kt1, Black would play 30 ......, P–R3; followed by ......, K–R2; with a reasonably good game), 28 ...., Q–B2; 29 R–K1, Q×Q; 30 B×Q, R–KB2; 31 P–Kt3, P×Pch.; 32 P×P, R–B1; 33 R–QKt1, R–B1; (the possession of the central point at White's K5 is of little account in this position) 34 R–Kt4, P–Kt4; 35 K–K3, K–B2; 36 P–Kt4, K–Kt3; 37 R–Kt1, P–R4; Draw.

3. It is possible to employ preventive measures when the opponent threatens to become too powerful on squares of one colour (see in No. 99 the 12th move recommended by us, B–QKt5,). It should be clear that we are inclined to give the last-mentioned method the preference.

Game No. 98.—Hanover, 1926.

Black: Mieses.

1 P–QB4	P–K4
2 Kt–QB3	Kt–KB3
3 Kt–B3	Kt–B3
4 P–K4	....

My own special Dresden Variation (compare Games 31 and 52).

4	B–Kt5
5 P–Q3	P–Q3
6 P–KKt3	B–QB4
7 B–Kt2	....

The preventive 7 P–KR3, could be considered.

7	Kt–KKt5
8 Castles	P–B4

With this move a position is reached which is difficult to assess: the second player is strong on Black-squared points (e.g.: his Q5 and KB7,) but White appears to be able to obtain counter-play on White squares.

9 Kt–Q5	....

Instead of the move in the text, two lines of play came under consideration: I. 9 P×P, B×P; 10 Kt–KKt5, Q–Q2; 11 B–Q5, R–KB1; 12 KKt–K4, B–QKt3; Black has the better game. II. 9 B–Kt5, Kt–B3; 10 P×P, B×P; 11 Kt–KR4, B–K3; 12 Kt–K4, Castles; 13 K–R1, if then ...., Q–Q2; there follows 14 B×Kt, P×B; 15 P–B4, K–R1; 16 P–B5, B–Kt1; 17 Kt×B, followed by 18 B–K4, Kt–Q5; with approximately even chances. Note (after

18 ...., Kt–Q5 ;) that the contrast between the White- and Black-squared formations was maintained, one could almost say, uncompromisingly, into the end-game (compare preliminary remarks to Chapter 7).

9 ....   P–KR3 ?

Impairs his own initiative on the Black squares, (for ...., P–KR3; spells loss of time) and fosters the opponent's plans on the White squares: more can hardly be expected of one move!

Instead of the text-move, 9 ...., Castles; is almost an obvious move.   After 9 ...., Castles; 10 B–Kt5, Q–K1; 11 Kt × BP, Q–R4; 12 Kt × R, could not be played (12 ...., P × P; 13 P × P, R × Kt;) and 12 P–KR3, would also lead to trouble for White, (12 ...., Kt × P; 13 R × Kt, B × Rch.; 14 K × B, P × P; 15 P × P, Q × B; 16 Kt × R, Kt–Q5; 17 R–B1, [........., B × P; was threatened] 17 ...., B × P; 18 R–R3, B–Kt5; 19 Kt–B7, Q–R4; 20 Kt–Kt5, B × Kt; 21 B × B, Q–R7ch.; 22 K–B1, Q–R8ch.; and wins.) White therefore could hardly play 10 B–Kt5, in reply to 9 Castles; After 10 P–KR3, (what else?) Kt × P; 11 R × Kt, B × Rch.; 12 K × B, P × P; 13 P × P, Kt–Q5; 14 B–K3, Kt × Kt; followed by ...., B × P; the games are approximately even.   After the text-move Black gets into difficulties.

10	P × P	B × P
11	Kt–R4	B–K3
12	Kt–Kt6	R–KKt1
13	P–KR3	....

In control of all the " White points " he now proceeds to oust the opponent from the " Black points " as well.

| 13 .... | Kt–B3 |
| 14 B–K3 | .... |

Preparing for P–QKt4, which, if played at once, allowed the parry ...., B–Q5.

| 14 .... | B × Kt |

Here 14 ...., B–B2; appeared indicated. The second player defends his position against the separate threats as they occur, but he does nothing towards restoring in a comprehensive manner the situation on the White squares. Incidentally it is interesting to note that 14 ...., Q–Q2; (intending ...., Q–B2;) would have been inadequate, e.g.: 15 P–QKt4, B × B; 16 P × B, Castles; (not ...., B × P; because of 17 R × Kt,) 17 Q–R4, K–Kt1; 18 P–Kt5, B × Kt; 19 P × Kt, B × P(B3); 20 B × B, P × B; 21 QR–Kt1ch., K–R1; 22 Kt–K7, and wins.

| 15 P × B | Kt–Q5 |

Or 15 ...., Kt–K2; 16 Kt × Kt, with 17 P–Q4, and the better game.

| 16 P–B4 | Q–Q2 |

Useless would be 16 ...., P × P; 17 R × P, Kt–K3; 18 B × B, Kt × R; 19 Q–K1ch., K–B2; 20 Kt × Kt, R–K1; 21 Kt–K6, and White maintains his advantage in material.

17 P–QKt4	B–Kt3
18 P × P	P × P
19 Kt × P	Q–K2
20 Kt–B4	....

Black of course is lost; the more commendable is Mieses' ingenuity in looking out for salvation.

| 20 .... | K–Q1 |

Castles QR would not do because of Kt × Bch., but now he plans ...., R–K1.

| 21 P–QR4 | .... |

A pity. There was an elegant win by 21 R–K1, namely:
21 ...., Q × P; 22 R–Kt1, Q–B6; 23 Q–R4, Kt–B7;
(there is nothing else) 24 B × B, Kt × R; 25 B × Pch., K × B;
26 R × Pch., K × R; 27 P–Q6 dis.ch., Kt × B; 28 Q–Kt5ch.,
and mate in three. 21 P–Q6, would also have won easily,
e.g.: 21 ...., P × P; 22 R–K1, Q–QB2; 23 P–QR4, P–R3;
24 Kt × B, Q × Kt; 25 Q–Q2, R–K1; 26 B–B2. The text-
move of course also wins.

21	....	R–K1
22	K–R2	Kt–K7
23	P–Q6	....

He lets himself be hoodwinked. Simply 23 Q × Kt,
B × B; 24 Q–B3, would have won fairly easily.

23	....	P × P
24	R–K1	B × B
25	R × Kt	B–Kt8ch.
26	Q × B	Q × R

Now White has to work again.

27	Kt × P	R–K2
28	P–R5	R–Q2
29	R–K1	Q–Q7
30	Kt–B4	Q × KtP
31	P–R6	....

The attack must win out.

31	....	R–B1

If 31 ...., P–QKt4; 32 Kt–K5, R–B1; 33 Kt × R,
Kt × Kt; 34 R–Kt1, Q–B4; 35 Q × Q, R × Q; 36 P–Q4,
R–B4; 37 B–B6. Or 31 ...., R–Kt1; 32 Kt–K5,
(threatening Q × P, which, if played at once would have
permitted the parry ...., P × P;) 32 ...., Q–Q5; (comparatively the best) 33 Kt–B7ch., K–B2; 34 R–B1ch.,
K–Kt3; 35 R–Kt1ch., K × P; 36 Q–QB1, Q × P; 37 B–B1.

32	R–Kt1	Q–R5
33	P × P	R–Kt1
34	Q–B5	R–QB2
35	Q–Q4ch.	Kt–Q2

Or 35 ...., R–Q2; 36 Q–K5, R–QB2; 37 Kt–R5,
with the deadly threat Kt–B6ch., R × Kt; Q × Rch., etc.

36	Q × KtP	R–B4
37	Q–R8ch.	K–B2
38	Q × P	Q–B7

39 Q–Q6ch.	K–Q1
40 R–KB1	K–K1
41 R–B8ch.	Resigns.

For the sequel could be 41 ...., Kt × R ; 42 Q × Rch., K–B2 ; 43 Q × Ktch., K × Q; 44 P–Kt8(Q)ch., K–B2; 45 Q × Pch., and Q × R.

The loss of the exchange altered the logical course of development, but it could not affect the essence of the situation, namely, the White-square attacking possibilities.

Game No. 99.—Copenhagen, 1923.

From three Simultaneous Consultation Games.

White: **Erik Andersen and J. W. Nielsen.**

1 P–K4	Kt–QB3
2 P–Q4	P–Q4
3 P × P	Q × P
4 B–K3	P–K3

In all probability 4 ...., P–K4; is objectively the right move here.

5 Kt–KB3   B–Q2

In order to intimidate the adversaries a little, for now Black " threatens " to throw the weight of the Q file into the scale. Objectively 5 ...., Kt–B3; is of course more correct, e.g.: 6 P–KR3, (preventing ...., Kt–KKt5; eventually). 6 ...., P–K4; 7 P × P, Q × Qch.; 8 K × Q, Kt–Q4; or 5 ...., Kt–B3; 6 P–KR3, Q–R4ch.; 7 P–B3, P–K4; 8 P–QKt4, Q–Q4; 9 P–Kt5, P × P; 10 P × P, Kt–K2; 11 Kt–B3, Q–Q1; with 12 ...., QKt–Q4; and Black's position is consolidated.

6 QKt–Q2   ....

Preferable was 6 B–K2, Castles; 7 Castles, Kt–B3; 8 P–B4, Q–KB4; 9 P–KR3, and Black's position on the Q side causes uneasiness. Probably the second player, after 6 B–K2, Castles; 7 Castles, would have had recourse to the phantastic-looking manœuvre 7 ...., P–B3; 8 P–B4, Q–KR4; 9 Kt–B3, Q–B2; after which his position would still have been difficult to defend.

6 ....   Castles
7 B–Q3   ....

A subtle thought. White foregoes herewith the obvious attacking line B–QB4, with Q–K2, and Castles QR, and, instead, leaves the Queen entirely unmolested. He did not think the Queen's presence on her Q4 undesirable; in this case the thrust ...., P–K4; could always be beaten off with a gain in time by P–B4, and P–Q5.

7	Kt–B3
8 Castles	P–KR3
9 P–B3	P–KKt4

In order to keep the Kt away from his K5; at the same time the development of the B at KKt2 is intended.

10 P–B4	....

This advance is now more than ever double-edged, though Black's Queen has to seek slightly unusual squares, which, however, turn out to be quite favourable. The logical procedure, arising from the 9th move was rather 10 P–QKt4, with the possible continuation 10 ...., P–Kt5; 11 Kt–K1, Q–KR4; 12 P–Kt5, Kt–K2; (not first ...., B–Q3; as P–Kt3, and P–QB4, would get the Bishop into trouble); 13 P–QB4, Kt–B4; 14 P–B5, Kt–Q4; with chances and counter-chances. After the manoeuvre in the text, White falls away surprisingly quickly.

10	Q–Q3
11 P–B5	Q–K2
12 Kt–B4	....

As Black is on the point of capturing White-squared territory, the resistance also should have had a White-squared tendency, therefore 12 B–Kt5.

12	Kt–Q4
13 KKt–K5	....

The offer of a sacrifice by 13 P–QKt4, was preferable here. After ...., Kt × KtP; 14 R–Kt1, White's attack should not be under-rated, linked as it would be with blockading effects.

13	B–Kt2
14 R–K1	Kt × Kt
15 Kt × Kt	B × Kt
16 P × B	B–B3

And now the first player's position is a " White squared " ruin. Note the smooth ease with which the rest develops quite naturally.

17 Q–B1	Kt–B5
18 B–B1	Kt–Q6
19 B × Kt	R × B
20 P–QKt4	Q–Q2

21	Q–B4	R–Q1
22	P–QR3	B–R5
23	KR–Kt1	B–Kt4
24	Q–B2	Q–Q4
25	R–K1	P–Kt5
26	Q–K2	P–KR4
27	P–QR4	B–B5
28	Q–B2	P–R5
29	Q–K2	R–Q5
30	Q–Kt2	R–Q6
31	Q–K2	R–Kt1
32	K–R1	P–R6

This new " White squared " weakness on White's KKt2 worthily joins those existing at QB6, Q5, QKt5, Q3, etc. It is indeed the last straw.

33	R–KKt1	P × Pch.
34	R × P	R–R6
35	Q–K1	R × R
36	Q × R	Q–B6
37	K–Kt1	R–Q1

Resigns.

8.—THE TRIUMPH OF THE " BIZARRE " AND " UGLY " MOVE.

Such were the extremely winsome epithets which used to be applied to our moves. To-day, after the modern idea has won all along the line, it is surprising to everybody how such a genuine, beautiful and deep line of play as the Hanham variation could ever be thought ugly.

After 1 P–K4, P–K4; 2 Kt–KB3, P–Q3; 3 P–Q4, Kt–KB3; 4 Kt–B3, QKt–Q2; Black intends to place another pawn in the centre with ...., P–B3; whereby he, at any rate, obtains there a certain superiority.   Compared to this, what importance can attach to the temporary non-development of the QB ?   But the pre-moderns had only one ideal : that of the free, untrammelled development of the pieces.   But we do not wish to " square accounts "; the school of formalism is dead, and you cannot flog a dead horse.   And if, in the following pages, we record a few criticisms from earlier times, the object is not to " square accounts " but is purely one of technical interest.

I.—1 P–K4, P–K3; 2 P–Q4, P–Q4; 3 P–K5, "the decisive mistake." This comment was, *inter alia*, intended to convey that this unjustified advance—unjustified because the Black KKt is not at his KB3, and there is, therefore, no attack —must be deemed ugly. In reality, as the author has maintained for fully twenty years (nobody would listen to him), 3 P–K5, is neither a mistake, nor ugly, but a good and rational move.   After 3 ...., P–QB4; White has no less than four (sic!) good equalising lines, namely : 4 P–QB3; 4 P × P, 4 Kt–KB3, 4 Q–Kt4! To-day the soundness of 3 P–K5, is universally admitted.

II.—1 P–K4, P–K4; 2 Kt–KB3, Kt–QB3; 3 B–B4, Kt–B3; 4 Kt–Kt5, a "duffer's" move. To-day everyone knows that 4 Kt–Kt5, is a logically well-founded attempt to castigate the opponent's premature development of the KKt (3 ...., Kt–B3;).

III.—1 P–K4, P–K4; 2 Kt–KB3, Kt–QB3; 3 B–Kt5, Kt–B3; 4 Castles, Kt × P; 5 P–Q4, B–K2; 6 Q Kt, Kt–Q3; 7 B × Kt, KtP × B; 8 P × P, Kt–Kt2; a glorious strategic retreat! Or rather a fighting withdrawal! On his retreat he inflicts two gaping wounds on the adversary : he deprives him of one of his Bishops and creates for his side a compact pawn-centre of dynamic value. Surely most captivating play! Not so in the judgment of the pre-moderns; they saw neither the dynamics of the retreat, nor the beauty of its conception : for them the whole manœuvre was and remained a pitiful Knight's move.

We present two games. In 101 we find the "Bishop at QKt5 in a close game," which formation, according to Tarrasch, is "less forgivable, in a master, than to leave a piece 'en prise.'" In reality, the Bishop on QKt5 appears to be well posted and could be placed there in 70 per cent. of close games without prejudice, probably even with advantage. In No. 100 we find the preparation (P–KKt3,) for a fianchetto which then "unaccountably" fails to materialise. And yet it is actually one of the most logically thought-out games. Also in its further course, the game makes an impression partly "mysterious," partly "discordant." But then, and that is the point, æsthetic feeling for Chess must be anchored in thought.

He who goes by appearances only, can easily arrive at that state in which moves will appear to him to be ugly, which by no means deserve the appellation. Beauty in Chess, after all is said and done, exists only in the thought.

Game No. 100.—New York, 1927.

Black: Dr. Alekhin.

1 Kt–KB3	Kt–KB3
2 P–QKt3	P–Q3
3 P–Kt3	P–K4
4 P–B4	....

" Bizarre "! He is not afraid of ...., P–K5; anyone else would have chosen 4 P–Q3.

4	P–K5

This move weakens the "black squared" points and sows the seeds of all future difficulties.

5 Kt–R4	....

So the square at KKt2 was not meant for a Bishop, pining for a fianchetto, but for the " bizarre " Knight.

5	P–Q4

This move which would have been good against 5 Kt–Q4, here only leads to an excursion by the Queen, which is not quite beyond cavil. There is, however, scarcely anything better.

6 P × P	Q × P
7 Kt–QB3	Q–B3
8 P–K3	....

The possibility of a fianchetto is thus given up permanently.

8	P–QR3

More consistent was 8 ...., B–KKt5; White's best continuation was then 9 Q × B, as the KKt loses a tempo when forced to withdraw, e.g.: 9 Q × Kt, Kt × Q; 10 B–Kt5, Kt–B3; 11 B–Kt2, P–QR3; 12 B × Qch., Kt × B; 13 Kt–K2, Kt–KKt5; 14 P–B3, (else there follows Kt–K4;) P × P; 15 Kt × P, Castles; with only a minute advantage to White. This variation provides an illustration of the second player's defensive resources : he evidently has counter-play on the White squares : if he plays his (none too numerous) trumps correctly, he has the chance of hemming in White's attack on the Black squares. The continuation selected by Alekhin renders the defence more difficult without being hopeless.

9 B–QKt2	B–KKt5
10 B–K2	B × B
11 Kt × B	QKt–Q2
12 R–QB1	Q–Kt3
13 Castles	....

13 Q–B2, deserved serious consideration, e.g.:
13 ...., B–Q3; 14 Kt–B5. But Black appears to have a
better line: 13 Q–B2, Kt–B4; 14 B–Q4, Kt–Q6ch.;
15 Q × Kt, P × Q; 16 B × Q, P × B; 17 Kt–Q4, (or 17 Kt–QB3,
B–R6; and White loses the QB file), B–B4; 18 R–B3,
Kt–Q4; 19 R × P, Kt–Kt5; 20 R–B3, B × Kt; with ....,
Kt × P; and Black has the better game.

Nevertheless the variation beginning with 13 Q–B2,
Kt–B4; appears favourable to White; only instead of
14 B–Q4, he should play 14 Castles, e.g.: 14 ...., Kt–Q6;
15 B × Kt, Q or P × B; 16 Kt–B4, (threatening Kt–Q5,) with
the better game. After moves other than ...., Kt–B4; we
should also prefer White's game, e.g.: 13 Q–B2,
Castles; 14 Castles, and Black is lacking a plausible
continuation. Not only that, but even the inferior text-move
should not allow the opponent to escape the pressure. The
missed opportunity of initiating " White-squared " counter-
play should not be allowed to recur. For that reason we view
with suspicion Alekhin's " White-squared " *coup d'état* in
the course of the next moves.

   13 ....   B–Q3
   14 P–B3   ....
Alekhin prefers 14 P–Q3.
   14 ....   B–K4

Very interesting ! He wishes at all cost to occupy White
squared territory (Q6). As to this, what can the logical conception of the game tell us ? We cannot help being in doubt :
Why and how should the White-squared points suddenly be
able to place those on the Black squares in the shade ? After
Black's lapse on the 8th move, the weakness of the second
player on the Black squares had become chronic. White has
made no mistake (for 13 Castles, could not be so termed). It

follows that Black's violent, if ingenious, attempt needs must
be in some way unsound.

15	B × B	Kt × B
16	P × P	Kt–Q6
17	R–QB3	Castles QR

18	Q–Kt1	Kt × P

No "coup d'état" without a "sacrifice." Whether
18 ...., Kt–B4; would have been better appears doubtful
after the further moves: 19 P–Q3, Kt–R5; 20 P × Kt,
Q × Pch.; 21 R–B2 (21 K–R1, Q × Kt; 22 KR–B1, would
also be promising), Kt–Kt5; 22 Q–KB1.

19	R × Kt	Kt × QP
20	R × Rch.	R × R
21	Q–B5ch.	K–Kt1
22	R–K1	....

Here 22 R–B1, also could be considered.

22	....	Q × Pch.
23	Q–B2	Q–Q6
24	Kt–B4	Q–QB6

There were good chances of a draw after 24 ....,
Q–B7; does this prove that the "coup d'état" was sound?
Or that "White" and "Black" points can assume power at
will? No, nothing of the kind. For, in the first place, the
draw (after 24 ...., Q–B7;) is not as yet certain; secondly,
it remains to be proved that White could not have improved
on his play at some stage (e.g., on move 22), and, finally,
there are unfortunately many positions in which a clearly
demonstrable superiority is not sufficient to enforce a win.
The victory by attrition should count.

25	R–K3	Q–B8ch.

There follows a bitter struggle. White wins, but only after many hours of the most stubborn contest.

26	K–Kt2	Q–B3ch.
27	Kt–B3	P–KKt4
28	Kt–Q3	Kt × Kt
29	Q × Kt	Q–B7ch.
30	Kt–B2	P–KB4
31	R–K2	Q–B4
32	Kt–Q3	Q–Q5
33	Kt–K5	P–B5
34	Kt–B4	....

According to Spielmann, 34 P–KKt4, was a safe road, for White would undoubtedly obtain a middle-game attack. But if it should come to an End-Game? Could not the passed pawn become troublesome?

34	....	P × P
35	R–Q2	Q–R1
36	R × Rch.	Q × R
37	P × P	Q–Q5
38	Q–B8ch.	K–R2
39	Q–B2	Q × Qch.
40	K × Q	P–KR4

The issue still trembles in the balance, and will depend on a line of play reminiscent of a study. See note to Black's 41st move.

   41 K–K3   ....
The sealed move.

   41 ....   P–B4
The main variation is: 41 ...., P–Kt4; 42 Kt–Q2, P–R5; 43 P–KKt4, P–R6; 44 K–B3, P–B4; 45 Kt–K4, P–B5; 46 P–Kt4, K–Kt3; for the Black King's participation looks unpleasant enough; the more so, because there is no

time to gather the KKtP. Now comes the point : 47 K–Kt3, and if 47 ...., K–B3; then (and not sooner) the pawn capture suddenly becomes possible : 48 Kt×P, P–B6; 49 Kt–B3, and wins.

42	P–R4	P–Kt4
43	P×P	P×P
44	Kt–Q2	K–Kt3
45	Kt–K4	P–R5
46	P–KKt4	P–R6
47	K–B3	P–Kt5

A last and ingenious flutter before darkness sets in.

48	Kt×KtP	P–B5
49	Kt–K4	P×P

If 49 ...., P–B6; 50 Kt–B2, with Kt–Q3.

50	P–Kt5	P–Kt7
51	Kt–Q2	K–B4
52	P–Kt6	P–R7
53	K–Kt2	K–Q5
54	P–Kt7	K–Q6
55	P–Kt8(Q)	K×Kt
56	Q–R2	K–B7
57	Q–B4ch.	Resigns.

A battle of giants.

Game No. 101.—Kecskemet, 1927.

Black: Gilg.

1	P–K4	P–QB4
2	Kt–KB3	Kt–QB3
3	B–Kt5	....

This move is far better than its reputation and secures a balanced game.

3	....	Q–B2

The best reply is probably ...., P–Q3.

4	P–B3	....

Now the usual and disagreeable reply to P–B3, namely ...., Kt–B3; is easily parried by Q–K2.

4	....	P–QR3
5	B–R4	Kt–B3
6	Q–K2	P–K4
7	Castles	B–K2
8	P–Q4	....

White offers a pawn which Black should have declined with ...., P-Q3.

    8 ....   BP × P

Equally insufficient would be 8 ...., Castles; 9 B × Kt, Q × B; 10 P × KP, Kt × P; 11 R-K1, P-B4; 12 P × P e.p., Kt × P(B3); 13 Q × B, R-K1; 14 Q × Rch., Kt × Q; 15 R × Ktch., K-B2; 16 Kt-K5ch., and remains with an extra piece.

    9 P × P   Kt × QP
   10 Kt × Kt   P × Kt
   11 P-K5   P-Q6

If 11 ...., Kt-Q4; 12 P-K6, P × P; 13 Q × KP, Kt-Kt3; 14 B KKt5, Q-Q1; 15 B × B, Kt × B; 16 Q-Kt3, Q × B; 17 Q × Kt, and White has the superior game. Less clear would be after 11 ...., Kt-Q4; 12 P-K6, P × P; 13 Q × KP, Kt-Kt3; the continuation 14 R-K1, Q-Q1; 15 B-KKt5, Kt × B; 16 Q × Bch., Q × Q; 17 R × Qch., with doubtful advantage.

   12 Q-K3   Kt-Q4

There was no salvation in 12 ...., B-B4; e.g.: 13 Q-Kt3, Kt-K5; 14 Q × P, B × Pch.; 15 K-R1, (not 15 R × B, because of ...., Q × Bch.; 16 R-B1, Q-K6ch.; and mate in 4) R-B1; 16 B-R6, B-B4; 17 P-K6, and wins.

   13 Q-Kt3   P-KKt3

If 13 ...., Castles; there comes first 14 B-Kt3.

   14 B-Kt3   Kt-Kt5
   15 B × Pch.   K-Q1
   16 B-R6   ....

This Bishop hardly looks as if he had an eye on QKt6, and yet such is the case!

   16 ....   Kt-B7
   17 Kt-B3   Kt-Q5

Despair. If 17 ...., Kt × R ; 18 Kt–Q5, Q–B3 (best) ; 19 B–K3, P–Q3 ; 20 B–Kt6ch., K–Q2 ; 21 P–K6, mate ! After the text move, White has a smashing win.

18	Q × QP	Q × P
19	KR–K1	Q–B3
20	R × B	Resigns.

For if ...., K × R ; 21 Kt–Q5ch., and if ...., Q × R ; 21 Q × Kt.

9.—THE DEFENCE ON HEROIC LINES.

One would, *a priori*, expect every department of the game to have been influenced to the same extent by the new ideas. This is far from being the case. In the realm of defence there seems to be a tendency stubbornly to eschew the invigorating influence of modern thought. It almost appears as if pre-modern spirit, ejected from all " positions " is entrenching itself in the territory in question. At the best progress there is infinitesimal. A mark of attack in the player's own camp creates fear and trembling, and in defence, a distinctly conventional trend seems, generally speaking, to take the upper hand. The cautious heed for niggling correctness in each move, the shy avoidance of untrodden paths, and particularly the fear of the " colossal " (of anything on a big scale)—how vividly does all this recall the so-called classic period of the dead and gone past !

The fault lies in the fact that too little use is made of newly found stratagems. The use of prophylaxis, restrictions, centralisation and over-protection can, in the sphere of defence, be of the greatest moment. We go so far as to say that the whole Art of Defence can thereby be lifted to a higher plane.

It surely makes a world of difference whether the section under fire by the enemy has to rely on its own resources, or whether the whole board radiates defensive energy. What could, for instance, centralisation mean other than designed co-ordination, as a matter of principle, over the whole board ? !

We bring forward four games, which are to illustrate defence by heroic measures. They show clearly an intensive fusion of the dictates mentioned above : in No. 102 a

restricted centre is thoroughly over-protected with the result
that the rather undeveloped formation acquires stability. The
retrograde selected for this purpose on moves 9 and 10 shows
a truly modern spirit. In No. 103, the most striking feature is
the unconcern with which the defence is conducted; a most
improbable-looking line, borrowed from the realm of End-
Game studies, is employed for defensive purposes. No. 104
is particularly noteworthy because the new defensive
technique comes into its own in a full measure : a violent
flank attack is brought to a standstill at the right moment by
counter-action in the centre, carried out with the utmost
intensity. This game is also significant on account of the
feature which, as mentioned above, is contrary to the spirit of
the so-called classics, namely, defensive manœuvres on a big
scale : attacks of immense power are neutralised by counter-
measures of equal vigour : as this widened scope is on the
whole only the product of a new perspective, but does not in
the main require a particularly high degree of playing
strength, it should by no means remain unattainable for less
experienced players.

In No. 105 also, the defensive technique, based on hyper-
modern principles, is fully triumphant. The opponent's
attack, based on the black squares, is held up, with the incidental use of the white squares, until an opportunity arises
to undertake a white-squared " coup d'état," returning at the
same time all the material gained. (Something similar
happened in No. 100, with the distinction that, unlike
Alekhin's " coup d'état," that in No. 105 was built up on a
sound basis).

The number of really great defensive players is very
small ; the author knows of the following only : Steinitz, Dr.
Em. Lasker, Amos Burn, Dr. O. S. Bernstein, Duras and
last, but not least, Louis Paulsen.

We hope that our research work will help to increase the
number of good defensive players. We wish to take this
opportunity of stating with gratification that a number of the
younger masters, for instance, the strategically brilliantly
gifted Sämisch, show interest for and adroitness in the
defence of difficult positions.

All hail to them !

Game No. 102.—Berlin, 1927.

White: Brinckmann.

1	P–K4	Kt–QB3
2	P–Q4	P–Q4
3	P × P	Q × P
4	B–K3	P–K3
5	B–K2	....

As explained in connection with No. 99, 5 Kt–KB3, would have caused the opponent trouble enough. But the B move is also strong.

5	....	Q × KtP

We have faith in the strength of the defence.

6	B–B3	Q–Kt3
7	Kt–K2	Kt–Kt5

The modern defensive technique sets in with sustained pressure. Centralisation with ...., Kt–Q4; is the object.

8	Kt–R3	Kt–Q4
9	Kt–QB4	....

The correct continuation was 9 Kt–Kt5, e.g. : 9 ...., P–QB3; 10 Kt–B4, Kt × Kt; 11 Kt–B7ch., K–Q2; 12 Kt × R, Kt–Kt7ch.; with the outcome uncertain (attempts by Dr. Lasker in conjunction with the author resulted in a draw).

9	....	Q–B3
10	Kt–Kt3	Q–Q1

What is the meaning of this manœuvre? Is it twofold! The Queen seeks security, and the idea of centralisation is sharply emphasised, for already three units are working against the break-through intended by White with P–QB4, and P–Q5, (naturally after moving the QKt). In short : the Knight in the centre is being over-protected. It remains clear that the retreat selected has a most neo-romantic effect,

for Black makes it clear that he is a believer in the power of
resistance of the initial position, whereas the so-called classics
were fanatics of quick development.

> 11 Q–Q2   KKt–B3

Sustained over-protection.

> 12 Kt–K5   P–B3

Over-protecting and marking time as well! He would
like to preserve the option of Castling on either side for as
long as possible, until his opponent has committed himself,
that is until he has Castled on one side or the other.   The
ability to wait is for Black's restricted position yet another
resource.   We would refer the reader to the 4th part of this
chapter (the restricted centre).

> 13 Castles KR   ....

If 13 Castles QR, there follows ...., B–Kt5; e.g.,
14 P–B3, B K2; and Black prepares for ...., Castles QR;
by ...., Q–B2; or ...., Q–R4; .. .., B–Q2; and
.........., KR–B1; but after the text-move, ..., Castles
QR; would be too dangerous.

> 13 ....   B–Q3
> 14 K–R1   Q B2
> 15 P–B4   Kt × B
> 16 Q × Kt   P–B4

A counter-attack has at all times an excellent effect, even
in a psychological sense; that was already known in bygone
days. On the other hand, the position is loosened by the text
move and 16 ...., Kt–Q2; therefore might have been
given preference.

> 17 Q–Kt5   ....

In order to punish the adversary for his " impudence."
More correct would be : 17 QR–K1, P × P; 18 Q × P, B–Q2;
although in this case also, Black would be in no real danger
(19 Kt–B5, P × Kt; 20 Kt–Kt6 dis. ch., B–K3; 21 Kt × R,
K–K2; and wins). There also came in question 17 Kt–Q3,
P × P; 18 Q × P.

> 17 ....   P × P
> 18 QR–K1   ....

If 18 Q × P, R–KKt1; 19 Q × Kt, B × Kt; with some
advantage to Black.

> 18 ....   K–B1

Wrong would be 18 ...., Castles; e.g. : 19 R–KKt1,
P–KR3; 20 Q–B4, B × Kt; 21 R × B, Kt–Q2; 22 Kt–R5,
Q × R ; 23 Q × RP, P–KKt3; 24 R–Kt5, Q–R1 ; 25 R × Pch.,
and mate in two.

	19 R–KKt1	P–KR3
	20 Q–B4	B × Kt
	21 Q × B	....

Or 21 R × B, Kt–Q2; etc.

	21	Q × Q
	22 R × Q	Kt–Q2

Simpler would be 22 ...., P–KKt3; 23 R–Q1, K–K2;
24 R × P, R–Q1 ; with a winning ending.

	23 R–QKt5	....

Black would have to overcome considerably greater
difficulties after 23 R–QR5.

	23	P–R3
	24 R–Kt3	....

Or 24 R–Kt4, Kt–K4; 25 B–Kt2, (B × P, R–QKt1 ;)
Kt–Q6; threatening ...., Kt × P; mate.

	24	Kt–B4
	25 R–R3	R–QKt1
	26 P–Kt4	Kt–Q2
	27 P–B5	Kt–K4
	28 R–K1	Kt × B
	29 R × Kt	B–Q2
	30 R–Q3	R–Q1
	31 K–Kt1	B–Kt4
	32 R–Q2	R–Q4
	33 Kt–K4	K–K2
	34 Kt–Q6	....

A mistake in a hopeless position. Relatively best was
34 P–B3, e.g.: ...., R–QKt1 ; 35 Kt–Q6, P–QKt3;
36 Kt × B, P × Kt ; 37 P × P, R × P ; and Black wins easily.

	34	R–Kt4ch.
	35 K–R1	B–B3ch.
	Resigns.	

Game No. 103.—Berlin, 1928.

White: Leonhardt.

1	P–K4	P–K3
2	P–Q4	P–Q4
3	Kt–QB3	B–Kt5
4	P × P	P × P
5	B–Q3	Kt–QB3
6	Kt–K2	KKt–K2
7	Castles	Castles
8	B–KB4	B–Kt5
9	P–KR3	………

Up to now the game has run on conventional lines, but with the text move Leonhardt suddenly makes preparations for an attack. But the following line would be simpler: 9 P–B3, B–KR4; 10 Q–Q2, or 10 B–K3, with 11 Kt–B4. The weakness at K3 is bearable.

9	………	B–KR4
10	Q–B1	B–R4

It cannot be said that White shuns untrodden paths. If 11 P–R3, (preventing ………, Kt–Kt5;) the intention was ………, B × QKt; 12 P × B, and the pawn lured on to QR3 would present a certain weakness in White's otherwise unexceptionable formation. Instead of 11 ……, B × QKt; (after 11 P–R3,) other moves are of course possible, e.g.: 11 ………, B–QKt3; or 11 ………, B–KKt3.

11	Q–K3	Kt–Kt5
12	Kt–Kt3	Kt × B
13	Kt × B	Kt × KtP
14	B–R6	………

The answer expected by Black.

14   ....   Kt–B5
15 Q–Kt5   ....

The main variation would have occurred after 15 Q–Kt3, 15 ...., Kt–B4; 16 Q–Kt4, P–KKt3; 17 B × R, B × Kt; and the White B has no retreat (a Rinck theme known as the "Bishop's Cross").

15   ....   Kt–KKt3
16 Kt × QP   P–KB3

At this point Black had two other good continuations. First of all the simple exchange 16 ...., Q × Q; 17 B × Q, P–KB3; 18 B–K3, QR–Q1; with a superiority on the White squares for the End-Game. Secondly, Kostich's suggestion: 16 ...., B–Q7; 17 Q × Q, QR × Q; 18 B × B, Kt × B; 19 KR–Q1, R × Kt; 20 R × Kt, R × Kt; etc., or 16 ...., B–Q7; 17 P–KB4, Q × Q; 18 B × Q, P–KB3; 19 P–B5, B × B; with an extra pawn, or finally, 16 ...., B–Q7; 17 Kt–K3, P × B; 18 Q × Q, (if Q × P, Q × P;) QR × Q; 19 Kt × Kt, R × P; 20 QR–Q1, KR–Q1; again winning a pawn.

The line of play selected appears to be stronger still.

17 QKt × Pch.   R × Kt

If ...., P × Kt; 18 Q–Kt5.

18 B × P   R–B2
19 B–B6   Q–Q3
20 QR–Q1   ....

If 20 Q–R6, there would follow 20 ...., R–K1; 21 P–KB4, R–K7; 22 P–B5, B–Q7; 23 P × Kt, B × Q; 24 P × Rch., K–B1; and Black wins, or 23 B–Kt5, (instead of P × Kt,) Kt–K6; and Black has not only an extra piece but also a very strong attack.

20   ....   QR–KB1
21 Q–Kt5   ....

If 21 Q–R6, P–B3; (threatening ...., B–Q1;) 22 P–KB4, Kt–K6; 23 P–B5, Kt × KR; 24 R × Kt, (24 P × Kt, Q–R7ch.; etc.) B–Q7; 25 Q × B, R × B; 26 Kt × Rch., Q × Kt; and Black wins.

21   ....   Q–B3
22 Q × Q   P × Q
23 B–Kt5   R–B4
24 P–B4   Kt–K6
25 P–Kt4   KR–B2
26 P–B5   Kt × KR
27 R × Kt   B–B6

28	R–Q1	Kt–K2
29	R–Q3	Kt–Q4
30	K–Kt2	R–Kt1
31	K–B3	R–Kt7
32	Kt–B6ch.	R × Kt

He does not wish to give up his handsome central Knight, but of course the simple 32 ...., Kt × Kt; 33 R × B, R–Kt3; would also have won without difficulty. The rest is easily understood.

33	B × R	R × RP
34	P–Kt5	R × P
35	B–K5	P–QR4
36	P–Kt6	P–R5
37	R–Q1	R–Q7
38	R–QKt1	B–Kt7
39	P × Pch.	K × P
40	R–Kt1	B × P

Saves everything.

41	R–Kt7ch.	K–R1
42	R–Kt2 dis. ch.	B × B
43	R × R	P–R6
44	R–K2	B–Kt7
45	R–K8ch.	K–Kt2
46	R–QR8	Kt–Kt5

Resigns.

Game No. 104.—Copenhagen, 1924.

White: Brinckmann.

1	P–Q4	P–KB4
2	P–K4	P × P
3	Kt–QB3	Kt–KB3
4	B–KKt5	P–QKt3

An innovation which looks extremely hazardous. After the customary 4 ...., Kt–B3; White can continue with 5 P–Q5, Kt–K4; 6 Q–Q4, Kt–B2; 7 B × Kt, KP × B; 8 Kt × P, P–KB4; 9 Kt–Kt3, P–KKt3; 10 Castles, B–R3ch.; 11 K–Kt1, Castles; 12 Kt–B3. But another as yet untried continuation is noteworthy: 4 ...., Kt–B3; 5 B × Kt, KP × B; 6 P–QR3, P–B4; 7 B–B4, Kt–K2; 8 P–Q5, and White is in readiness suitably to exploit the weakness which ...., P–Q3; would create.

5	B–QB4	....

Far better seems the clearance indicated in the preceding note: 5 B × Kt, KP × B; 6 P–QR3, with serious difficulties for Black.

5	P–K3
6 B × Kt	Q × B
7 Kt × P	Q–K2

Only a few moves have been played and the position already offers many fanciful possibilities. Note, for instance, the following variations: 7 ...., Q–Kt3; 8 Q–B3, B–Kt2; (not 8 ...., P–Q4; because of 9 B–Q3,) 9 Kt–Q6ch, ? B × Kt; 10 Q × B, Castles; 11 Q × R, Kt–B3; followed by ...., Q × KtP; or else 9 Kt–B6ch., (instead of Kt–Q6ch.,) Q × Kt; 10 Q × B, Q × P; 11 Q × R, B–Kt5ch.; 12 P–B3, B × Pch.; 13 K–B1, Castles; and Black must win. Finally 7 ...., Q–Kt3; 8 Q–B3, B–Kt2; 9 B–Q3, B–Kt5ch.; 10 P–B3, R–B1; 11 Kt–Q6ch., K–K2; 12 Kt × B, R × Q; 13 B × Q, R × QBP; 14 K–K2, R–B5; 15 B–Q3, R × P; 16 P–QR3, and White should win.

The attempt 7 ...., Q–Kt3; is, on balance, unfavourable to Black.

8 B–Q3	Kt–B3
9 P–QB3	B–Kt2
10 Kt–B3	Castles

Now Black has happily reached a position which, according to generally accepted views, cannot be accounted as tenable. But generally accepted views are not always well-founded. For instance, very few positions are supposed to be defensible, whereas the majority could in reality be held. I may add that, at this point, 10 ...., P–Q4; followed by ...., P–K4; appears to be playable, e.g.: 10 ...., P–Q4; 11 QKt–Kt5, P–K4; 12 P × P, Kt × P; 13 Castles, Kt × Kch., 14 Kt × Kt, Castles; Black would remain with certain weaknesses on the K file and on White-squared points, e.g.: 15 Q–R4, K–Kt1; 16 QR–K1, Q–B3; 17 Kt–K5. This outcome is not surprising, for a sudden plunge into the open game only seldom evolves without repercussions.

11 Castles	R–Kt1

Intent on centralisation, the idea being ...., P–KKt4–Kt5; relieving his K4. Instead, " liberation " by 11 ...., P–Q4; 12 Kt–Kt3, P–K4; might again be thought of, but it would be a mistake because of 13 Kt × P, Kt × Kt; 14 R–K1.

But the following variation, somewhat beyond the ken of modern book-learning, would be playable: 11 ...., P–Q4; 12 Kt–Kt3, P–KR4; 13 P–KR4, and now 13 ...., P–K4; as the capture quoted above (Kt × KP,) now fails because the White KRP is in the air.

12	Q–K2	K–Kt1
13	P–QR4	....

Perhaps 13 B–R6, deserved the preference, the storming by pawns could wait.

13	....	P–QR4

The QRP, unhindered by a White B at QR6 demonstrates its mobility.

14	KR–Kt1	P–KKt4
15	P–QKt4	P–Q4

Well timed, as the Knight can no longer move to the favourable square at Q2. For if 16 QKt–Q2, P × P; and the intended P–R5, is not workable because of ...., P × BP; attacking the Kt.

16	Kt–Kt3	P × P
17	P–R5	P–Kt5
18	Kt–K5	Kt × Kt
19	P × Kt	P–B4

White could win with 20 RP × P, compel the remarkable sequence of moves which his adversary intended, namely: 20 RP × P, P–B5; 21 P × P, R–B1; (it would be fatal for Black to open the QB file with 21 ...., P × B; 22 Q–R2, etc.) 22 Q–R2, R–B3; 23 Q–R7ch., K–B1; 24 P–Kt5, R–B4; such an odd situation for a Rook does not occur every day. The resulting position is full of tension; powerful attacks crumble up against the equally mighty resources of the defence; the position is throughout of an heroic nature. As an illustration we give : 25 B–K2, B–Kt2 ; 26 B × KtP, B × P ; 27 R–K1, R × B ; 28 R × B, P–B6 ; 29 Kt–B5, Q–Q2 ; 30 Q–R3, R(Kt5)–QB5 ; 31 Kt–K3, Q × P ; 32 Kt × R, Q × Kt ; 33 R × KP, P–B7 ; 34 KR–K1, and White would probably win. However, Black can improve on his defence by : 25 B–K2, B–Kt2 ; 26 B × KtP, B × P ; 27 R–K1, P–Q5 ; with vast complications.

20	BP × P	BP × P
21	R–QB1	………

If 21 P × P, then simply ………, Q–B4.

21	………	B–KR3
22	KR–QKt1	Q–B4
23	P × P	Q × P
24	R–R4	B–KB1
25	Kt–R5	………

The Knight threatens to settle at KB6.

25	………	B–B4
26	Kt–B6	R–Kt2
27	B–Kt5	B–QB1
28	KR–R1	B–Kt2

Black is given no peace.

29	K–R1	………

White, who has conducted the game with remarkable élan, should again have played R–QKt1.

29	………	B–Q5
30	QKt1	B–B6
31	Kt–K8	R–Kt4
32	Q–B1	R × P
33	Kt–B6	Q–Q3
34	Kt × KtP	R–Kt4
35	P–B3	QR–Kt1

Black in abruptly sounding the attack on the K wing, temporarily forsakes his main object (play in the centre against flank-attack !). Correct and more conformable is ………, KR–Kt1.

| 36 B–R6 | Q–Kt3 |
| 37 Q–Q3 | R–QB1 |

The immediate return of the Rooks is compulsory.

38 B × B	K × B
39 Q × RPch.	R–B2
40 Q–Q3	R–Kt1
41 P–R3	....

Better was Kt–K3, threatening Kt–Q1, or Kt–B2.

41	KR–QB1
42 Kt–K3	R–B4
43 P–B4	Q–Kt4

Consolidation.

44 Q–Q1	R–QR1
45 R × R	K × R
46 P–B5	....

A mistake, but against Black's B and passed pawns the position is untenable in any event.

46	P–Q5
47 P–B6	P × Kt
48 Q–B3ch.	Q–B3
49 Q × P	B × P
50 R–KB1	....

Or 50 R × P, R–B8ch.; 51 K–R2, Q–Q3ch.; 52 R–B4, B–K4.

50	R–B7
51 Q–KKt3	B–K4
52 Q–Kt8ch.	K–Kt2

Resigns.

Game No. 105.—Carlsbad, 1923.

White: Rubinstein.

1	P–K4	P–QB4
2	Kt–KB3	Kt–QB3
3	P–Q4	P × P
4	Kt × P	P–Q4

This innovation, first tried on this occasion, leads to complicated positions and cannot therefore be recommended to the player, who only knows one strictly correct way, namely, the wide main road. A tour in the mountains which leads over precipices, but on the other hand opens a wonderful outlook is, of course, not for timid souls.

5	P × P	....

Respecting the main variation at this point 5 B–QKt5, P × P; compare No. 44. It may be added that Dr. Lasker recommends here 5 Kt × Kt, P × Kt; 6 P × P, Q × P; 7 Kt–B3, Q × Qch.; 8 Kt × Q, but White's end-game advantage thus obtained is of a problematic nature.

5	....	Q × P
6	B–K3	P–K3

Bad would be 6 ...., P–K4; because of 7 Kt–Kt5. The square at Black's K4 is required for the Queen. If his QRP were at its third, which can be done in the Sicilian, ..., P–K4; would be playable, but not fitted for giving the second player an easy or comfortable journey. The game is designed for defence on heroic lines and not for placid wood-shifting.

Compare the opening moves of our game against Norman-Hansen (Black), July, 1923. 1 P–QB4, P–K4; 2 P–QR3, (White now plays a Sicilian with a move thrown in) Kt–KB3; 3 Kt–QB3, P–Q4; 4 P × P, Kt × P; 5 P–Q4, P × P; 6 Q × P, B–K3; 7 P–K4, Kt–QB3; 8 B–QKt5, Kt–K2; 9 KKt–K2, P–QR3; 10 B–R4, P–QKt4; 11 Q × Qch., R × Q; 12 B–B2, Kt–K4; (Kt–R4; could also be considered) and Black obtained playing space in the centre. The "energetic" thrust 7 P–K4, should have been abandoned in favour of the more restrained 7 P–K3, e.g.: 7 ...., Kt–QB3; 8 B–Kt5. If now .... Kt–K2; 9 Q–K4. Even after 9 Kt–B3, (instead of 9 Q–K4,) White would have a better (because firmer) position than in the game. 9 ...., P–QR3; 10 B–R4, P–QKt4; 11 Q × Qch., R × Q; 12 B–B2. The facile thrust P–K4, on either side in these games does not seem to fit into the weighty scheme of things.

7 Kt–B3	B–Kt5
8 Kt–Kt5	....

Here 8 B–K2, KKt–K2; (8 ...., Q × KtP; 9 B–B3,) 9 Castles, could be entertained.

8	Q–K4

The brighter side of the restrained 6 ...., P–K3; is now manifest.

9 P–QR3	B × Ktch.

Good enough would be the retreat 9 ...., B–K2; e.g.: 10 B K2, P–QR3; 11 Kt–Q4, Kt–B3; intending ...., Castles; and ...., R–Q1. But the continuation adopted is more consistent, for the "Black squared" assault, which the first player is now able to launch, can surely be endured. The avoidance of complications would be out of keeping with the whole lay-out of the game. Now comes a terrific struggle.

10 P × B	....

After 10 Kt × B, Kt–B3; White has the two Bishops, but Black is better centralised. The continuation in the text allows the entry at Q6, but at the price of a pawn.

10	P–QR3
11 Kt–Q6ch.	K–K2
12 Kt–B4	Q × Pch.
13 B–Q2	Q–Q5

In order to parry 14 B–Kt4ch., by ...., Kt × B; etc.

14 B–Q3	P–QKt4

In order to drive the Knight off "Black squared" points; at the same time a counter-action, based on White squares (........., B–Kt2;) is set in motion.

15 Kt–R5	Q–K4ch.
16 B–K2	Kt × Kt
17 B × Kt	B–Kt2

To force the exchange of Queens by ...., Q–Q4; in the event of White's Castling.

18 P–KB3	Kt–B3

At last Black has found time and leisure to develop the unhappy Knight: but the opportunities now offered at Black's Q4 and K6 are ample compensation for the protracted delay.

19 B–Kt4ch.	K–K1

Le Roi s' amuse.

20 Castles	R–Q1
21 B–Q3	Kt–Q4
22 B–R5	R–Q2
23 R–K1	Q–Q5 ch.

" The Queen always seems to find a way out with check," is the astonished comment of the book of the tournament!

24 K–R1	Kt–B5

To make an end of " the two Bishops." That this is possible is due to intensive centralisation.

25 Q–Q2	Kt × B
26 P × Kt	P–R4

With one piece out of play Black must decline with thanks the capture of the QP; instead, he plans the manœuvre ...., P–R5; with ...., R–R4–Q4; or else ...., R–R3–Kt3; etc.

27 QR–B1	R–R3
28 B–B3	....

Here 28 R–K3, (with QR–K1,) would be more apposite; for one thing the QP is less untouchable than White—rather optimistically—appears to think, and, in addition, Black's manœuvre ...., P–B3; and ...., K–B2; would be checked.

28	Q × P
29 Q–B4	Q–Q3
30 Q–Kt5	....

An anti-prophylactic move which actually helps Black's intended manœuvre ...., P–B3; with ...., K–B2; as indicated in the preceding note. Q–K3, would be appropriate.

30	P–B3
31 Q–K3	P–K4
32 B–Kt4	....

He is still filled with Black-square malevolence.

32	Q–Q5
33 Q–Kt3	Q–Q4
34 Q–B2	Q–Q6
35 Q–B5	K–B2
36 R–B2	R–R1

Black has at last achieved the complete development of his forces.

37	R–Q2	Q–B4
38	R × Rch.	Q × R
39	Q–QB2	B–B1

If 39 ...., R–QB1 ; 40 Q–R7.

| 40 | R–Q1 | Q–B4 |

The defence runs of course on " White squared " lines.

41	Q–B7ch.	K–Kt3
42	P–R3	R–K1
43	R–QB1	Q–B5
44	R–B6	B–B4

With the threat ...., R–QB1 ; etc.

| 45 | Q–Q6 | P–R5 |

Stronger than ...., R–K3.

| 46 | B–Q2 | Q–Kt6 |

| 47 | R–B3 | P–R4 |

A " coup d'état " : he gives up the whole of his gains in material ; but he obtains a combined attack on both wings. (see the next note).

48	P–B4	Q–B7
49	R–KB3	Q–K7
50	P × P	R × P
51	R–B4	P–Kt5
52	P × P	P–R5
53	R × P	P–R6
54	K–R2	P–R7

White is hopelessly lost : on one side he has to tame an advanced passed pawn and on the other he faces a mating attack. The finish, however, is still very interesting.

55	B–B3	Q–K6
56	B–Kt2	....

If 56 B × R, Q × Bch. ; 57 Q × Q, P × Q ; and the RP Queens.

56	....	Q–K8
57	Q–Q4	R–K6

Threatening ...., Q–Kt6ch.; etc.

58	Q–KB4	R–K5
59	Q–Kt3ch.	Q × Qch.
60	K × Q	R–K7
61	B–Q4	R–Q7

Resigns.

There might follow 62 B–R1, R–Q8; 63 B–Kt2, R–QKt8; 64 B–Q4, R–Kt6ch.; with ...., R × KtP; and ...., R × B; and ...., P–R8 (Q.) The tragedy for White (in the final phase) was that he had to pay too high a price for the capture of Black's KRP, namely: the displacement of his Rook.

The Black Queen's moves are a noteworthy feature of the game: they appeared only to serve the warding off at the moment of each threatening danger, and therefore to lack any correlative basis idea. In reality, we have a well-planned employment of central territory giving prominence at the same time to existing counter-chances on White squares. In short, centralisation and White-square counter-play on one side; powerful Black-square pressure on the other side. The victory of the second player can be proclaimed, in these circumstances, a triumph of the " heroic defence " based on modern stratagems.

Finally, an ending demonstrating with plastic clearness the basis on which the " heroic defence " rests.

Game (Ending) No. 106.—Riga, 1909.

Black: C. Behting.

Black, with the move, made an obvious sacrifice:

1	Kt–B6ch.
2 P×Kt	Q×RP
3 B–Q4ch.	K–Kt1
4 P×P	R–B6

And now White, not wishing tamely to submit to a draw, scorned the safe parry 5 KR–K1, and entered upon a hair-raising adventure, in the course of which he had to give up a whole Rook to ward off a mate, remaining with the exchange and a pawn to the bad, apparently without any compensation, when——there set in the wonder of the fantastic adventure.

5 R–B8ch.	K–R2
6 KR–B1	Q–Kt5ch.
7 K–B1	R×KP
8 KR–B7ch.	K–Kt3
9 R Kt7ch.	K R4
10 R×Pch.	P×R
11 R–R8ch.	K–Kt3

Now White is at least rid of the terrible mating threat at R3 (........., Q–R6ch.; K–Kt1, R–Kt5; mate), but at what cost! And in addition both Queen and Bishop *en prise*. And no sign of an attack for White anywhere!

12 Q–B2   ....

This completes the defensive formation.   The White defenders in their floating, disjointed oddity are in almost humorous contrast with the massively co-ordinated, brutally threatening trio, Black's Queen and two Rooks.   But of what use are callisthenics?   White is the exchange down and must lose?   No!   White's " heroic defence " was based on centralisation and his Bishop and Queen (this last aiming at KKt6 over K4) appear as central forces.   The central energy, concentrated for defensive purposes, is also available, as is now shown, for attack, and, quite surreptitiously, a sharp threat has arisen, namely: 13 R–Kt8ch., K–R2; 14 Q–B7ch., K×R; 15 Q–Kt7, mate.

12	Q–B4
13 Q–B7	....

With a variety of incisive threats.

13 ....   R–K8ch.

Luckily for Black he still has a loop-hole.

14 K×R	Q–Kt8ch.
15 K–K2	Q–Q6ch.

And draws by perpetual check.

In this game the "heroic defence" was based entirely on centralisation. Let the attentive reader try to establish the kind and extent of the functional changes which each unit of the White trio (QB2, BQ4, RKR8,) undergoes on the 12th move. That move, as we know, was the turning point of the game, when White's defensive pieces, at one stroke, were turned into storm-troops.

This concludes the 9th section, devoted to the "Heroic Defence."

10.—COMBINATIONS WHICH " SLUMBER BENEATH A THIN COVERLET."

This excellent description Professor Adolf Anderssen applied to the combinations in close games; if this grand old master of the classic period were alive to-day, he would probably have included all combinations of the hyper-modern creed. Indeed it seems as if it were a feature of the modern combinational play to be studiously unassuming: combinations flit in ghostly fashion, so to speak, between the lines, too shy to appear in the text, and even when, on the crest of a wave, they emerge from obscurity into the turmoil of practical play, they still are full of restraint (entirely devoid of thunder and lightning), and their modest appearance (see for instance No. 107, 17 ...., Kt–Kt3; in the note to move 16) is often in—one might almost say deliberate—contrast with the intellectual depth of their conception.

We are, of course, far from wishing to state that modesty is typical of our times; but there is an offshoot of modesty which appears to be typical of modern thought, namely, the voluntary subordination of self to the whole, (Reinhardt, Stanislawsky; consider the film " Potemkin " in which there is only one principal, the " people "!).

Besides modesty, another factor which also typifies our epoch may be taken into consideration : loving care of the purely technical. Of importance may also be the campaign, which has also been conducted by the author, and which aims at replacing the existing æsthetics of chess with a new type. Beautiful is neither the accumulation of minute advantages, nor the game played on text-book lines, beautiful is any-and everything which links up the heterogeneous chess happenings with the laws of nature, thus revealing how kindly and beautifully Dame Nature discharges her duties.

We have been quoting just now from our dissertation on " What is beautiful?" which appeared in K.N.N. Ex. 1926, page 484, and we cull therefrom the following description of a struggle, which, to us, represents a shining example of the new æsthetics in chess.

" Through careless play Black gets on a downward path. By dint of a tremendous exertion of will-power, he finds a move which only just holds the position. An end is put to the downward trend. And then there comes the advance, contrary to all positional probabilities, and the game is an easy draw. Why then does the second player win? Well, because the dissolution, which was brought to a stop by a violent effort of will, was bound to unleash the latent powers in Black's position, which then surprisingly burst forth. The lung specialist well knows the symptoms. Once the growth of the disease is suspended, there comes unfailingly an upward tendency, then—the cure."

Lack of space forbids us to go into details, and we refer instead to the above-mentioned article. But we believe that we have made it clear, by these short remarks, that the modern combination is less ostentatious, that it rather eschews cheap brilliancy and is more ready to subordinate itself to strategical exigencies, than was the case with the combination of the old school.

In short, the modern combination fully lives up to the characteristics described by Anderssen (though ascribed to another).

Game No. 107.

Played by Correspondence, 1912-1913.

White: Dr. G. Fluss, Budapest.

1	P–K4	P–K4
2	Kt–KB3	Kt–QB3
3	Kt–B3	Kt–B3
4	B–B4	B–B4
5	P–Q3	P–Q3
6	B–KKt5	P–KR3
7	B–R4	P–KKt4
8	B–KKt3	B–KKt5
9	P–KR3	B–R4
10	P–KR4	....

If at once 9 P–KR4, Kt–KR4; would have been very strong, e.g.: 9 P–KR4, Kt–KR4; 10 P×P, Kt×B; 11 P×Kt, Kt–Q5; 12 Kt–Q5, B×Kt; 13 P×B, Q×P; and wins, (14 P–KKt4, P–QB3; 15 R–R5, P×Kt; etc.).

$$\begin{array}{lll} 10 & \text{.........} & \text{P–Kt5} \\ 11 & \text{Kt–Q2} & \text{P–R3} \end{array}$$

A waiting move which also is to prevent B–QKt5, at any time.

$$\begin{array}{lll} 12 & \text{Kt–Q5} & \text{Kt×Kt} \\ 13 & \text{B×Kt} & \text{Kt–K2} \end{array}$$

A pawn sacrifice with a very unusual point.

$$\begin{array}{lll} 14 & \text{B×KtP} & \text{R–R2} \\ 15 & \text{B–Q5} & \text{P–B4} \end{array}$$

$$16 \quad \text{P–KB4} \qquad \text{.........}$$

The natural continuation 16 B–K6, P–B5; 17 B–R2, would have brought out the point of the sacrifice. Black would have spurned the flashy 17 ...., B×Pch.; and selected the defensive 17 ...., Kt–Kt3; a move alluring in its humility. After 17 ...., B×Pch.; 18 K–B1, B–K6; 19 Kt–B4, Kt–Kt3; (the only way to cover the important KtP,) 20 B–Kt1, B×B; 21 B×P, and White has the advantage. But 17 ...., Kt–Kt3; is very effective, (if then 18 B×KtP, Q×P; it is to be noted that after 18 B×KtP, Q×P; the Kt at Kt3 interrupts a check by 19 B×B,) 18 P–KKt3, P–B6; and the QB is shut in. Or 17 ...., Kt–Kt3; 18 B–Kt1, P–B6; 19 P×P, P×P; with ...., Kt–B5; and advantage to Black. We believe that the renunciatory sacrifice 17 ...., Kt–Kt3; (and not 17 ...., B×Pch.;) is most significant in the sense of the

introductory remarks. In the position under review, instead
of B–K6, 16 Q–K2, also came into consideration. There
would follow 16 ...., Kt × B ; 17 P × Kt, Q–R1 ; 18 P–QB4,
(best ; not 18 B × P, because of ...., Castles ;) P–B3 ;
19 P × P, Q × P ; and Black, with *inter alia*, a very mobile
QR—observe the possibilities ...., R–K2 ; and ....,
R–KKt2 ;—should have a decided advantage. The move in
the text, 17 P–KB4, also has its drawbacks.

16	....	P × P e.p.
17	P × P	Kt × B
18	P × Kt	R–Kt1
19	Kt–B1	....

If 19 B–B2, the continuation would be ...., B × Bch. ;
20 K × B, P–B3 ; which move gives the Q and QR deadly
mobility, e.g. : 21 P × P, Q–Kt3ch. ; 22 K–B1, QR–KKt2 ;
and mate in a few moves.

19	....	Q–Kt1

Much stronger than ...., P–K5 ; which would be
answered by Q–Q2, threatening Q × P, and eventually check
at K6.

20	P–Q4	....

A last attempt to save the situation, for if 20 P–Kt3,
Q–Kt5ch. ; 21 K–K2, P–K5 ; or 20 R–QKt1, R–QKt2 ;
21 P–Kt3, although the deadly Q check at Kt5 is lacking,
a similar result is obtained. 21 ...., B–Kt5ch. ; 22 K–B2,
Q R2ch. ; 23 P–Q4, B–B6 ; and wins.

20	....	B × QP
21	P–B3	....

A sort of Evans Gambit ; if ...., B–B4 ; P–Kt4.

21	....	Q × P

An elegant final combination.

22	P × B	Q–B6ch.
23	K–B2	R–QKt2

There is no reply.

24	R–B1	....

Or 24 R–R2, with a similar conclusion.

24	....	R–Kt7ch.
25	K–Kt1	R × Bch.

Resigns.

The same sacrifice arises after 24 R–R2, (instead of
R–B1,). In that case, after ...., Q–K6ch. ; White still has
K–R1, which is, however, of no avail against B × Pch.

Game No. 108.—Copenhagen, 1924.

Black: Dr. O. H. Krause.

This game is far from making a combinative impression. And yet it is simply crowded with brilliant, colourful combinations, which, however, do not appear in the text, but brightly and lightly hover in the background. The reader is strongly advised to play over, with special care, the analysis of the variations given in the notes.

1	P–Q4	P–KB4
2	Kt–KB3	Kt–KB3
3	B–B4	P–Q3

Dr. Krause's special variation, which he also plays in reply to 3 P–B4. The point lies in the plan to enforce ...., P–K4; even at the price of a pawn. Compare move 6 by Black.

4	P–K3	P–KR3
5	P–KR4	....

Anticipating the adversary's threatened expansion— ...., P–KKt4; and ...., B–Kt2;

5	....	Kt–B3
6	P–Q5	....

Has to be played at once if at all. A waiting policy, 6 P–B4, or 6 QKt–Q2, would of course call forth 6 ...., Kt–KKt5; and the variations beginning with 7 P–Q5, P–K4; would be less favourable for White than those in the text, (for 6 ...., Kt–KKt5; would mean a valuable extra tempo for Black).

6	....	P–K4

Dr. Krause's prescription, which, however, does not appear quite adequate in this case.

7	P × Kt	P × B
8	B–Kt5	....

But not 8 P × KtP, B × P; 9 P × P, Q–K2ch.; 10 B–K2, B × Kt; and White has a trebled KBP.

8 ....   P–QKt3

Dr. Krause recommends 8 ...., K–B2; as the better move. Indeed, in reply, both I. 9 P × BP, and II. 9 Castles, would seem to be bad for White, e.g.: I. 9 P × BP, Q–K2ch.; (not 9 ...., Q–K1ch., because of 10 Kt–K5ch., P × Kt; 11 P × KtP, and wins.) 10 Q–K2, Q × Qch.; 11 K × Q, P × P; 12 B × P, R–QKt1; or II. 9 Castles, P × KP; 10 Kt–K5ch., K–Kt1; 11 P × KP, Q–K2; 12 Kt–Kt6, Q × Pch.; 13 K–R1, Q–KKt6; 14 Kt × R, Kt–Kt5; and wins. However, simple centralisation by 9 Q–Q4, leads to a superior game for White; examine the following line of play: 8 ...., K–B2; 9 Q–Q4, P × KP; 10 P × KP, P–Q4; 11 Kt–K5ch., K–Kt1; 12 Kt–Q2, P–QKt3; 13 P–QKt4, (directed against ...., B–B4;) and White is clearly superior. It is remarkable how Q–Q4, had a calming effect on the combinatively seething position! The intermingling of positional moves is typical of the modern combination.

9 P × P	P–Q4
10 Castles	B–B4
11 P–KKt3	Kt–K5
12 K–Kt2	P–Kt4

Probably the best, certainly the most incisive chance. To be considered was 12 ...., Q–Q3; with the probable continuation 13 Kt–K5?, B–K3; 14 P–KB3, Kt–B3; threatening ...., P–Q5; with ...., Kt–Q4–K6; or 13 P–QB3, P–QR4; 14 Kt–Q4, and White has the better game.

13 Kt–K5   Castles

Faulty of course would be 13 ...., P–Kt5; 14 Kt–Q7, P–Q5; 15 P–Kt4, B × P; 16 Q × QP, and wins a piece. After the text-move the critical position in the following diagram is reached.

14 RP × P   ....

The logical reply : the immediate 14 Q–R5, fails against the piquant reply 14 ......, Q–K1 ; 15 Q × RP, R–B3 ; and so the Q at R5 is to be protected, if necessary, by R–R1, therefore 14 RP × P, P × P ; 15 Q–R5, Q–K1 ; 16 R–R1. The less consistent move 14 P–KB3, (i.e., unpositional obstruction of the important Diagonal Q1–R5) would have led to an extremely lively game, e.g. : 14 P–KB3, Kt–Q3 ; 15 Q × Pch., K–R2 ; 16 RP × P, (16 Kt–B3, Kt × B ; 17 Q × Q, R × Q ; 18 Kt × Kt, R–Q7ch. ; gives White only a draw) 16 ...., Kt × B ; 17 Kt–B3, Kt × Kt ? ; 18 R–R1, and wins, e.g. : 18 ...., Q–B3 ; (mate in three was threatened,) 19 P × Q, Kt × Q ; 20 R × Pch., and mate in a few moves. After 14 P–KB3, Kt–Q3 ; 15 Q × Pch., K–R2 ; 16 RP × P, Kt × B ; 17 Kt–B3, Black could have exchanged Queens instead of 17 ...., Kt × Kt ; e.g. : 17 ...., Q × Q ; 18 Kt × Q—the position would then be difficult. For instance, 18 ...., P × P ; would lead to an overwhelming attack by 19 R–R1ch., K–Kt2 ; 20 R–R5, but a tenacious resistance could be organised by 18 ...., R–R1 ; e.g. : 19 P–R4, (19 Kt–B7 ?, B–K3 ; 20 Kt × R, B × Kt ; etc.) 19 ......, Kt Q5, 20 Kt × BP, R–QKt1 ; 21 R–R1, K–Kt2 ; 22 P × Pch., K–R2 ; (but not 22 ...., R × P ; because of an interpolated Kt check at K8, with an exchange of Rooks and mate, 23 Kt–K8ch., K–R2 ; 24 R × Rch., K × R ; 25 R–R1, mate) ; 23 Kt–Q5, R–B1 ; (mate was threatened) 24 P–B3, and White will still have to work hard for a win.

The logical continuation in the text was therefore to be preferred, which is not surprising for even in imaginative positions, logic holds its sway.

14 ....   P × P
15 Q–R5   Q–B3

16 P–KB3   ....

Puts an end to the spook! White has no fear of ghosts.
16 ...., P × P; 17 P × Kt, Q × Kt; 18 Kt–B3, and White's
KP is taboo! If 18 ...., R–B2; which some thought
sufficient, 19 R × P, would have followed and Black must
hold back his trump-card ...., R–R2; for 19 ....,
R–R2; would have brought on the catastrophe 20 R–Kt4ch.,
K–R1; 21 Q × Rch. There is nothing better, therefore,
than development by 19 ...., B–K3! The win could be
then forced by a study-like manœuvre as follows: 19 ....,
B–K3; 20 P × BP, B × P; 21 R–R1, (threatening R × B,)
B–K5ch.; Black must now seek simplification. 22 Kt × B,
Q × Q; 23 R × Q, R × R; 24 Kt × B, R–QKt5; 25 Kt–R6,
R × B; 26 P–QKt4!, and wins, (but by no means 26 Kt × P,
because of 26 ...., R × P; 27 Kt × R, R × Pch.; 28 K–B3,
R × BP; winning the Kt and drawing the game.) The very
unusual position reached after 26 P–QKt4, deserves a
Diagram.

Variation to Game 108.

In the game, however, the Kt retired to Q3. (See
preceding Diagram).

16	....	Kt–Q3
17	Kt–B3	B–K3
18	P × P	Q × Kt
19	Q–Kt6ch.	Q–Kt2
20	Q × Bch.	Q–B2
21	Q × Qch.	K × Q
22	B–Q3	B–Q5

If 22 ...., P–Q5; 23 Kt–Q5, threatening P–QKt4, etc.

23	Kt × P	B × P
24	QR–K1	QR–K1
25	Kt × BP	R × R
26	R × R	R–B1
27	Kt–Q5	....

More precise than 27 Kt–K6, R–K1; 28 P–B7, R × Kt; 29 B–B4. White has in view a dreadful stalemate of all the Black pieces.

27	....	R × P
28	R–K7ch.	Resigns.

For if 28 ...., K–Kt3; the sequel is 29 Kt–B4ch., K × P; 30 R–K6, B–B3; 31 P–B4, and Black dies of Zugzwang. It was fated in this game that the combinations should not be consummated; but who shall say that they did not, nevertheless, strongly influence the course of play?

As a tail-piece, a short and exciting game, which, however, cannot lay particular claims to soundness. Black first makes a perfectly correct combination, but then, in order to avoid the exchange of Queens, he throws himself headlong into an adventure, which could have turned out badly.

Game No. 109.—Stockholm, 1920.

White: Spielmann.

1	P–K4	Kt–QB3
2	P–Q4	P–Q4
3	P–K5	B–B4

Simpler than 3 ...., P–B3.

4	Kt–K2	....

More natural would be 4 Kt–KB3.

4	....	P–K3
5	Kt–Kt3	B–Kt3
6	P–KR4	P–KR4
7	B–K2	B–K2

Thus White's manœuvre is justified. But Black could have played better, namely: 7 ...., Kt–Kt5; 8 Kt–R3,

P–QB4; 9 P–QB3, Kt–QB3; and White's efforts against Black's KRP appear to be excessive in view of the serious situation in the centre.

8	B × P	B × B
9	Kt × B	P–KKt3
10	Kt–B4	R × P
11	R × R	B × R
12	Q–Q3	....

Preventing 12 ...., B–Kt4; as then 13 Kt × KP, would win.

12	....	KKt–K2 !
13	P–KKt3	Kt–B4
14	P × B	KKt × QP

There is now a double threat, namely: 14 ...., Kt–Kt5; 15 Q × Kt, Kt × Pch.; and 14 ...., Kt × KP; 15 Q × Kt, Kt–B6ch.; a neat two-fold turn.

15	Kt–QR3	Q × P

Simpler would be 15 ...., Kt × P; 16 Q–R3, Kt(Q5)–B6ch.; 17 K–B1, Q × P; with a promising ending, but Black wished to avoid the exchange of Queens.

16	Q–R3	....

In order to force the exchange.

16 ....   Q–Kt4

With the idea 17 Q–R8ch., K–Q2; 18 Q × R, Q–Kt8ch.;
19 K–Q2, Q × Pch.; 20 K–B3, Kt–Kt6 ! !; (after the game
was over, they found the dual 20 ...., Kt–B6;). Never-
the less 16 ...., Q × Q; was necessary.

17 B–K3   ....

For now 17 Kt–Q3, could have been played to White's
advantage, e.g.: 17 ...., Q–Kt8ch.; 18 K–Q2, Kt × KP;
19 Kt × Kt, Q × Pch.; which would be insufficient (as would
also be the other possible continuation, 17 Kt–Q3, Q–Kt8ch.;
18 K–Q2, K–Q2; 19 Kt–B5ch., (not 19 P–QB3, because of
........., R–R1; 20 Q × R, Q–Kt4ch.; with perpetual check,)
19 ...., K–K2; 20 Q–R4ch., K–K1; (or 20 ....,
P–Kt4; 21 Q–Kt3,) 21 Q–R8ch., K–K2; 22 Q–B6ch., and
23 P–QB3.

17	....	Q–Kt8ch.
18	Q–B1	Kt–B6ch.
19	K–K2	KKt–Q5ch.
20	K–Q2	Kt–B6ch.
21	K–K2	QKt–Q5ch.
22	K–Q3	....

Fatal.   For better or for worse, White should have
embarked upon 22 B × Kt, Kt × Bch.; 23 K–Q3, Q–Kt4;
although his position then would scarcely have been enviable
If 13 ...., Castles; there follows first 14 B–Kt3.

22	....	Q–Kt4
23	Q–R3	Q × P
24	R–KB1	Castles
25	P–Kt3	P–QKt4
26	QKt × P	Q–K5ch.
27	K–B3	Q × Pch.
28	K–Kt4	P–B4ch.
	Resigns.	

Here I close this book and bid farewell to my readers.

INDEX TO GAMES.

Number.	Opponent.	Opponent's Colour.	Venue.	Date.	Page.
1	Ahues	B	Berlin	1928	3
2	Bogoljubow	W	London	1927	5
3	v. Schewe	B	Ostend	1907	8
4	E. Cohn	W	Ostend	1907	10
5	Spielmann	W	Carlsbad	1923	12
6	Yates	W	London	1927	13
7	Allies	W	Oslo	1921	17
8	Löwenfisch	B	Carlsbad	1911	21
9	Yates	W	Semmering	1926	24
10	Réti	W	Marienbad	1925	27
11	Löwenfisch	W	Wilna	1912	30
12	Tartakower	W	London	1927	32
13	Sämisch	W	Berlin	1928	36
14	Dr. Alekhin	W	St. Petersburg	1913	41
15	Dr. Alekhin	B	Semmering	1926	43
16	Romih	B	London	1927	47
17	Grünfeld	W	Kecskemet	1927	49
18	L. Steiner	B	Niendorf	1927	53
19	Alapin	W	Carlsbad	1911	55
20	Dr. Alekhin	W	Kecskemet	1927	57
21	Marshall	B	New York	1927	61
22	Vukovic	B	Kecskemet	1927	64
23	Duras	B	San Sebastian	1912	65
24	Breyer	B	Gothenburg	1920	74
25	Tartakower	B	Gothenburg	1920	77
26	Marshall	B	New York	1927	80
27	Sämisch	W	Carlsbad	1923	82
28	Buerger	W	London	1927	87
29	Van Vliet	W	Ostend	1907	92
30	Buerger	B	London	1927	97
31	Sämisch	B	Dresden	1926	101
32	Colle	B	London	1927	103
33	Janowski	W	St. Petersburg	1914	108
34	Johner	W	Dresden	1926	112
35	Dr. Vidmar	B	Carlsbad	1907	117
36	Marshall	W	New York	1927	121
37	Réti	B	Carlsbad	1923	125
38	Ahues	W	Berlin	1927	127
39	Ahues	W	Kecskemet	1927	130
40	Schweinburg	W	Berlin	1927	133
41	Colle	W	Baden	1925	135
42	Hage	W	Arnstadt	1926	138
43	Blümich	W	Breslau	1926	140
44	v. Holzhausen	W	Dresden	1926	144
45	Duhm	B	Hanover	1926	148
46	Brinckmann	W	Kolding	1922	150
47	Leonhardt	B	San Sebastian	1912	153
48	Ahues	B	Niendorf	1927	154
49	Dr. Vajda	W	Kecskemet	1927	159
50	Kmoch	W	Niendorf	1927	162
51	Brinckmann	W	Niendorf	1927	166
52	L. Steiner	W	Dresden	1926	170
53	K. Behting	W	Riga	1910	175
54	Schlechter	W	Carlsbad	1907	179
55	Wendel	W	Stockholm	1921	181
56	Yates	W	London	1927	185

INDEX TO GAMES—Continued.

Number.	Opponent.	Opponent's Colour.	Venue.	Date.	Page.
57	Morrison	W	London	1927	188
58	Hakansson	B	Kristianstad	1922	190
59	Szekely	B	Kecskemet	1927	192
60	Bogoljubow	W	St. Petersburg	1913	195
61	Jacobsen	B	Copenhagen	1923	201
62	Allies	B	Dorpat	1910	204
63	Dr. O. H. Krause	W	Correspondence	1924/5	207
64	Janowski	B	Carlsbad	1907	209
65	Rubinstein	W	Carlsbad	1907	213
66	Dr. Vidmar	B	New York	1927	215
67	Dr. Tarrasch	W	Hamburg	1910	218
68	Brekke	W	Oslo	1921	221
69	Leonhardt	B	Ostend	1907	224
70	M. E. Goldstein	W	London	1927	225
71	Schlage	W	Berlin	1928	230
72	von Gottschall	W	Hanover	1926	235
73	von Holzhausen	W	Hanover	1926	238
74	Buerger	B	London	1927	241
75	Dr. Antze	B	Hanover	1926	245
76	S. Petersen	B	Copenhagen	1928	250
77	E. Cohn	W	Carlsbad	1911	253
78	Michell	W	Marienbad	1925	256
79	W. Nielsen	W	Copenhagen	1928	259
80	Dr. Vidmar	W	New York	1927	262
81	Przepiorka	W	Kecskemet	1927	264
82	Spielmann	B	New York	1927	265
83	Rubinstein	B	Semmering	1926	268
84	A. Nilsson	B	Copenhagen	1924	274
85	Yates	W	Carlsbad	1923	277
86	Gemsöe	B	Copenhagen	1928	281
87	P. Johner	W	Berlin	1928	284
88	C. Nilsson	W	Eskilstuna	1921	286
89	Capablanca	W	New York	1927	290
90	E. Jacobsen	W	Copenhagen	1923	292
91	E. Hansen	W	Copenhagen	1928	296
92	Möller	W	Copenhagen	1922	300
93	Enoch	W	Berlin	1927	304
94	Marshall	W	New York	1927	307
95	Tartakower	B	Carlsbad	1923	310
96	Allies	W	Oslo	1922	312
97	Stoltz	W	Berlin	1928	317
98	Mieses	W	Hanover	1926	322
99	Allies	W	Copenhagen	1923	326
100	Dr. Alekhin	B	New York	1927	330
101	Gilg	B	Kecskemet	1927	334
102	Brinckmann	W	Berlin	1927	338
103	Leonhardt	W	Berlin	1928	341
104	Brinckmann	W	Copenhagen	1924	343
105	Rubinstein	W	Carlsbad	1923	348
106	K. Behting	B	Riga	1909	352
107	Dr. Fluss	W	Correspondence	1912/13	355
108	Dr. Krause	B	Copenhagen	1924	358
109	Spielmann	W	Stockholm	1920	362

REGISTER OF STRATAGEMS.

(COMPLEMENTARY TO TABLE OF CONTENTS.)

The numbers refer to the games.

LINES, open, with or without outposts : 1, 2, 3, 9, 10, 12, 14, 21, 28, 34, 43, 53, 68, 73, 76, 81, 84, 90, 92, 93, 99.
Line, neutralised : 80, 93.

SEVENTH RANK : 12, 14, 21, 24, 27, 45, 49, 51, 56, 58, 92, 107.
Seventh Rank Absolute plus passed pawn : 12, 32.
Seventh Rank, neutralised : 97.
Eighth Rank : 25, 45, 51, 78, 84.

PASSED PAWNS : 7, 9, 21, 41, 51, 56, 70, 71, 72, 73, 79, 97, 105.
Fight against the blockader : 7, 9, 17, 70, 73, 76.
Lust to expand : 15 (move 41), 78, 96.
Reserve blockader : 70.

PAWN-CHAINS : 8, 23, 29, 30, 35, 38, 49, 50, 58, 59, 60, 84.

PINNING : 37, 80, 98, 99, 101.
Unpinning : 2, 44.

DISCOVERED CHECK : 1, 27, 70, 75, 78, 83, 93.

THE KING IN THE END-GAME : 10, 41, 53, 62, 65, 72, 74, 84, 87, 97.
The King's flight from perpetual check : 13, 27, 68, 75, 77.

CENTRALISATION : 1-23 incl., 71, 78, 81, 83, 92, 102, 104, 105, 106, 108.
Faulty Centralisation : 1-6, 78, 104.
Omission of a central attack : 5.
Omission of central consolidation : 1, 2, 4, 6, 23.

PROPHYLAXIS : 13, 15, 20, 21, 24, 25, 32, 33, 36, 38-41, 43, 49, 51, 53, 54, 55, 56, 60, 63, 69, 70, 72, 73, 74, 75, 81, 87, 88, 90, 105.

RESTRICTION of a body of pawns ready to advance : 19, 23, 67, 70, 74.
Restriction of liberating moves : 24, 25, 35, 48.
Blockade : 35, 36, 42, 59, 62, 67, 70, 73.

OVER-PROTECTION : 20, 44, 57, 58, 59, 60, 62, 102.

ALTERNATING PLAY : 16, 60, 67, 71-78 incl.

ISOLATED PAWNS : 61, 62, 63, 64, 72, 76.
Isolated pair of pawns : 62.
The two hanging pawns : 65-68 incl.

THE TWO BISHOPS : 15, 19, 46, 50, 60, 63, 67, 69, 70, 95, 96.
Diagonal outposts : 61, 73, 95, 97.

BREAK-THROUGH : 4, 12, 14, 28, 30, 38, 43, 48, 50, 71, 73, 78, 85, 97.
Parried break-through : 4, 54, 102.
Attempted break-through : 8, 44, 59, 65.

DIFFICULT DEFENCE : 63, 84, 85, 102-105 incl.

SQUARE-WEAKNESSES OF A SPECIFIED COLOUR : 20, 46, 49, 50, 59, 62, 72, 81, 86, 88, 91, 98, 99, 100, 105.

CONCERNING FIRM AND LOOSE FORMATIONS :
The restricted centre : 89, 90, 102.
Overloading the restricted centre : 89.
Manœuvres on inner lines : 89, 90.
Consolidation by retreat : 11, 71, 79, 85, 94, 102.
Loose formations : 91.
Frustrated consolidation : 96.
Reducing his own choice of moves : 97.
Localising the enemy break-through : 15 (move 23).

VARIOUS POSITIONAL SUBTLETIES :
  Positional feelers : 17, 18.
  Reconnoitring expedition : 96.
  Waiting moves : 18, 53, 54, 81, 102, 107.
  Intermediate moves : 59, 74, 108.
  Discreet threats : 88.
  Transcendental intervention : 36, 64.
  Reflex-weakness : 90.
  Point of inertia. 86.

WHAT THE PRACTICAL PLAYER MUST KNOW :
  Returning extra material : 1, 10, 105.
  Interesting saving attempts : 41, 50, 51, 86, 94 (a piquant draw : 49).
  Mummification : 34, 41, 43, 50, 84, 88.
  " Coup d'état " : 100, 105.

END-GAMES :
  Queens : 13, 27, 75.
  Rook (or Rooks) : 7, 21, 22, 23, 32, 33, 37, 50, 53, 61, 73, 84, 97.
  Queens and Rooks : 14, 22, 77.
  Rook and Bishop v. Rook and Knight : 32, 33, 61, 81, 90.
  Rook and Knight v. Rook and Knight : 51, 73, 79, 87.
  Rook and Knight v. Rook and pawns : 68.
  Two Bishops v. Bishop and Knight : 96.
  Bishops : 61.
  Bishops of opposite colours : 25, 36, 50, 72, 96, 99, 105.
  Bishop v. Knight : 41, 62, 64, 65, 67.
  Knight v. pawns : 100.
  Pawns : 23, 61, 90, 97.

INDEX TO OPENINGS.

The numbers refer to the games.

OPEN GAMES :

    King's Gambit : 53.
    Scotch Opening : 64, 69.
    Giuoco Piano : 107.
    Ruy Lopez : 18, 24, 54.
    Philidor's Defence (Hanham variation) : 19, 48.

SEMI-OPEN GAMES :

    French Defence :
        a. Exchange Variation : 40, 73, 93.
        b. 1 P–K4, P–K3 ; 2 P–Q4, P–Q4 ; 3 Kt–QB3, B–Kt5 ; 4 P×P, :
            7, 9, 36, 92, 94, 103.
        c. Giving up the centre : 20.
        d. 1 P–K4, P–K3 ; 2 P–Q4, P–Q4 ; 3 Kt–QB3, Kt–KB3 ; : 13, 60.
        e. 1 P–K4, P–K3 ; 2 P–Q4, P–Q4 ; 3 P–K5, : 8, 23, 47, 58, 59.
        f. Irregular : 57, 72.
    Sicilian Defence :
        a. 1 P–K4, P–QB4 ; 2 Kt–KB3, Kt–KB3 ; : 6, 56, 71, 78, 79.
        b. 1 P–K4, P–QB4 ; 2 Kt–KB3, Kt–QB3 ; : 44, 52, 101, 105.
        c. Other variations : 45, 66, 97.
    Caro-Kann : 5, 11, 63.
    Niemzowitsch Defence : 1 P–K4, Kt–QB3 ; : 40, 49, 50, 51, 55, 73, 88,
        99, 102, 109.
    Alekhin Defence : 15.

CLOSE GAMES :

    Queen's Gambit and Queen's Pawn Games :
        a. Tarrasch Defence, 3 ...., P–QB4 ; : 62, 65, 67.
        b. The Modern Defence (wrongly called Orthodox) : 16, 61, 70.
        c. Stonewall Defence : 4.
        d. With obstructed QBP : 35.
        e. With P–QKt3, : 29.
    Indian :
        a. 1 P–Q4, Kt–KB3 ; 2 P–QB4, P–K3 ; 3 Kt–QB3, B–Kt5, 17, 33,
        34, 38.
        b. 1 P–Q4, Kt–KB3 ; 2 Kt–KB3, P–K3 ; 3 P–B4, B–Kt5ch. ; : 80.
        c. 1 P–Q4, Kt–KB3 ; 2 P–QB4, P–QKt3 ; : 27, 32, 81, 87, 90.
        d. With B–KKt5, : 89, 90.
        e. 1 P–Q4, P–K3 ; 2 Kt–KB3, Kt–KB3 ; 3 P–K3, P–QKt3 ; (or with
        inverted colours) : 12, 21, 100.
    The Bremen Opening : 1, 2, 28, 37, 74, 91.
    Dutch Defence : 25, 39, 41, 42, 95, 104, 108.
    Dutch Opening : 30, 76, 82, 83.
    Irregular Defences against 1 P–Q4, or 1 P–QB4, : 26, 68, 75.
    Irregular Openings : 43, 84, 85, 86, 96.

A CATALOGUE OF SELECTED DOVER BOOKS
IN ALL FIELDS OF INTEREST

A CATALOGUE OF SELECTED DOVER BOOKS
IN ALL FIELDS OF INTEREST

LEATHER TOOLING AND CARVING, Chris H. Groneman. One of few books concentrating on tooling and carving, with complete instructions and grid designs for 39 projects ranging from bookmarks to bags. 148 illustrations. 111pp. 7⅞ x 10.
23061-9 Pa. $2.50

THE CODEX NUTTALL, A PICTURE MANUSCRIPT FROM ANCIENT MEXICO, as first edited by Zelia Nuttall. Only inexpensive edition, in full color, of a pre-Columbian Mexican (Mixtec) book. 88 color plates show kings, gods, heroes, temples, sacrifices. New explanatory, historical introduction by Arthur G. Miller. 96pp. 11⅜ x 8½.
23168-2 Pa. $7.50

AMERICAN PRIMITIVE PAINTING, Jean Lipman. Classic collection of an enduring American tradition. 109 plates, 8 in full color—portraits, landscapes, Biblical and historical scenes, etc., showing family groups, farm life, and so on. 80pp. of lucid text. 8⅜ x 11¼.
22815-0 Pa. $4.00

WILL BRADLEY: HIS GRAPHIC ART, edited by Clarence P. Hornung. Striking collection of work by foremost practitioner of Art Nouveau in America: posters, cover designs, sample pages, advertisements, other illustrations. 97 plates, including 8 in full color and 19 in two colors. 97pp. 9⅜ x 12¼.
20701-3 Pa. $4.00
22120-2 Clothbd. $10.00

THE UNDERGROUND SKETCHBOOK OF JAN FAUST, Jan Faust. 101 bitter, horrifying, black-humorous, penetrating sketches on sex, war, greed, various liberations, etc. Sometimes sexual, but not pornographic. Not for prudish. 101pp. 6½ x 9¼.
22740-5 Pa. $1.50

THE GIBSON GIRL AND HER AMERICA, Charles Dana Gibson. 155 finest drawings of effervescent world of 1900-1910: the Gibson Girl and her loves, amusements, adventures, Mr. Pipp, etc. Selected by E. Gillon; introduction by Henry Pitz. 144pp. 8¼ x 11⅜.
21986-0 Pa. $3.50

STAINED GLASS CRAFT, J.A.F. Divine, G. Blachford. One of the very few books that tell the beginner exactly what he needs to know: planning cuts, making shapes, avoiding design weaknesses, fitting glass, etc. 93 illustrations. 115pp.
22812-6 Pa. $1.50

CREATIVE LITHOGRAPHY AND HOW TO DO IT, Grant Arnold. Lithography as art form: working directly on stone, transfer of drawings, lithotint, mezzotint, color printing; also metal plates. Detailed, thorough. 27 illustrations. 214pp.
21208-4 Pa. $3.00

DESIGN MOTIFS OF ANCIENT MEXICO, Jorge Enciso. Vigorous, powerful ceramic stamp impressions — Maya, Aztec, Toltec, Olmec. Serpents, gods, priests, dancers, etc. 153pp. 6⅛ x 9¼.
20084-1 Pa. $2.50

AMERICAN INDIAN DESIGN AND DECORATION, Leroy Appleton. Full text, plus more than 700 precise drawings of Inca, Maya, Aztec, Pueblo, Plains, NW Coast basketry, sculpture, painting, pottery, sand paintings, metal, etc. 4 plates in color. 279pp. 8⅜ x 11¼.
22704-9 Pa. $4.50

CHINESE LATTICE DESIGNS, Daniel S. Dye. Incredibly beautiful geometric designs: circles, voluted, simple dissections, etc. Inexhaustible source of ideas, motifs. 1239 illustrations. 469pp. 6⅛ x 9¼.
23096-1 Pa. $5.00

JAPANESE DESIGN MOTIFS, Matsuya Co. Mon, or heraldic designs. Over 4000 typical, beautiful designs: birds, animals, flowers, swords, fans, geometric; all beautifully stylized. 213pp. 11⅜ x 8¼
22874-6 Pa. $5.00

PERSPECTIVE, Jan Vredeman de Vries. 73 perspective plates from 1604 edition; buildings, townscapes, stairways, fantastic scenes. Remarkable for beauty, surrealistic atmosphere; real eye catchers. Introduction by Adolf Placzek. 74pp. 11⅜ x 8¼.
20186-4 Pa. $2.75

EARLY AMERICAN DESIGN MOTIFS, Suzanne E. Chapman. 497 motifs, designs, from painting on wood, ceramics, appliqué, glassware, samplers, metal work, etc. Florals, landscapes, birds and animals, geometrics, letters, etc. Inexhaustible. Enlarged edition. 138pp. 8⅜ x 11¼.
22985-8 Pa. $3.50
23084-8 Clothbd. $7.95

VICTORIAN STENCILS FOR DESIGN AND DECORATION, edited by E.V. Gillon, Jr. 113 wonderful ornate Victorian pieces from German sources; florals, geometrics; borders, corner pieces; bird motifs, etc. 64pp. 9⅜ x 12¼.
21995-X Pa. $2.75

ART NOUVEAU: AN ANTHOLOGY OF DESIGN AND ILLUSTRATION FROM THE STUDIO, edited by E.V. Gillon, Jr. Graphic arts: book jackets, posters, engravings, illustrations, decorations; Crane, Beardsley, Bradley and many others. Inexhaustible. 92pp. 8⅛ x 11.
22388-4 Pa. $2.50

ORIGINAL ART DECO DESIGNS, William Rowe. First-rate, highly imaginative modern Art Deco frames, borders, compositions, alphabets, florals, insectals, Wurlitzer-types, etc. Much finest modern Art Deco. 80 plates, 8 in color. 8⅜ x 11¼.
22567-4 Pa. $3.00

HANDBOOK OF DESIGNS AND DEVICES, Clarence P. Hornung. Over 1800 basic geometric designs based on circle, triangle, square, scroll, cross, etc. Largest such collection in existence. 261pp.
20125-2 Pa. $2.50

150 MASTERPIECES OF DRAWING, edited by Anthony Toney. 150 plates, early 15th century to end of 18th century; Rembrandt, Michelangelo, Dürer, Fragonard, Watteau, Wouwerman, many others. 150pp. 8⅜ x 11¼.   21032-4 Pa. $3.50

THE GOLDEN AGE OF THE POSTER, Hayward and Blanche Cirker. 70 extraordinary posters in full colors, from Maîtres de l'Affiche, Mucha, Lautrec, Bradley, Cheret, Beardsley, many others. 9⅜ x 12¼.   22753-7 Pa. $4.95
21718-3 Clothbd. $7.95

SIMPLICISSIMUS, selection, translations and text by Stanley Appelbaum. 180 satirical drawings, 16 in full color, from the famous German weekly magazine in the years 1896 to 1926. 24 artists included: Grosz, Kley, Pascin, Kubin, Kollwitz, plus Heine, Thöny, Bruno Paul, others. 172pp. 8½ x 12¼.   23098-8 Pa. $5.00
23099-6 Clothbd. $10.00

THE EARLY WORK OF AUBREY BEARDSLEY, Aubrey Beardsley. 157 plates, 2 in color: Manon Lescaut, Madame Bovary, Morte d'Arthur, Salome, other. Introduction by H. Marillier. 175pp. 8½ x 11.   21816-3 Pa. $3.50

THE LATER WORK OF AUBREY BEARDSLEY, Aubrey Beardsley. Exotic masterpieces of full maturity: Venus and Tannhäuser, Lysistrata, Rape of the Lock, Volpone, Savoy material, etc. 174 plates, 2 in color. 176pp. 8½ x 11.   21817-1 Pa. $4.00

DRAWINGS OF WILLIAM BLAKE, William Blake. 92 plates from Book of Job, Divine Comedy, Paradise Lost, visionary heads, mythological figures, Laocoön, etc. Selection, introduction, commentary by Sir Geoffrey Keynes. 178pp. 8½ x 11.
22303-5 Pa. $3.50

LONDON: A PILGRIMAGE, Gustave Doré, Blanchard Jerrold. Squalor, riches, misery, beauty of mid-Victorian metropolis; 55 wonderful plates, 125 other illustrations, full social, cultural text by Jerrold. 191pp. of text. 8⅛ x 11.
22306-X Pa. $5.00

THE COMPLETE WOODCUTS OF ALBRECHT DÜRER, edited by Dr. W. Kurth. 346 in all: Old Testament, St. Jerome, Passion, Life of Virgin, Apocalypse, many others. Introduction by Campbell Dodgson. 285pp. 8½ x 12¼.   21097-9 Pa. $6.00

THE DISASTERS OF WAR, Francisco Goya. 83 etchings record horrors of Napoleonic wars in Spain and war in general. Reprint of 1st edition, plus 3 additional plates. Introduction by Philip Hofer. 97pp. 9⅜ x 8¼.   21872-4 Pa. $3.00

ENGRAVINGS OF HOGARTH, William Hogarth. 101 of Hogarth's greatest works: Rake's Progress, Harlot's Progress, Illustrations for Hudibras, Midnight Modern Conversation, Before and After, Beer Street and Gin Lane, many more. Full commentary. 256pp. 11 x 14.   22479-1 Pa. $7.00
23023-6 Clothbd. $13.50

PRIMITIVE ART, Franz Boas. Great anthropologist on ceramics, textiles, wood, stone, metal, etc.; patterns, technology, symbols, styles. All areas, but fullest on Northwest Coast Indians. 350 illustrations. 378pp.   20025-6 Pa. $3.50

MOTHER GOOSE'S MELODIES. Facsimile of fabulously rare Munroe and Francis "copyright 1833" Boston edition. Familiar and unusual rhymes, wonderful old woodcut illustrations. Edited by E.F. Bleiler. 128pp. 4½ x 6⅜. 22577-1 Pa. $1.00

MOTHER GOOSE IN HIEROGLYPHICS. Favorite nursery rhymes presented in rebus form for children. Fascinating 1849 edition reproduced in toto, with key. Introduction by E.F. Bleiler. About 400 woodcuts. 64pp. 6⅞ x 5¼. 20745-5 Pa. $1.00

PETER PIPER'S PRACTICAL PRINCIPLES OF PLAIN & PERFECT PRONUNCIATION. Alliterative jingles and tongue-twisters. Reproduction in full of 1830 first American edition. 25 spirited woodcuts. 32pp. 4½ x 6⅜. 22560-7 Pa. $1.00

MARMADUKE MULTIPLY'S MERRY METHOD OF MAKING MINOR MATHEMATICIANS. Fellow to Peter Piper, it teaches multiplication table by catchy rhymes and woodcuts. 1841 Munroe & Francis edition. Edited by E.F. Bleiler. 103pp. 4⅝ x 6.
22773-1 Pa. $1.25
20171-6 Clothbd. $3.00

THE NIGHT BEFORE CHRISTMAS, Clement Moore. Full text, and woodcuts from original 1848 book. Also critical, historical material. 19 illustrations. 40pp. 4⅝ x 6. 22797-9 Pa. $1.00

THE KING OF THE GOLDEN RIVER, John Ruskin. Victorian children's classic of three brothers, their attempts to reach the Golden River, what becomes of them. Facsimile of original 1889 edition. 22 illustrations. 56pp. 4⅝ x 6⅜.
20066-3 Pa. $1.25

DREAMS OF THE RAREBIT FIEND, Winsor McCay. Pioneer cartoon strip, unexcelled for beauty, imagination, in 60 full sequences. Incredible technical virtuosity, wonderful visual wit. Historical introduction. 62pp. 8⅜ x 11¼ 21347-1 Pa. $2.50

THE KATZENJAMMER KIDS, Rudolf Dirks. In full color, 14 strips from 1906-7; full of imagination, characteristic humor. Classic of great historical importance. Introduction by August Derleth. 32pp. 9¼ x 12¼. 23005-8 Pa. $2.00

LITTLE ORPHAN ANNIE AND LITTLE ORPHAN ANNIE IN COSMIC CITY, Harold Gray. Two great sequences from the early strips: our curly-haired heroine defends the Warbucks' financial empire and, then, takes on meanie Phineas P. Pinchpenny. Leapin' lizards! 178pp. 6⅛ x 8⅜. 23107-0 Pa. $2.00

WHEN A FELLER NEEDS A FRIEND, Clare Briggs. 122 cartoons by one of the greatest newspaper cartoonists of the early 20th century — about growing up, making a living, family life, daily frustrations and occasional triumphs. 121pp. 8½ x 9½.
23148-8 Pa. $2.50

THE BEST OF GLUYAS WILLIAMS. 100 drawings by one of America's finest cartoonists: The Day a Cake of Ivory Soap Sank at Proctor & Gamble's, At the Life Insurance Agents' Banquet, and many other gems from the 20's and 30's. 118pp. 8⅜ x 11¼. 22737-5 Pa. $2.50

THE BEST DR. THORNDYKE DETECTIVE STORIES, R. Austin Freeman. The Case of Oscar Brodski, The Moabite Cipher, and 5 other favorites featuring the great scientific detective, plus his long-believed-lost first adventure — 31 New Inn — reprinted here for the first time. Edited by E.F. Bleiler. USO 20388-3 Pa. $3.00

BEST "THINKING MACHINE" DETECTIVE STORIES, Jacques Futrelle. The Problem of Cell 13 and 11 other stories about Prof. Augustus S.F.X. Van Dusen, including two "lost" stories. First reprinting of several. Edited by E.F. Bleiler. 241pp.
20537-1 Pa. $3.00

UNCLE SILAS, J. Sheridan LeFanu. Victorian Gothic mystery novel, considered by many best of period, even better than Collins or Dickens. Wonderful psychological terror. Introduction by Frederick Shroyer. 436pp.   21715-9 Pa. $4.00

BEST DR. POGGIOLI DETECTIVE STORIES, T.S. Stribling. 15 best stories from EQMM and The Saint offer new adventures in Mexico, Florida, Tennessee hills as Poggioli unravels mysteries and combats Count Jalacki. 217pp.   23227-1 Pa. $3.00

EIGHT DIME NOVELS, selected with an introduction by E.F. Bleiler. Adventures of Old King Brady, Frank James, Nick Carter, Deadwood Dick, Buffalo Bill, The Steam Man, Frank Merriwell, and Horatio Alger — 1877 to 1905. Important, entertaining popular literature in facsimile reprint, with original covers. 190pp. 9 x 12.   22975-0 Pa. $3.50

ALICE'S ADVENTURES UNDER GROUND, Lewis Carroll. Facsimile of ms. Carroll gave Alice Liddell in 1864. Different in many ways from final Alice. Handlettered, illustrated by Carroll. Introduction by Martin Gardner. 128pp. 21482-6 Pa. $1.50

ALICE IN WONDERLAND COLORING BOOK, Lewis Carroll. Pictures by John Tenniel. Large-size versions of the famous illustrations of Alice, Cheshire Cat, Mad Hatter and all the others, waiting for your crayons. Abridged text. 36 illustrations. 64pp. 8¼ x 11.   22853-3 Pa. $1.50

AVENTURES D'ALICE AU PAYS DES MERVEILLES, Lewis Carroll. Bué's translation of "Alice" into French, supervised by Carroll himself. Novel way to learn language. (No English text.) 42 Tenniel illustrations. 196pp.   22836-3 Pa. $2.50

MYTHS AND FOLK TALES OF IRELAND, Jeremiah Curtin. 11 stories that are Irish versions of European fairy tales and 9 stories from the Fenian cycle — 20 tales of legend and magic that comprise an essential work in the history of folklore. 256pp.   22430-9 Pa. $3.00

EAST O' THE SUN AND WEST O' THE MOON, George W. Dasent. Only full edition of favorite, wonderful Norwegian fairytales — Why the Sea is Salt, Boots and the Troll, etc. — with 77 illustrations by Kittelsen & Werenskiöld. 418pp.
22521-6 Pa. $4.00

PERRAULT'S FAIRY TALES, Charles Perrault and Gustave Doré. Original versions of Cinderella, Sleeping Beauty, Little Red Riding Hood, etc. in best translation, with 34 wonderful illustrations by Gustave Doré. 117pp. 8⅛ x 11.   22311-6 Pa. $2.50

EARLY NEW ENGLAND GRAVESTONE RUBBINGS, Edmund V. Gillon, Jr. 43 photographs, 226 rubbings show heavily symbolic, macabre, sometimes humorous primitive American art. Up to early 19th century. 207pp. 8⅜ x 11¼.

21380-3 Pa. $4.00

L.J.M. DAGUERRE: THE HISTORY OF THE DIORAMA AND THE DAGUERREOTYPE, Helmut and Alison Gernsheim. Definitive account. Early history, life and work of Daguerre; discovery of daguerreotype process; diffusion abroad; other early photography. 124 illustrations. 226pp. 6⅙ x 9¼. 22290-X Pa. $4.00

PHOTOGRAPHY AND THE AMERICAN SCENE, Robert Taft. The basic book on American photography as art, recording form, 1839-1889. Development, influence on society, great photographers, types (portraits, war, frontier, etc.), whatever else needed. Inexhaustible. Illustrated with 322 early photos, daguerreotypes, tintypes, stereo slides, etc. 546pp. 6⅛ x 9¼. 21201-7 Pa. $5.95

PHOTOGRAPHIC SKETCHBOOK OF THE CIVIL WAR, Alexander Gardner. Reproduction of 1866 volume with 100 on-the-field photographs: Manassas, Lincoln on battlefield, slave pens, etc. Introduction by E.F. Bleiler. 224pp. 10¾ x 9. 22731-6 Pa. $5.00

THE MOVIES: A PICTURE QUIZ BOOK, Stanley Appelbaum & Hayward Cirker. Match stars with their movies, name actors and actresses, test your movie skill with 241 stills from 236 great movies, 1902-1959. Indexes of performers and films. 128pp. 8⅜ x 9¼. 20222-4 Pa. $2.50

THE TALKIES, Richard Griffith. Anthology of features, articles from Photoplay, 1928-1940, reproduced complete. Stars, famous movies, technical features, fabulous ads, etc.; Garbo, Chaplin, King Kong, Lubitsch, etc. 4 color plates, scores of illustrations. 327pp. 8⅜ x 11¼. 22762-6 Pa. $6.95

THE MOVIE MUSICAL FROM VITAPHONE TO "42ND STREET," edited by Miles Kreuger. Relive the rise of the movie musical as reported in the pages of Photoplay magazine (1926-1933): every movie review, cast list, ad, and record review, every significant feature article, production still, biography, forecast, and gossip story. Profusely illustrated. 367pp. 8⅜ x 11¼. 23154-2 Pa. $6.95

JOHANN SEBASTIAN BACH, Philipp Spitta. Great classic of biography, musical commentary, with hundreds of pieces analyzed. Also good for Bach's contemporaries. 450 musical examples. Total of 1799pp.

EUK 22278-0, 22279-9 Clothbd., Two vol. set $25.00

BEETHOVEN AND HIS NINE SYMPHONIES, Sir George Grove. Thorough history, analysis, commentary on symphonies and some related pieces. For either beginner or advanced student. 436 musical passages. 407pp. 20334-4 Pa. $4.00

MOZART AND HIS PIANO CONCERTOS, Cuthbert Girdlestone. The only full-length study. Detailed analyses of all 21 concertos, sources; 417 musical examples. 509pp. 21271-8 Pa. $4.50

THE FITZWILLIAM VIRGINAL BOOK, edited by J. Fuller Maitland, W.B. Squire. Famous early 17th century collection of keyboard music, 300 works by Morley, Byrd, Bull, Gibbons, etc. Modern notation. Total of 938pp. 8⅜ x 11.
ECE 21068-5, 21069-3 Pa., Two vol. set $14.00

COMPLETE STRING QUARTETS, Wolfgang A. Mozart. Breitkopf and Härtel edition. All 23 string quartets plus alternate slow movement to K156. Study score. 277pp. 9⅜ x 12¼.
22372-8 Pa. $6.00

COMPLETE SONG CYCLES, Franz Schubert. Complete piano, vocal music of Die Schöne Müllerin, Die Winterreise, Schwanengesang. Also Drinker English singing translations. Breitkopf and Härtel edition. 217pp. 9⅜ x 12¼.
22649-2 Pa. $4.50

THE COMPLETE PRELUDES AND ETUDES FOR PIANOFORTE SOLO, Alexander Scriabin. All the preludes and etudes including many perfectly spun miniatures. Edited by K.N. Igumnov and Y.I. Mil'shteyn. 250pp. 9 x 12.
22919-X Pa. $5.00

TRISTAN UND ISOLDE, Richard Wagner. Full orchestral score with complete instrumentation. Do not confuse with piano reduction. Commentary by Felix Mottl, great Wagnerian conductor and scholar. Study score. 655pp. 8⅛ x 11.
22915-7 Pa. $10.00

FAVORITE SONGS OF THE NINETIES, ed. Robert Fremont. Full reproduction, including covers, of 88 favorites: Ta-Ra-Ra-Boom-De-Aye, The Band Played On, Bird in a Gilded Cage, Under the Bamboo Tree, After the Ball, etc. 401pp. 9 x 12.
EBE 21536-9 Pa. $6.95

SOUSA'S GREAT MARCHES IN PIANO TRANSCRIPTION: ORIGINAL SHEET MUSIC OF 23 WORKS, John Philip Sousa. Selected by Lester S. Levy. Playing edition includes: The Stars and Stripes Forever, The Thunderer, The Gladiator, King Cotton, Washington Post, much more. 24 illustrations. 111pp. 9 x 12.
USO 23132-1 Pa. $3.50

CLASSIC PIANO RAGS, selected with an introduction by Rudi Blesh. Best ragtime music (1897-1922) by Scott Joplin, James Scott, Joseph F. Lamb, Tom Turpin, 9 others. Printed from best original sheet music, plus covers. 364pp. 9 x 12.
EBE 20469-3 Pa. $6.95

ANALYSIS OF CHINESE CHARACTERS, C.D. Wilder, J.H. Ingram. 1000 most important characters analyzed according to primitives, phonetics, historical development. Traditional method offers mnemonic aid to beginner, intermediate student of Chinese, Japanese. 365pp.
23045-7 Pa. $4.00

MODERN CHINESE: A BASIC COURSE, Faculty of Peking University. Self study, classroom course in modern Mandarin. Records contain phonetics, vocabulary, sentences, lessons. 249 page book contains all recorded text, translations, grammar, vocabulary, exercises. Best course on market. 3 12" 33⅓ monaural records, book, album.
98832-5 Set $12.50

MANUAL OF THE TREES OF NORTH AMERICA, Charles S. Sargent. The basic survey of every native tree and tree-like shrub, 717 species in all. Extremely full descriptions, information on habitat, growth, locales, economics, etc. Necessary to every serious tree lover. Over 100 finding keys. 783 illustrations. Total of 986pp.
20277-1, 20278-X Pa., Two vol. set $8.00

BIRDS OF THE NEW YORK AREA, John Bull. Indispensable guide to more than 400 species within a hundred-mile radius of Manhattan. Information on range, status, breeding, migration, distribution trends, etc. Foreword by Roger Tory Peterson. 17 drawings; maps. 540pp. 23222-0 Pa. $6.00

THE SEA-BEACH AT EBB-TIDE, Augusta Foote Arnold. Identify hundreds of marine plants and animals: algae, seaweeds, squids, crabs, corals, etc. Descriptions cover food, life cycle, size, shape, habitat. Over 600 drawings. 490pp.
21949-6 Pa. $5.00

THE MOTH BOOK, William J. Holland. Identify more than 2,000 moths of North America. General information, precise species descriptions. 623 illustrations plus 48 color plates show almost all species, full size. 1968 edition. Still the basic book. Total of 551pp. 6½ x 9¼. 21948-8 Pa. $6.00

AN INTRODUCTION TO THE REPTILES AND AMPHIBIANS OF THE UNITED STATES, Percy A. Morris. All lizards, crocodiles, turtles, snakes, toads, frogs; life history, identification, habits, suitability as pets, etc. Non-technical, but sound and broad. 130 photos. 253pp. 22982-3 Pa. $3.00

OLD NEW YORK IN EARLY PHOTOGRAPHS, edited by Mary Black. Your only chance to see New York City as it was 1853-1906, through 196 wonderful photographs from N.Y. Historical Society. Great Blizzard, Lincoln's funeral procession, great buildings. 228pp. 9 x 12. 22907-6 Pa. $6.00

THE AMERICAN REVOLUTION, A PICTURE SOURCEBOOK, John Grafton. Wonderful Bicentennial picture source, with 411 illustrations (contemporary and 19th century) showing battles, personalities, maps, events, flags, posters, soldier's life, ships, etc. all captioned and explained. A wonderful browsing book, supplement to other historical reading. 160pp. 9 x 12. 23226-3 Pa. $4.00

PERSONAL NARRATIVE OF A PILGRIMAGE TO AL-MADINAH AND MECCAH, Richard Burton. Great travel classic by remarkably colorful personality. Burton, disguised as a Moroccan, visited sacred shrines of Islam, narrowly escaping death. Wonderful observations of Islamic life, customs, personalities. 47 illustrations. Total of 959pp. 21217-3, 21218-1 Pa., Two vol. set $10.00

INCIDENTS OF TRAVEL IN CENTRAL AMERICA, CHIAPAS, AND YUCATAN, John L. Stephens. Almost single-handed discovery of Maya culture; exploration of ruined cities, monuments, temples; customs of Indians. 115 drawings. 892pp.
22404-X, 22405-8 Pa., Two vol. set $8.00

CONSTRUCTION OF AMERICAN FURNITURE TREASURES, Lester Margon. 344 detail drawings, complete text on constructing exact reproductions of 38 early American masterpieces: Hepplewhite sideboard, Duncan Phyfe drop-leaf table, mantel clock, gate-leg dining table, Pa. German cupboard, more. 38 plates. 54 photographs. 168pp. 8⅜ x 11¼. 23056-2 Pa. $4.00

JEWELRY MAKING AND DESIGN, Augustus F. Rose, Antonio Cirino. Professional secrets revealed in thorough, practical guide: tools, materials, processes; rings, brooches, chains, cast pieces, enamelling, setting stones, etc. Do not confuse with skimpy introductions: beginner can use, professional can learn from it. Over 200 illustrations. 306pp. 21750-7 Pa. $3.00

METALWORK AND ENAMELLING, Herbert Maryon. Generally coneeded best all-around book. Countless trade secrets: materials, tools, soldering, filigree, setting, inlay, niello, repoussé, casting, polishing, etc. For beginner or expert. Author was foremost British expert. 330 illustrations. 335pp. 22702-2 Pa. $3.50

WEAVING WITH FOOT-POWER LOOMS, Edward F. Worst. Setting up a loom, beginning to weave, constructing equipment, using dyes, more, plus over 285 drafts of traditional patterns including Colonial and Swedish weaves. More than 200 other figures. For beginning and advanced. 275pp. 8¾ x 6⅜. 23064-3 Pa. $4.00

WEAVING A NAVAJO BLANKET, Gladys A. Reichard. Foremost anthropologist studied under Navajo women, reveals every step in process from wool, dyeing, spinning, setting up loom, designing, weaving. Much history, symbolism. With this book you could make one yourself. 97 illustrations. 222pp. 22992-0 Pa. $3.00

NATURAL DYES AND HOME DYEING, Rita J. Adrosko. Use natural ingredients: bark, flowers, leaves, lichens, insects etc. Over 135 specific recipes from historical sources for cotton, wool, other fabrics. Genuine premodern handicrafts. 12 illustrations. 160pp. 22688-3 Pa. $2.00

THE HAND DECORATION OF FABRICS, Francis J. Kafka. Outstanding, profusely illustrated guide to stenciling, batik, block printing, tie dyeing, freehand painting, silk screen printing, and novelty decoration. 356 illustrations. 198pp. 6 x 9. 21401-X Pa. $3.00

THOMAS NAST: CARTOONS AND ILLUSTRATIONS, with text by Thomas Nast St. Hill. Father of American political cartooning. Cartoons that destroyed Tweed Ring; inflation, free love, church and state; original Republican elephant and Democratic donkey; Santa Claus; more. 117 illustrations. 146pp. 9 x 12. 22983-1 Pa. $4.00 23067-8 Clothbd. $8.50

FREDERIC REMINGTON: 173 DRAWINGS AND ILLUSTRATIONS. Most famous of the Western artists, most responsible for our myths about the American West in its untamed days. Complete reprinting of Drawings of Frederic Remington (1897), plus other selections. 4 additional drawings in color on covers. 140pp. 9 x 12. 20714-5 Pa. $3.95

HOW TO SOLVE CHESS PROBLEMS, Kenneth S. Howard. Practical suggestions on problem solving for very beginners. 58 two-move problems, 46 3-movers, 8 4-movers for practice, plus hints. 171pp. 20748-X Pa. $2.00

A GUIDE TO FAIRY CHESS, Anthony Dickins. 3-D chess, 4-D chess, chess on a cylindrical board, reflecting pieces that bounce off edges, cooperative chess, retrograde chess, maximummers, much more. Most based on work of great Dawson. Full handbook, 100 problems. 66pp. 7⅞ x 10¾. 22687-5 Pa. $2.00

WIN AT BACKGAMMON, Millard Hopper. Best opening moves, running game, blocking game, back game, tables of odds, etc. Hopper makes the game clear enough for anyone to play, and win. 43 diagrams. 111pp. 22894-0 Pa. $1.50

BIDDING A BRIDGE HAND, Terence Reese. Master player "thinks out loud" the binding of 75 hands that defy point count systems. Organized by bidding problem—no-fit situations, overbidding, underbidding, cueing your defense, etc. 254pp. EBE 22830-4 Pa. $2.50

THE PRECISION BIDDING SYSTEM IN BRIDGE, C.C. Wei, edited by Alan Truscott. Inventor of precision bidding presents average hands and hands from actual play, including games from 1969 Bermuda Bowl where system emerged. 114 exercises. 116pp. 21171-1 Pa. $1.75

LEARN MAGIC, Henry Hay. 20 simple, easy-to-follow lessons on magic for the new magician: illusions, card tricks, silks, sleights of hand, coin manipulations, escapes, and more —all with a minimum amount of equipment. Final chapter explains the great stage illusions. 92 illustrations. 285pp. 21238-6 Pa. $2.95

THE NEW MAGICIAN'S MANUAL, Walter B. Gibson. Step-by-step instructions and clear illustrations guide the novice in mastering 36 tricks, much equipment supplied on 16 pages of cut-out materials. 36 additional tricks. 64 illustrations. 159pp. 6⅝ x 10. 23113-5 Pa. $3.00

PROFESSIONAL MAGIC FOR AMATEURS, Walter B. Gibson. 50 easy, effective tricks used by professionals —cards, string, tumblers, handkerchiefs, mental magic, etc. 63 illustrations. 223pp. 23012-0 Pa. $2.50

CARD MANIPULATIONS, Jean Hugard. Very rich collection of manipulations; has taught thousands of fine magicians tricks that are really workable, eye-catching. Easily followed, serious work. Over 200 illustrations. 163pp. 20539-8 Pa. $2.00

ABBOTT'S ENCYCLOPEDIA OF ROPE TRICKS FOR MAGICIANS, Stewart James. Complete reference book for amateur and professional magicians containing more than 150 tricks involving knots, penetrations, cut and restored rope, etc. 510 illustrations. Reprint of 3rd edition. 400pp. 23206-9 Pa. $3.50

THE SECRETS OF HOUDINI, J.C. Cannell. Classic study of Houdini's incredible magic, exposing closely-kept professional secrets and revealing, in general terms, the whole art of stage magic. 67 illustrations. 279pp. 22913-0 Pa. $2.50

THE MAGIC MOVING PICTURE BOOK, Bliss, Sands & Co. The pictures in this book move! Volcanoes erupt, a house burns, a serpentine dancer wiggles her way through a number. By using a specially ruled acetate screen provided, you can obtain these and 15 other startling effects. Originally "The Motograph Moving Picture Book." 32pp. 8¼ x 11. 23224-7 Pa. $1.75

STRING FIGURES AND HOW TO MAKE THEM, Caroline F. Jayne. Fullest, clearest instructions on string figures from around world: Eskimo, Navajo, Lapp, Europe, more. Cats cradle, moving spear, lightning, stars. Introduction by A.C. Haddon. 950 illustrations. 407pp. 20152-X Pa. $3.00

PAPER FOLDING FOR BEGINNERS, William D. Murray and Francis J. Rigney. Clearest book on market for making origami sail boats, roosters, frogs that move legs, cups, bonbon boxes. 40 projects. More than 275 illustrations. Photographs. 94pp. 20713-7 Pa. $1.25

INDIAN SIGN LANGUAGE, William Tomkins. Over 525 signs developed by Sioux, Blackfoot, Cheyenne, Arapahoe and other tribes. Written instructions and diagrams: how to make words, construct sentences. Also 290 pictographs of Sioux and Ojibway tribes. 111pp. 6⅛ x 9¼. 22029-X Pa. $1.50

BOOMERANGS: HOW TO MAKE AND THROW THEM, Bernard S. Mason. Easy to make and throw, dozens of designs: cross-stick, pinwheel, boomabird, tumblestick, Australian curved stick boomerang. Complete throwing instructions. All safe. 99pp. 23028-7 Pa. $1.50

25 KITES THAT FLY, Leslie Hunt. Full, easy to follow instructions for kites made from inexpensive materials. Many novelties. Reeling, raising, designing your own. 70 illustrations. 110pp. 22550-X Pa. $1.25

TRICKS AND GAMES ON THE POOL TABLE, Fred Herrmann. 79 tricks and games, some solitaires, some for 2 or more players, some competitive; mystifying shots and throws, unusual carom, tricks involving cork, coins, a hat, more. 77 figures. 95pp. 21814-7 Pa. $1.25

WOODCRAFT AND CAMPING, Bernard S. Mason. How to make a quick emergency shelter, select woods that will burn immediately, make do with limited supplies, etc. Also making many things out of wood, rawhide, bark, at camp. Formerly titled Woodcraft. 295 illustrations. 580pp. 21951-8 Pa. $4.00

AN INTRODUCTION TO CHESS MOVES AND TACTICS SIMPLY EXPLAINED, Leonard Barden. Informal intermediate introduction: reasons for moves, tactics, openings, traps, positional play, endgame. Isolates patterns. 102pp. USO 21210-6 Pa. $1.35

LASKER'S MANUAL OF CHESS, Dr. Emanuel Lasker. Great world champion offers very thorough coverage of all aspects of chess. Combinations, position play, openings, endgame, aesthetics of chess, philosophy of struggle, much more. Filled with analyzed games. 390pp. 20640-8 Pa. $3.50

CATALOGUE OF DOVER BOOKS

SLEEPING BEAUTY, illustrated by Arthur Rackham. Perhaps the fullest, most delightful version ever, told by C.S. Evans. Rackham's best work. 49 illustrations. 110pp. 7⅞ x 10¾. 22756-1 Pa. $2.00

THE WONDERFUL WIZARD OF OZ, L. Frank Baum. Facsimile in full color of America's finest children's classic. Introduction by Martin Gardner. 143 illustrations by W.W. Denslow. 267pp. 20691-2 Pa. $2.50

GOOPS AND HOW TO BE THEM, Gelett Burgess. Classic tongue-in-cheek masquerading as etiquette book. 87 verses, 170 cartoons as Goops demonstrate virtues of table manners, neatness, courtesy, more. 88pp. 6½ x 9¼. 22233-0 Pa. $1.50

THE BROWNIES, THEIR BOOK, Palmer Cox. Small as mice, cunning as foxes, exuberant, mischievous, Brownies go to zoo, toy shop, seashore, circus, more. 24 verse adventures. 266 illustrations. 144pp. 6⅝ x 9¼. 21265-3 Pa. $1.75

BILLY WHISKERS: THE AUTOBIOGRAPHY OF A GOAT, Frances Trego Montgomery. Escapades of that rambunctious goat. Favorite from turn of the century America. 24 illustrations 259pp. 22345-0 Pa. $2.75

THE ROCKET BOOK, Peter Newell. Fritz, janitor's kid, sets off rocket in basement of apartment house; an ingenious hole punched through every page traces course of rocket. 22 duotone drawings, verses. 48pp. 6⅞ x 8⅜. 22044-3 Pa. $1.50

PECK'S BAD BOY AND HIS PA, George W. Peck. Complete double-volume of great American childhood classic. Hennery's ingenious pranks against outraged pomposity of pa and the grocery man. 97 illustrations. Introduction by E.F. Bleiler. 347pp. 20497-9 Pa. $2.50

THE TALE OF PETER RABBIT, Beatrix Potter. The inimitable Peter's terrifying adventure in Mr. McGregor's garden, with all 27 wonderful, full-color Potter illustrations. 55pp. 4¼ x 5½. USO 22827-4 Pa. $1.00

THE TALE OF MRS. TIGGY-WINKLE, Beatrix Potter. Your child will love this story about a very special hedgehog and all 27 wonderful, full-color Potter illustrations. 57pp. 4¼ x 5½. USO 20546-0 Pa. $1.00

THE TALE OF BENJAMIN BUNNY, Beatrix Potter. Peter Rabbit's cousin coaxes him back into Mr. McGregor's garden for a whole new set of ·dventures. A favorite with children. All 27 full-color illustrations. 59pp. 4¼ x 5½. USO 21102-9 Pa. $1.00

THE MERRY ADVENTURES OF ROBIN HOOD, Howard Pyle. Facsimile of original (1883) edition, finest modern version of English outlaw's adventures. 23 illustrations by Pyle. 296pp. 6½ x 9¼. 22043-5 Pa. $2.75

TWO LITTLE SAVAGES, Ernest Thompson Seton. Adventures of two boys who lived as Indians; explaining Indian ways, woodlore, pioneer methods. 293 illustrations. 286pp. 20985-7 Pa. $3.00

HOUDINI ON MAGIC, Harold Houdini. Edited by Walter Gibson, Morris N. Young. How he escaped; exposés of fake spiritualists; instructions for eye-catching tricks; other fascinating material by and about greatest magician. 155 illustrations. 280pp. 20384-0 Pa. $2.50

HANDBOOK OF THE NUTRITIONAL CONTENTS OF FOOD, U.S. Dept. of Agriculture. Largest, most detailed source of food nutrition information ever prepared. Two mammoth tables: one measuring nutrients in 100 grams of edible portion; the other, in edible portion of 1 pound as purchased. Originally titled Composition of Foods. 190pp. 9 x 12. 21342-0 Pa. $4.00

COMPLETE GUIDE TO HOME CANNING, PRESERVING AND FREEZING, U.S. Dept. of Agriculture. Seven basic manuals with full instructions for jams and jellies; pickles and relishes; canning fruits, vegetables, meat; freezing anything. Really good recipes, exact instructions for optimal results. Save a fortune in food. 156 illustrations. 214pp. 6⅛ x 9¼. 22911-4 Pa. $2.50

THE BREAD TRAY, Louis P. De Gouy. Nearly every bread the cook could buy or make: bread sticks of Italy, fruit breads of Greece, glazed rolls of Vienna, everything from corn pone to croissants. Over 500 recipes altogether. including buns, rolls, muffins, scones, and more. 463pp. 23000-7 Pa. $3.50

CREATIVE HAMBURGER COOKERY, Louis P. De Gouy. 182 unusual recipes for casseroles, meat loaves and hamburgers that turn inexpensive ground meat into memorable main dishes: Arizona chili burgers, burger tamale pie, burger stew, burger corn loaf, burger wine loaf, and more. 120pp. 23001-5 Pa. $1.75

LONG ISLAND SEAFOOD COOKBOOK, J. George Frederick and Jean Joyce. Probably the best American seafood cookbook. Hundreds of recipes. 40 gourmet sauces, 123 recipes using oysters alone! All varieties of fish and seafood amply represented. 324pp. 22677-8 Pa. $3.00

THE EPICUREAN: A COMPLETE TREATISE OF ANALYTICAL AND PRACTICAL STUDIES IN THE CULINARY ART, Charles Ranhofer. Great modern classic. 3,500 recipes from master chef of Delmonico's, turn-of-the-century America's best restaurant. Also explained, many techniques known only to professional chefs. 775 illustrations. 1183pp. 6⅝ x 10. 22680-8 Clothbd. $17.50

THE AMERICAN WINE COOK BOOK, Ted Hatch. Over 700 recipes: old favorites livened up with wine plus many more: Czech fish soup, quince soup, sauce Perigueux, shrimp shortcake, filets Stroganoff, cordon bleu goulash, jambonneau, wine fruit cake, more. 314pp. 22796-0 Pa. $2.50

DELICIOUS VEGETARIAN COOKING, Ivan Baker. Close to 500 delicious and varied recipes: soups, main course dishes (pea, bean, lentil, cheese, vegetable, pasta, and egg dishes), savories, stews, whole-wheat breads and cakes, more. 168pp. USO 22834-7 Pa. $1.75

Cookies from Many Lands, Josephine Perry. Crullers, oatmeal cookies, chaux au chocolate, English tea cakes, mandel kuchen, Sacher torte, Danish puff pastry, Swedish cookies — a mouth-watering collection of 223 recipes. 157pp.
22832-0 Pa. $2.00

Rose Recipes, Eleanour S. Rohde. How to make sauces, jellies, tarts, salads, pot-pourris, sweet bags, pomanders, perfumes from garden roses; all exact recipes. Century old favorites. 95pp.
22957-2 Pa. $1.25

"Oscar" of the Waldorf's Cookbook, Oscar Tschirky. Famous American chef reveals 3455 recipes that made Waldorf great; cream of French, German, American cooking, in all categories. Full instructions, easy home use. 1896 edition. 907pp. 6⅝ x 9⅜.
20790-0 Clothbd. $15.00

Jams and Jellies, May Byron. Over 500 old-time recipes for delicious jams, jellies, marmalades, preserves, and many other items. Probably the largest jam and jelly book in print. Originally titled May Byron's Jam Book. 276pp.
USO 23130-5 Pa. $3.00

Mushroom Recipes, André L. Simon. 110 recipes for everyday and special cooking. Champignons à la grecque, sole bonne femme, chicken liver croustades, more; 9 basic sauces, 13 ways of cooking mushrooms. 54pp.
USO 20913-X Pa. $1.25

Favorite Swedish Recipes, edited by Sam Widenfelt. Prepared in Sweden, offers wonderful, clearly explained Swedish dishes: appetizers, meats, pastry and cookies, other categories. Suitable for American kitchen. 90 photos. 157pp.
23156-9 Pa. $2.00

The Buckeye Cookbook, Buckeye Publishing Company. Over 1,000 easy-to-follow, traditional recipes from the American Midwest: bread (100 recipes alone), meat, game, jam, candy, cake, ice cream, and many other categories of cooking. 64 illustrations. From 1883 enlarged edition. 416pp.
23218-2 Pa. $4.00

Twenty-Two Authentic Banquets from India, Robert H. Christie. Complete, easy-to-do recipes for almost 200 authentic Indian dishes assembled in 22 banquets. Arranged by region. Selected from Banquets of the Nations. 192pp.
23200-X Pa. $2.50

Prices subject to change without notice.
Available at your book dealer or write for free catalogue to Dept. GI, Dover Publications, Inc., 180 Varick St., N.Y., N.Y. 10014. Dover publishes more than 150 books each year on science, elementary and advanced mathematics, biology, music, art, literary history, social sciences and other areas.